英語で楽しむ
折り紙
Fun with Origami

Lily

監修◉奥田光雄
Mitsuo Okuda

Swan

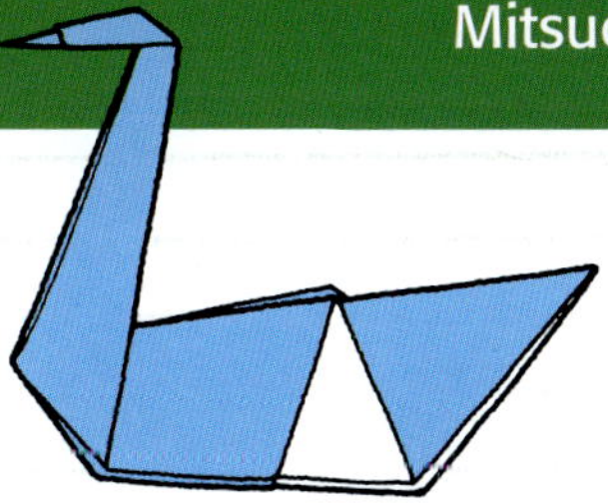

Crab

Hand Basket

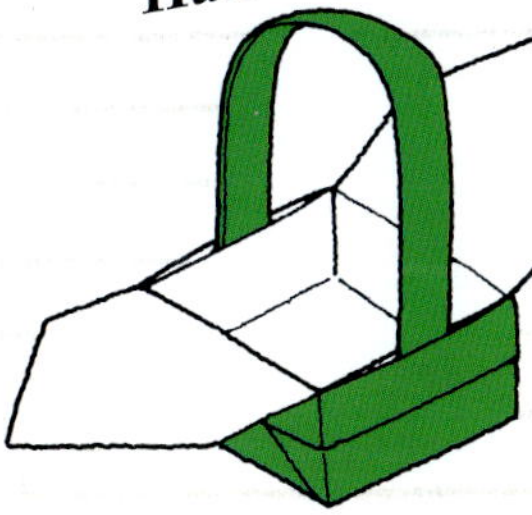

大泉書店

伝統的な折り紙
Traditional Origami

鶴
Crane

See p30

こま
Top

See p38～39

ふきごま

Pinwheel

See p49～52

六角形のオーナメント

Hexagonal Ornament

See p88～90

楽しく使おう

Useful Origami

ようじ入れ

Toothpick case

See p65～67

かざり箱

Decorative Box

See p68～69

花を折る

Flowers

花・チューリップ・葉と茎

Flower・Tulip・Leaf&Stem

See p99～102

あやめ

Ayame

See p95～96

かわいい動物たち

Animals

つばめ
Swallow

See p122

ダックスフンド
Dachshund

See p125～126

きつね
Fox

See p111～112

水辺の生き物たち

Aquatic Animals

かに

Crab

See p134～136

海ガメ

Sea Turtle

See p143～145

金魚

Goldfish

See p141～142

昆虫たち
Insects

かたつむり
Snail

See p154～156

カマキリ
Mantis

See p160～163

はじめに

折り紙は、おとなでも子どもでも、折り紙になじみのない外国の人でも親しめる、とても楽しい紙遊びです。折り方図の約束事を頭に入れておけば、あとは「折る」という単純な作業を繰り返すだけ。道具も必要ありません。紙さえあれば、どこででもできますし、ひとりでも楽しむことができます。

わたしは30数年前、負傷したきき手のリハビリのために折り紙を始めました。現在、創作折り紙作家として、年に数回は海外の折り紙展などの作品展に出品し、作品集も出しています。そして、古来より伝承されてきた折り紙の美しさ、楽しさを、日本だけでなく世界中の人たちにも知っていただきたいと願っています。

折り紙は、けっして難しいものではありません。どんな複雑な作品でも、丁寧に根気よく折っていくことで、誰でもきれいに折れるようになるのです。また、自分なりに折りを少し変えてみることで、作品にオリジナリティをもたせることができるのも、折り紙の大きな魅力でしょう。基本形に折りを重ねることによって形が変化する楽しさ、たった１枚の紙からさまざまな作品を作り出す楽しさを、ぜひ皆さんにも味わっていただきたいと思います。

奥田光雄

Preface

Origami is create fun for people of all ages. Anyone can do it. You don't need special training or tools.

You just need to learn a few basic shapes that are the foundation of all Origami figures. As long as you have a piece of paper, you can do Origami anywhere, anytime.

I began learning Origami some 30 years ago as rehabilitation for a hand injury. Today, I display my original creations at exhibitions all over the world. I want all people to appreciate the joy and beauty of this age-old Japanese tradition.

Origami is not at all difficult. With a little care and patience, you can make beautiful, complex figures. You can make small changes to the figures and delight in your own creativity. You can watch with joy as the figure emerges with each additional fold. You can see the amazing number of figures that can be made from a single sheet of paper, I want everyone to experience the delights of Origami.

Mitsuo Okuda

もくじ
CONTENTS

折り紙の約束ごと　The rules of Origami——18

CHAPTER 1 かんたんな折り紙 Easy Origami

鶴　Crane——30
ふうせん　Balloon——31
ハンドバッグ　Handbag——32
いえ　House——33
しゅりけん　Syuriken——34
おひなさま　Ohinasama——36
こま　Top——38
コップ　Cup——40
教会　Church——41
紙でっぽう　Popgun——43
UFO・くす玉——44
UFO・Decorative Ball
王冠　Crown——46
小鳥型飛行機　Airplane——47
ふきごま　Pinwheel——49

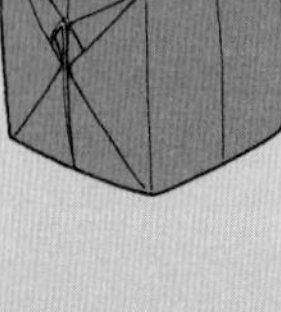

CHAPTER 2

つかえる折り紙
Useful Origami

コースター　Coaster————54
フォトフレーム　Photo Frame————55
しおり　Bookmark————56
ティッシュ入れ　Tissue Case————57
ナプキンリング　Napkin ring————58
ナプキン立て　Napkin Stand————59
和紙の菓子入れ　Candy Dishes————62
ようじ入れ　Toothpick Case————65
かざり箱　Decorative Box————68
持ち手のついたかご　Hand Basket————70
さいふ　Wallet————72
小銭入れ　Coin Purse————73
ソーイングボックス　Sewing Box————75
ギフトバッグ　Gift Bag————77
新聞紙のゴミ入れ　Trash Box————78
なべしき　Pot Mat————80
とりの小物入れ　Case————81
花びらの入れ物　Case————83

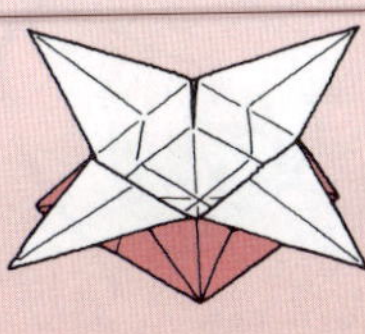

花のかご　Flower Basket——85
絵馬　Ema——86
六角形のオーナメント——88
Hexagonal Ornament
クリスマスのかざり——91
Christmas decoration

CHAPTER 3 花を折る Flowers

つりがねそう　Bellflower——94
あやめ　Ayame——95
ゆり　Lily——97
花•チューリップ・葉と茎——99
Flower • Tulip • Leaf & Stem
かきつばた　Iris——103
つきみそう　Evening primrose——106

CHAPTER 4 かわいい動物たち Animals

ライオン　Lion — 108
ぶた　Pig — 109
きつね・たぬき　Fox・Racoon Dog — 110
ねずみ　Mouse — 115
おうむ　Parrot — 116
おんどり・ひよこ　Cock・Chick — 117
うし　Cow — 120
つばめ　Swallow — 122
さる　Monkey — 123
ダックスフンド　Dachshund — 125

CHAPTER 5 水辺の生き物たち Aquatic Animals

とび魚　Flying fish — 128
魚・シャチ　Fish・Orc — 130
かめ　Turtle — 133

カニ　Crab——134
白鳥　Swan——137
ペンギン　Penguin——138
たこ　Octopus——139
金魚　Goldfish——141
海ガメ　Sea Turtle——143
ピョンピョンがえる　Jumping Frog——146
えび　Shrimp——148
カジキマグロ　Tuna——149
エイ　Ray——151

CHAPTER 6 昆虫たち Insects

かたつむり　Snail——154
とんぼ　Dragonfly——157
バッタ　Grasshopper——159
カマキリ　Mantis——160
ちょうちょう　Butterfly——164
飛ぶちょうちょう　Flying Butterfly——165

監修／奥田光雄
編集・構成／造事務所
文／石川直子
英訳／AIDEN・GREW
撮影／安田仁志
イラスト／三国淳
ブックデザイン／安田ナオミ

折り紙の約束ごと
The rules of Origami

作品を完成させる3つのカギ　The 3 key points for making the works

- 約束記号　Symbols
- 折り方記号　Basic Folds
- 折り方基本形　Basic Shapes

これらの約束ごとさえわかれば、むずかしい作品だって、できたも同然!
まずは、しっかり覚えてください。

If you master these rules, you can make any works.
First, let's learn these rules.

約束記号 *Symbols*

山折り線
Line for Yama-Ori (mountain fold)

谷折り線
Line for Tani-Ori (valley fold)

折りすじ
Crease

前方に折る
Fold forward

裏側に折る
Fold backward

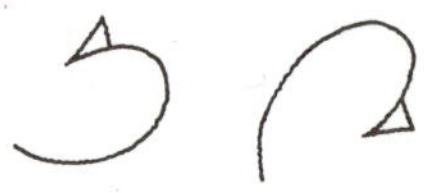

切る
Cut with scissors

切り込み線
Cut along this line

ふくらます
Inflate by blowing

開く
Open

ひっくり返す
Turn over

折り方記号
Basic Fold

山折り　Yama-Ori

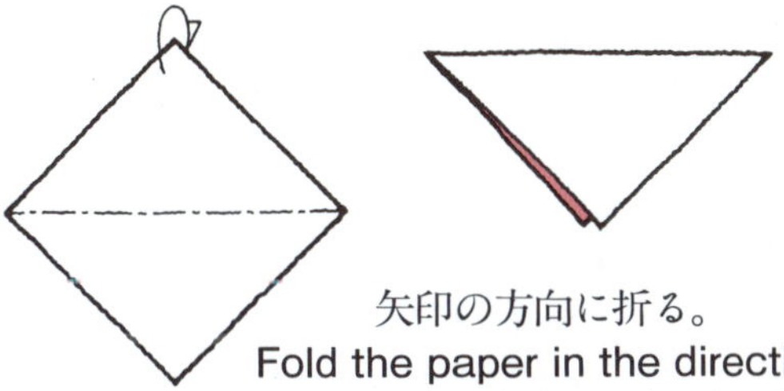

矢印の方向に折る。
Fold the paper in the direction of the arrow to make a peak.

谷折り　Tani-Ori

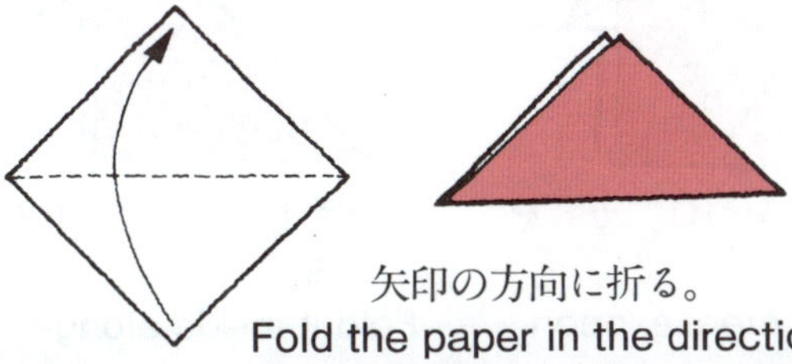

矢印の方向に折る。
Fold the paper in the direction of the arrow to make a trough.

折りすじをつける
Make a crease

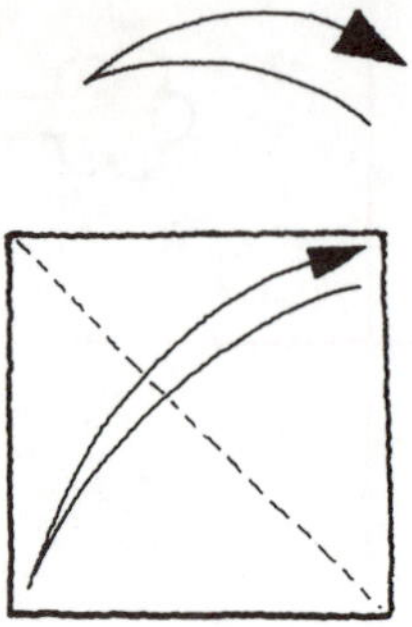

カドを合わせて半分に折り、折りすじをつける。
Fold the paper in half to make a crease.

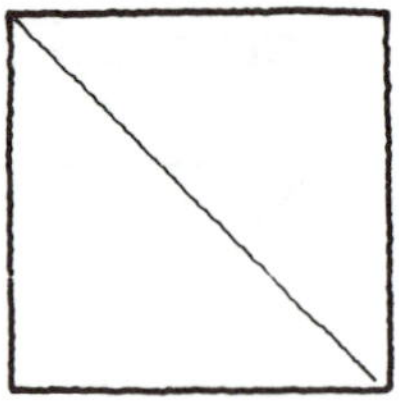

もとに戻す。
Unfold.

だん折り
Dan-Ori

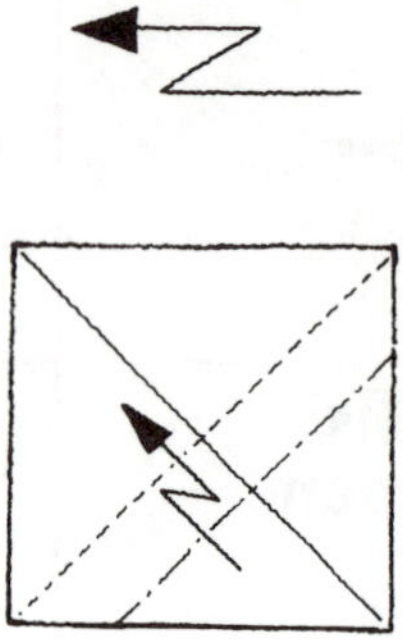

初めに谷折り、次に山折りをして、だんに折る。
Fold the paper in by Tani-Ori, then fold it forward by Yama-Ori.

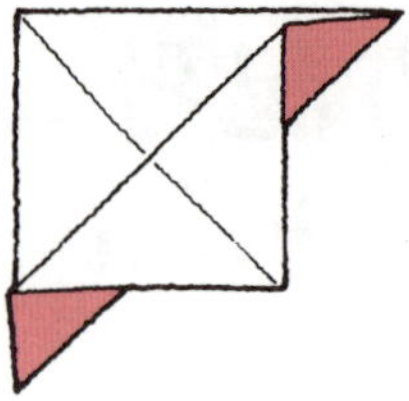

中わり折り　Nakawari-Ori

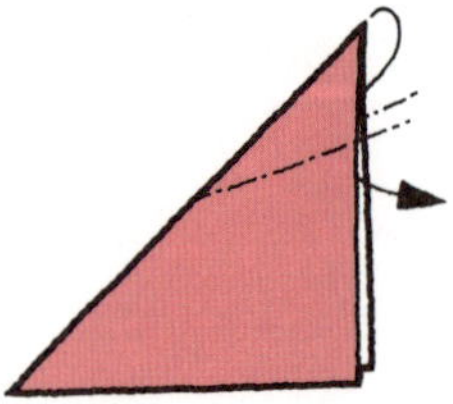

①

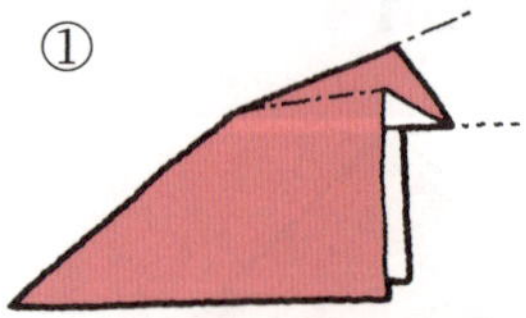

折りすじをつけ、カドを開く。
Make a crease, open the corner.

②

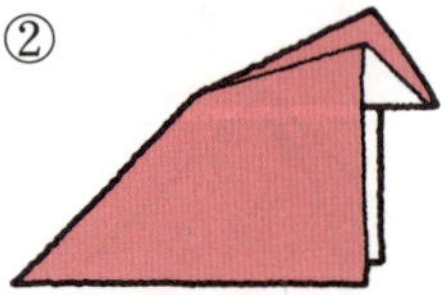

折りすじに沿って、内側に折る。
Fold it inside along the crease.

かぶせ折り　Kabuse-Ori

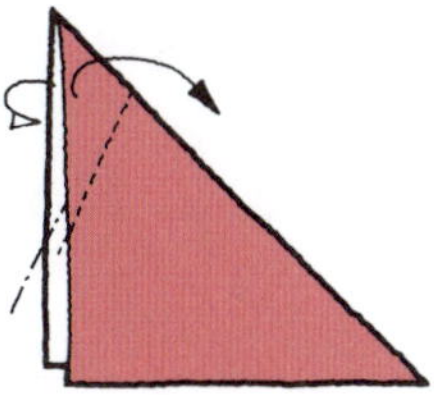

①

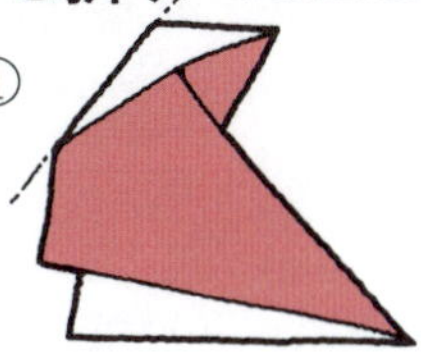

折りすじをつけ、カドを開く。
Make a crease, open the corner.

②

折りすじに沿って、外側に折る。
Fold it outside along the crease.

ひきよせ折り　Hikiyose-Ori

①

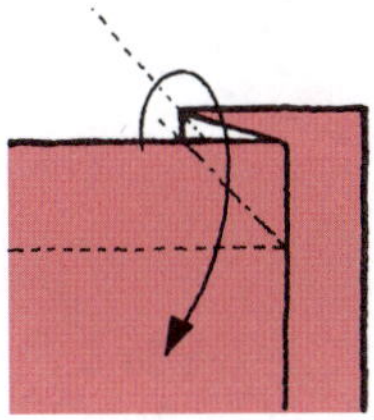

カドに斜めの折りすじをつけ、手前にひきよせるように三角部分を広げる。
Make a diagonal crease in the upper corner, and draw the top sheet towards you to open the triangle.

②

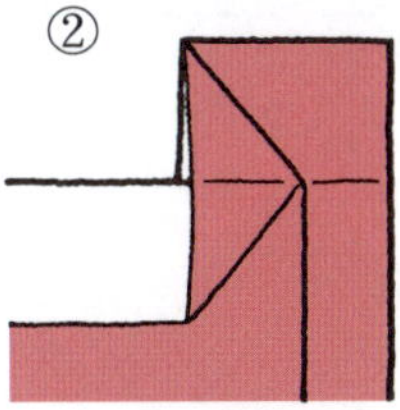

三角をつぶす。
Flatten the triangle.

つまみ折り　Tumami-Ori

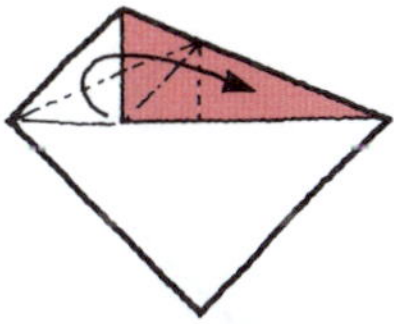

①

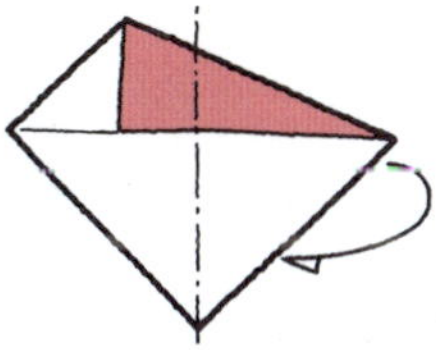

中心線に合わせて折り下げ、半分に山折りする。
Fold the top corner down to the center line, and fold in half backward.

②

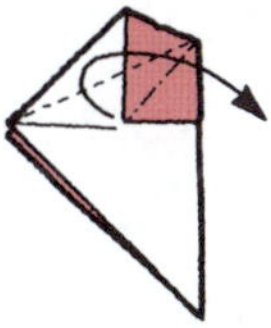

袋になっている部分を開いて、つぶす。
Open the pocket and flatten.

③

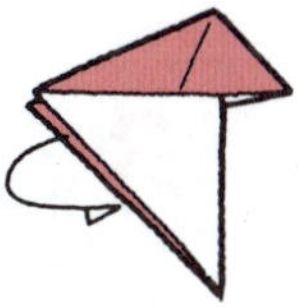

開く。
Unfold.

④

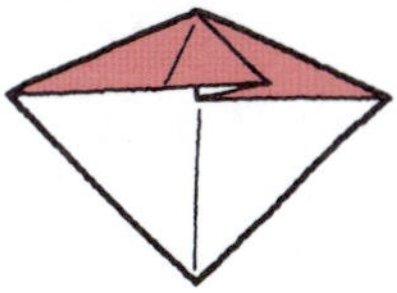

中央の三角部分を右へ倒すように折る。
Fold the flap to the right.

折り方基本形
Basic Shapes

凧の基本形
Basic Kite

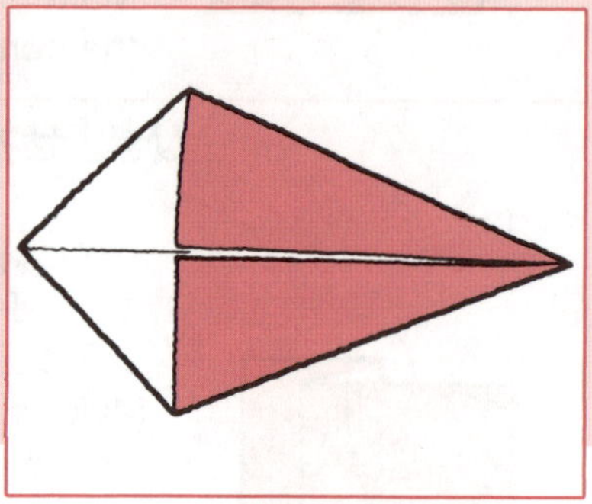

1 裏を出し、折りすじをつける。
Fold in half. Unfold.

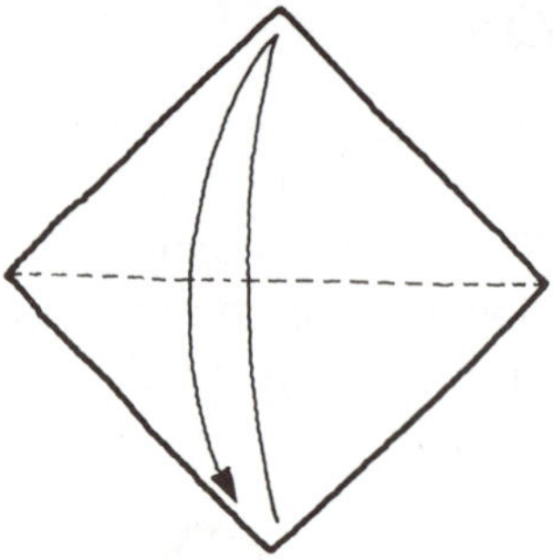

2 中心に合わせて上下を折る。
Fold the top and bottom corners to the center.

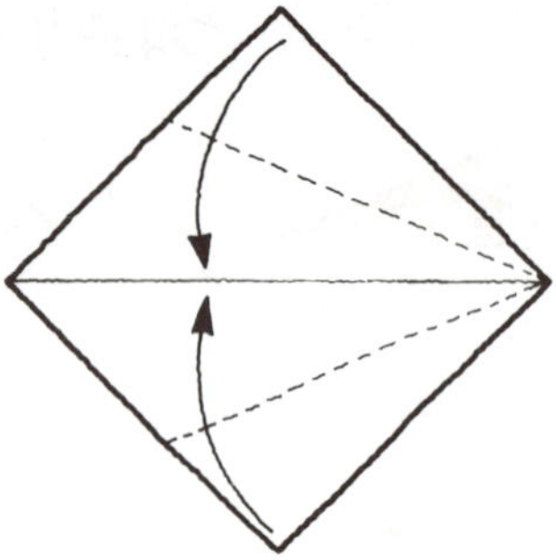

3 できあがり。
It should look like this.

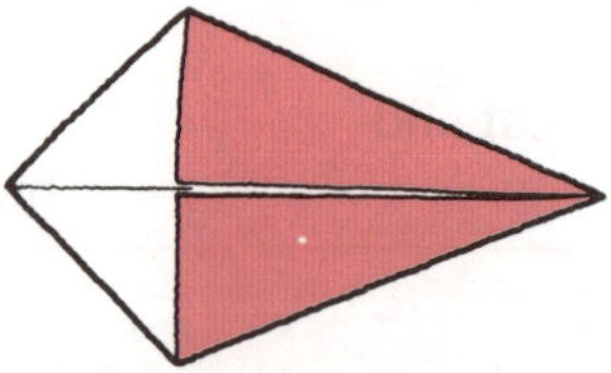

ざぶとん基本形
Basic Zabuton

1 裏を出し、カドを合わせるように折りすじをつける。
Make a cross shaped crease.

2 4つのカドを合わせて上下に折る。
Fold each corner to the center.

3 できあがり。
It should look like this.

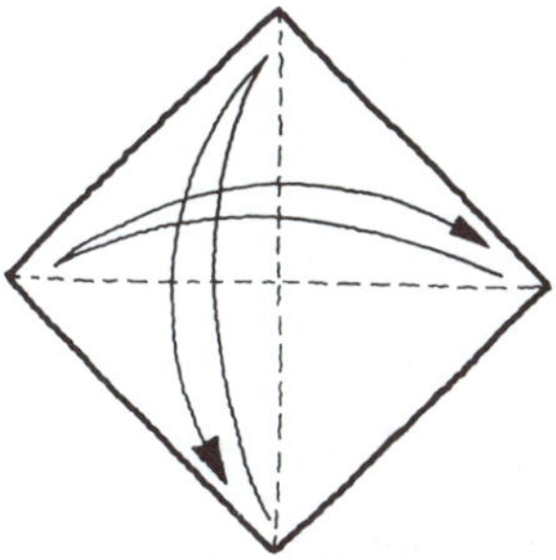

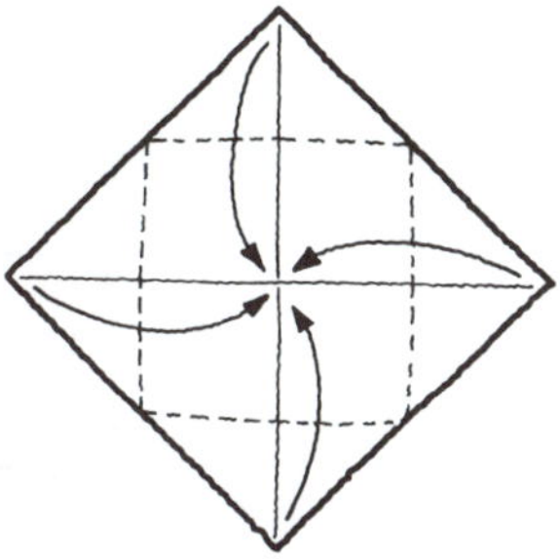

二そう船基本形
Basic Nisoubune

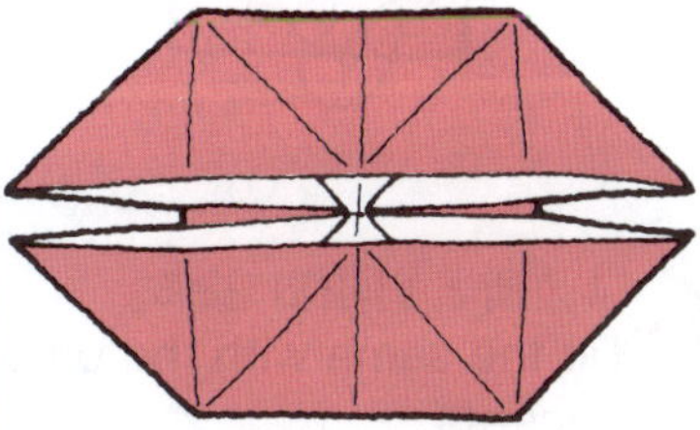

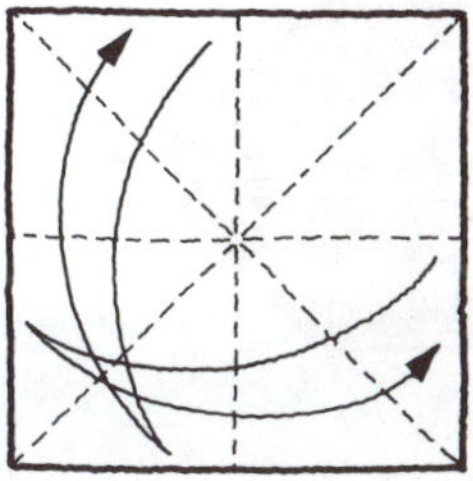

1 裏を出して2本の対角線とタテ、ヨコ半分の折りすじをつける。
Crease the paper vertically, horizontally and diagonally.

2 表を出して、４つのカドを中心に合わせて、折りすじをつける。
Turn over. Fold each corner to the center. Unfold.

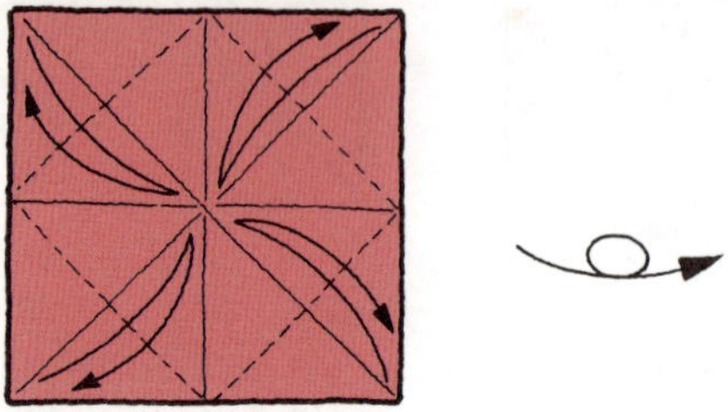

3 ひっくり返し、両側の辺を中心の折りすじに合わせて折る。
Turn over. Fold the left and right sides to the center.

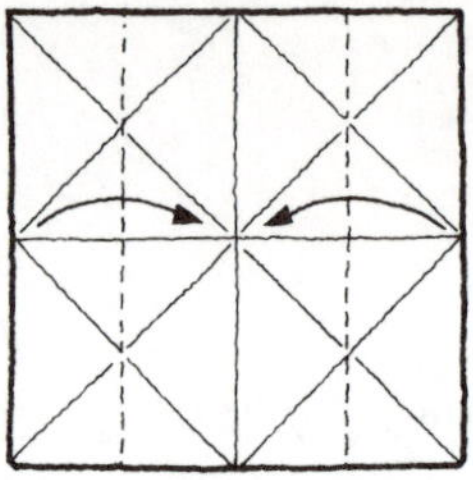

4 上下の辺を、中心の折りすじに合わせて折る。
Fold the top and bottom edges to the center.

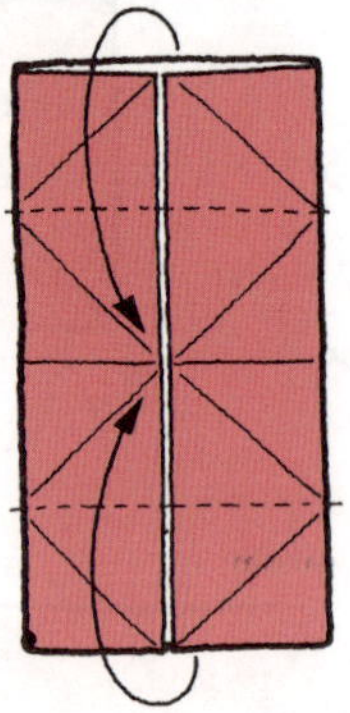

5 内側を広げてカドを引き出し、折りすじどおりにつぶして折る。
Open the pocket and pull the corner out, and flatten along the crease.

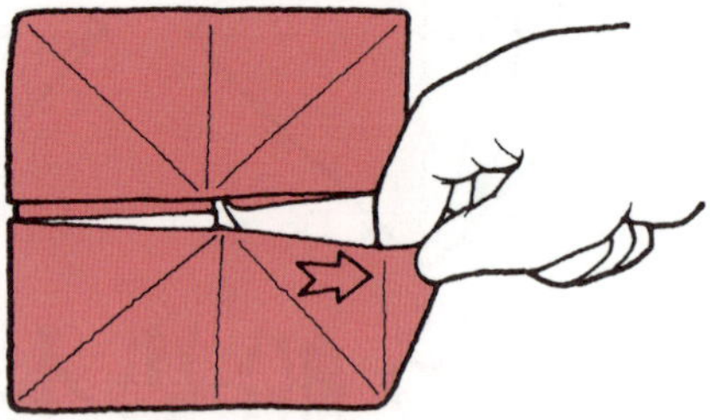

6 ４カ所とも同様に折る。
Do the same with the other pockets.

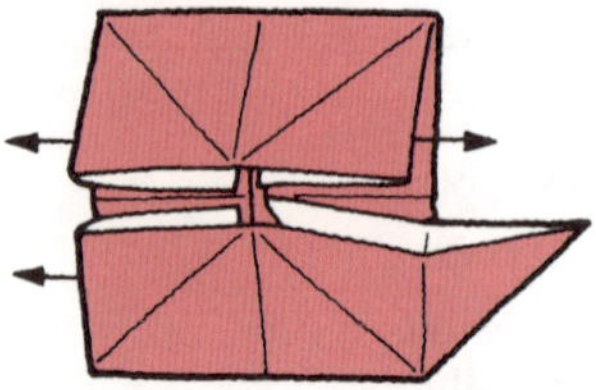

7 できあがり。
It should look like this.

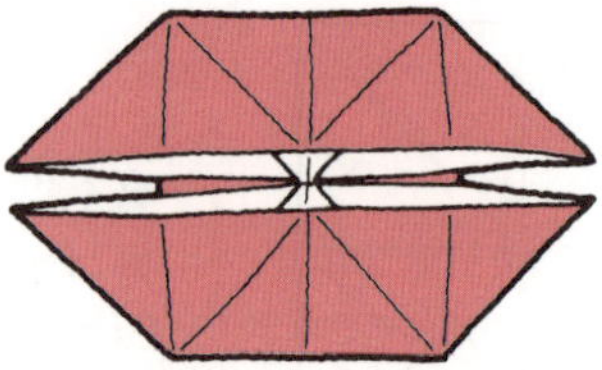

正方基本形

Basic Square

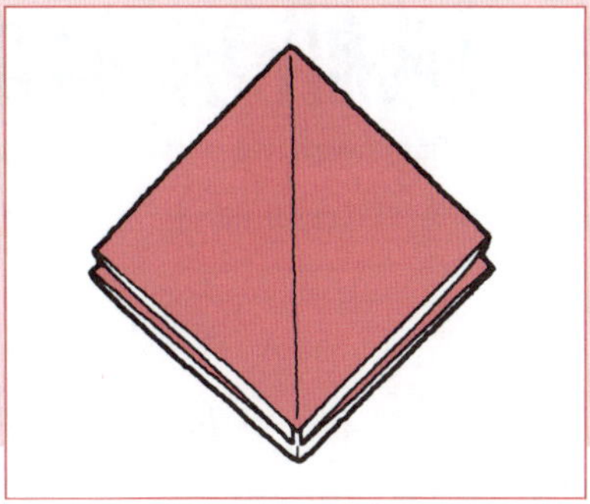

1 表を出し、向かい合うカドとカドを合わせて十字の折りすじをつける。
Make a cross shaped crease.

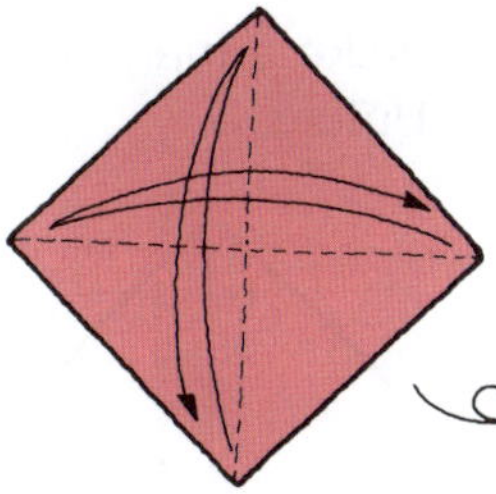

2 ひっくり返してから、タテ、ヨコ半分の折りすじをつける。
Turn over. Fold in half to make diagonal creases as shown.

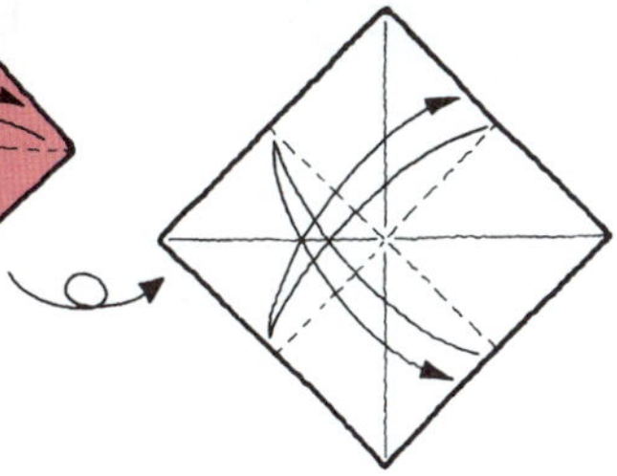

3 3つのカドを、ひとつのカドに合わせるように折っていく。
Fold the 3 corners to meet at the bottom corner. Unfold.

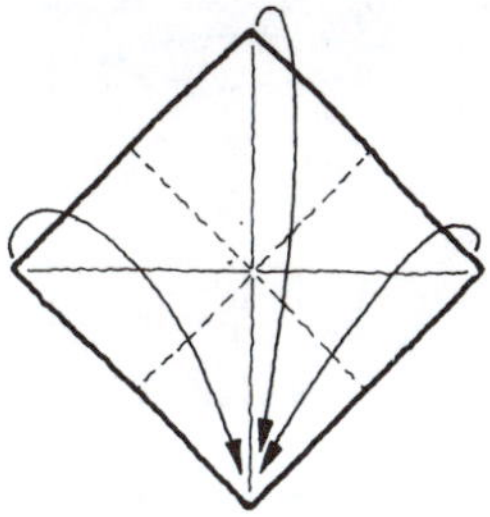

4 折りすじどおりに、たたむようにする。
Bring the 3 corners towards the bottom corner. Fold it along the creases.

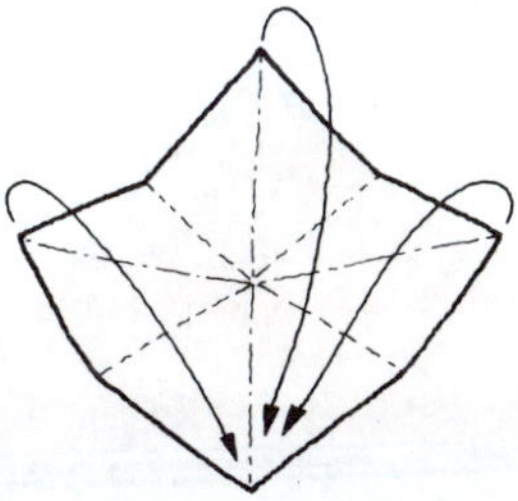

5 3つのカドが、ひとつに重なる。
Make sure the corners meet at the bottom corner.

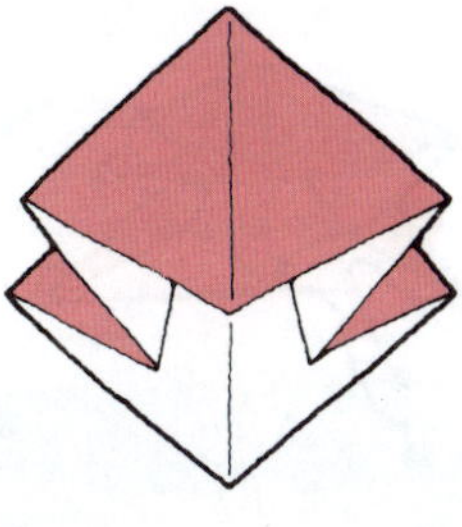

6 できあがり。
It should look like this.

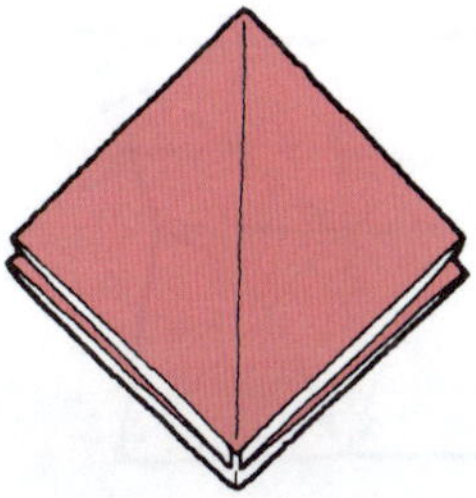

風船基本形

Basic Fūsen

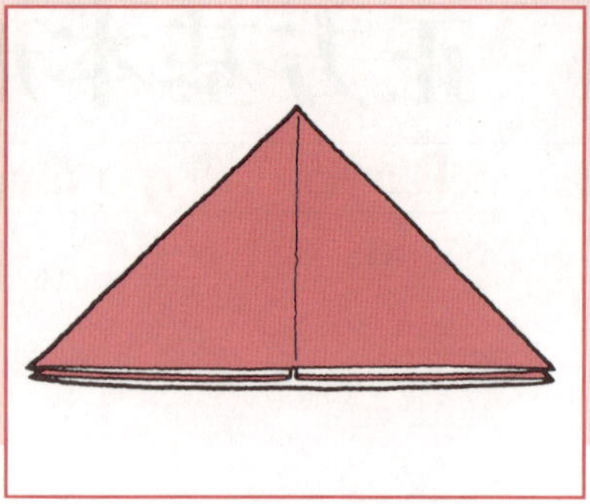

1 表を出し、タテ、ヨコ半分の折りすじをつける。
Make vertical and horizontal creases.

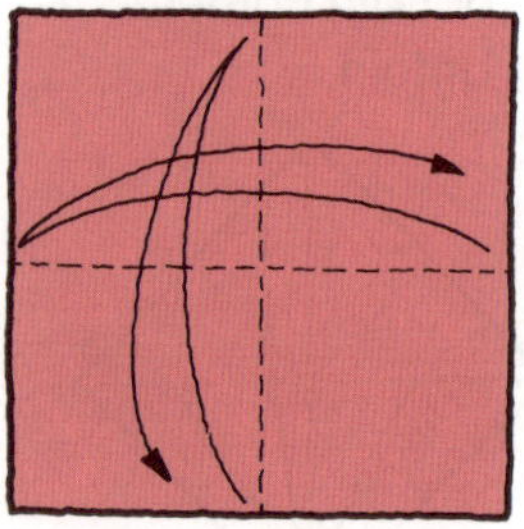

2 ひっくり返して、向かい合うカドとカドを合わせ、折りすじをつける。
Turn over.
Make diagonal creases.

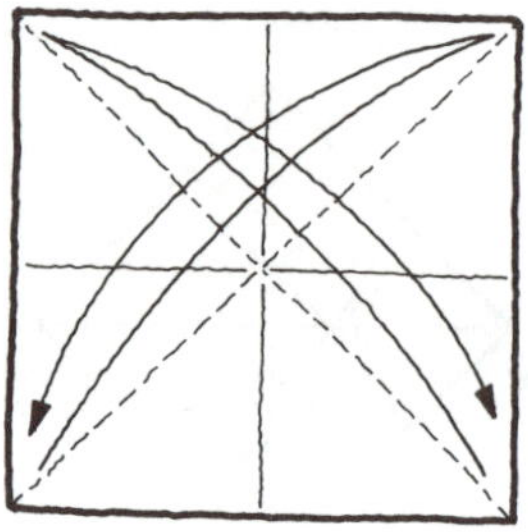

3 下の辺の中心に、上と左右の中心を合わせるように折っていく。
Fold the top and the corners in and down to make a triangle.
Unfold.

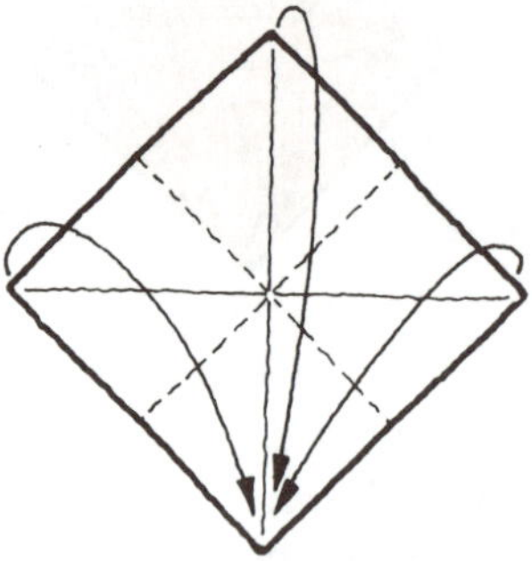

4 折りすじどおりに、たたむようにする。
Follow the creases and fold the top down while tucking the sides in.

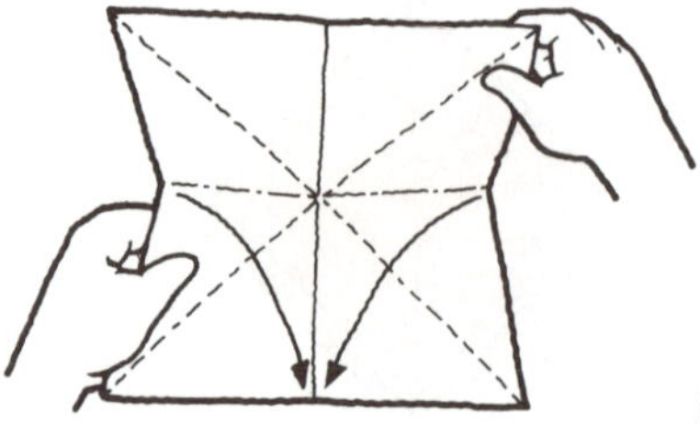

5 3つの辺の中心が、ひとつの辺の中心に重なる。
Make sure the edges are aligned at the bottom.

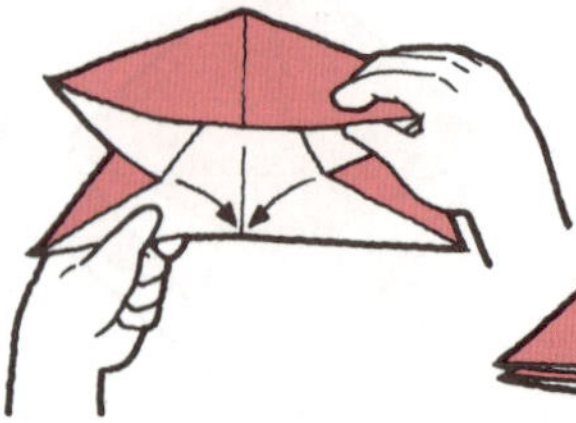

6 できあがり。
It should look like this.

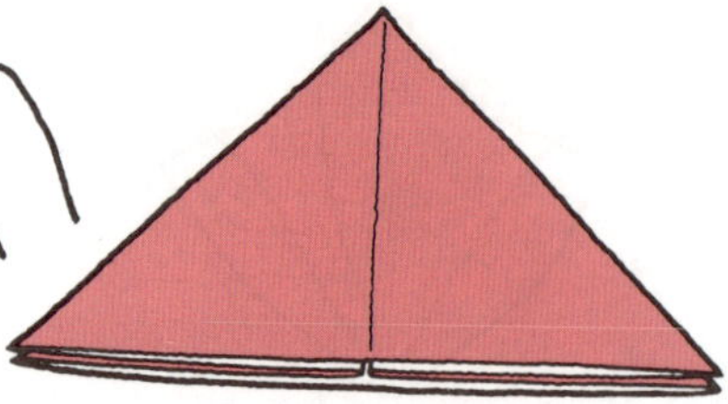

鶴の基本形

Basic Turu

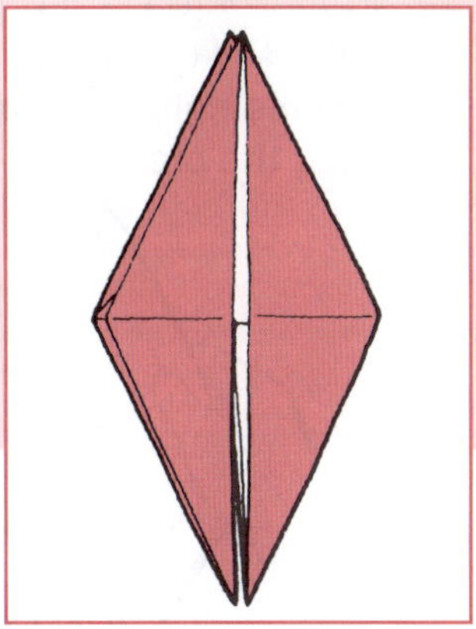

1 正方基本形を折る（P 25参照）。
Begin with the "Basic Square" (See P25).

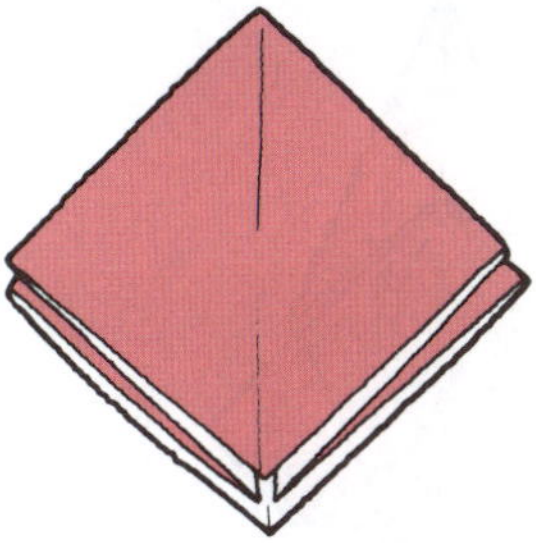

2 左右を中心に合わせて折る。
Fold the front left and right flaps to the center.

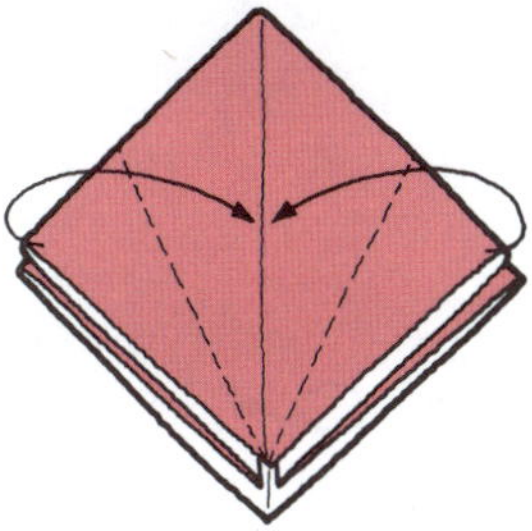

3 裏側も同様に折る。
Do the same with the back flaps.

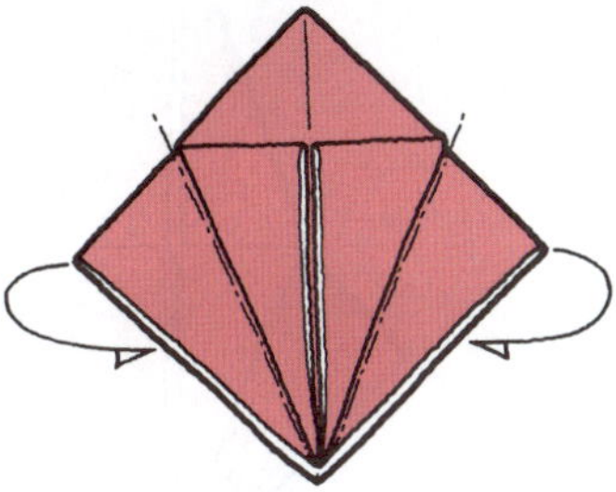

4 上のカドを折り下げる。
Fold the top triangle down and crease.

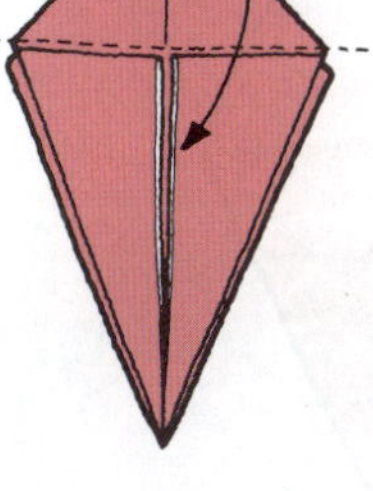

5 折りすじをしっかりつけてからひらき、1の形までもどす。
Open it to shape in drawing-1.

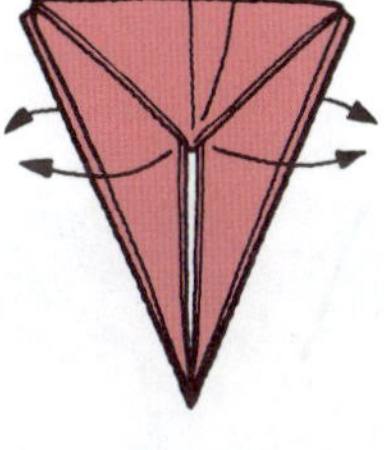

6 上の１枚を持ち上げ、内側を広げてつぶすように折る。
Raise, open and flatten the front sheet.

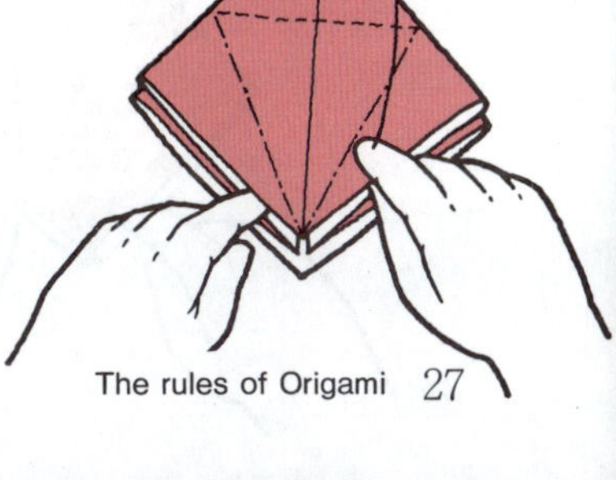

7 上のカドを倒すようにして、折りすじどおりにつぶす。
Fold the right side flap inside along the creases.

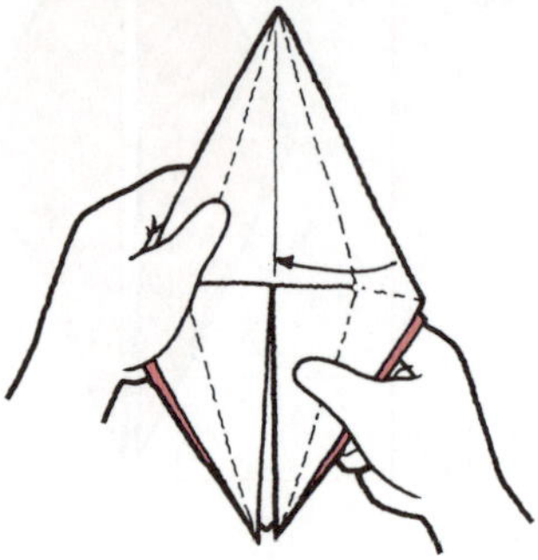

8 左側も同様に折る。
Do the same with the left side.

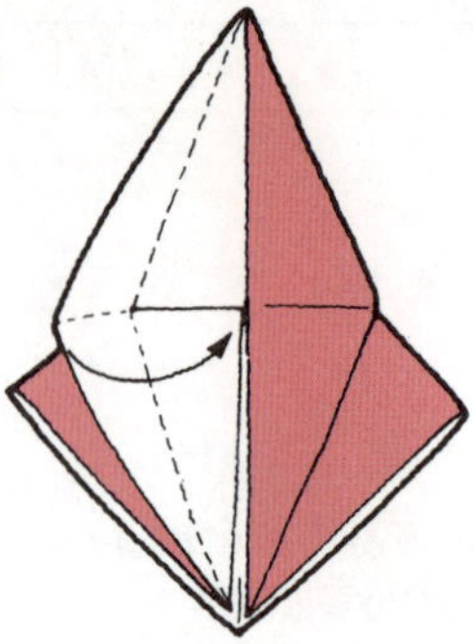

9 ひっくり返す。
Turn over.

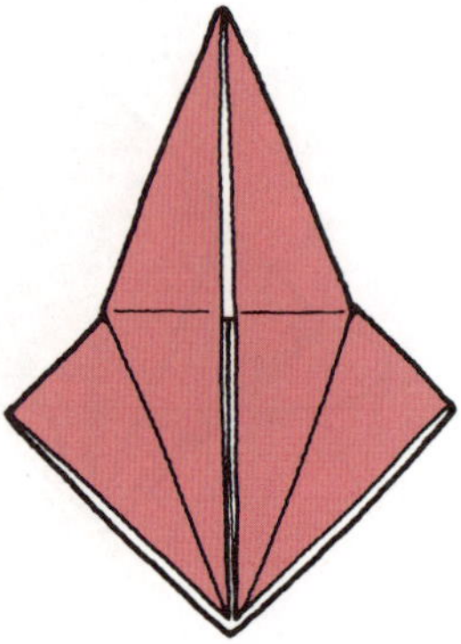

10 上のカドを折り下げて、折りすじをつける。
Fold the corner down to make a crease. Unfold.

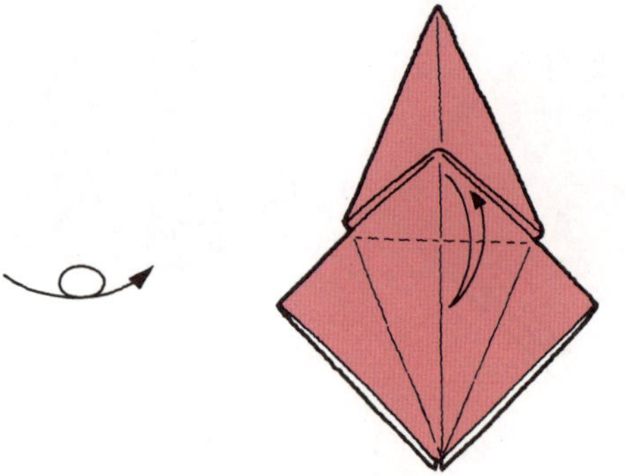

11 6〜8を繰り返す。
Repeat steps 6〜8.

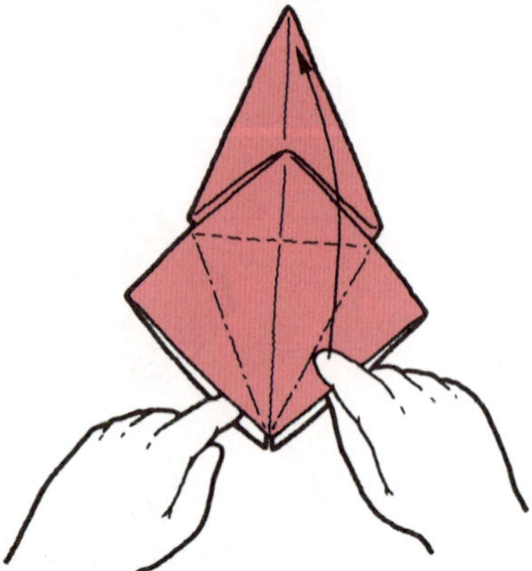

12 できあがり。
It should look like this.

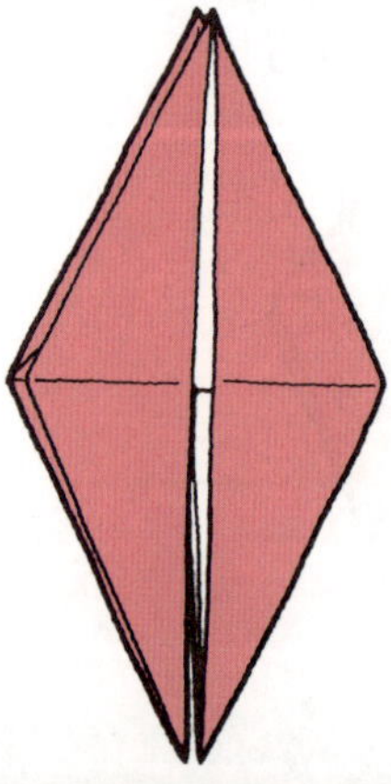

Chapter 1

かんたんな折り紙
Easy Origami

鶴

Crane

●材料　materials

15×15cmの折り紙(以下、特別な指定がないかぎりは、このサイズの折り紙だけを使います)。

15×15cm Origami (Use this size unless you find any instructions in this book.)

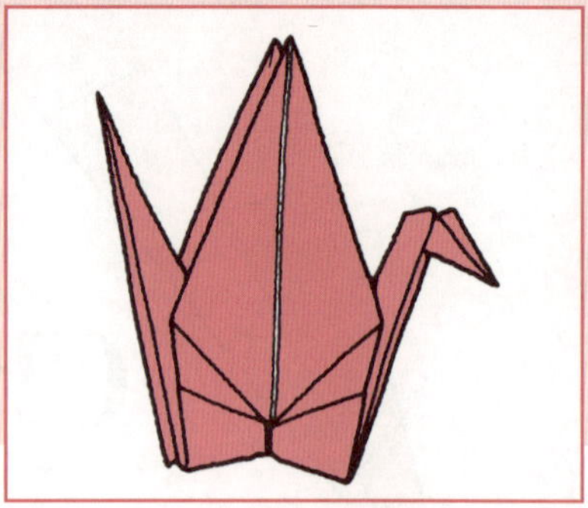

1 鶴の基本形(P27参照)を作り、中心に合わせて折る。裏側も同様に。

Begin with "Basic Turu" (See P27). Fold both sides in. Do the same with the reverse side.

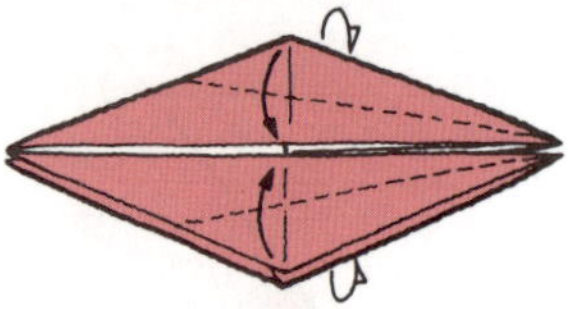

2 上の1枚を左に折る。裏側も同様に。

Fold the right flap to the left. Do the same with the reverse side.

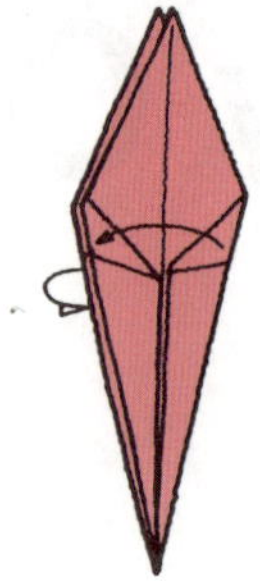

3 折り上げる。裏側も同様に折る。

Fold the bottom flap up. Do the same with the reverse side.

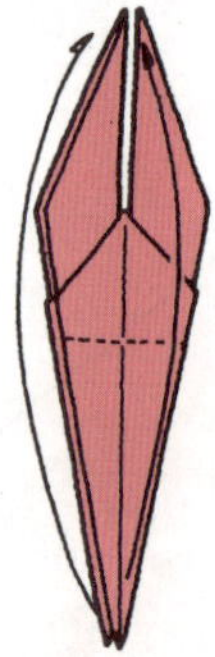

4 上の1枚を左に重ねる。裏側も同様に折る。

Fold the front flap to the left. Do the same with the reverse side.

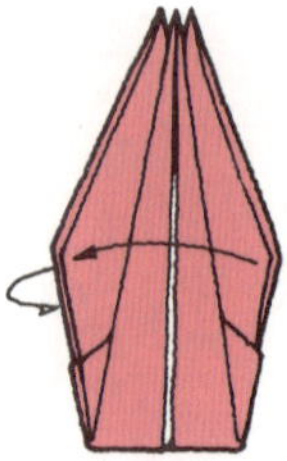

5 中わり折りをして、口ばしを作る。

Do "Nakawari-Ori" on the right flap to make a bill.

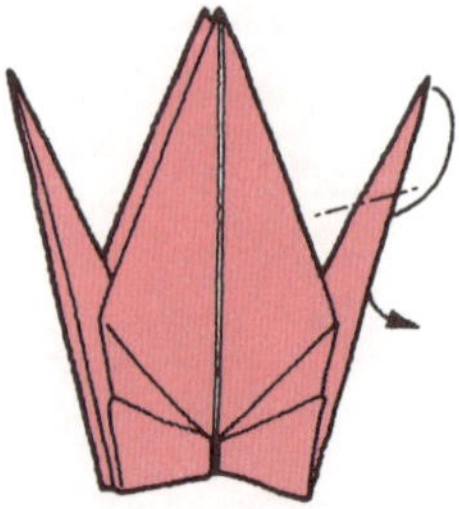

Finished

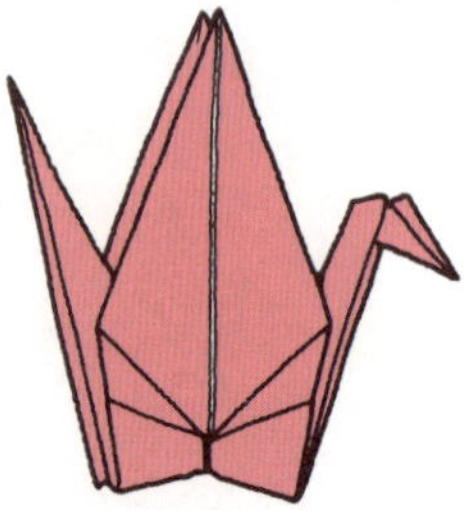

ふうせん

Balloon

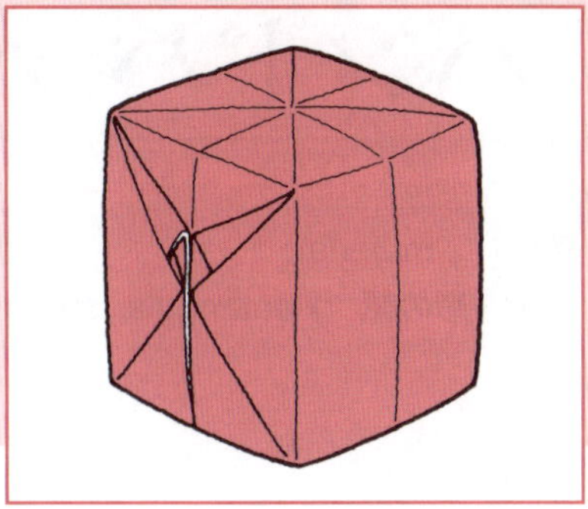

1 風船基本形（P26参照）から始める。上の１枚を折り上げる。
Begin with "Basic Fūsen" (See P26). Fold the corners of the front flap up diagonally.

2 中心に合わせて、左右を折る。
Fold the upper left and right corners in to meet at the center.

3 カドを、三角形の袋にさし込む。
Put the top corners into the trianglar pockets.

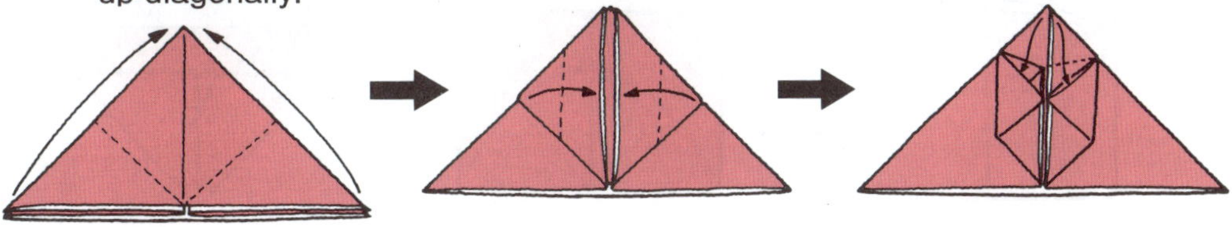

4 裏側も、1から同じように折る。
Repeat steps 1～3 on the reverse side.

5 息を吹き込んで、ふくらます。
Inflate a balloon by blowing.

Finished

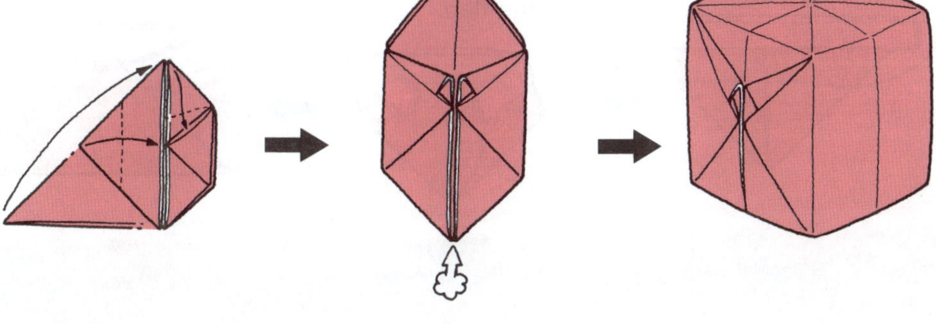

ハンドバッグ

Handbag

●材料　materials

長方形の紙　Rectangular sheet

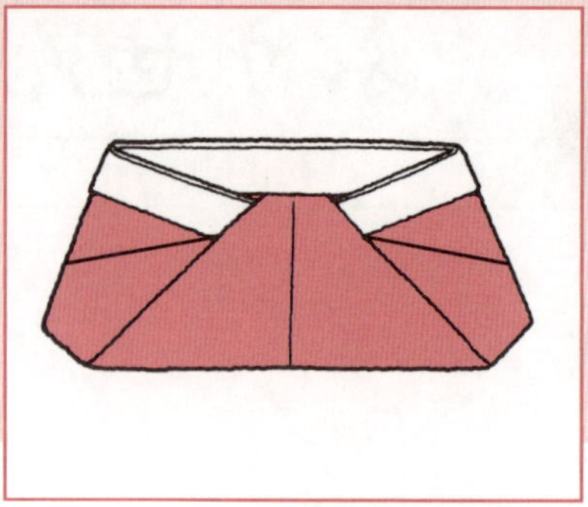

1 長方形の紙を半分に折って、広げる。
Fold a rectangular sheet in half. Unfold.

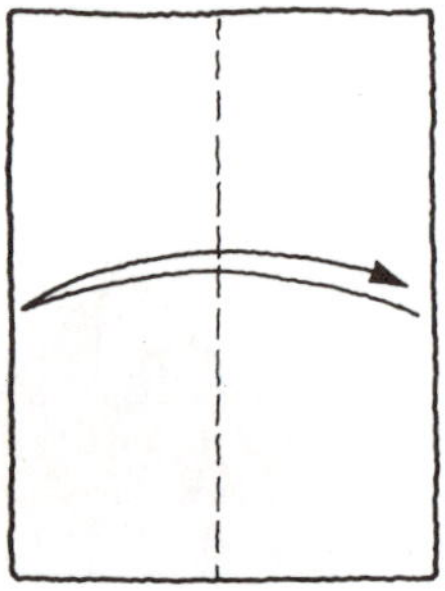

2 半分に折り、カドを折りすじに合わせて折る。
Fold in half again to the top edge, and fold the bottom corners to the center.

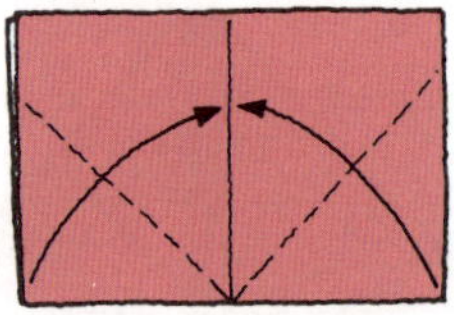

3 上の部分を半分に２回折る。反対側も同様に。
Fold in half to the edge of the triangle, and fold it down again. Do the same with the reverse side.

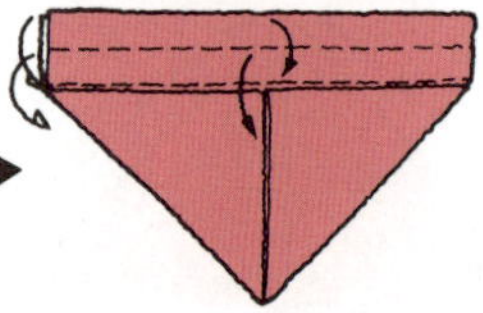

4 両はじを斜めに折る。
Fold both sides in diagonally.

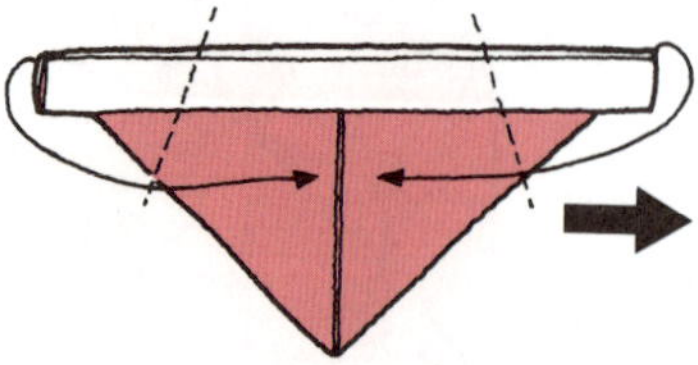

5 三角形のところを、すきまに差し込む。
Fold the bottom corner up and tuck it under the flap.

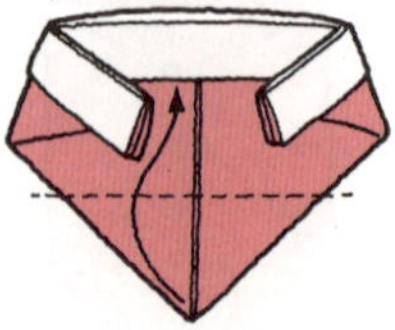

Finished

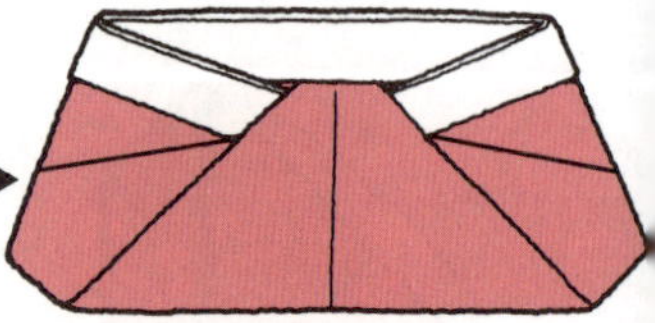

いえ

House

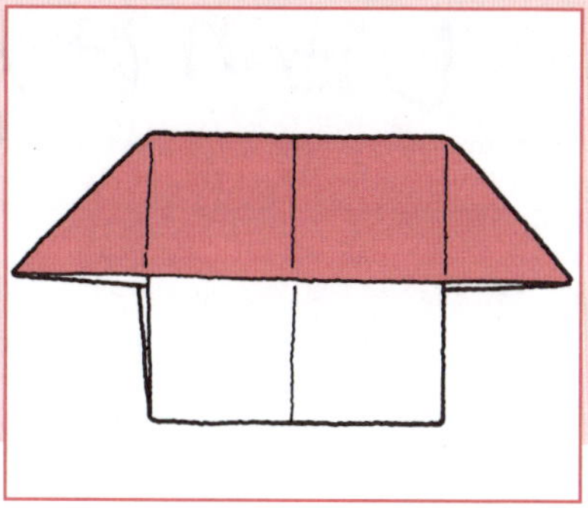

1 折り紙の裏を出す。タテ、ヨコ、半分に折りすじをつけ、もとに戻す。
Make a cross shaped crease.

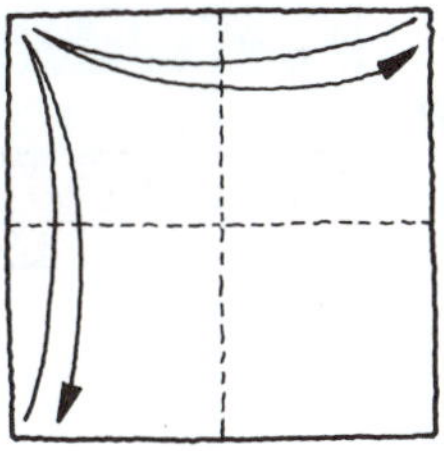

2 中心の折りすじに合わせて、半分に折る。
Fold the top edge down to the center.

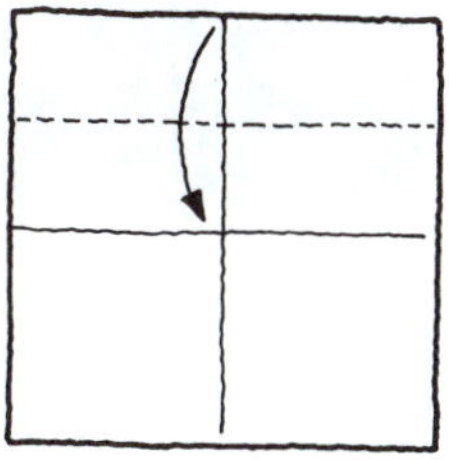

3 ひっくり返す。中心の折りすじに合わせ、左右を折る。
Turn over. Fold both sides to the center.

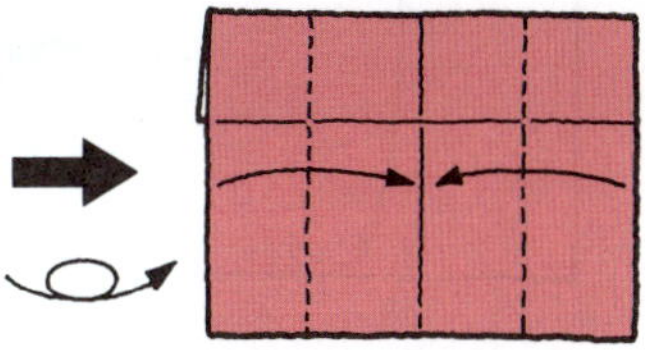

4 ●と○を広げるように折る（●を右に、○を左に引っぱるようにする）。
Pull ○ to the left and ● to the right, then flatten.

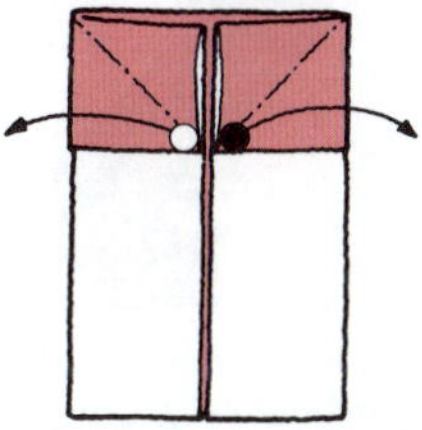

5 半分に折る。
Fold the bottom edge up to the center line.

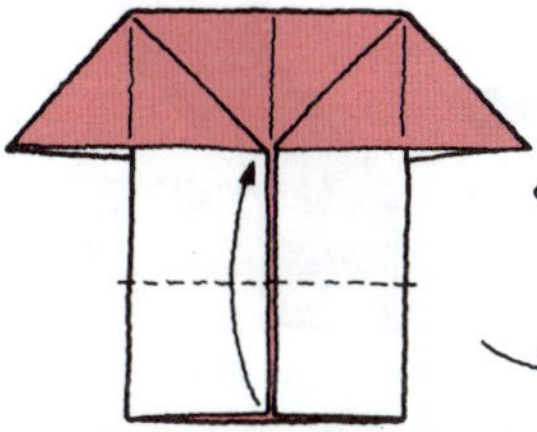

6 ひっくり返す。
Turn over.

Finished

しゅりけん

Syuriken

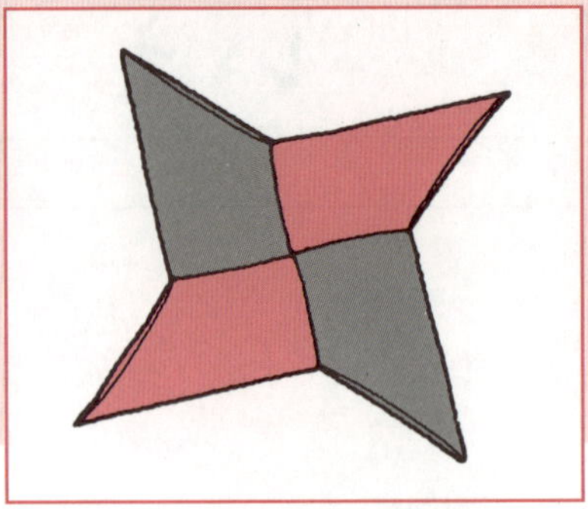

1 半分に折る。
Fold in half.

2 半分に折る。
Fold in half again.

3 もう1枚同じものを作る。
Make another piece.

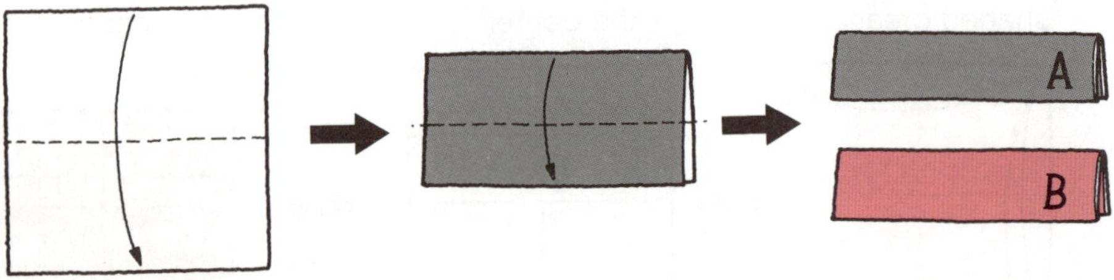

4 中心に折りすじをつけ、斜めに折る。
Make a crease in the center and fold both sides diagonally.

5 図のように置く。
Place it as shown.

6 ひっくり返す。矢印のほうに折る。
Turn over. Fold in the direction of the arrows.

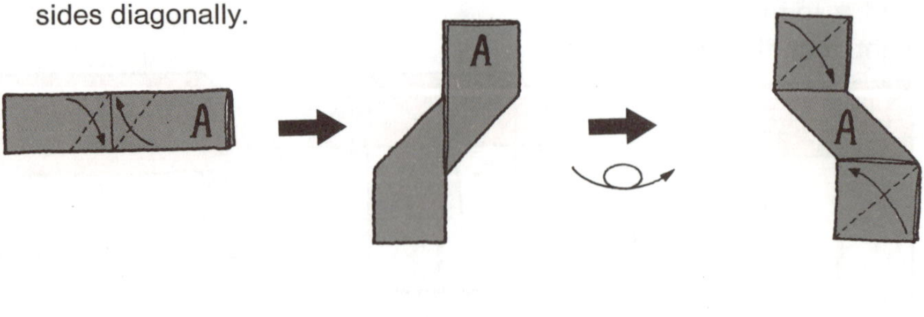

7 Aと同じく、中心に折りすじをつけ、斜めに折る。
Repeat steps 4 ~6 on piece "B".

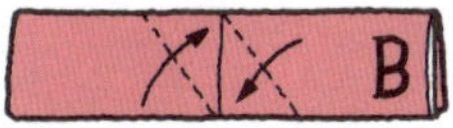

8 Bも図のように置く。ひっくり返す。
Place it as shown. Turn over.

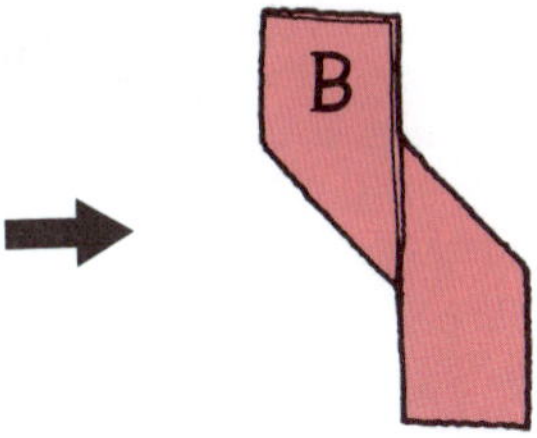

9 矢印のほうに折る。
Fold in the direction of the arrows.

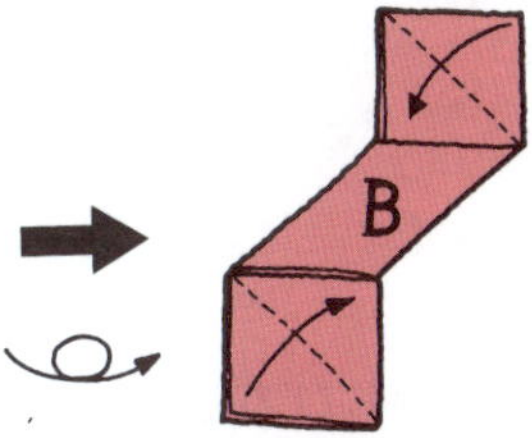

10 ひっくり返すと、図のようになる。
Turn over. It should look like this.

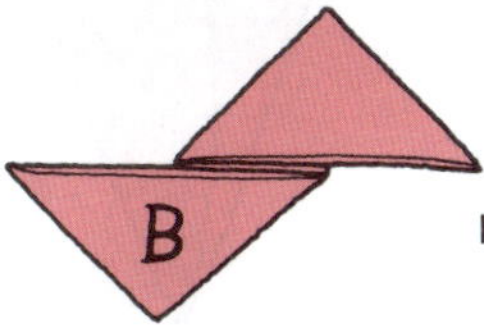

11 Aの☆部分にBを重ねる。
Put B on the ☆ of A.

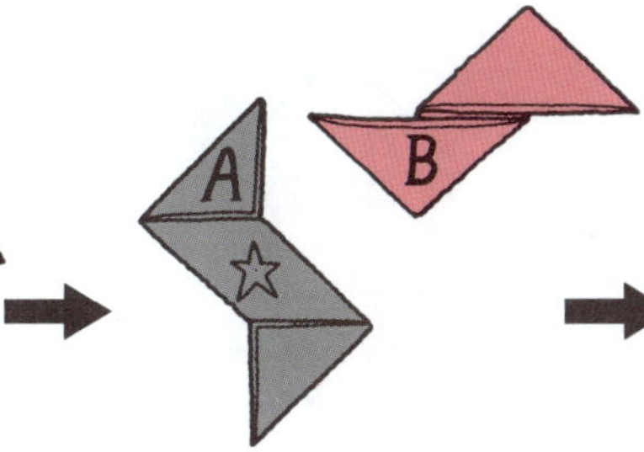

12 ①をBの●の袋へ折り込む。
Fold the tips① of A into ● of B.

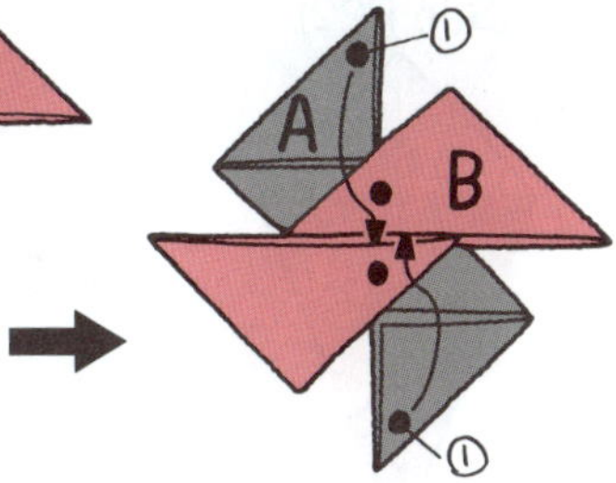

13 ひっくり返す。
Turn over.

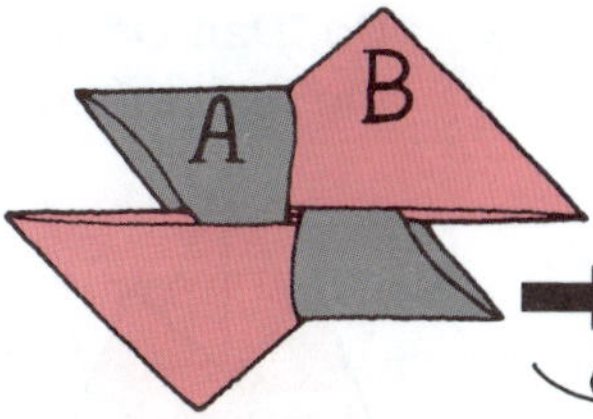

14 ②をAの●の袋へ折り込む。
Fold the tips② of B into ● of A.

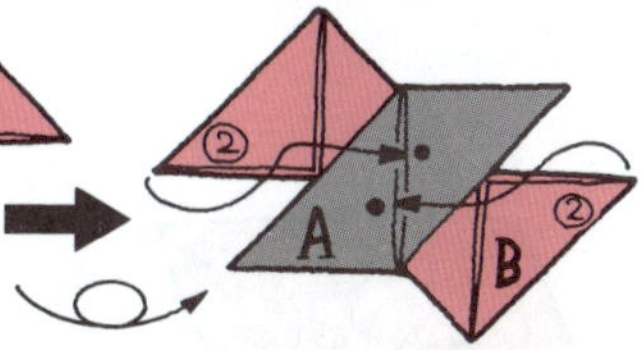

Finished

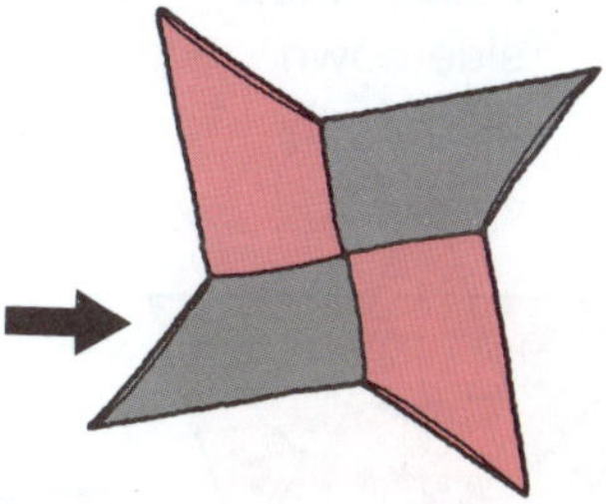

おひなさま

Ohinasama

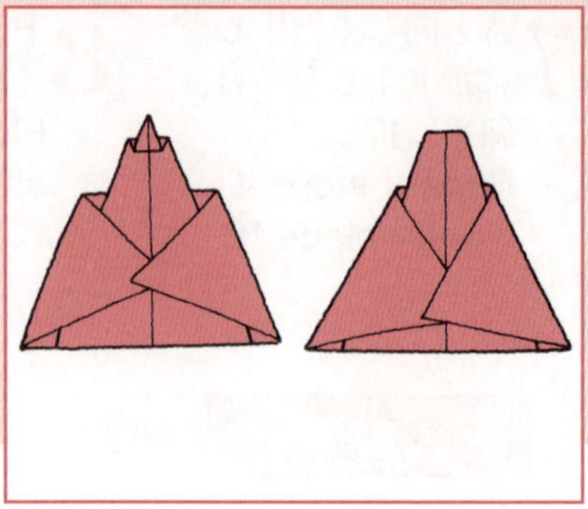

おびな
Obina

1 凧の基本形（P22参照）から始める。
Begin with "Basic Kite" (See P22).

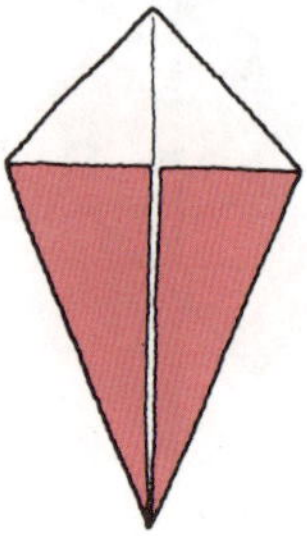

2 白い三角部分を折り下げる。
Fold the white triangle down.

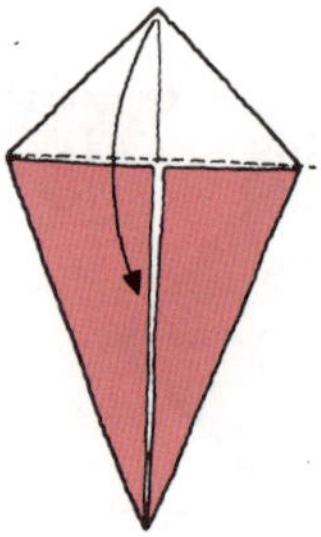

3 下の三角部分を折り上げる。
Fold the bottom corner up.

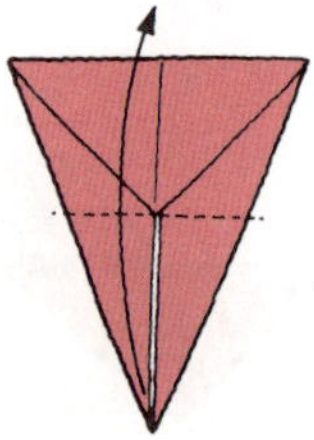

4 左の三角を斜めに折り下げる。
Fold the left side down diagonally.

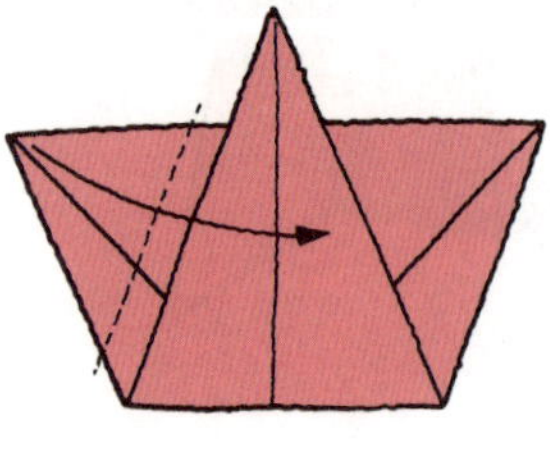

5 右側も同様に折り下げる。
Do the same with the right side.

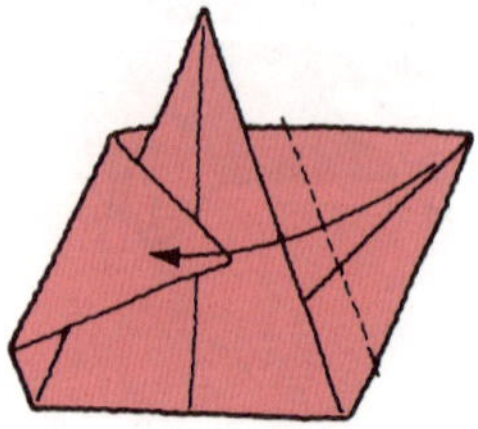

6 上の三角部分をだん折り（P17参照）にする。
Do "Dan-Ori" on the top corner.

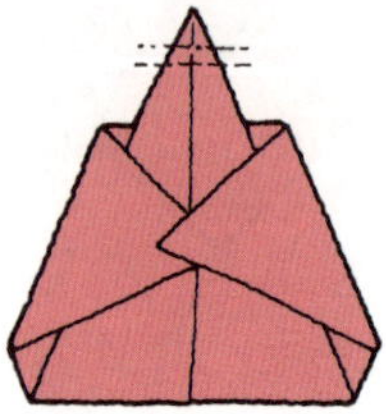

7 下を少し折る。
Fold the bottom backward a little.

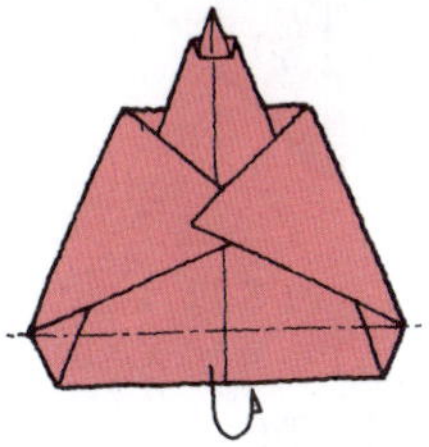

Finished

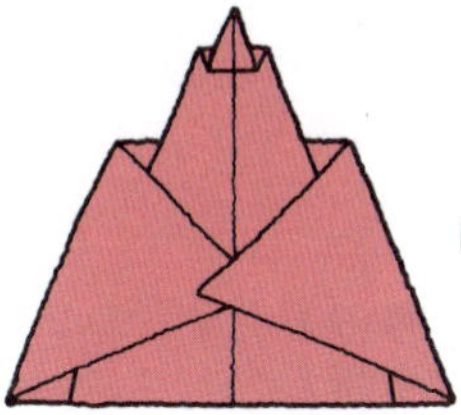

めびな
Mebina

1 おびなの4から始め、左を折る。
Repeat obina steps 1~3. Fold the flap down.

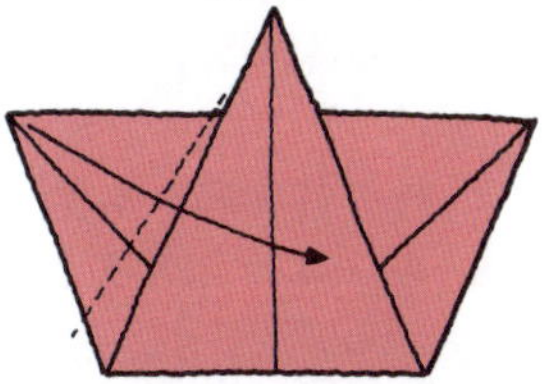

2 右側も同様に折り下げる。
Do the same with the right side.

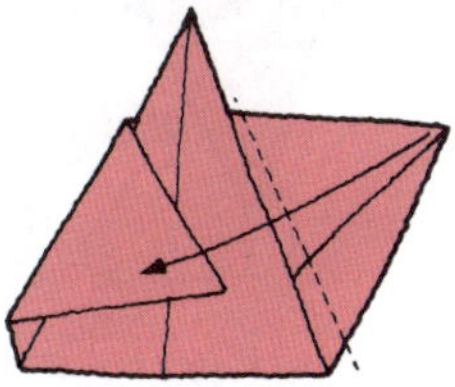

3 上の三角部分を裏側に折る。
Fold the top corner backward.

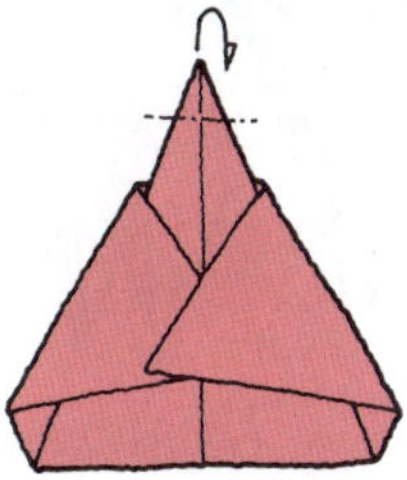

4 下を少し折る。
Fold the bottom backward a little.

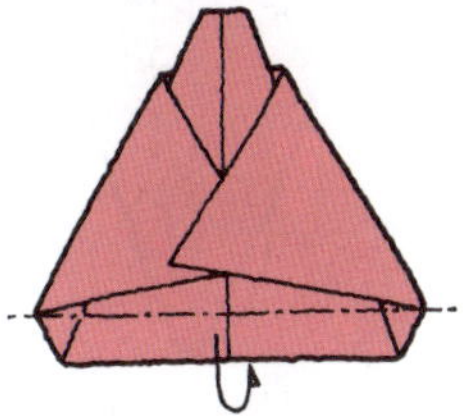

Finished

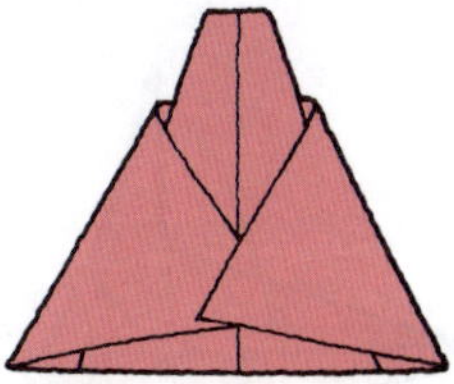

※おびなとめびなを並べて飾る。
Place Obina & Mebina side by side.

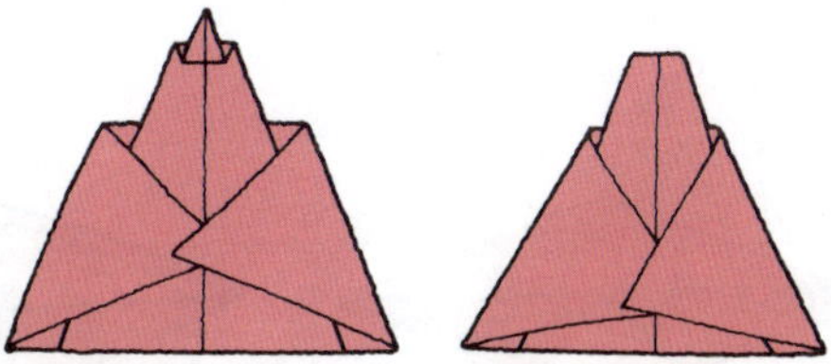

●日本には、ひなまつりという伝統的な行事があります。おひなさまはそのときに、女児の息災を願って飾られます。
●Hinamaturi is one of traditional festivals in Japan. Ohinasama (special dolls for Hinamaturi) are decorated to wish the healthy growth of girls.

こま

Top

●材料　materials

マッチ棒　match stick

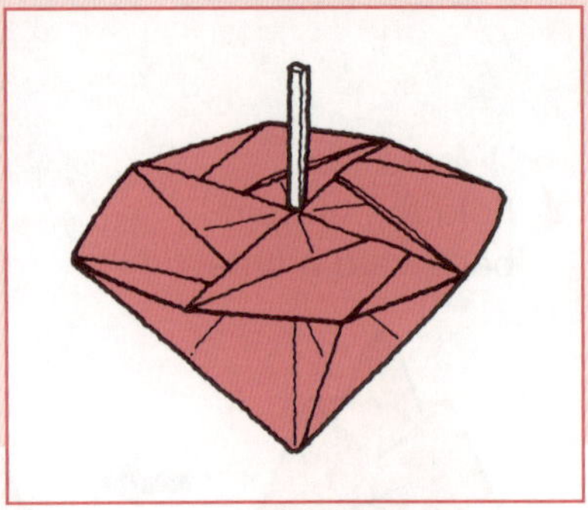

1 鶴の基本形から始め、カドを折り下げる。
Begin with "Basic Turn".
Fold the flaps down.

2 ●のカドを合わせて折る。
Fold the left edge up so that ● and ● meet.

3 引っぱられるほうも、しっかり折る。裏側も同様に。
Open it and flatten the resulting inner flap to the left. The reverse side too.

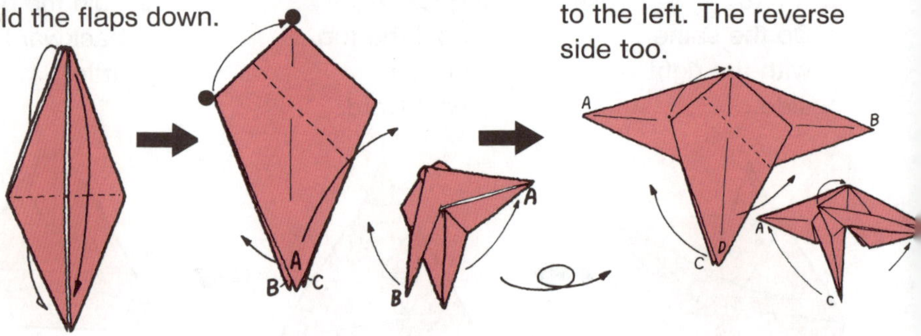

4 右側を折り上げる。
Fold the front right flap up.

5 右手前のカドを向こう側に折り上げる。
Bring the front right flap up to the top.

6 折り上げたカドを折り下げる。
Fold the top right flap down to the front.

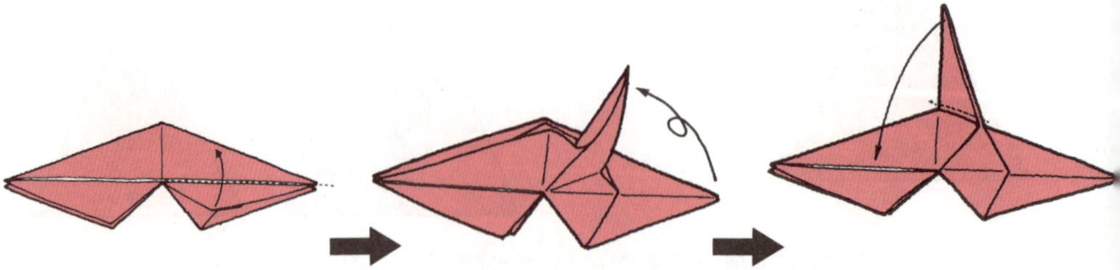

7 左を折り上げる。
Fold the bottom left flap up to the upper edge.

8 折り下げる。
Fold the left end down to the front.

9 裏返して同様に折る。
Turn over.
Repeat steps 4～8.

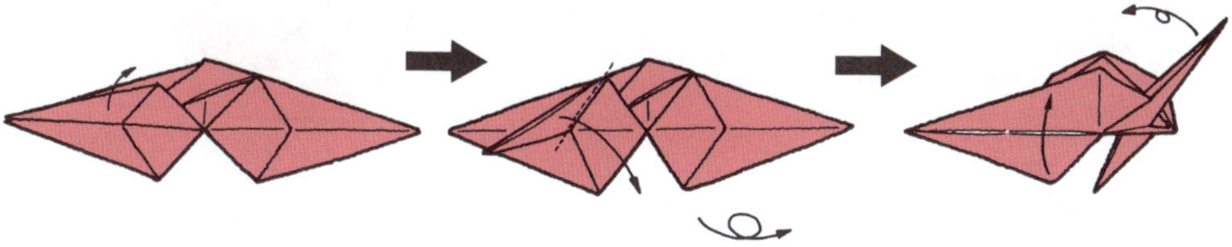

10 開く。
Open it.

11 カドを差し込む。
Tuck the tips into the front slit.

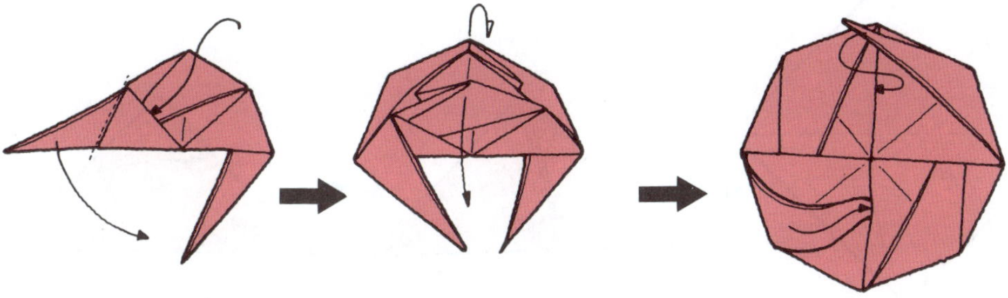

12 中心にマッチ棒を差し込む（先のところは取る）。
Insert a match stick in the center and spin.
(Break off the tip of the match stick)

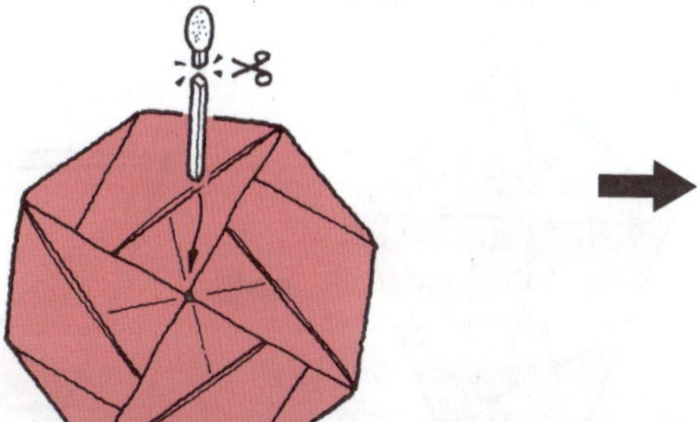

Finished

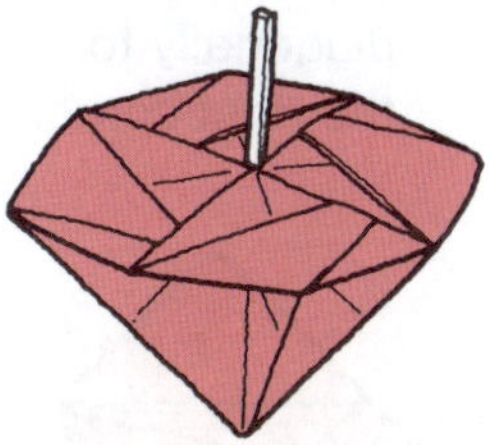

コップ

Cup

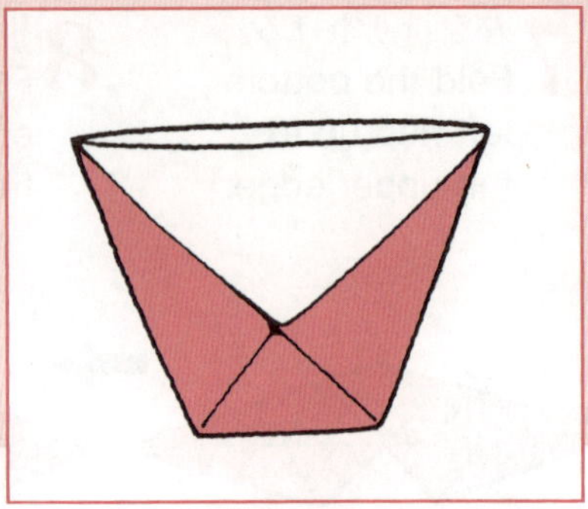

1 半分に折る。
Fold in half to the top corner.

2 上の１枚を折って、戻す。
Fold the front sheet down to the bottom edge. Unfold.

3 ○のところを合わせるように折る。
Fold the right corner to the left to meet ○.

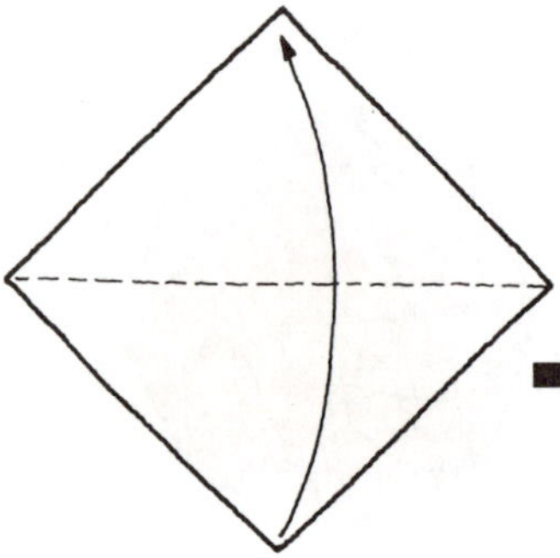

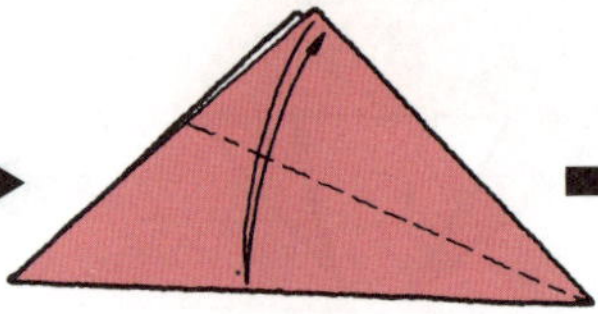

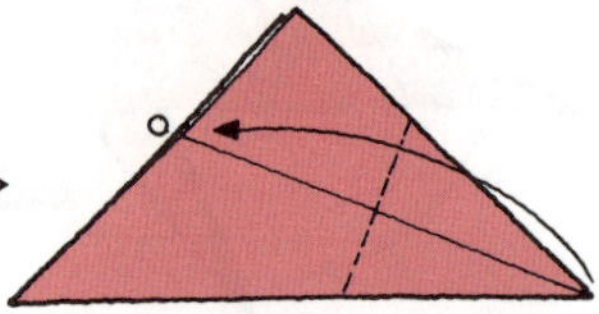

4 カドを合わせるように折る。
Fold the left corner up diagonally to the right corner.

5 上の１枚を折る。反対側も同様に。
Fold the front flap down. Do the same with the reverse side.

Finished

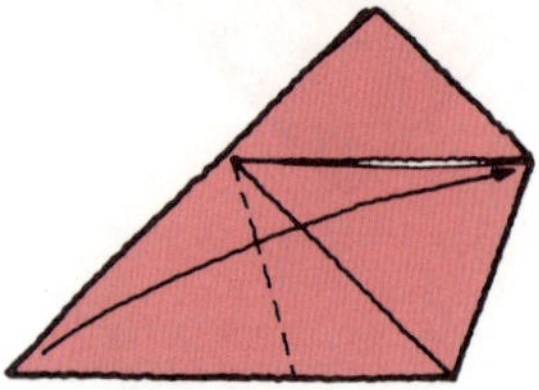

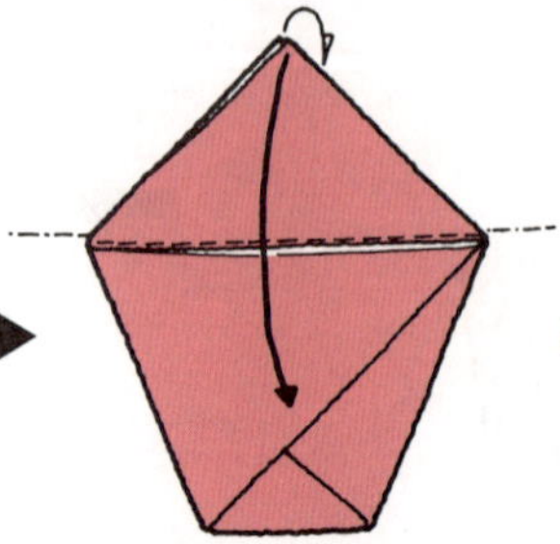

教会

Church

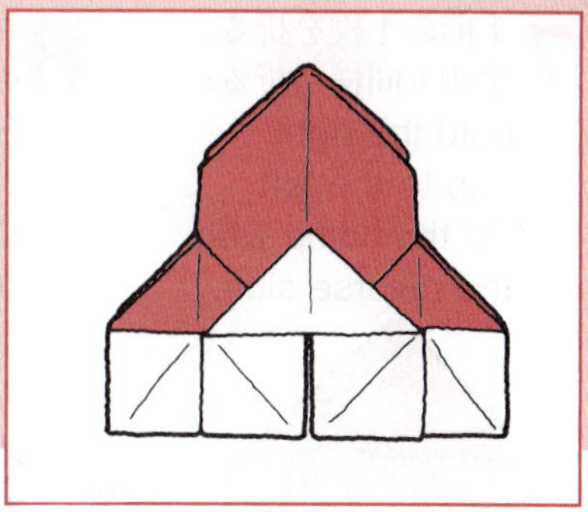

1 風船基本形（P 26 参照）から始める。
Begin with "Basic Fūsen" (See P26).

2 カドを折り上げる。
Fold both corners up to the top corner.

3 裏側も同様に折る。
Do the same with the reverse side.

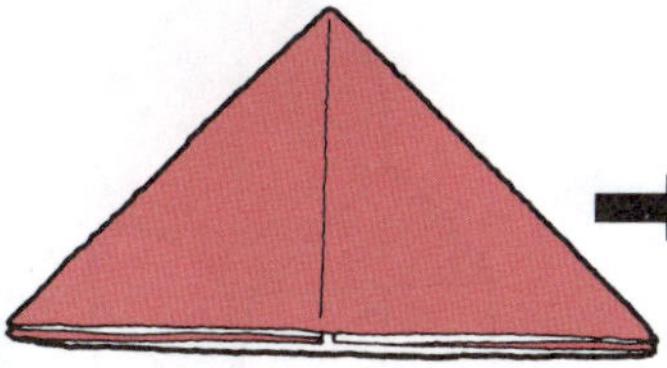

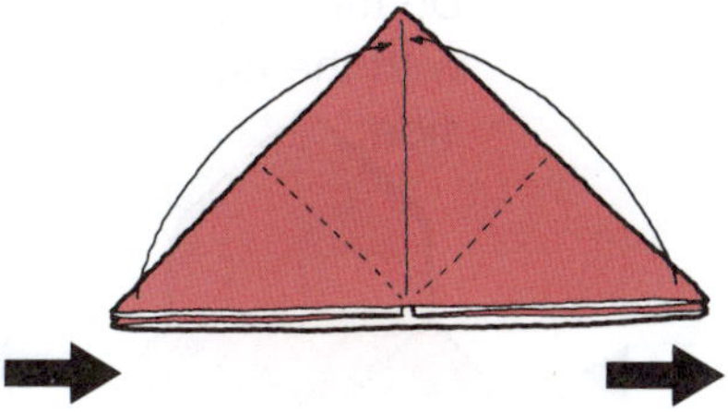

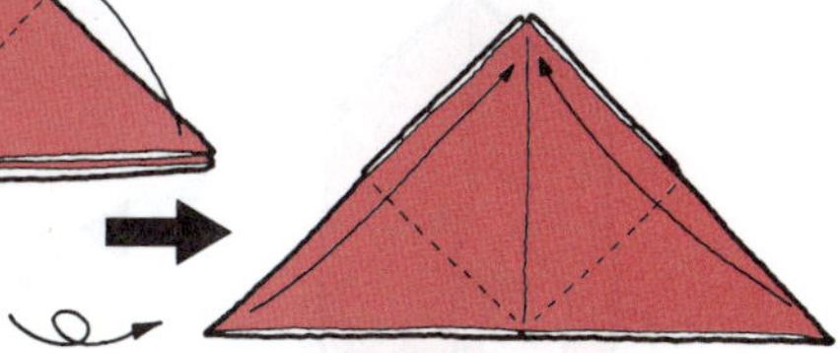

4 内側を広げて、つぶすように折る。
Open the pocket to make a square and flatten.

5 反対側も同様に。
Do the same with the right side.

6 裏側も同様に折る。
Do the same with the reverse side.

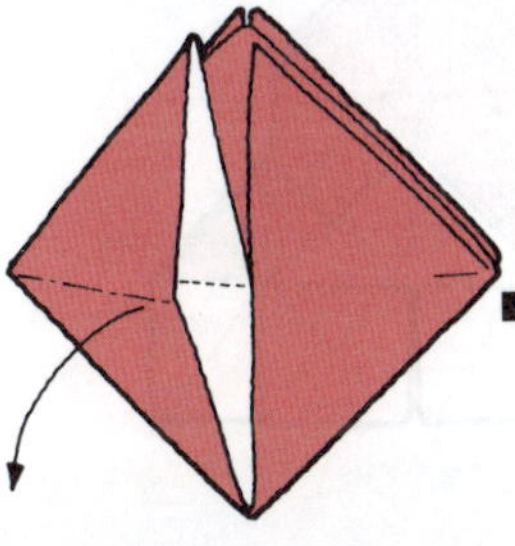

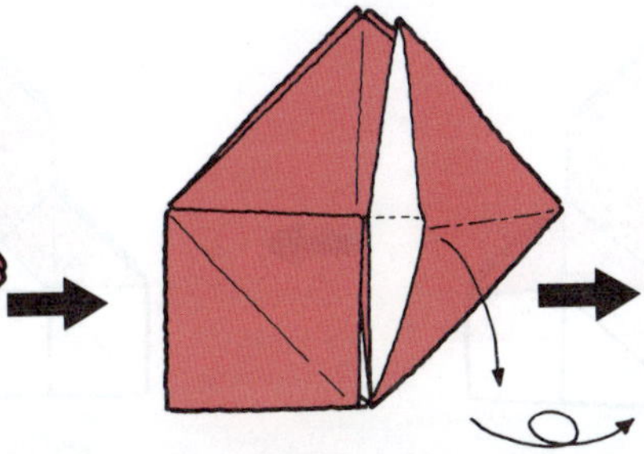

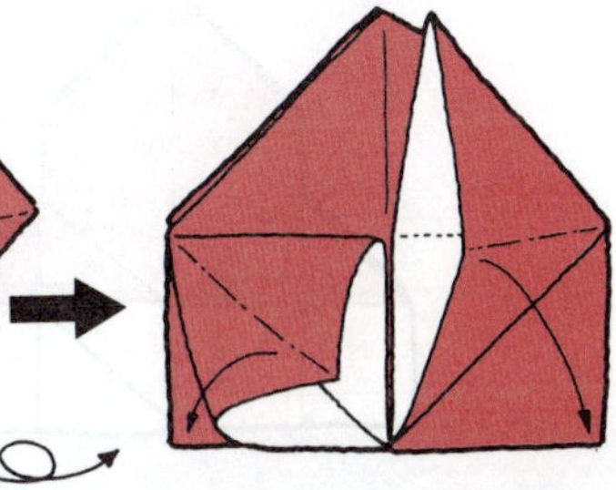

7 手前の１枚を折る。裏側も同様に折る。
Fold the right flap to the left. Do the same with the reverse side.

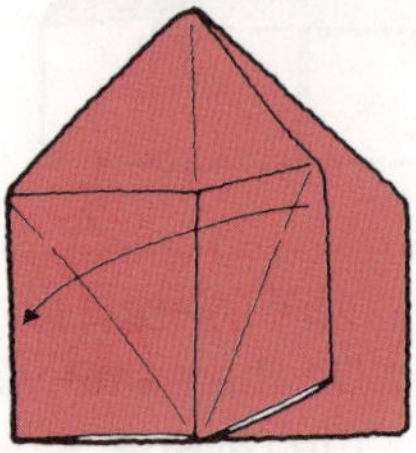

8 中央に合わせて折る。裏側も同様に。
Fold both sides to the center. Do the same with the reverse side.

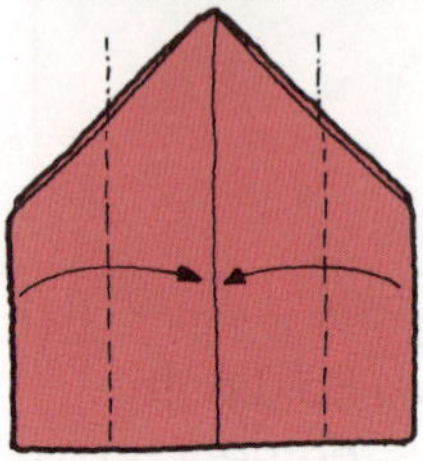

9 手前の１枚を折る。裏側も同様に折る。
Fold the right flap to the left. Do the same with the reverse side.

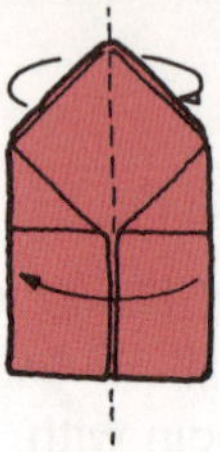

10 内側を広げ、つぶすように折る。
Open the pocket and flatten.

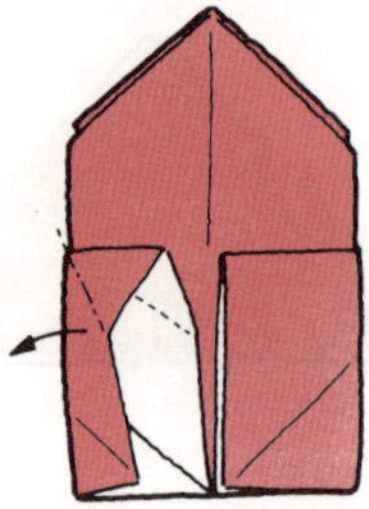

11 反対側も同様に折る。
Do the same with the right side.

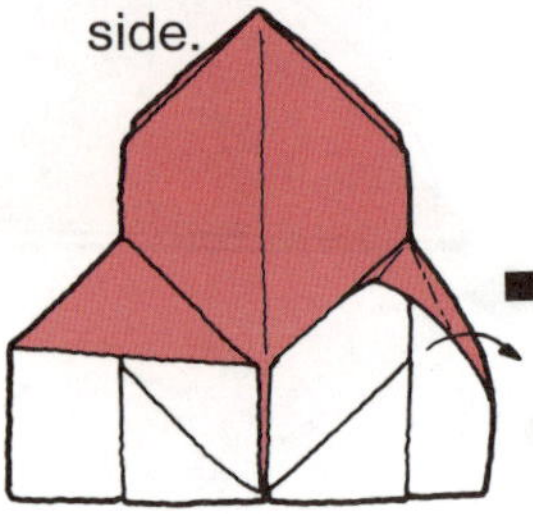

12 裏側も同様に。
Do the same with the reverse side.

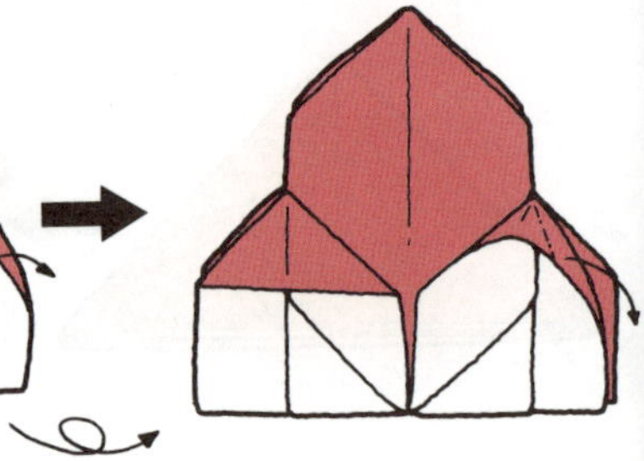

13 三角形の部分を折り上げる。裏側も同様に折る。
Fold the bottom corner of the lower triangle upward. Do the same with the reverse side.

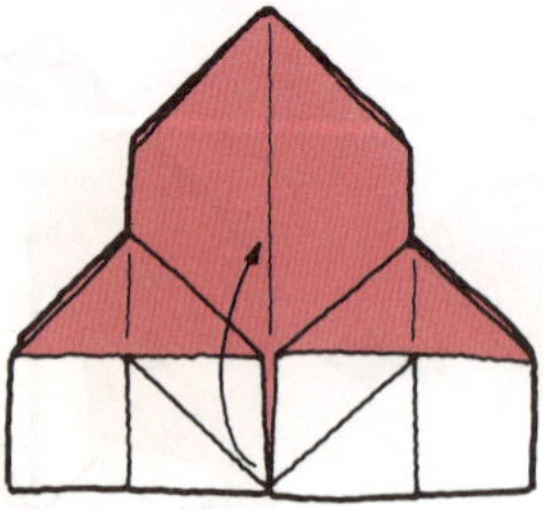

Finished

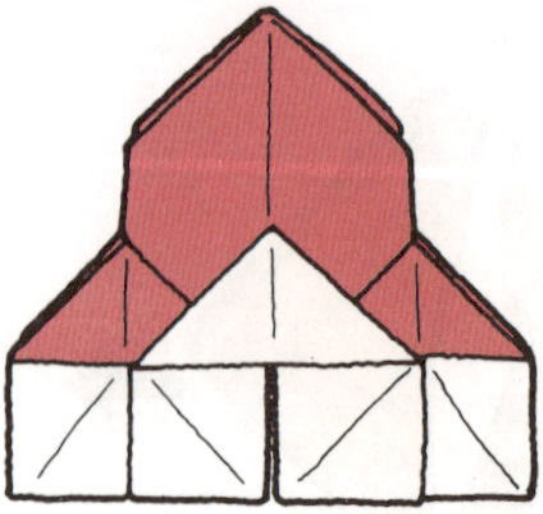

紙でっぽう

Popgun

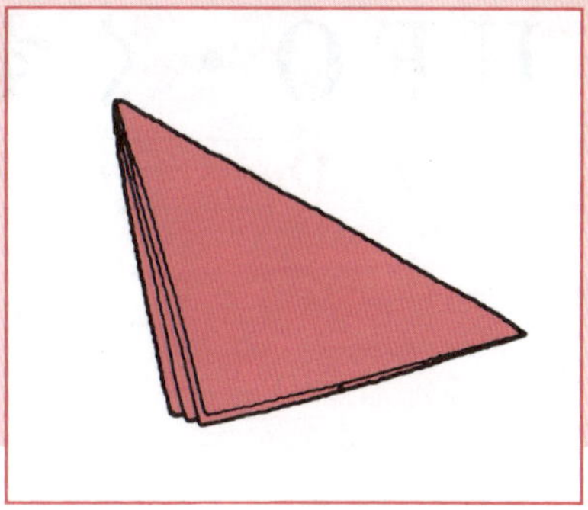

●材料　materials
新聞紙　newspaper

1 折りすじをつけ、もとにもどす。四すみを中心に合わせて折る。
Make a crease. Unfold. Fold the 4 corners to the center.

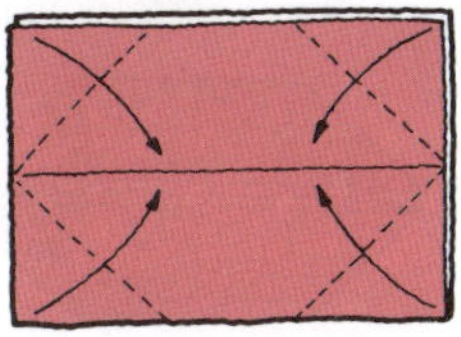

2 半分に折る。
Fold in half from the left.

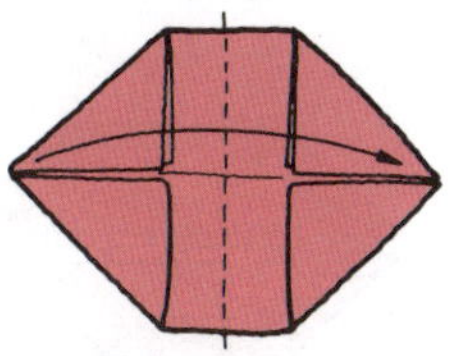

3 半分に折る。
Fold in half from the bottom.

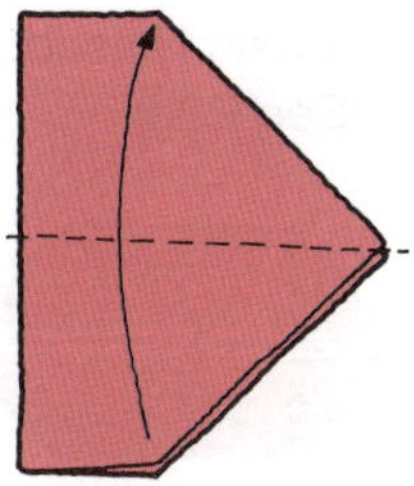

4 袋になっている部分を開いて折る。裏側も同様に折る。
Open the pocket and flatten. Do the same with the reverse side.

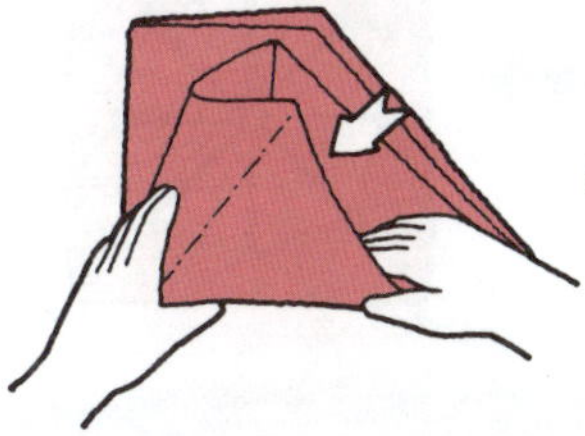

5 上の１枚を折り下げる。裏側も同様に折る。
Fold the top flap down. Do the same with the reverse side.

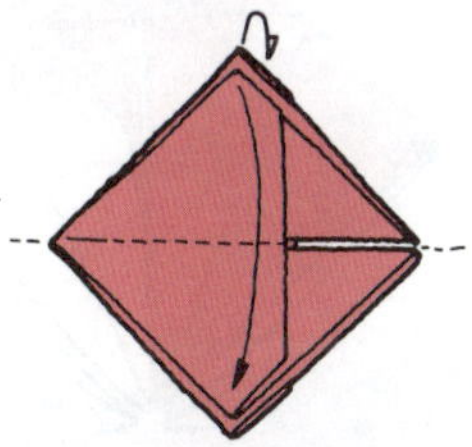

Finished

※右はじを持って思いきり振り下ろそう。
Hold the right side, then swing down quickly to make a "pop" sound.

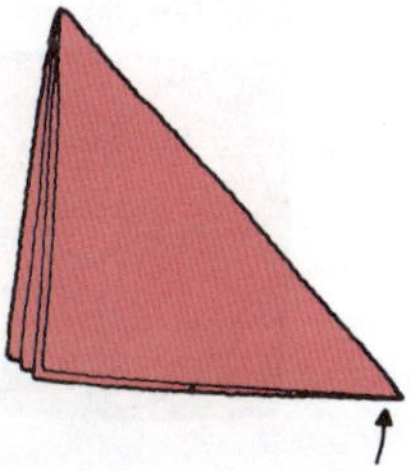

UFO・くす玉

UFO • Decorative Ball

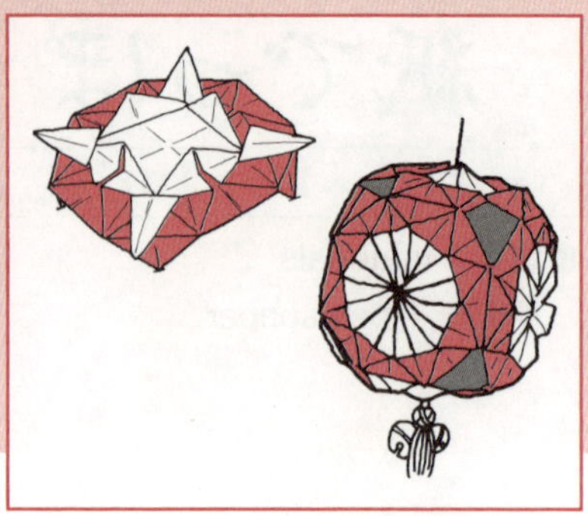

ＵＦＯ
UFO

1 二そう船基本形(Ｐ23参照)から始める。
Begin with "Basic Nisoubune" (See P23).

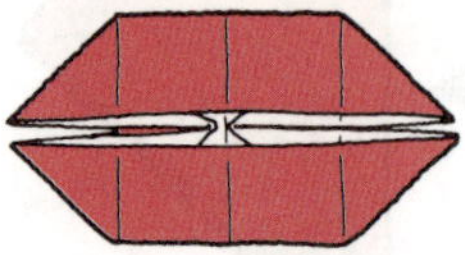

2 四すみを矢印の方向に折る。
Fold the 4 corners in the direction of the arrows.

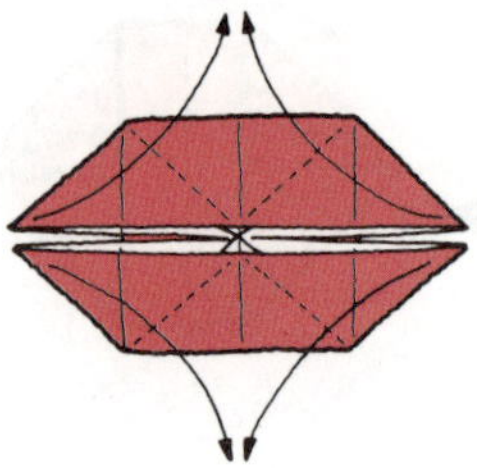

3 ４つの袋を開いて四角形に折る。
Open the 4 pockets and flatten to form squares.

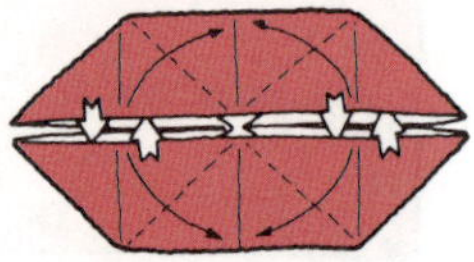

4 中心の折りすじに合わせ、８カ所を三角形に折る。
Fold the left and right flaps of each square in to meet in the center.

5 袋になっている部分を８カ所開く。
Open the pocket of all eight triangles.

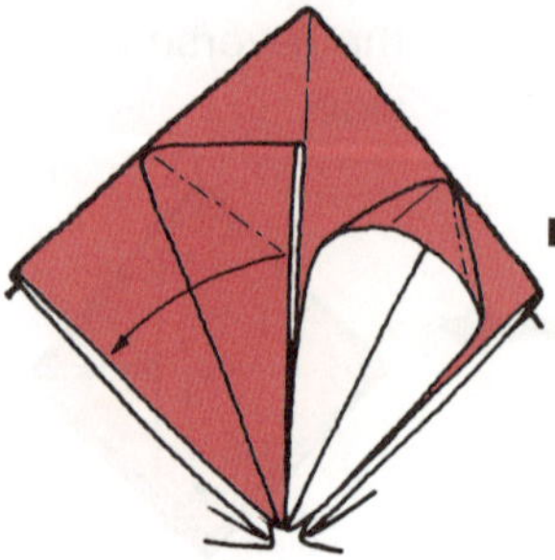

6 四すみを山折りにする。
Fold the 4 corners backward.

7 上のとがった部分を外側に折る。
Fold the 4 triangles A outside.

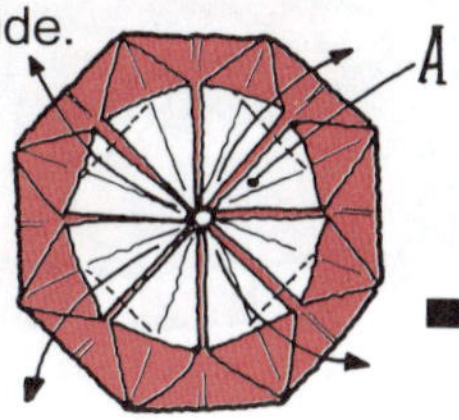

8 内側の部分を図のように立てる。
Fold the 4 triangles B to stand upward as shown.

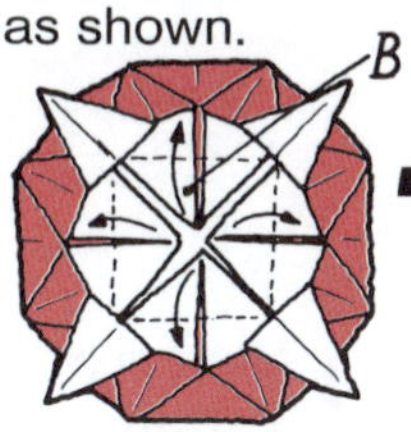

Finished

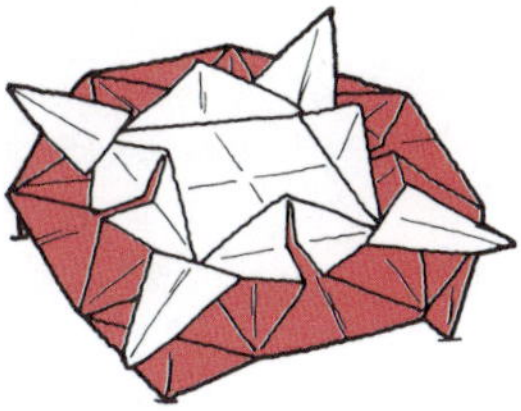

くす玉
Decorative Ball

1 ＵＦＯの**6**の形を６枚作る。四すみを山折りにしてもとに戻す。
Repeat steps **1〜6**, make 6 UFO pieces. Unfold the corners.

2 折りすじをつけた６枚の四すみにのりづけをする。
Glue each corner of the 6 pieces.

3 まず、４枚をつなぎ合わす。
Glue 4 pieces together.

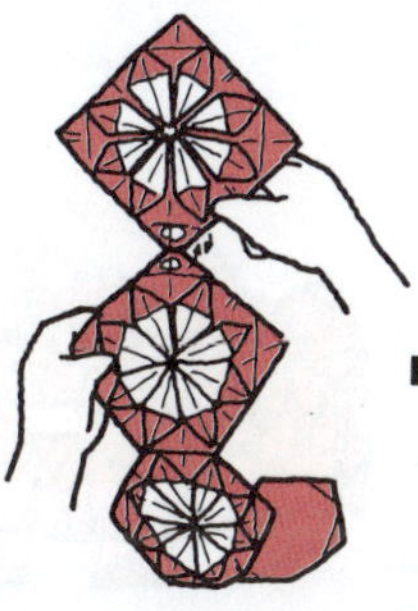

4 左右残りの２枚をはり合わす。
Glue 2 other pieces on the left and right sides.

Finished

王冠

Crown

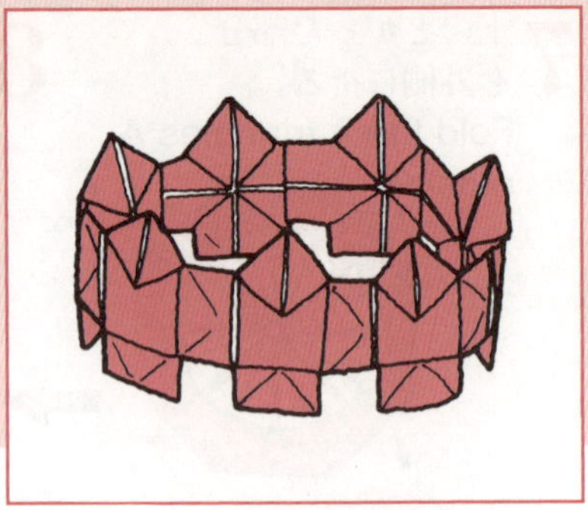

1 ざぶとん基本形(P23参照)から始める。
Begin with "Basic Zabuton" (See P23).

2 ひっくり返し、四すみを中心に合わせて折る。
Turn over.
Fold the corners to the center.

3 もう一度ひっくり返す。四すみを、中心に合わせる。
Turn over again and repeat step 2.

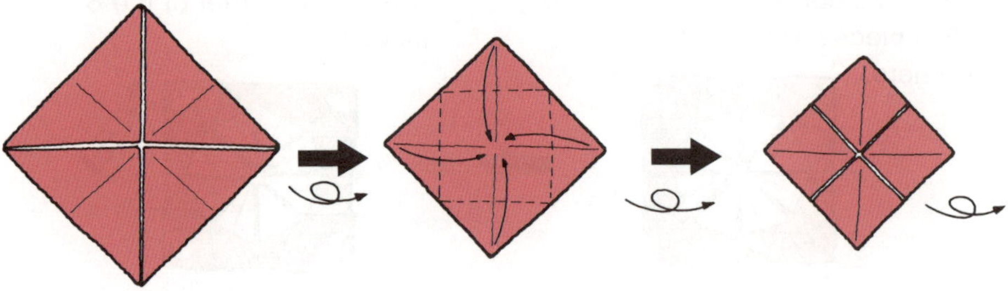

4 ひっくり返す。袋の部分を3カ所とも、長方形に開く。
Turn over.
Open the 3 lower pockets to make rectangles.

5 これを7～8つ用意し、つなぎ合わせる。
Make 7～8 pieces, and glue together as shown.

6 輪にする。
Make a ring.

Finished

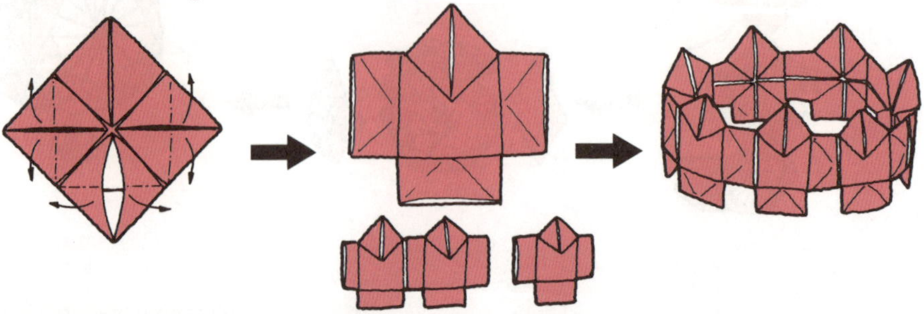

小鳥型飛行機

Airplane

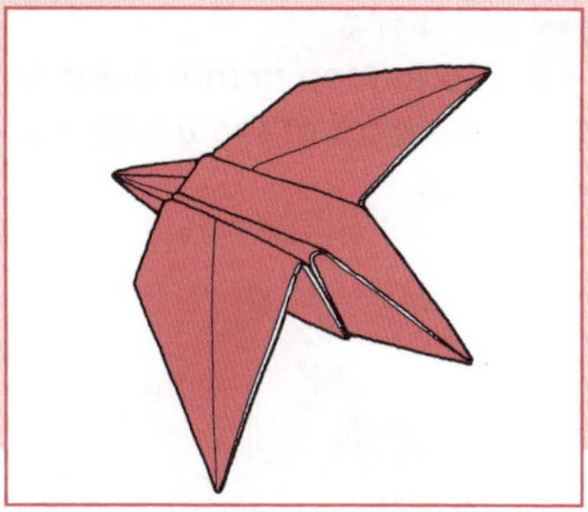

1 裏を出し、半分に折る。
Fold in half to the bottom corner.

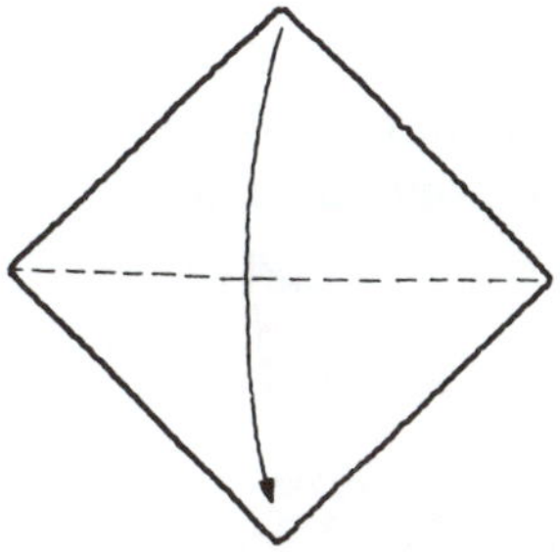

2 左右のカドを下に合わせて折る。
Fold both corners down to the bottom corner.

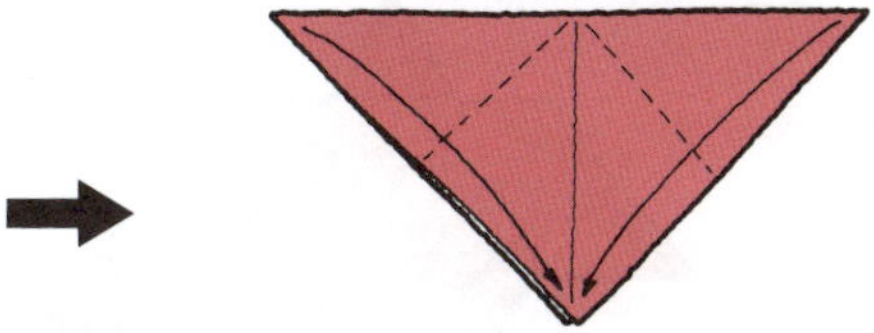

3 図のようになる。
It should look like this.

4 中心に合わせて左右を折る。裏側は折らずにはね出す。
Fold the left and right edges to the center, then pull the back flaps to each side to form a triangle.

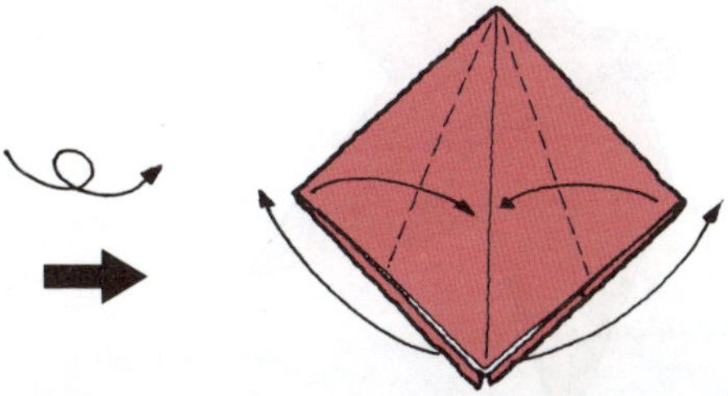

5 折り下げる。
Fold the top corner down to the center of the triangular edge.

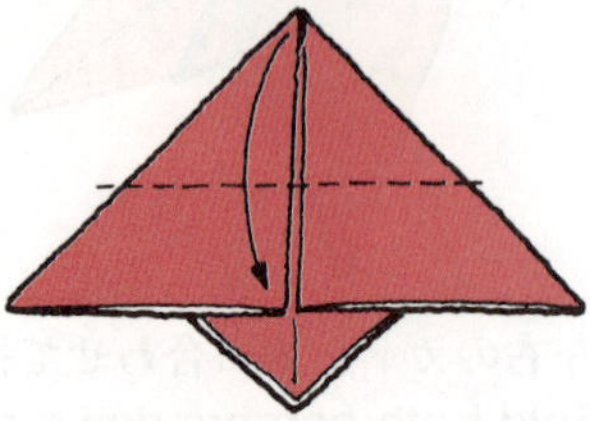

6 点線にそって折り上げる。
Fold the bottom corner of the front flap up along the dotted line.

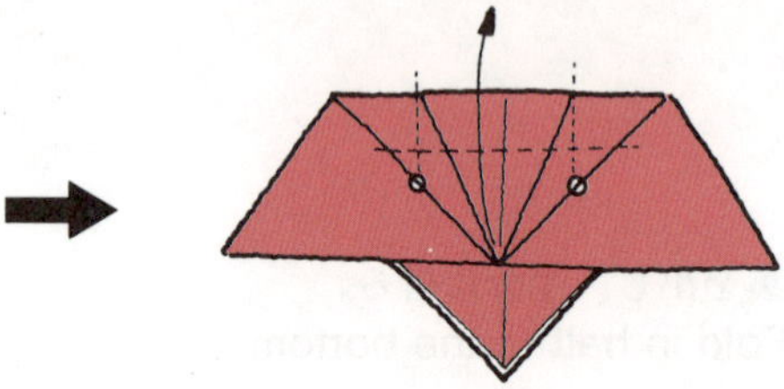

7 ひっくり返して、半分に折る。
Turn over. Fold in half to the right.

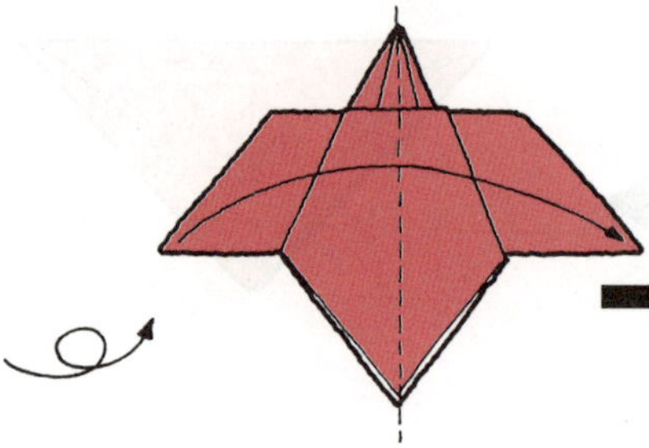

8 はねの部分を折り下げる。裏側も同様に折る。
Fold the front flap down to the bottom corner. Do the same with the reverse side.

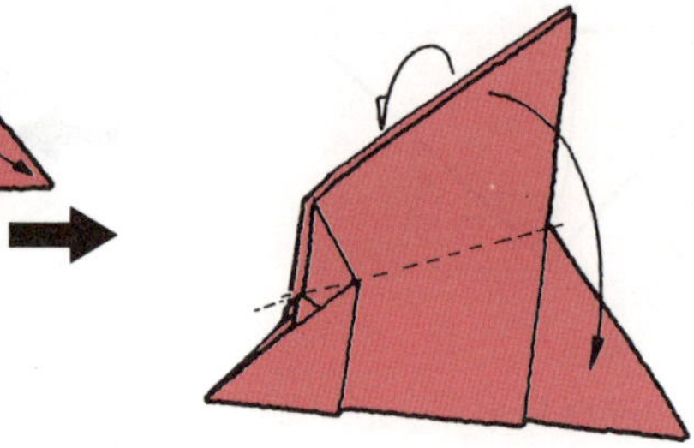

Finished

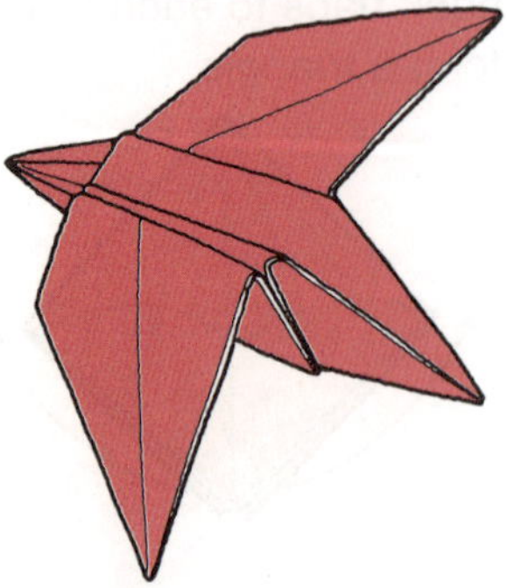

ふきごま

Pinwheel

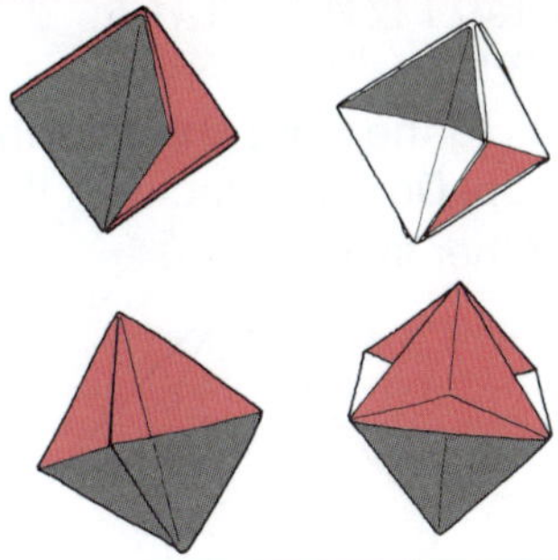

ふきごま①
Pinwheel①

1 色を表に出して、正方基本形（P25参照）を２枚作る。
Begin with "Basic" Square (See P25). Make 2 different coloured pieces.

2 ４枚のはねが均等になるように、左右のカドを起こす。
Open each piece slightly.

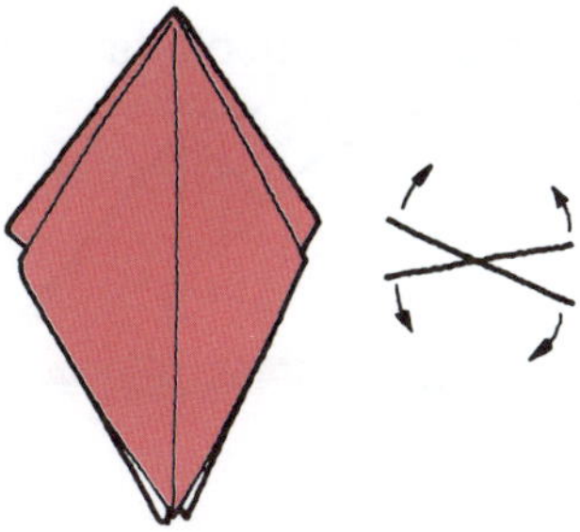

3 開いている側を、交互に差し込む。
Insert the tips of each piece into the pockets of the other.

Finished

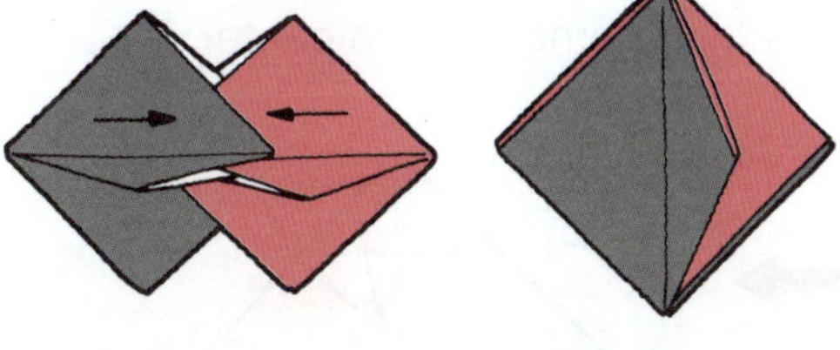

ふきごま②
Pinwheel②

1 表を中にして正方基本形を２枚作る。
Begin with "Basic Square". Make 2 different coloured pieces.

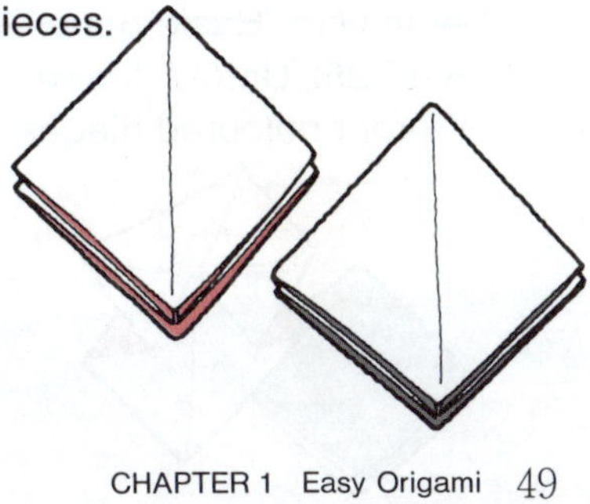

2 上の１枚を折り上げる。裏側も同様に。
Fold the front sheet to the top. Do the same with the other side.

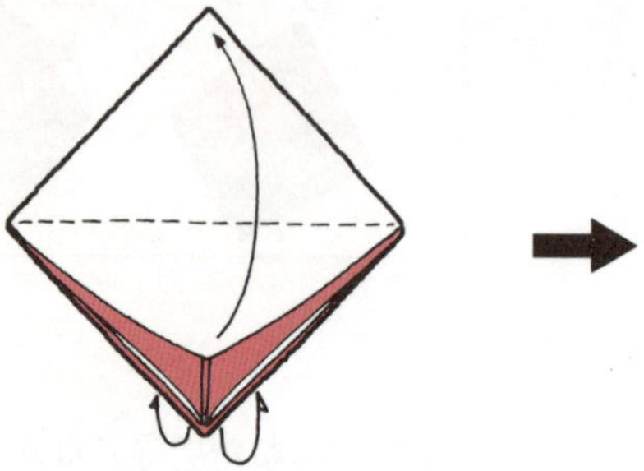

3 ４枚のはねが均等になるように、左右のカドを起こす。
Open each piece slightly.

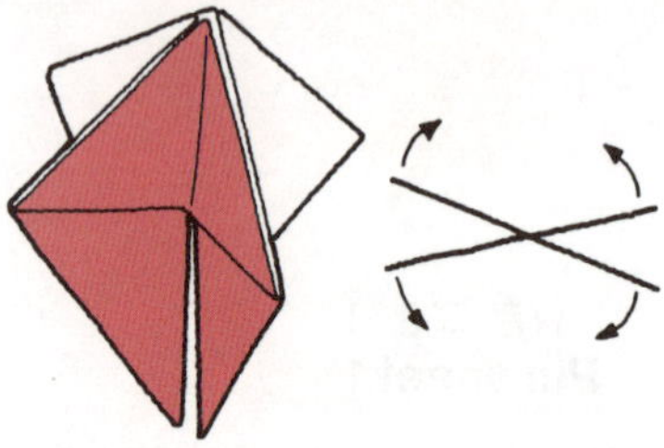

4 それぞれの開いている側を、交互に差し込む。
Insert the pointed tips of each piece into the pockets of the other.

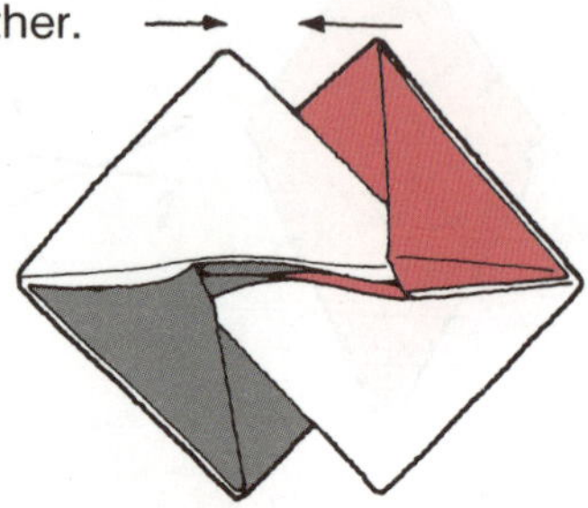

Finished

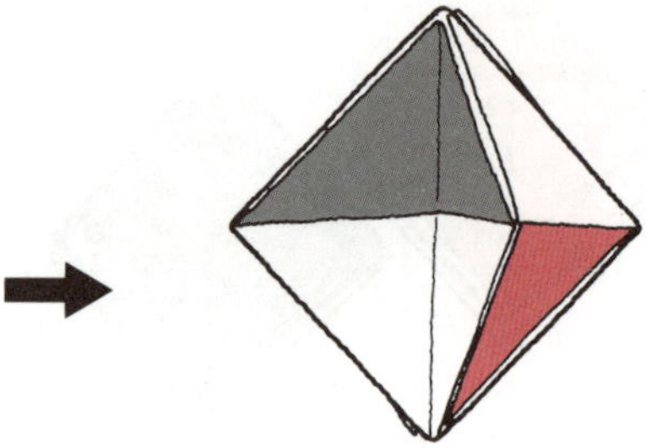

ふきごま③
Pinwheel③

1 色を表に出して、正方基本形（P25参照）を２枚折り、それぞれ広げる。
Begin with "Basic Square" (See P25). Unfold. Make 2 different coloured pieces.

2 裏返して、上下のカドを中心に合わせて折る。
Fold the top and bottom corners to the center.

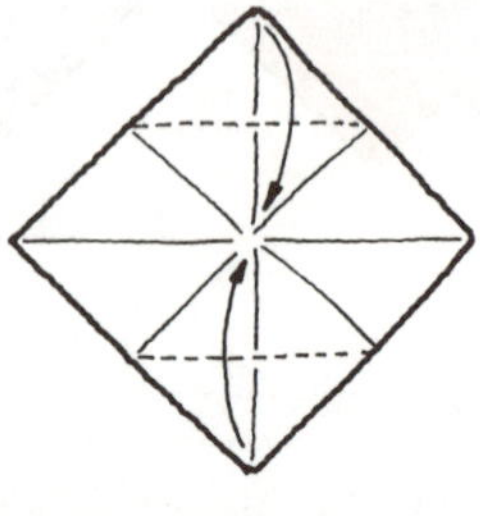

3 折りすじどおりにたたむ。
Using the creases, fold both sides in and up to the center.

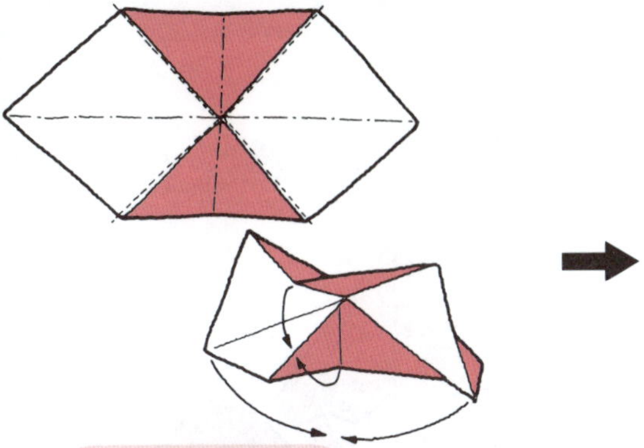

4 開いている側を図のように交互に差し込む。
Insert the pointed tips of each piece into the pockets of the other.

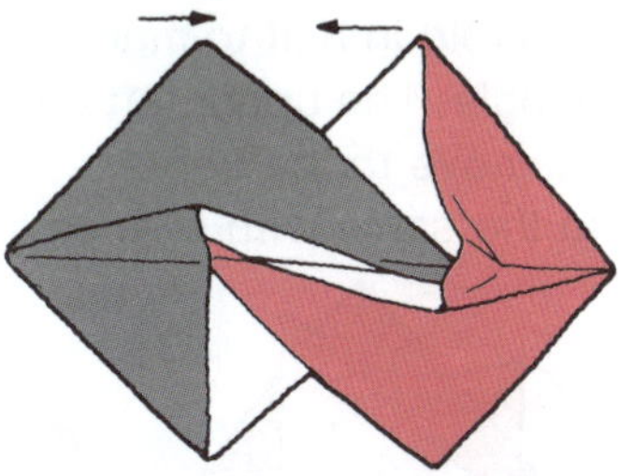

Finished

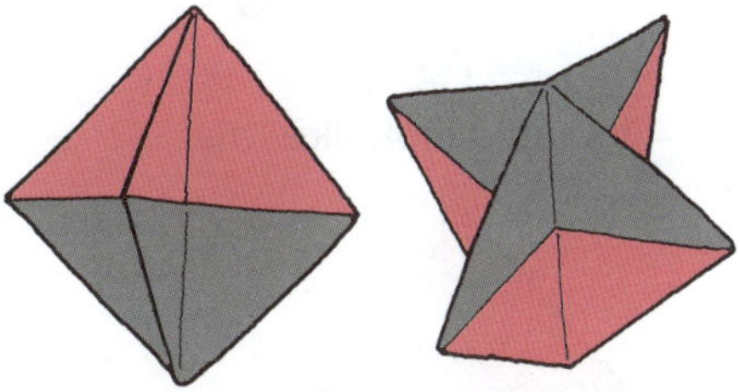

ふきごま④
Pinwheel④

1 色を表に出して、正方基本形を２枚折る。
Begin with "Basic Square". Make 2 different coloured pieces.

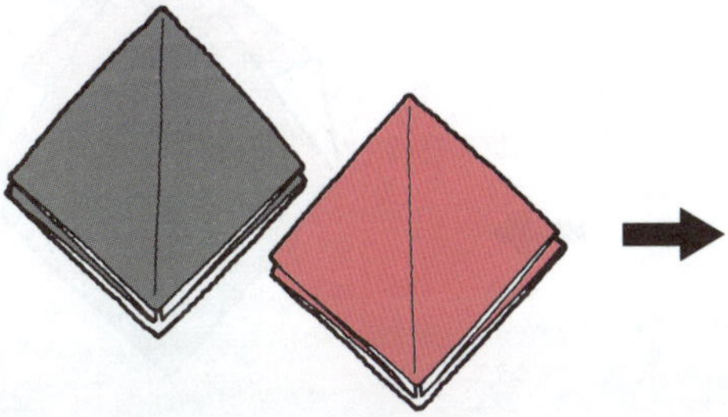

2 上の１枚を折り上げる。裏側も同様に。
Fold the front sheet to the top. Do the same with the reverse side.

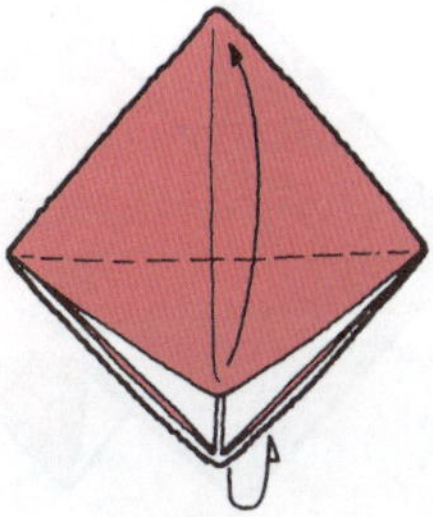

3 上のカドを右のカドに合わせ、重なった部分を手前に折りたたむ。引っぱられる左半分は、垂直に立たせる。裏側も同様に折る。
Bring the bottom corner of the front flap to the right corner, then fold in half to make a triangle. The upper left edge will move to the center.
Do the same with reverse side.

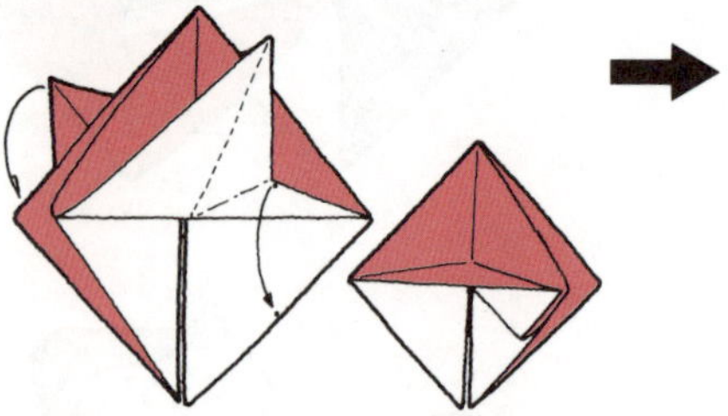

4 三角の部分を裏側に折り込む。
Fold both small triangles backward.

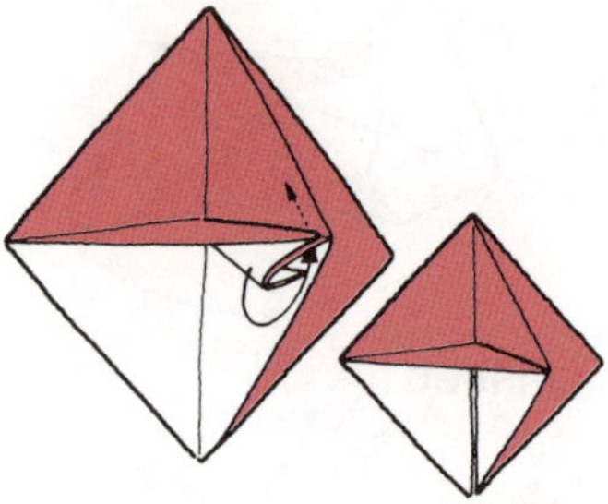

5 一カ所だけ少し折り上げる。
※差し込みやすくするため。
Fold the bottom corner of one piece a little.

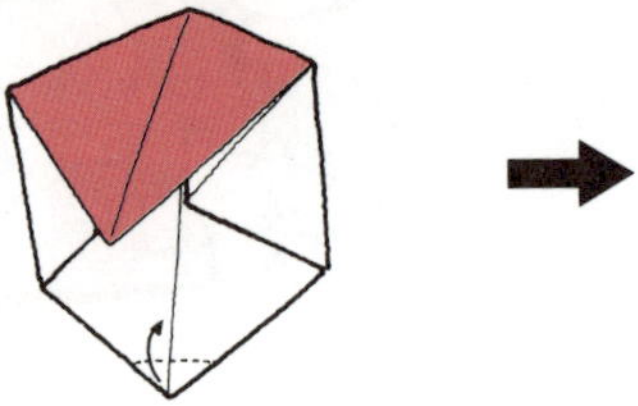

図のようになる。
It should look like this.

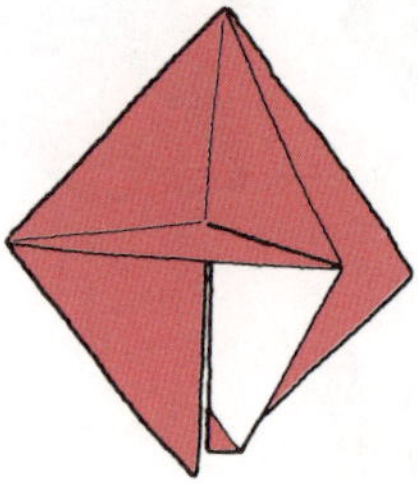

6 開いている側を、図のように交互に差し込む。
Insert the tips of each piece into the pockets of the other as shown.

Finished

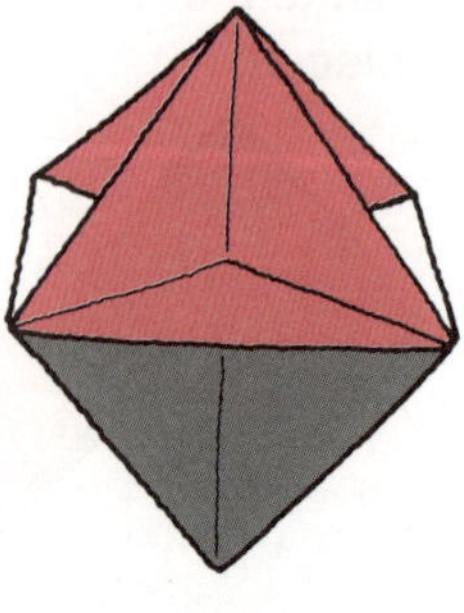

Chapter 2

つかえる折り紙
Useful Origami

コースター

Coaster

●材料　materials

3.5×20㎝

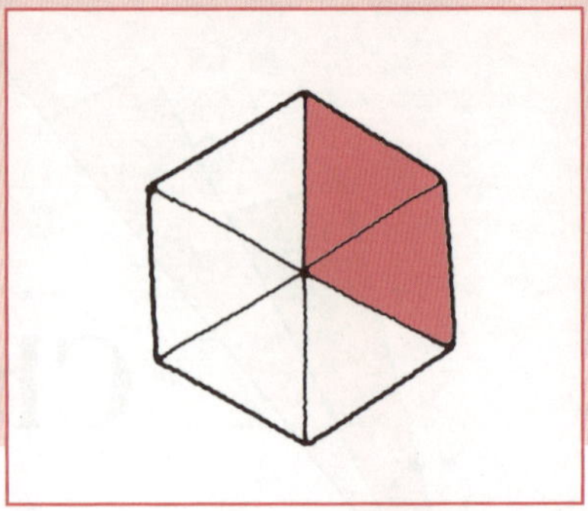

1 中心に折りすじをつけ、カドを中心線に合わせて折る。
Fold the left corner down to the center line.

2 辺と辺を合わせるようにして、正三角形を作っていく。
Fold the edge down to make an equilateral triangle.

3 端まで折って開く。
Repeat step 2 to the end.
Unfold.

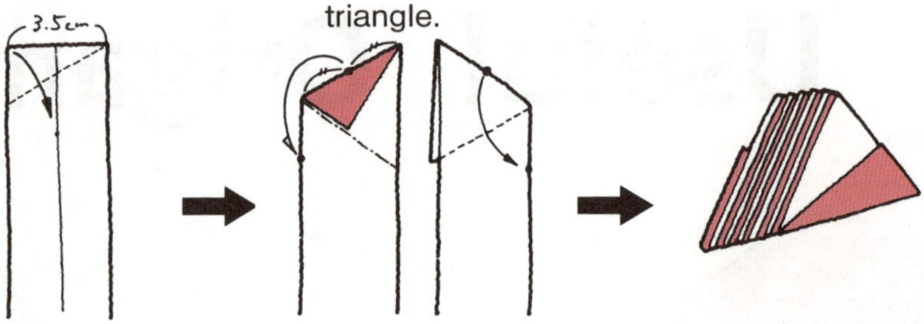

4 3番目の三角の辺で折っていく。
Fold every 3rd triangle backward.

5 あまった部分は間にはさむ。
Tuck in the ends.

Finished

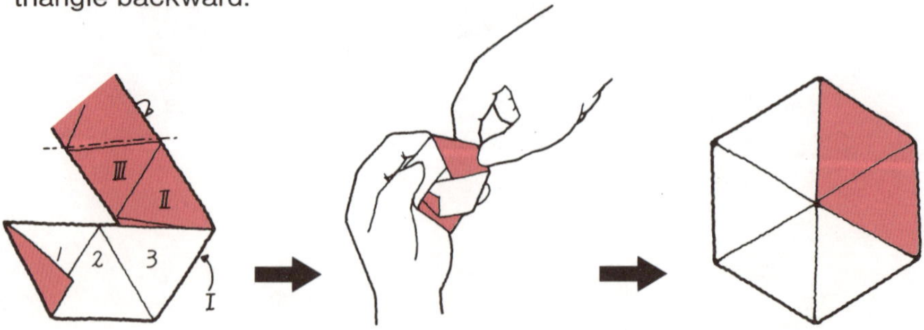

フォトフレーム

Photo Frame

1 二そう舟基本形(P23参照)から始める。
Begin with "Basic Nisoubune" (See P23).

2 4カ所ともカドを四角形につぶす。
Open the corners to form squares and flatten.

3 中心に集まっているカドを4すみにもどす。
Fold the flaps outward.

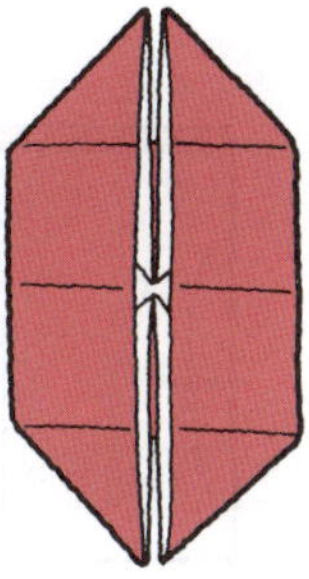

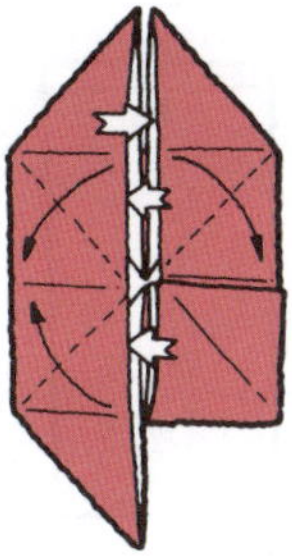

4 裏側へ折り返す。8カ所とも折る。
Raise a flap. Fold the point back to the center line. Repeat with the other 7 flaps.

5 中心に集まっている4つのカドを、外に向けて折る。
Fold each triangle outside.

Finished

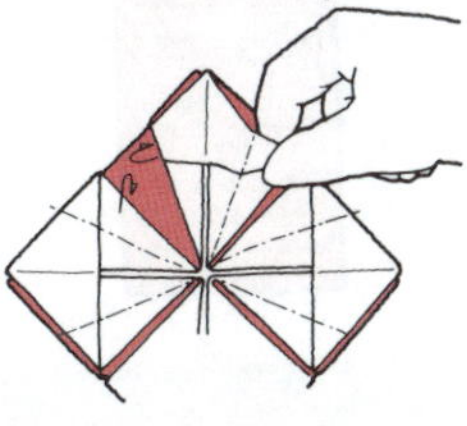

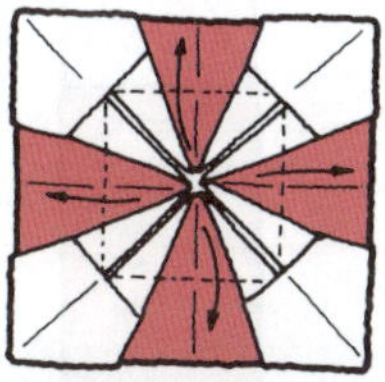

しおり

Bookmark

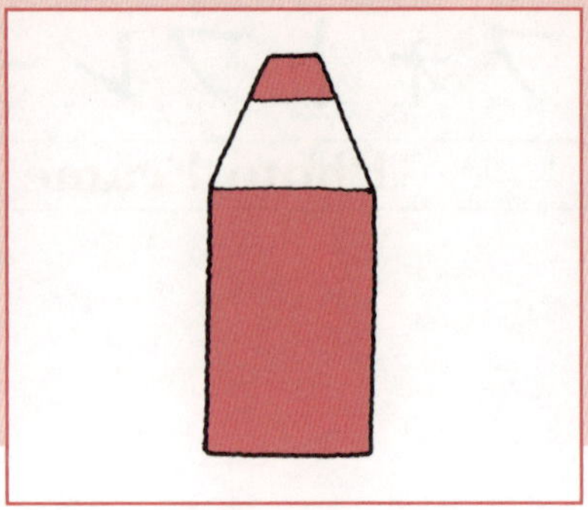

1 半分に切る。
Cut in two.

2 裏を出し、上から0.5cmのところを折り下げる。
Fold 0.5cm down from the top edge.

3 下から約５cmくらいのところを折り上げる。
Fold 5cm up from the bottom edge.

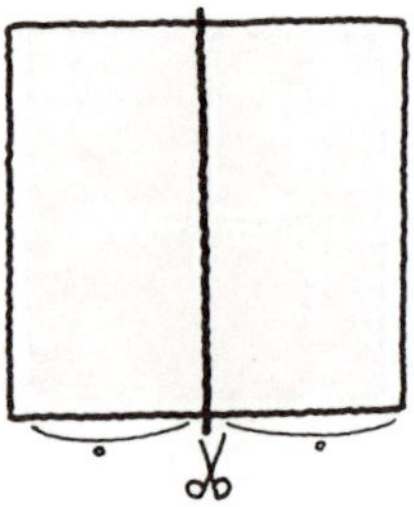

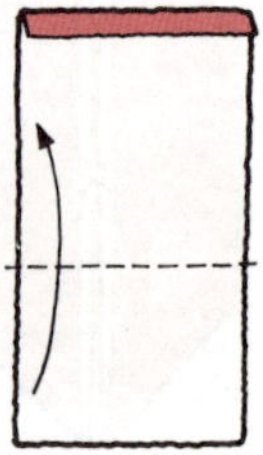

4 左右を裏で折り合わせる。
Fold the left and right edges backward.

5 左右の三角部分を斜めに折る。
Fold the upper corners backward diagonally.

Finished

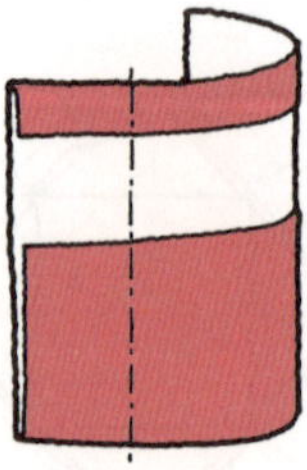

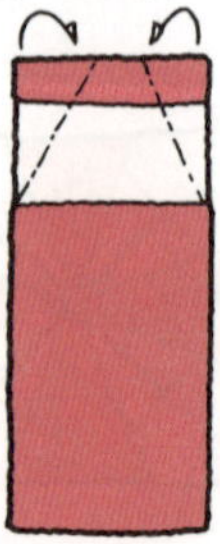

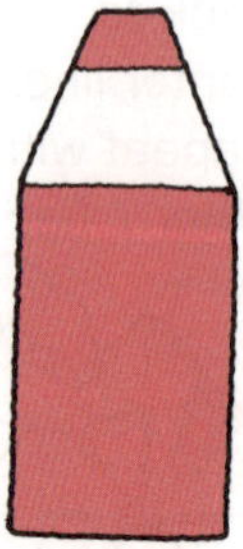

ティッシュ入れ

Tissue Case

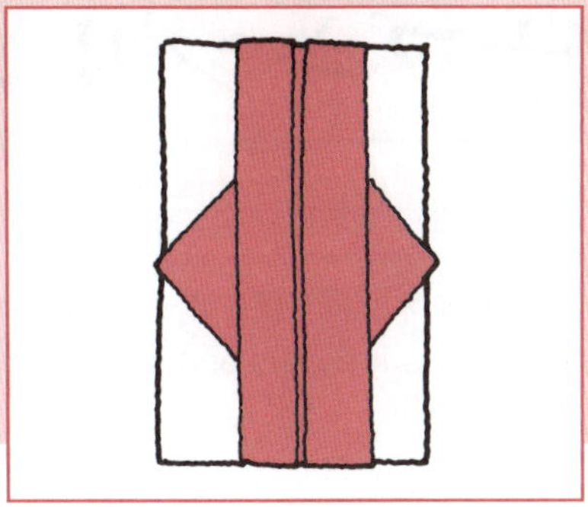

1 表を出し、中心に折りすじをつける。左のカドを右に向けて折る。
Make a crease in the center. Fold the left corner to the right as shown.

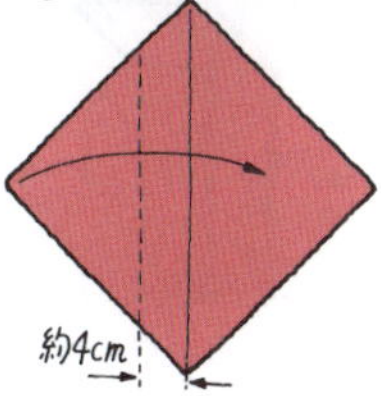

2 中心の折りすじに合わせて、左側に返す。
Fold the front flap outside along the center line.

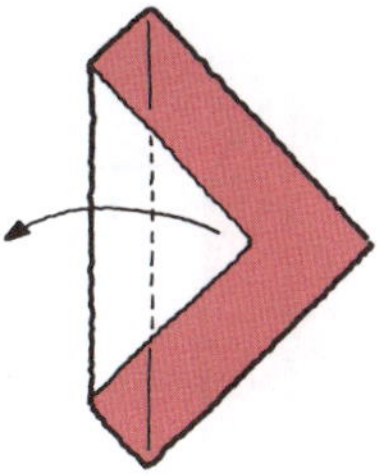

3 右側のカドを左カドに合わせる。
Fold the right corner over to meet the left corner.

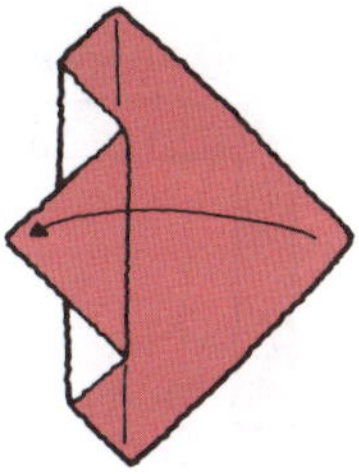

4 中心線で折り返し右側に返す。
Fold the front flap to the right along the center line.

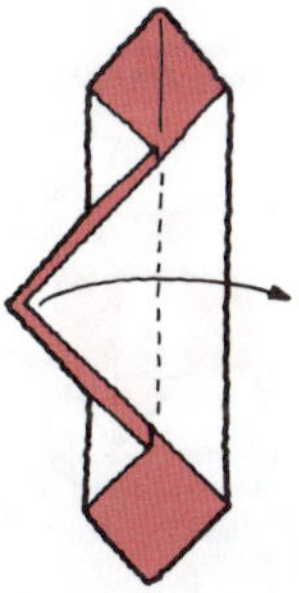

5 左右を図のように折る。
Fold the triangles as shown.

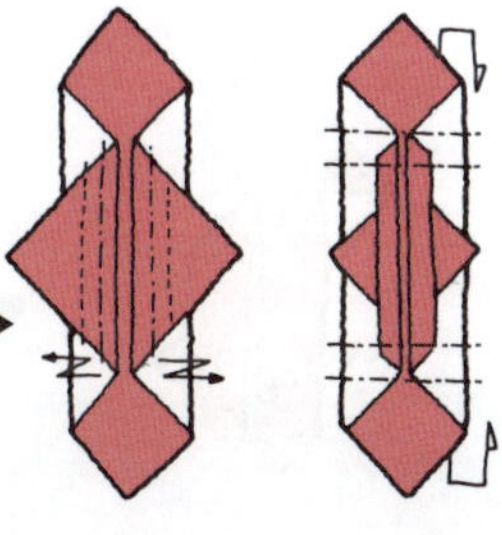

Finished

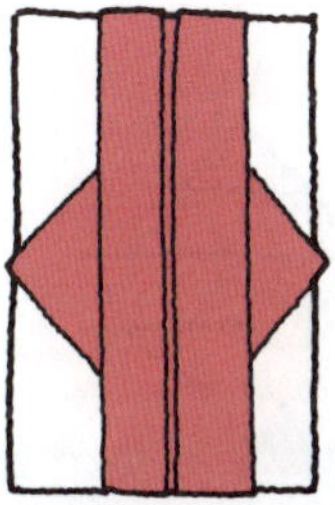

ナプキンリング

Napkin ring

●材料　materials

1×80cm×2(折り紙を切って、のりでつなぎ合わせる。 Cut papers and glue them together.)

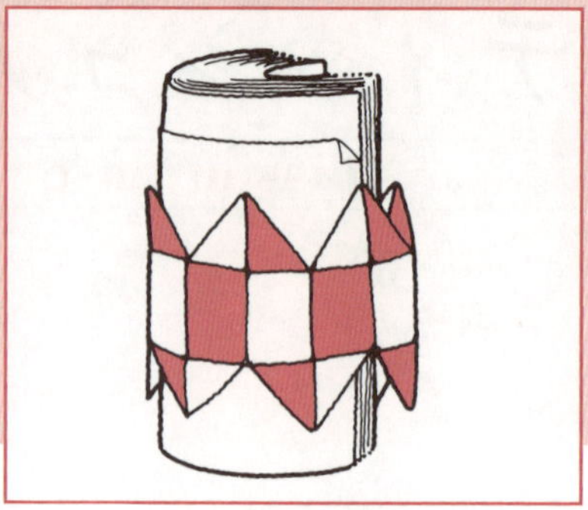

1 2色の折り紙を外表にしてはり合わせる。
Cut 2 coloured papers as shown and glue them together.

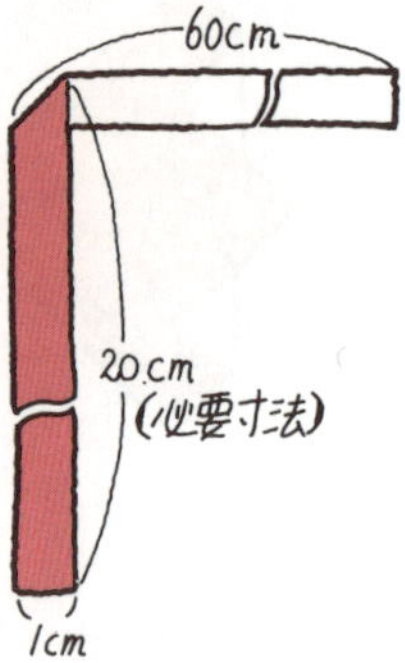

2 必要寸法をはかったほうを、下にたらし、長いほうを巻きつけていく。
Wind the longer paper round the shorter one.

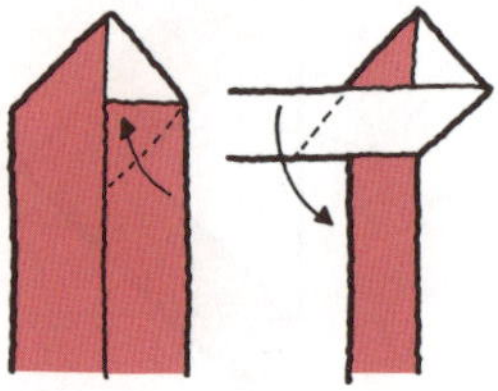

3 折り込んでいく。
Twist as shown.

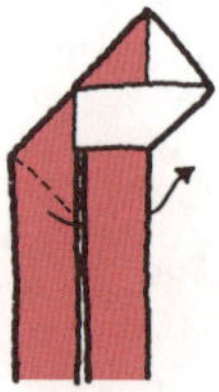

4

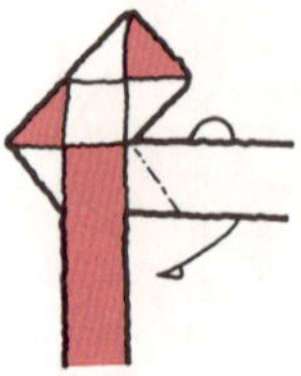

5 また3から、同様に折っていく。
Repeat from drawing-3.

輪にする。
Make a ring.

Finished

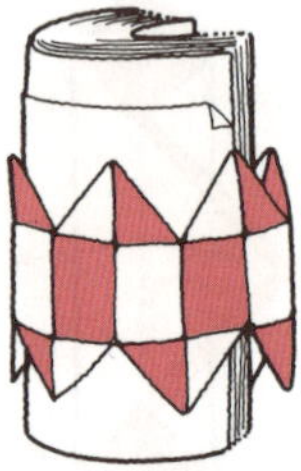

ナプキン立て

Napkin Stand

1 裏を出して、半分に折る。
Fold in half to the upper edge.

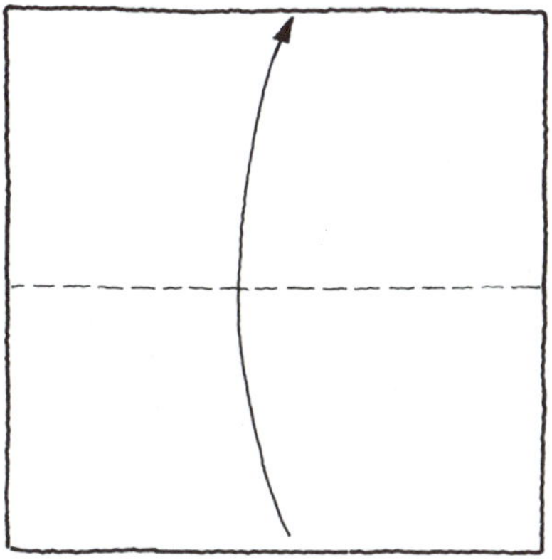

2 折りすじをつける。
Fold in half again to the bottom edge. Unfold.

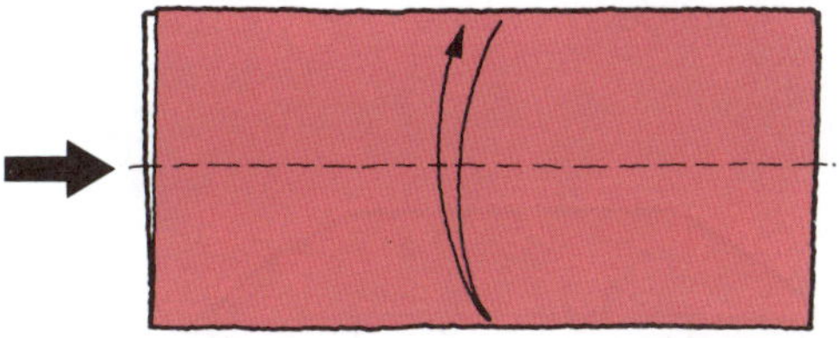

3 折りすじをつける。
Fold the left and right bottom corners up to the center. Unfold.

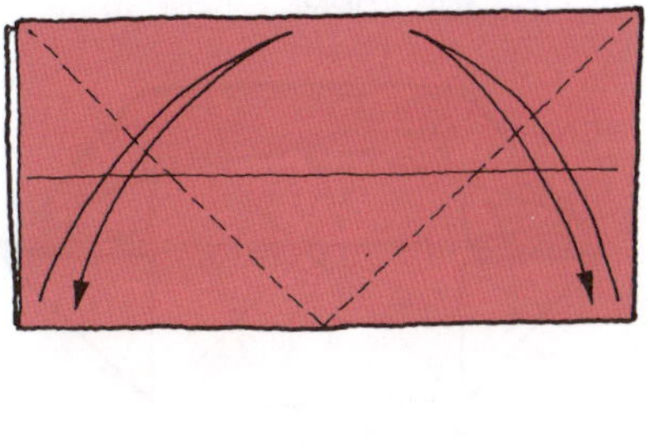

4 折りすじをつける。
Fold the left and right top corners down to the center. Unfold.

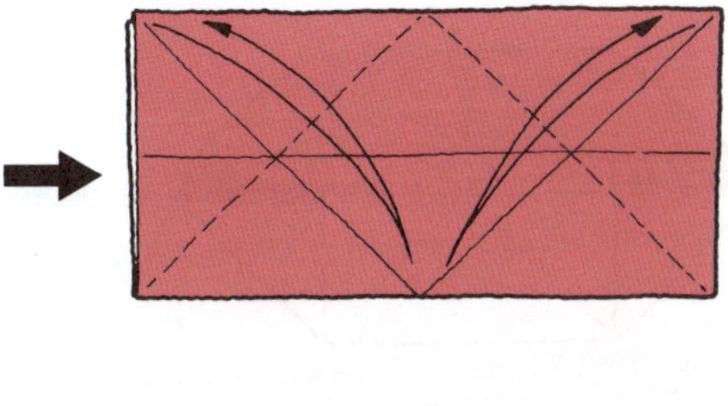

5 半分に折って折りすじに合わせて、両端を中わり折りにする。
Fold in half to the upper edge, then do Nakawari-ori on both ends.

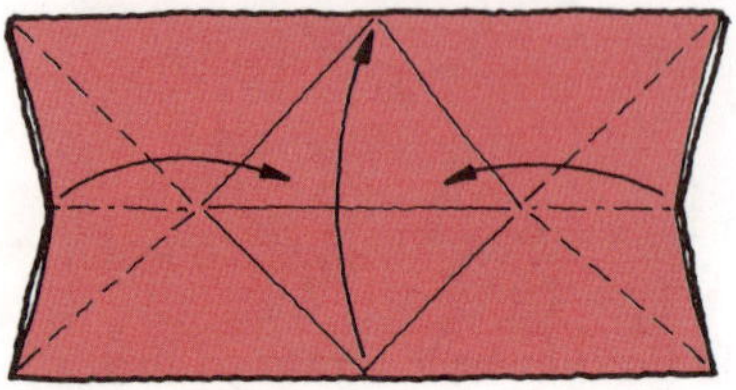

6 ２枚合わせになった部分の内側を引き出す。
Pull the middle flap up as shown.

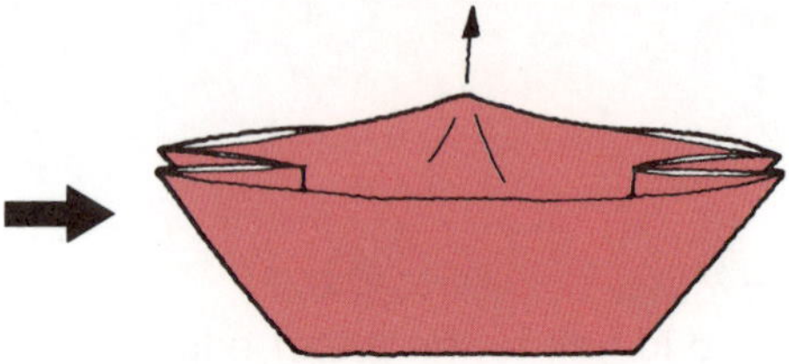

7 両カドを引き出す。
Pull both bottom corners outside.

8 手前に折る。
Fold the bottom corners to make triangles.

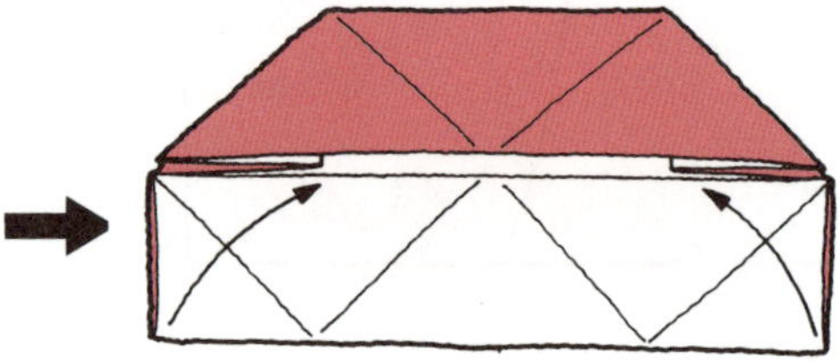

9 上の部分を少し持ち上げる。
Lift the top sheet up a little.

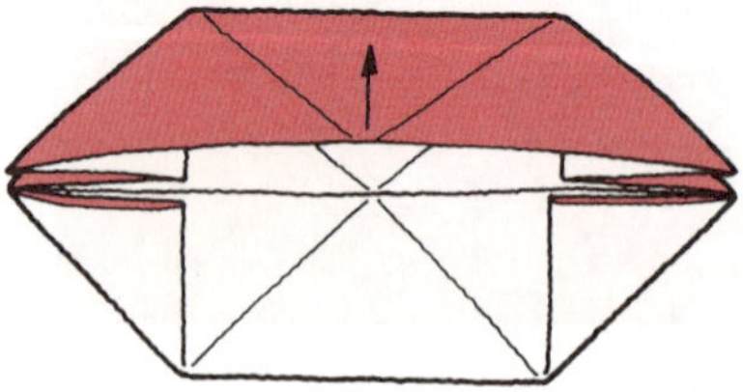

10 指で上を広げながら、下半分を中に入れ込む。
Insert the lower half under the top sheet.

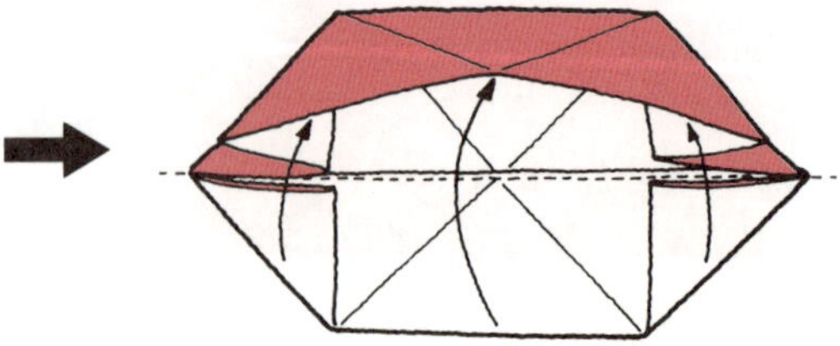

11 上の２枚を引っ張り上げて、折りすじどおりにつぶす。
Raise the two front sheets. Open and flatten along the creases as shown.

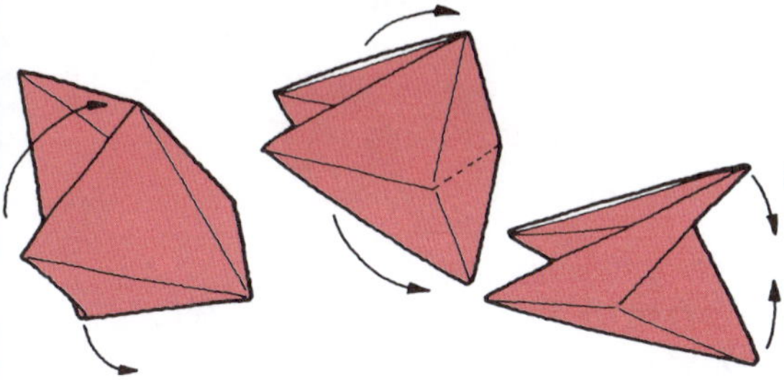

12 左へ折る。裏側も同様に。
Fold in half to the left. Do the same with the reverse side.

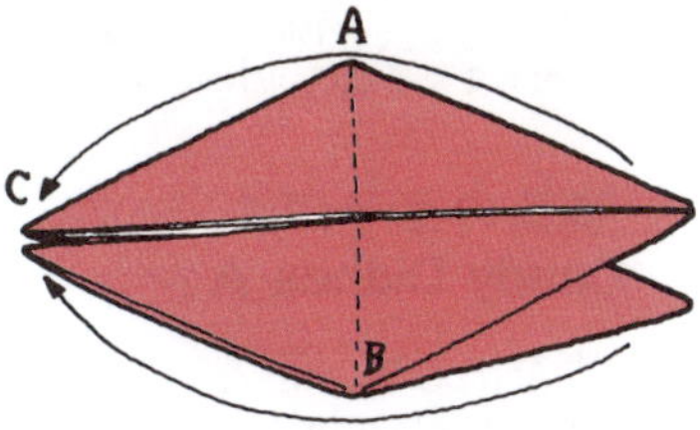

13 折り上げる。裏側も同様に。
Fold the bottom corner up to the edge. Do the same with the reverse side.

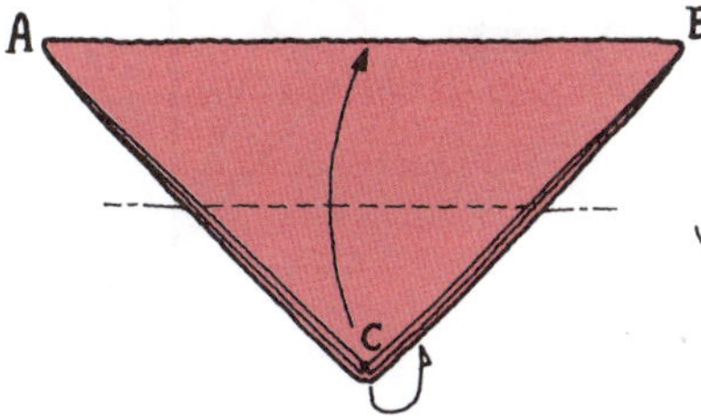

14 ひっくり返して、上のカドを左右いっぱいに引っぱり、しっかりつぶす。
Turn upside down.
Pull both triangles to the left and right.

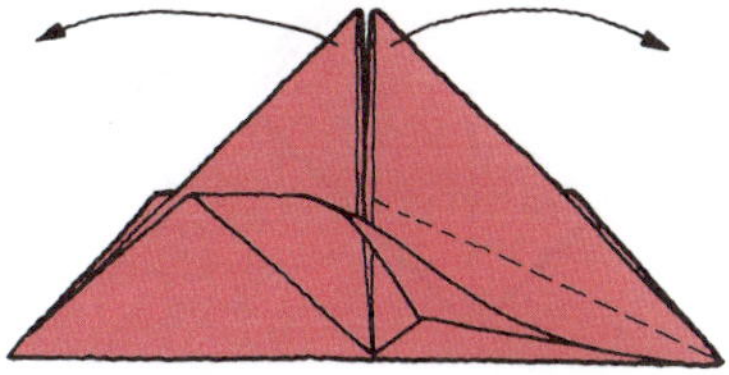

15 カドをかぶせ折りにする。
Do“kabuse-Ori”on the top corners.

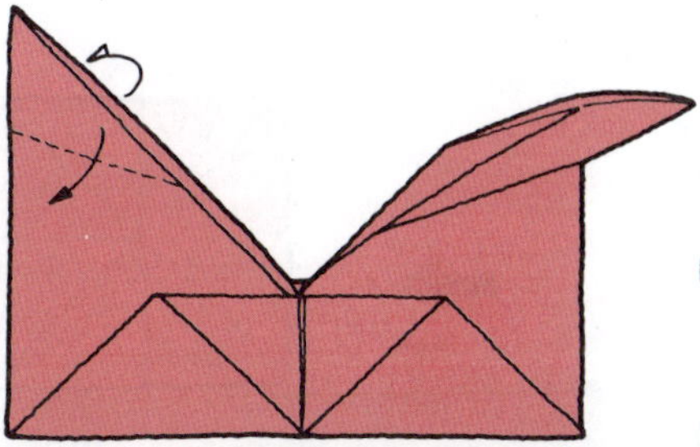

中を広げる。
Spread the bottom, shape it.

Finished

和紙の菓子入れ

Candy Dishes

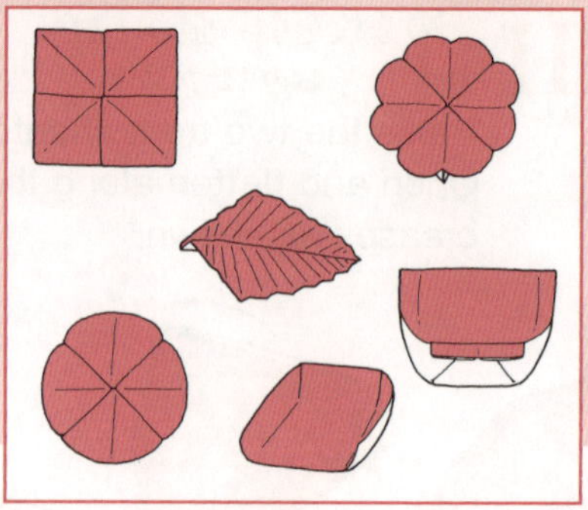

●材料　materials

和紙の菓子皿　Candy Dishes／A・B 28×28cm、C 25×25cm、D 32×32cm、26×26cm
葉っぱの皿　Leaf Dishes／16×16cm、10×10cm
深さのある菓子皿　Dishes／24×24cm

和紙の菓子皿 A
Candy Dishes A

1 表を出して、正方基本形（P 25参照）から始める。
Begin with "Basic Square" (See P25).

2 中心に合わせて、折り合わせる。
Fold both of the top flaps to the center line.

3 裏側も同様に折る。
Do the same with the reverse side.

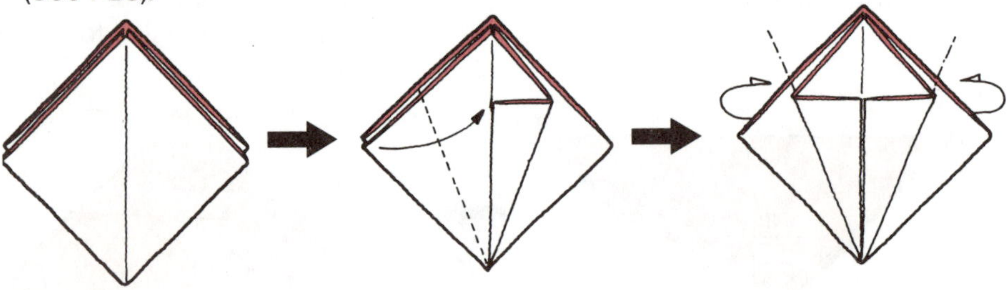

4 半分のところに折り目をつける。
Make a crease in the middle.

5 上の1枚を折り下げる。
Holding the back flap, fold the front flap down.

手前の1枚を押さえ、残りを広げる。
Flatten to form a square.

Finished

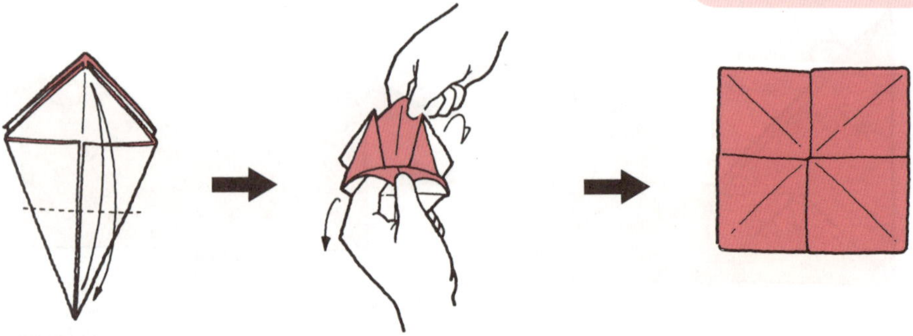

和紙の菓子皿B
Candy Dishes B

1 Aの4から始める。4枚いっしょに切って、開く。
Repeat A steps 1 ～4. Cut the top(4 sheets) as shown, then open.

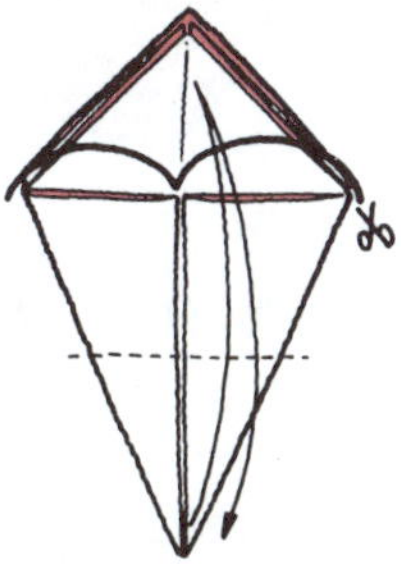

Finished

和紙の菓子皿C
Candy Dishes C

1 Aの4から始める。4枚いっしょに切って、開く。
Repeat A steps 1 ～4. Cut the top(4 sheets) as shown, then open.

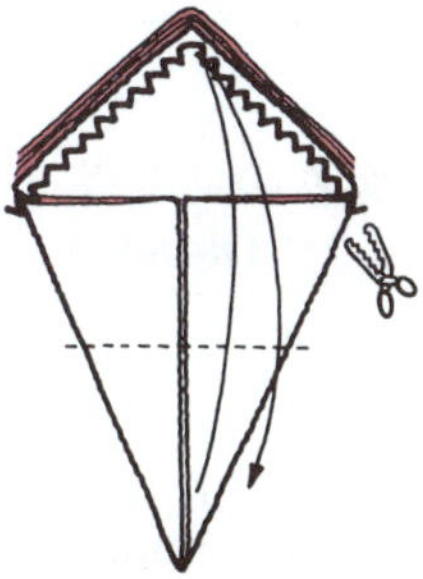

Finished

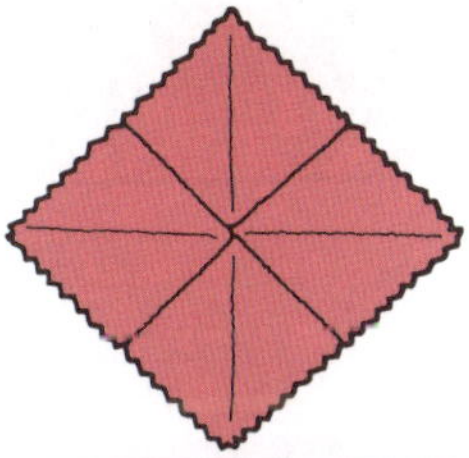

和紙の菓子皿D
Candy Dishes D

1 Aの4から始める。4枚いっしょに切って、開く。
Repeat A steps 1 ～4. Cut the top(4 sheets) as shown, and open.

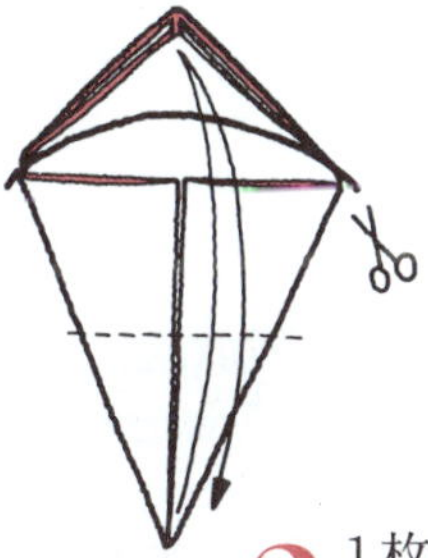

Finished

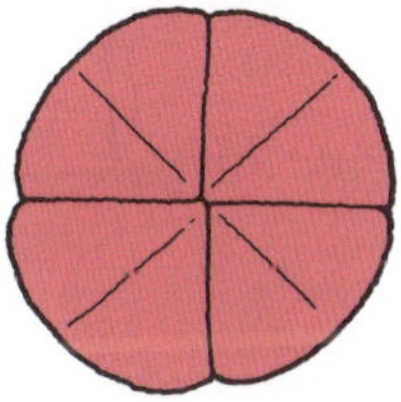

葉っぱの皿
Leaf Dishes

1 表を出し、三角形をつくる。
Fold in half to make a triangle.

2 1枚折り下げる。裏側も同様に。
Fold the upper flap down.
Do the same with the reverse side.

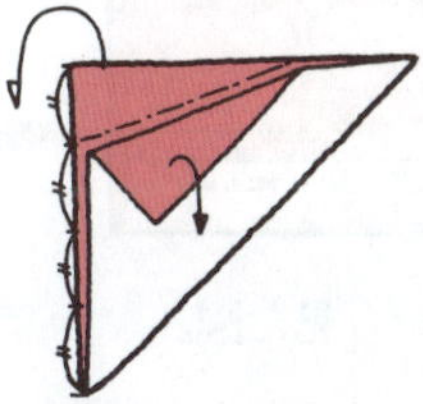

3 1.5cmの間隔でジャバラ折りをする。
Repeat “Tani-Ori” and“Yama-Ori” at intervals of 1.5 cm.

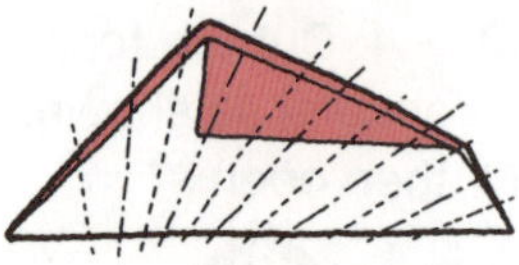

4 少し弓なりに折り上げる。
Arch the bottom slightly.

中をひらく。※大は、左端を裏に折る。
Open. ※If you used a big piece of paper, fold the left edge backward.

Finished

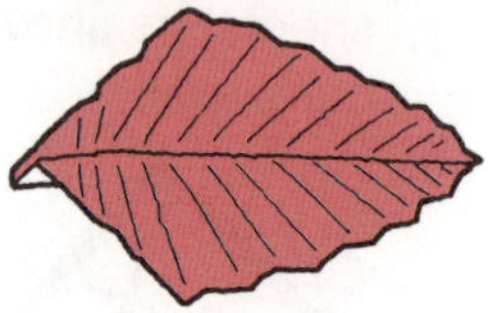

深さのある菓子皿
Dishes

1 裏側を出し、下から1.5cmのところで折り上げる。全部で4カ所すじをつけておく。
Fold up 1.5cm from the bottom edge, and make quarter creases as shown.

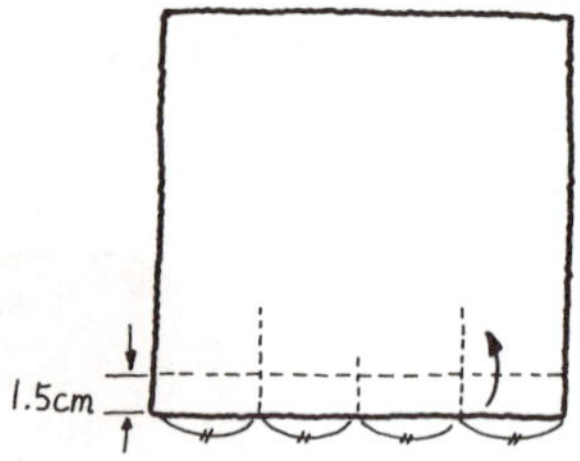

2 裏返して、左右に折りすじをつける。
Turn over.
Crease both bottom corners.

3 左右のカドを中心に引き合わせる。
Fold both corners to meet at the center.

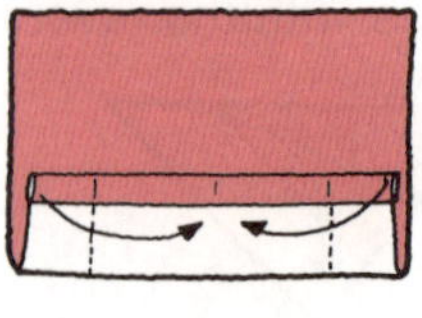

正面から見た図。

4 最初に折った1.5cmの部分を折り下げる。
Fold down the 1.5 cm strip.

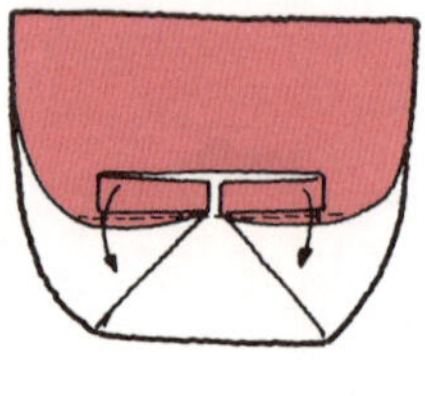

Finished

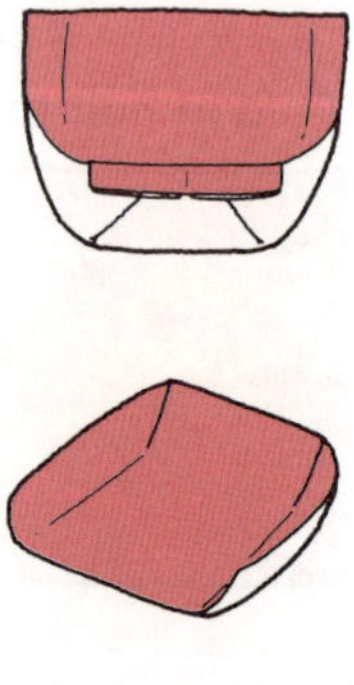

ようじ入れ

Toothpick Case

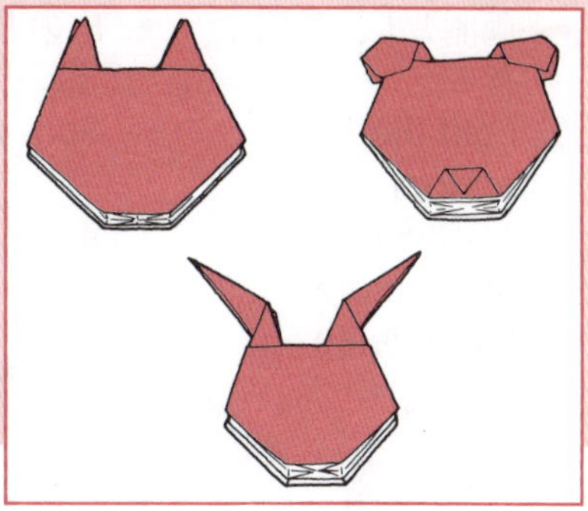

うさぎ
Rabbit

1 表を中にした正方基本形(P25参照)から始める。
Begin with "Basic Square" (See P25).

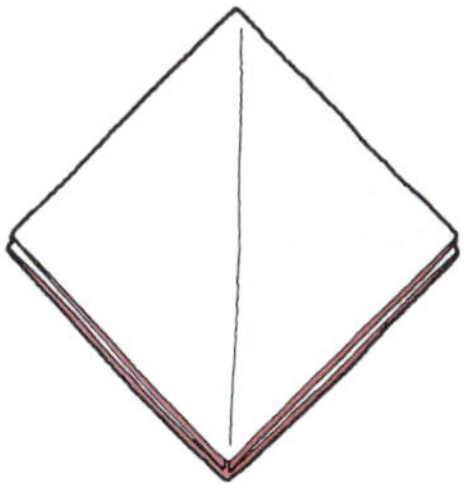

2 手前に折る。裏側も同様に折る。
Fold the front flap up.
Do the same with the reverse side.

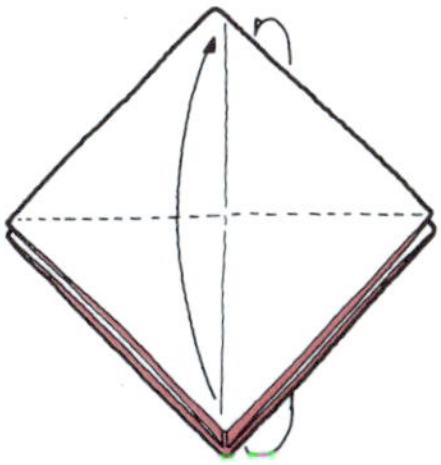

3 左に倒すように折る。裏側も同様に。
Fold the front flap to the left.
Do the same with the reverse side.

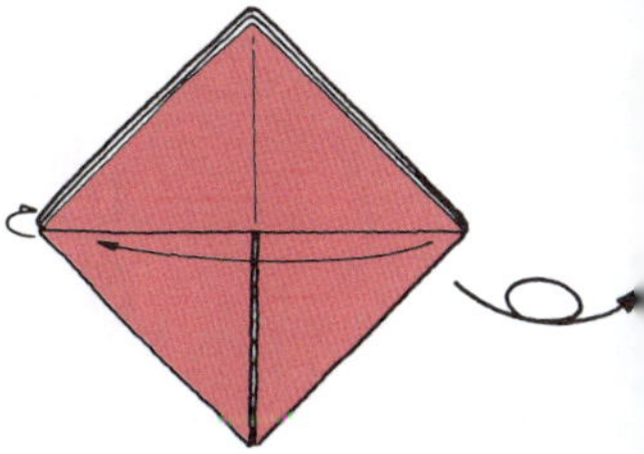

4 中心に合わせて折る。裏側も同様に。
Fold the front flaps in. Do the same with the reverse side.

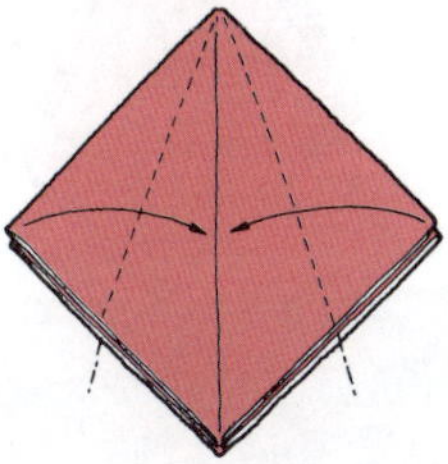

5 半分に折る。裏側も同様に折る。
Fold the right flap. Do the same with the reverse side.

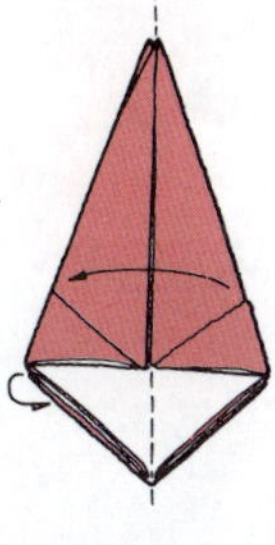

6 中割り折りをする。
Do "Nakawari-Ori" on the top triangles.

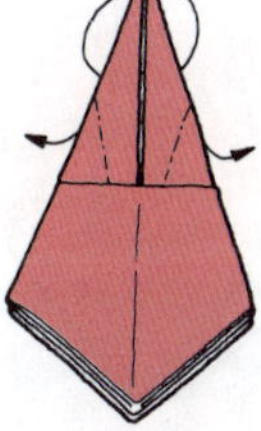

7 両側とも、内側に折る。
Fold the front bottom flap backward. Do the same with the reverse side.

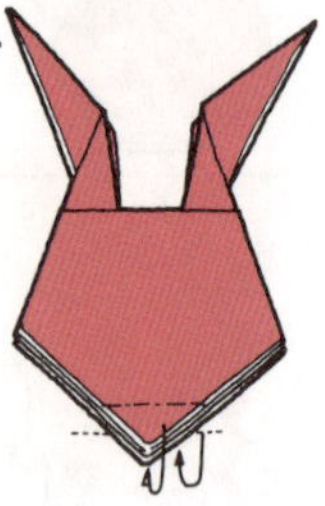

底のところをつぶすように広げる。
Spread the bottom.

Finished

ねこ
Cat

1 うさぎの**5**から始める。
Repeat Rabbit steps **1〜4**.

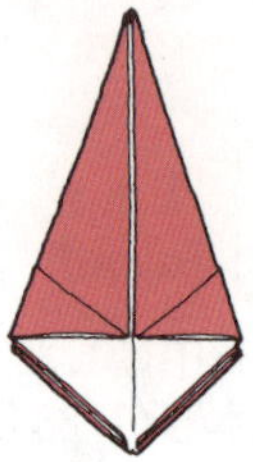

2 上のカドをAのところまで手前に折る。反対側も同様に折る。
Fold the top corner down to point A. Do the same with the reverse side.

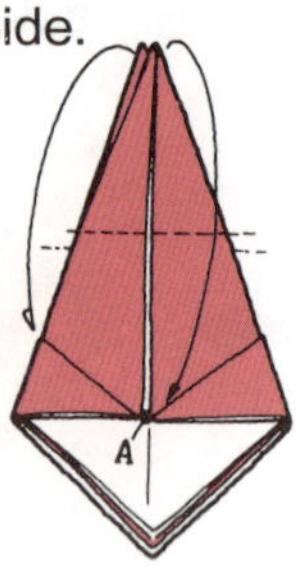

3 表側と裏側を開くように折る。
Fold the right flap to the left. Do the same with the reverse side.

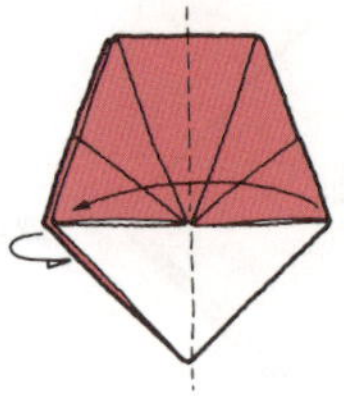

4 中わり折りをする。
Do “Nakawari-Ori” on the top trapezoid.

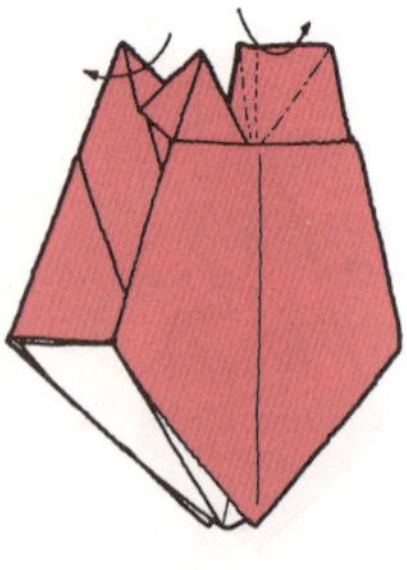

5 両側とも折り込む。
Fold the bottom flap. Do the same with the reverse side.

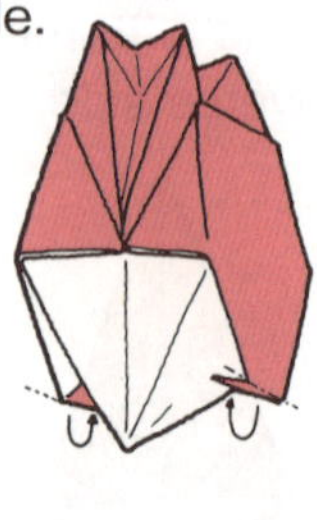

6 中わり折りをする。
Do “Nakawari-Ori” to form ears.

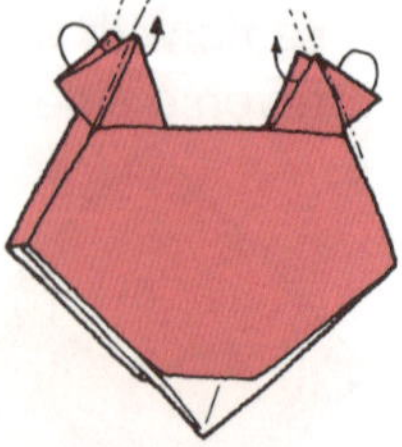

底のところをつぶすように広げる。
Spread the bottom.

Finished

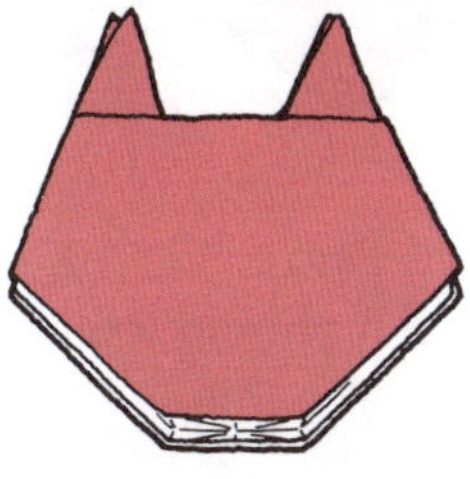

ぶた
Pig

1 うさぎの6から始める。
Repeat Rubbit steps 1～5.

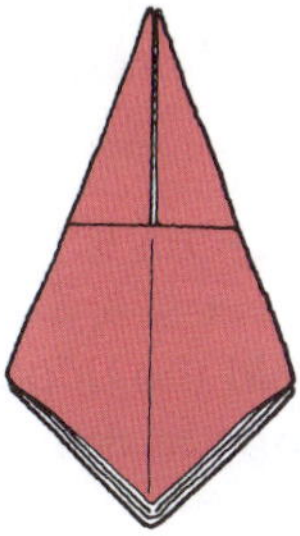

2 中わり折りをする。
Do "Nakawari-Ori" on the top triangles.

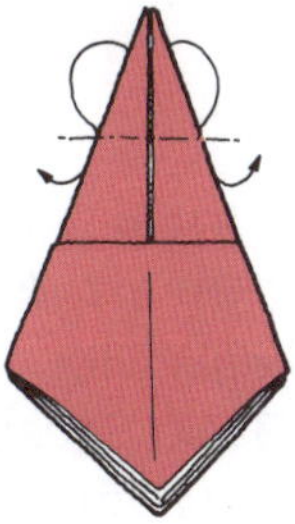

3 中わり折りをする。
Do "Nakawari-Ori" again.

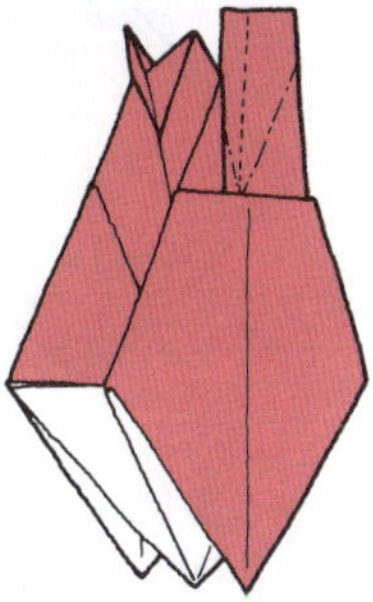

4 カドを折り上げる。反対側も同様に折る。
Fold the front bottom flap up. Do the same with the reverse side.

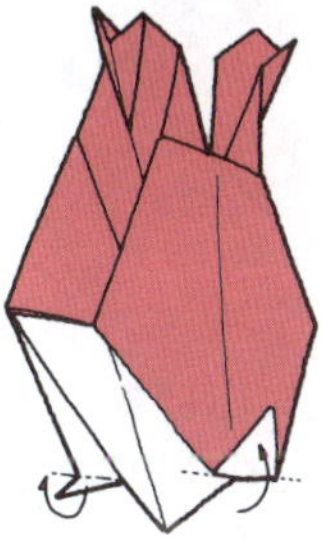

5 折り上げたカドを、下に折る。
Fold the top of the triangle down a little.

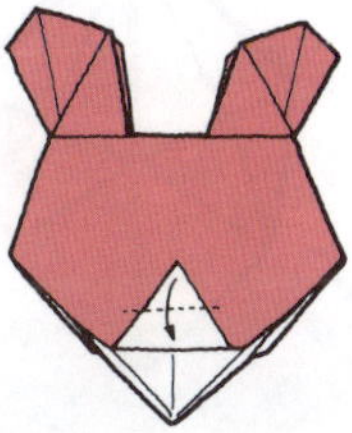

6 かぶせ折りをする。
Do "Kabuse-Ori" to form ears.

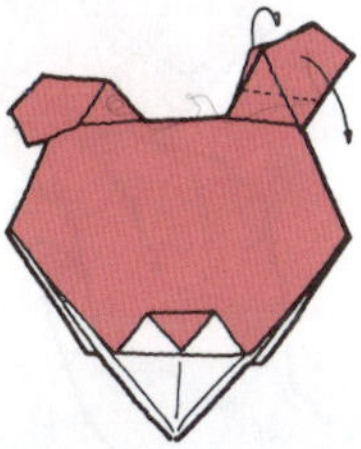

底のところをつぶすように広げる。
Spread the bottom.

Finished

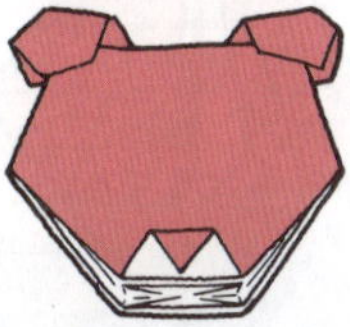

かざり箱

Decorative Box

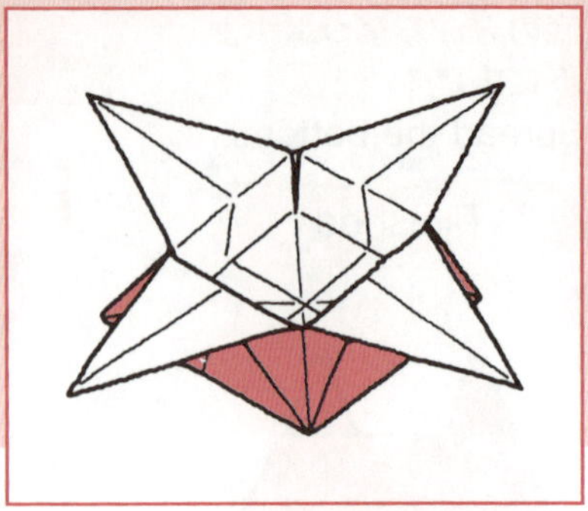

1 正方基本形（P25参照）から始める。
Begin with "Basic Square" (See P25).

2 中心の折りすじに合わせて折る。
Fold the upper flaps to the center.

3 図のようになる。
It should look like this.

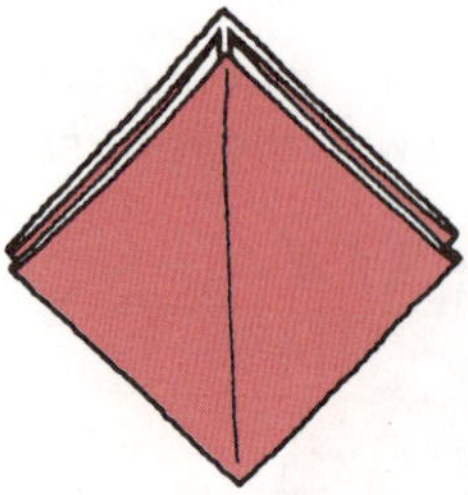

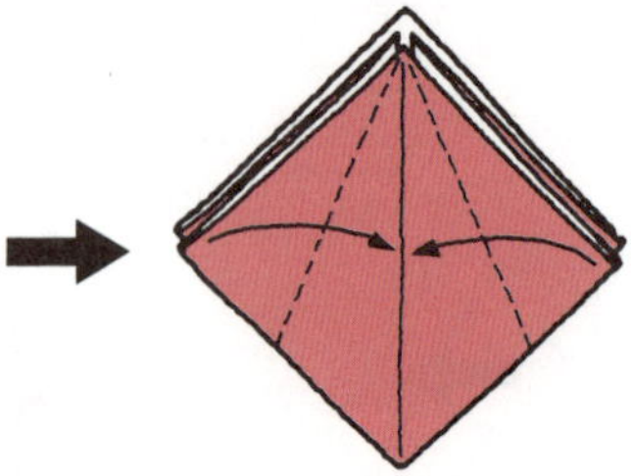

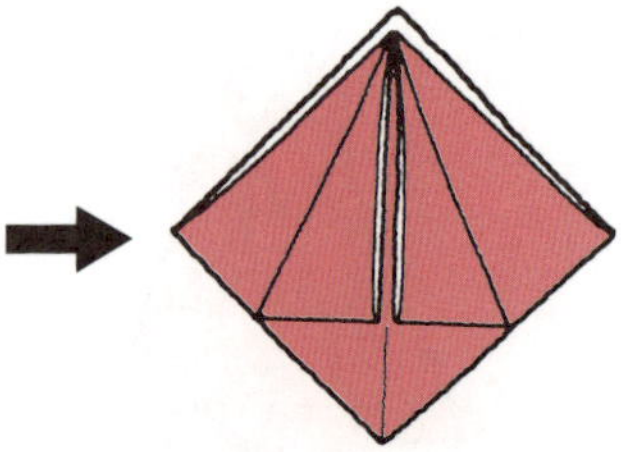

4 袋を左右に広げる。
Open the pockets and flatten.

5 裏側も同様に折る。
Do the same with the reverse side.

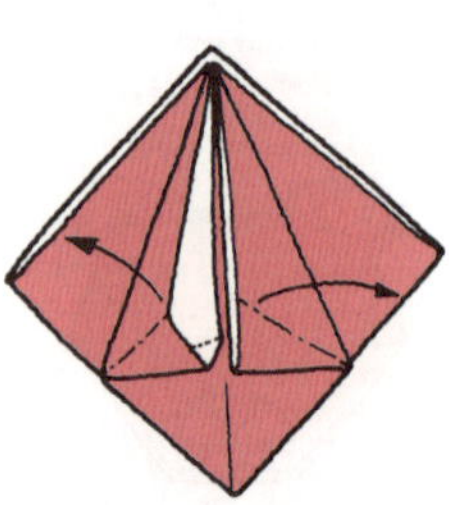

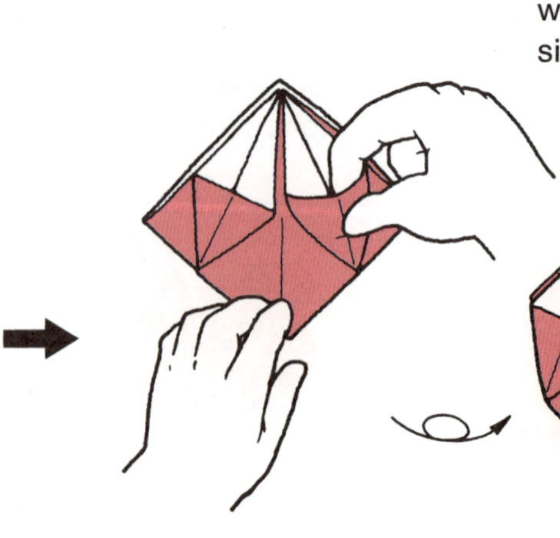

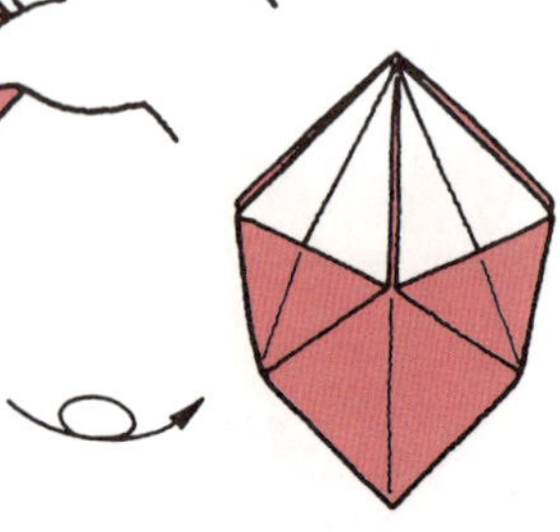

6 上の１枚を反対側へ重ね、裏側も同様に折る。
Fold the upper flap to the right. Do the same with the reverse side.

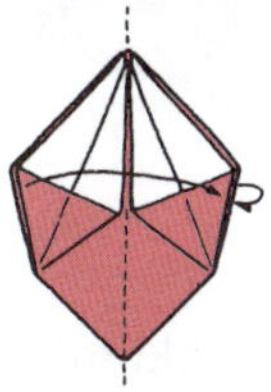

7 中心の折りすじに合わせて折る。裏側も同様に折る。
Fold the upper flaps to the center line. Do the same with the reverse side.

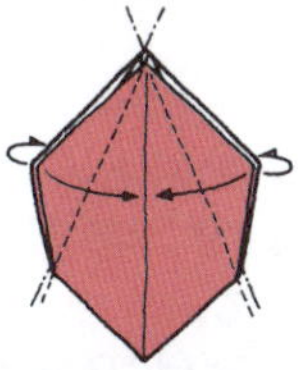

8 上の１枚を折り下げる。裏側も同様に折る。
Fold the upper tip down. Do the same with the reverse side.

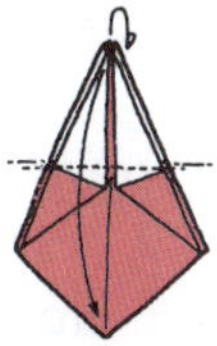

9 上の１枚を反対側へ重ねる。裏側も同様に折る。
Fold the flap to the right. Do the same with the reverse side.

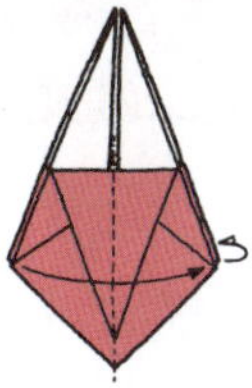

10 １枚折り下げる。裏側も同様に。
Fold the upper tip down. Do the same with the reverse side.

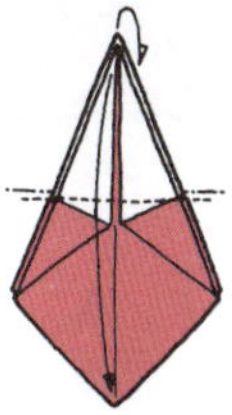

11 箱の形に広げる。
Open to a box shape.

12 箱の中に、指を入れて、形を整える。
Shape into a box.

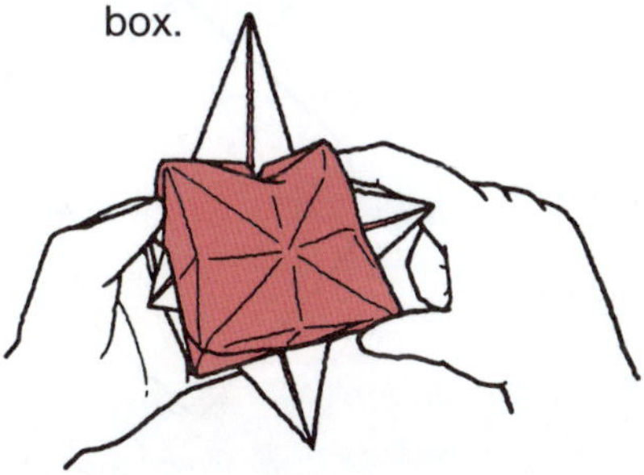

Finished

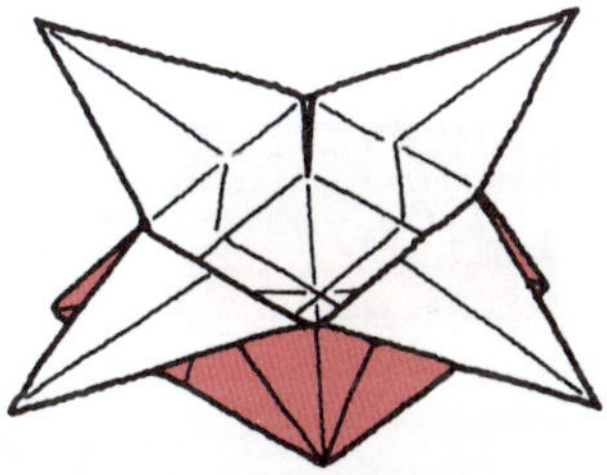

持ち手のついたかご

Hand Basket

●材料　materials
かご　Basket／28×28㎝
持ち手　Handle／7×45㎝

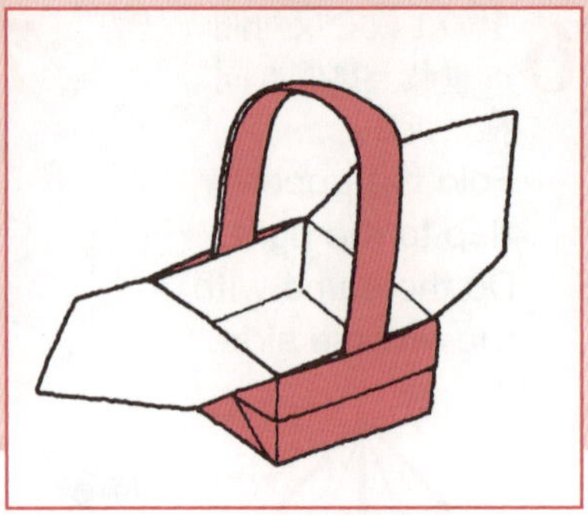

1 折り目をつけて、もとにもどす。
Make a cross shaped crease. Unfold.

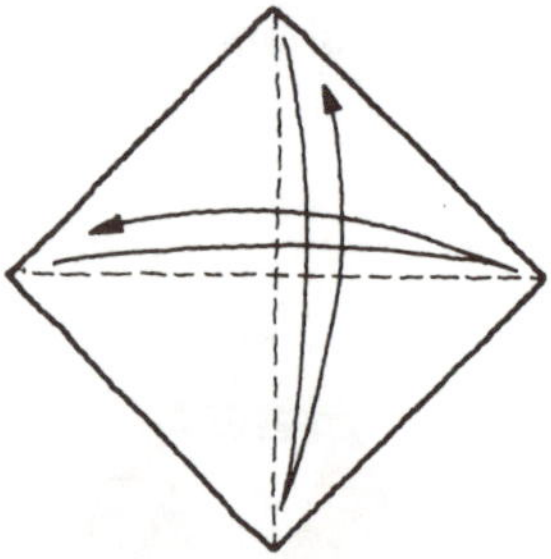

2 ざぶとん基本形（P23参照）を折る。
Fold "Basic Zabuton".

3 中心の線に合わせ、上下を折る。
Fold the upper and bottom edges to meet in the center.

4 中心の線に合わせ、左右を折る。
Fold the left and right sides to the center.

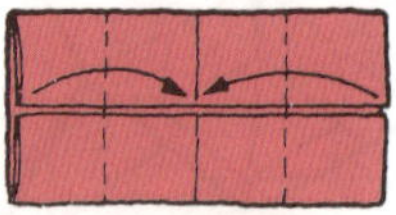

5 開く。A、Bの位置を確認する。
Open. Confirm the position A & B.

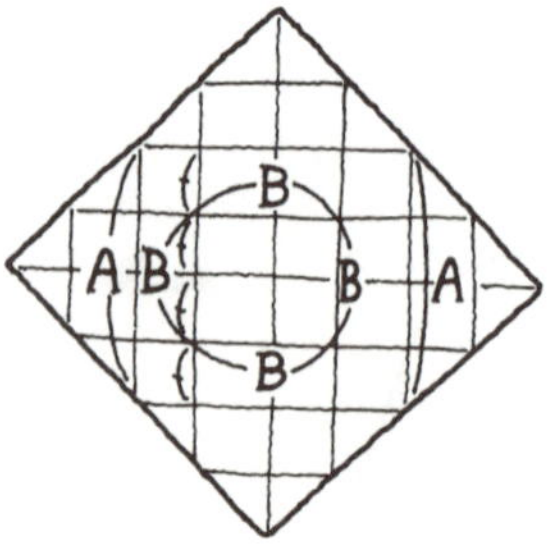

6 左右のカドをAの線に合わせて折る。
Fold the left and right corners to the line A.

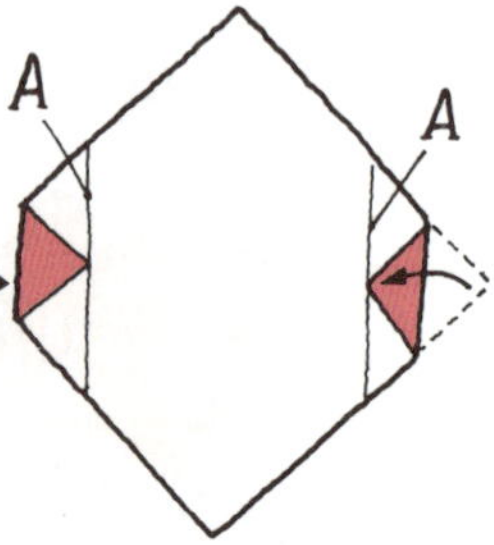

7 Aの線に合わせて半分に折る。
Fold the sides in half.

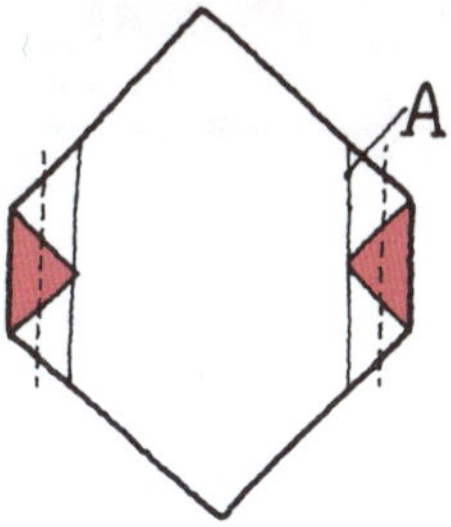

8 Aの線で裏側に折る。
Fold both sides backward at line A.

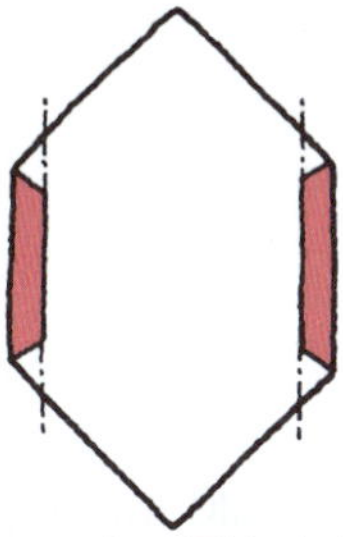

9 左右のBの線を直角に立てる。上下のBも直角に立てるようにする。
Fold each line B to stand upright.

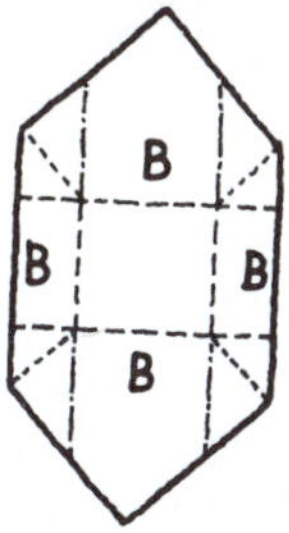

10 でっぱった両側の三角部分を折り合わせる。
Fold both triangles inside.

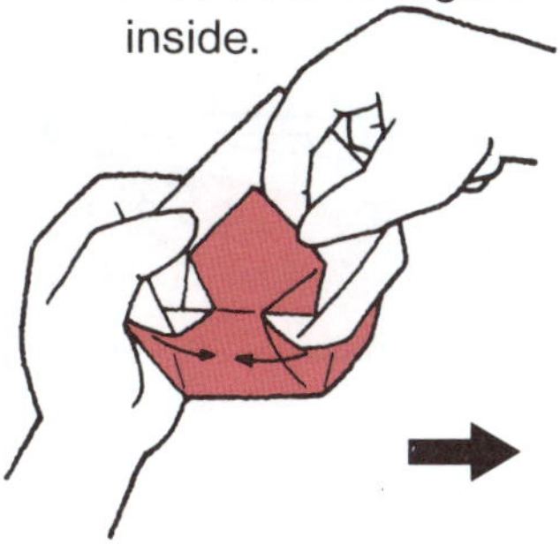

11 上の三角を折り下げる。
Fold the top triangles outside.

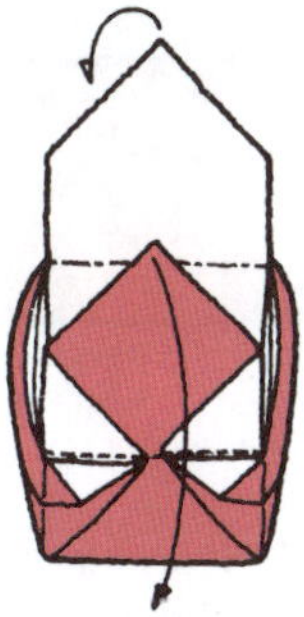

12 かごのできあがり。
It should look like this.

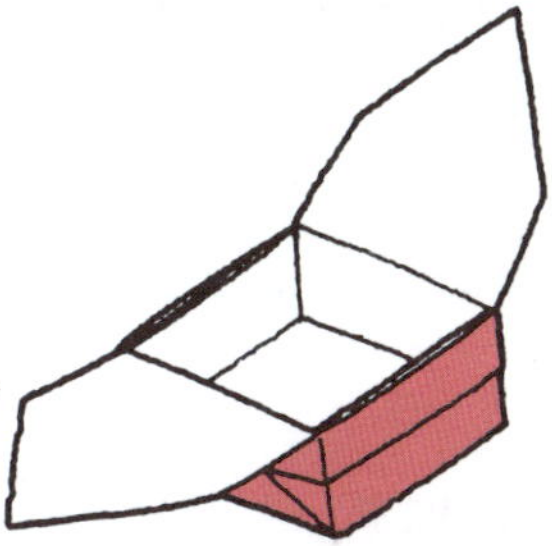

13 太さ2.8cmの持ち手を作る。
Make a handle as shown.

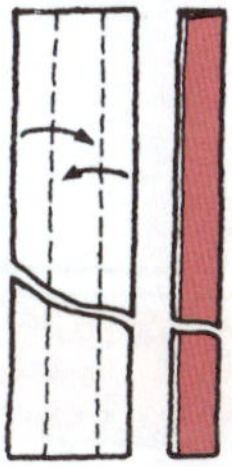

14 かごの左右のすきまに、持ち手をのりづけする。
Glue the handle into the side slots of the basket.

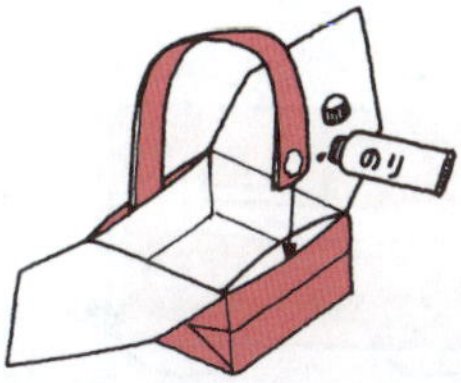

Finished

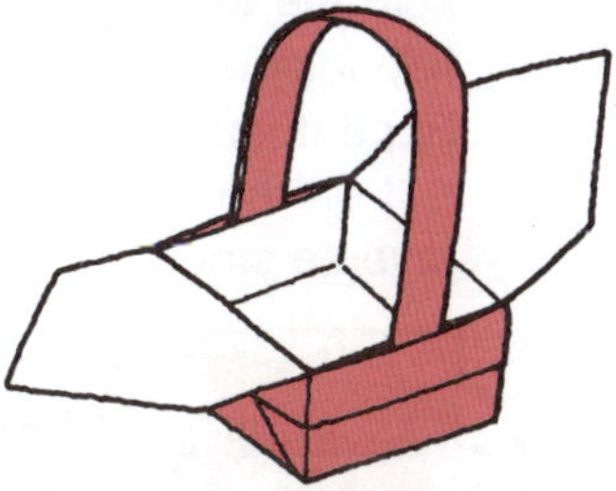

さいふ

Wallet

●材料　materials
30×25cm

1 中表にふたつ折りにする。上の1枚を折り上げる。
Fold in half, then fold the front flap up.

2 やや左を深めに折り下げる。
Fold the upper flap down diagonally.

3 図のようになる。
paper should look like this.

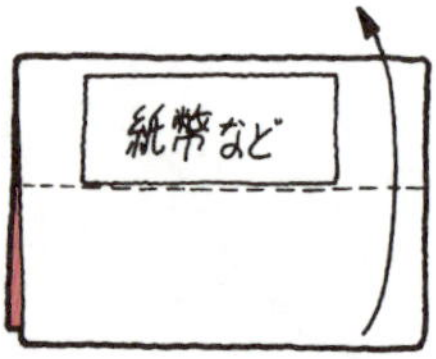

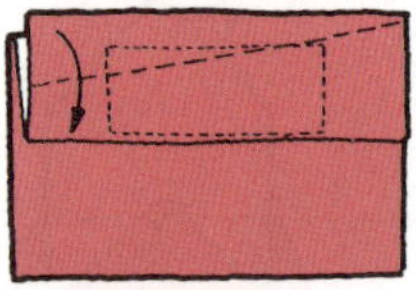

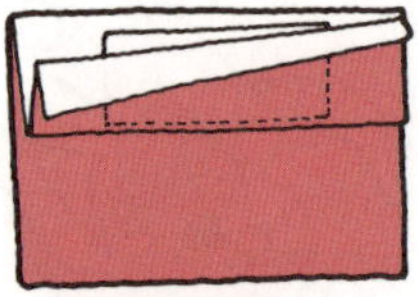

4 3で折った部分を内側に返す。1〜3の順に裏側も同様に折る。
Fold the top flap inside. Repeat steps 1〜3 on the reverse side.

5 中心線を開き、左右を裏側に折る。
Open, then fold both sides backward.

6 中心線をもとのように山折りにする。
Fold in half as shown.

Finished

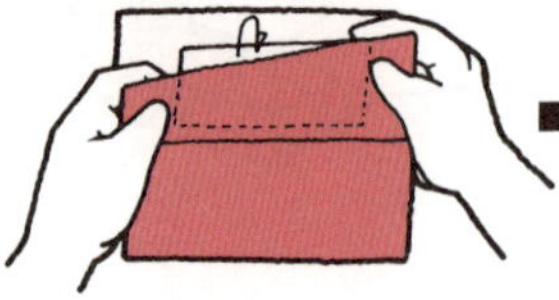

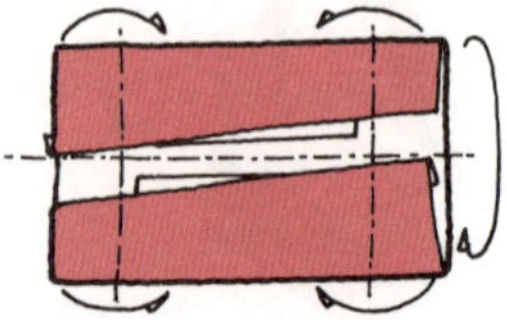

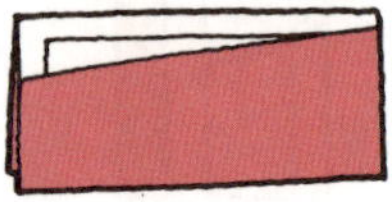

小銭入れ

Coin Purse

●材料　materials
厚めの台紙　thick paper

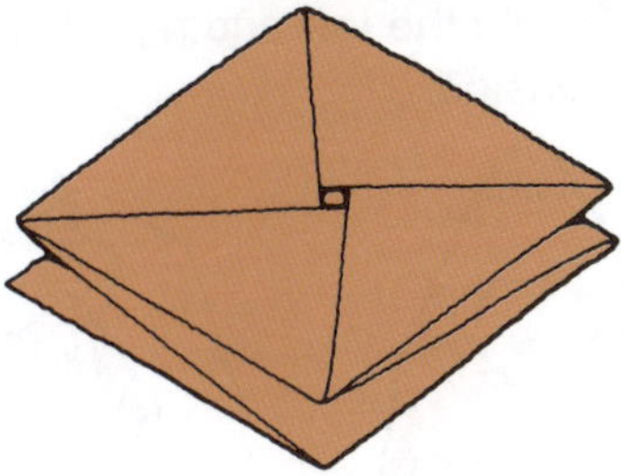

1 ざぶとん基本形(P23参照)から始める。
Begin with "Basic Zabuton".

2 3等分に折る。
Fold in trisection.

3 戻す。
Unfold.

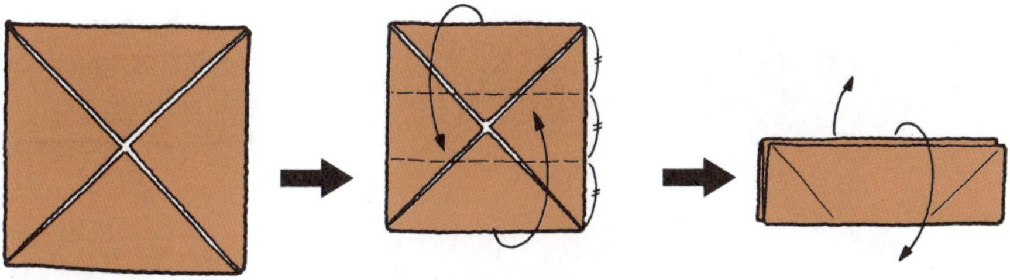

4 上下だけ開く。
Open the top and bottom flaps.

5 3等分に折る。
Fold in trisection as shown.

6 戻す。
Unfold.

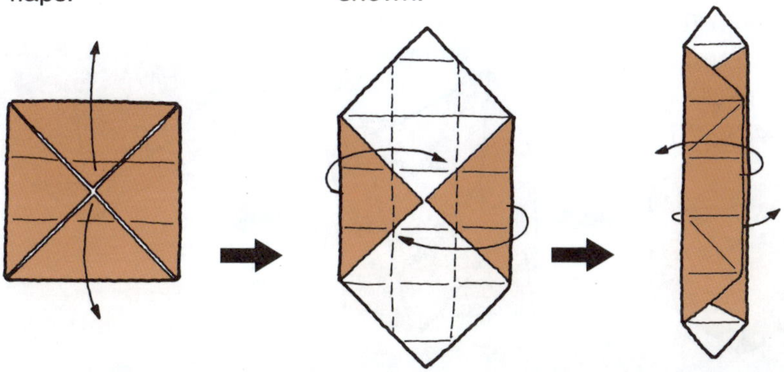

7 内側にたたみ、起こすように折る。
Fold the left and right flaps inside.

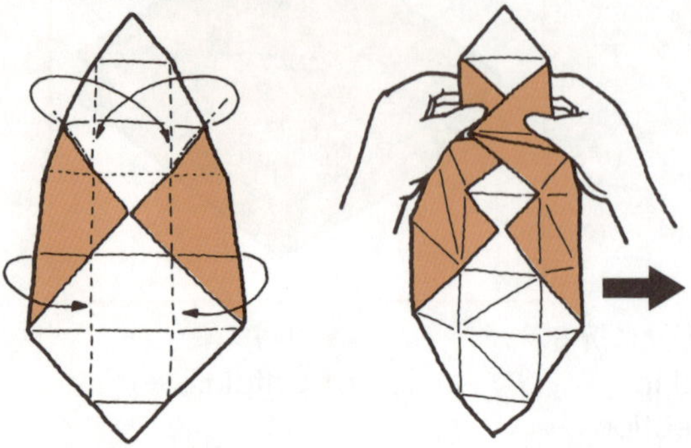

8 内側にしまうように折る。
Fold the top flap inside.

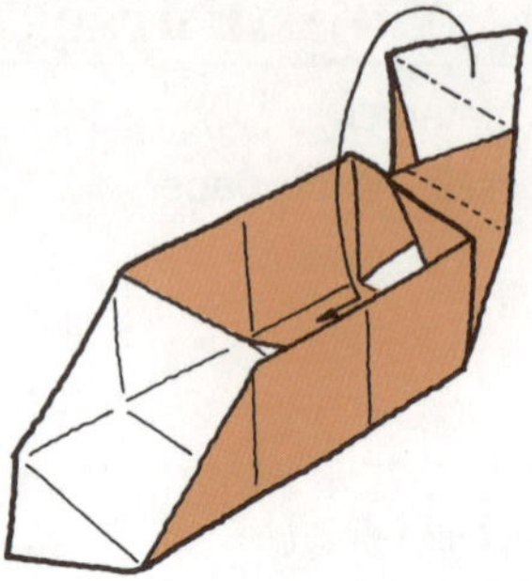

9 7と同様に折る。
Repeat step 7 on the other end.

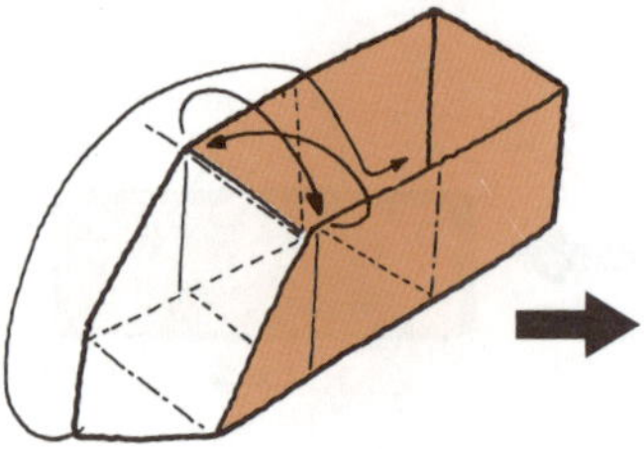

10 内側に折る。
Fold the triangle inside.

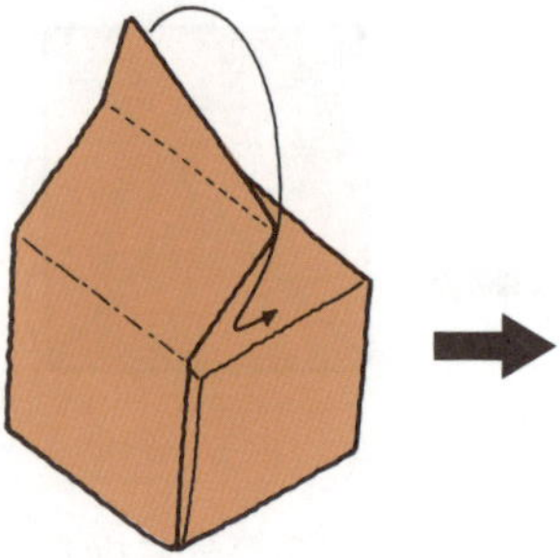

11 厚めの紙を底に敷く。
Put thick paper on the bottom.

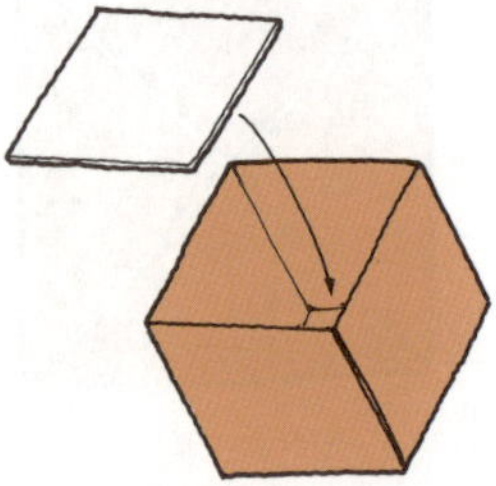

12 図のように折りすじをつける。
Make creases as shown.

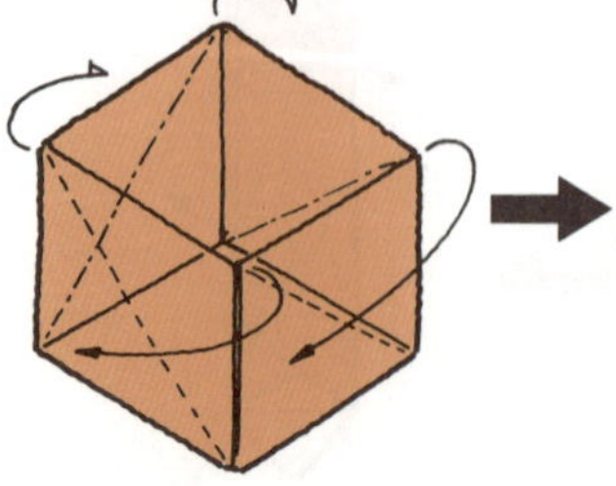

13 ねじるように4辺をたたむ。
Fold the 4 flaps as shown.

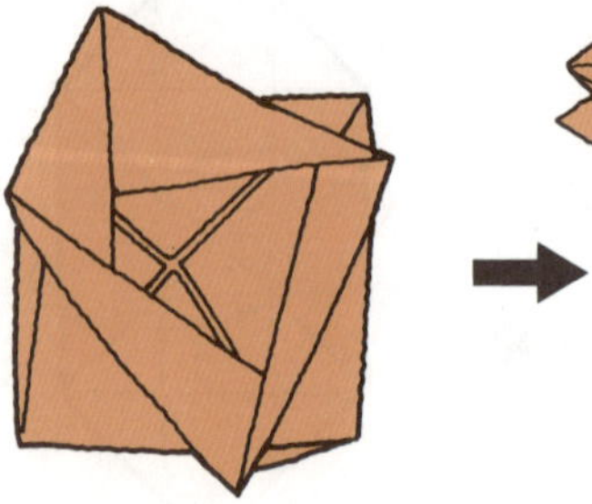

Finished

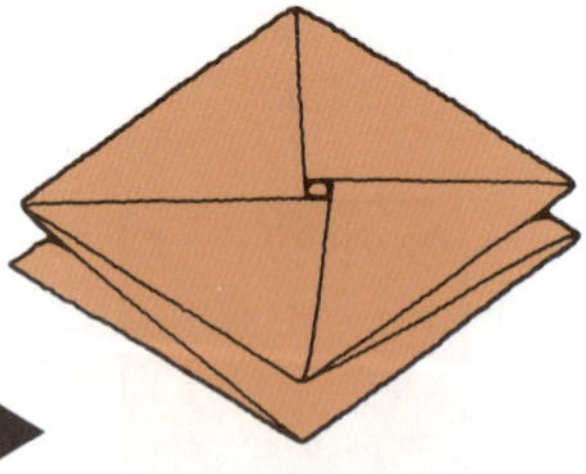

ソーイングボックス

Sewing Box

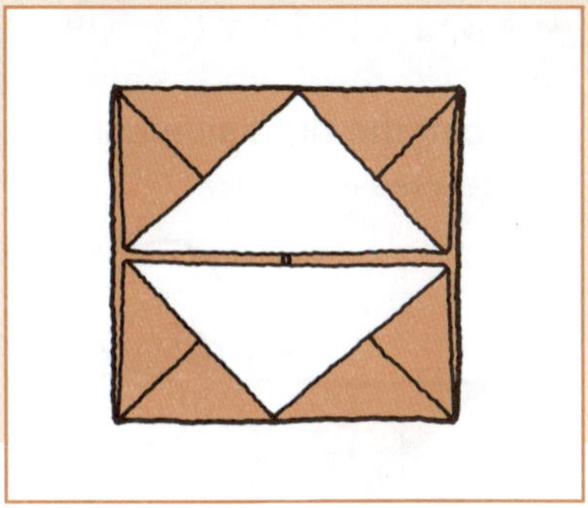

1 裏をだし、ざぶとん基本形（P23参照）から始める。左右は開く。
Fold "Basic Zabuton" (See P23), then open the left and right flaps.

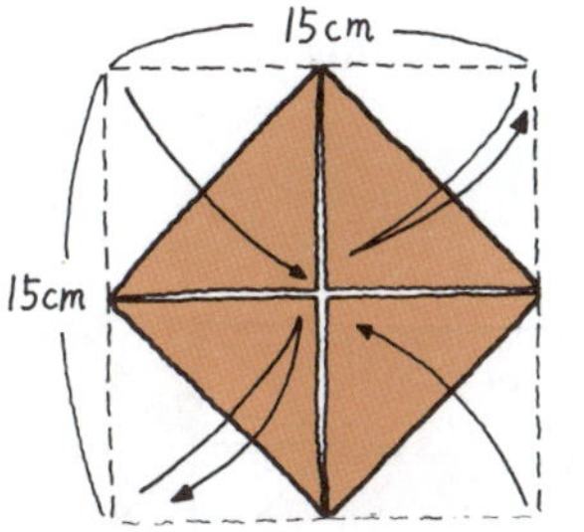

2 内側に三角部分を折り込む。
Fold the tips inside.

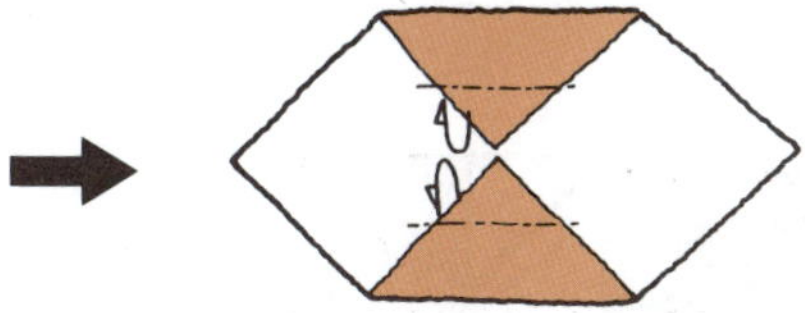

3 中心に合わせて上下折り合わせる。左右の三角部分を裏に折り込む。
Fold the top and bottom edges in to meet at the center. Fold the left and right triangles backward.

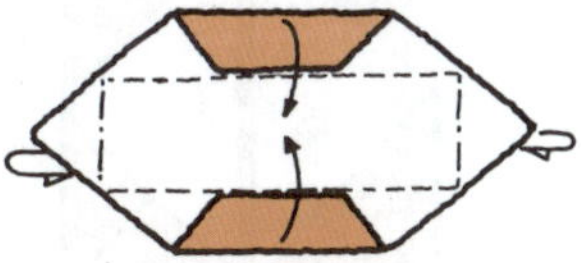

4 図のように折りすじをつける。
Make creases as shown.

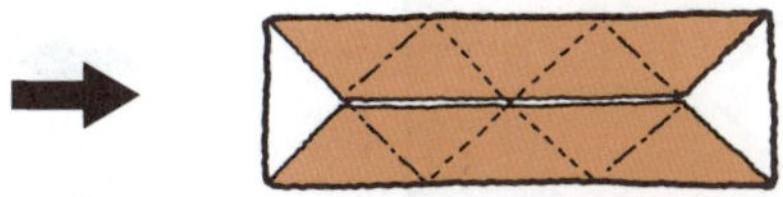

5 図のように折りすじを利用して開く。
Open the right side using the creases as shown.

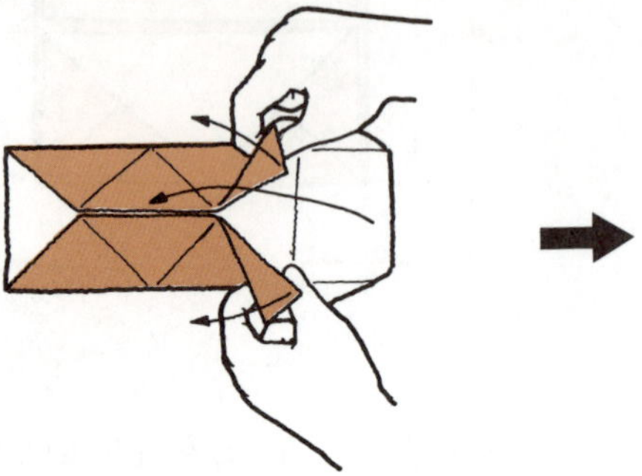

6 上下の三角を折る。
Fold the top and bottom triangles to the center.

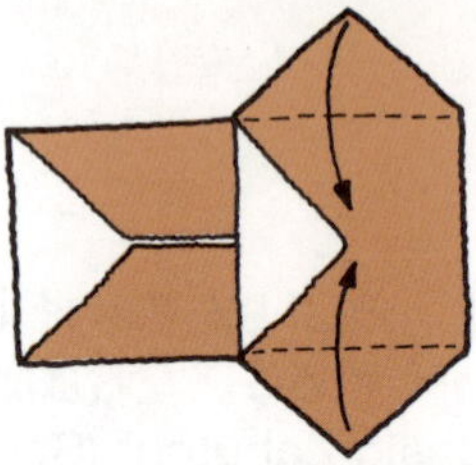

7 三角部分を折る。
Fold both corners to the center.

8 三角部分を右側に折り返す。
Fold the top corner of the white triangle to the right.

9 左側も**5**から同じように折る。
Repeat steps **5**~**8** on the left side.

Finished

ギフトバッグ

Gift Bag

●材料　materials

包装紙　Wrapping paper／48×38cm、テープ　Strip of paper／1.5×50cm

1 裏側を出し、図のように折る。右の2cm部分をのりづけし、輪にする。

Fold the paper as shown. Glue a 2cm strip of the right side.

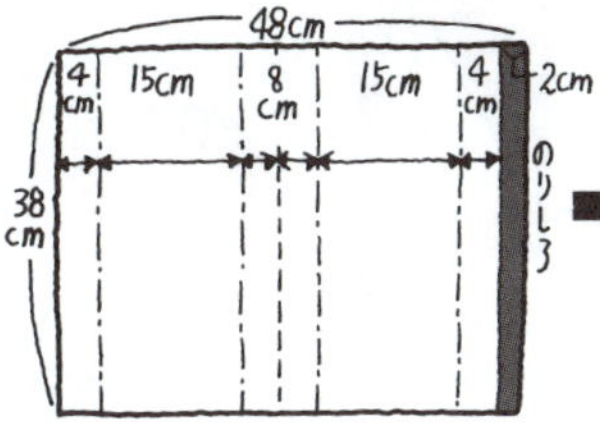

2 下から10cmの部分に折り目をつける。

Make a crease 10cm from the bottom edge.

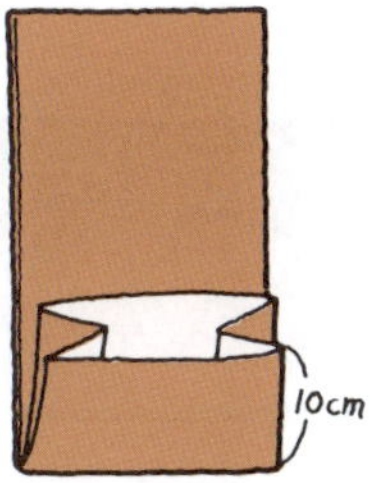

3 図のように底になる部分を開いてつぶす。

Open the bottom and flatten.

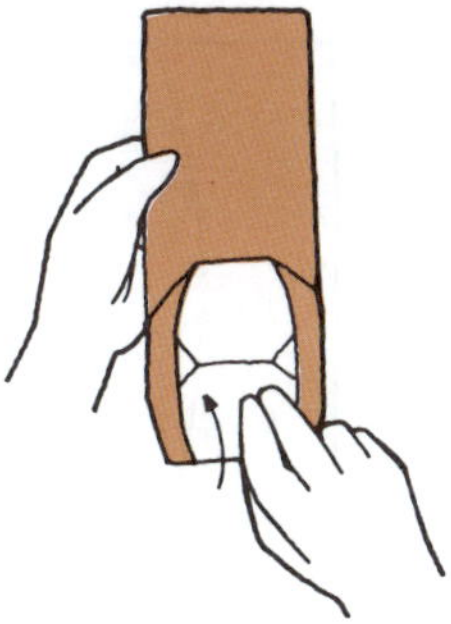

4 上下を折り合わせ、のりづけをし、底をつくる。

Fold both edges to the center. Glue the edge to make the bottom.

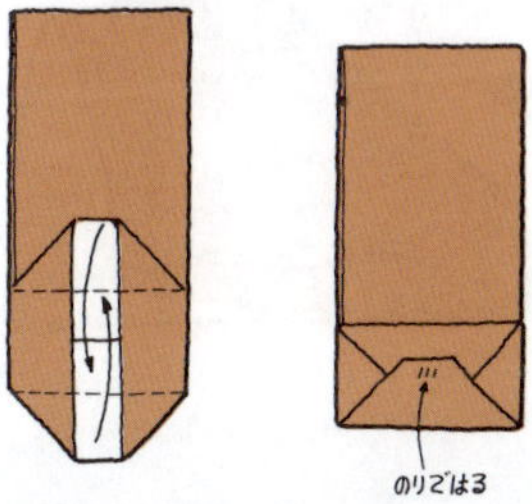

5 入り口を折り下げ、その間に1.5cmの紙テープをはさむ。

Fold the top edge down. Insert a 1.5cm strip of paper.

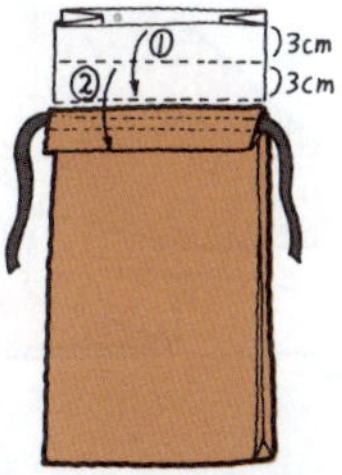

カドを折り下げ、テープを結ぶ。

Fold the corners down, then make a tie.

Finished

新聞紙のゴミ入れ

Trash Box

●材料　materials
新聞紙　２面続きを２枚
2sheets of newspaper

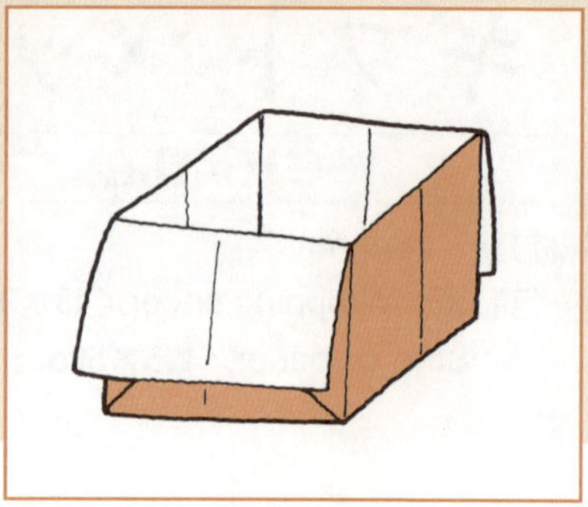

1 新聞紙を２枚重ねる。重ねたままタテに半分折る。
Fold 2 sheets of newspaper in half.

2 ヨコに、半分に折る。
Fold in half to the right.

3 上の１枚（２枚ひと組み）を左側に開く。
Open the upper flap (2sheets) and flatten.

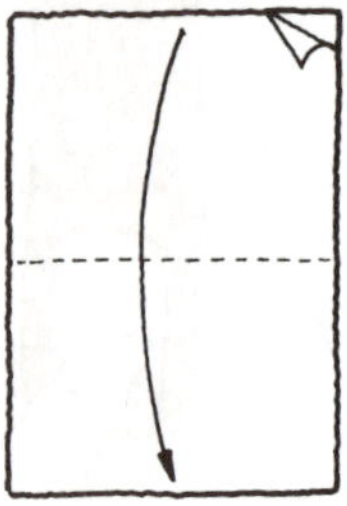

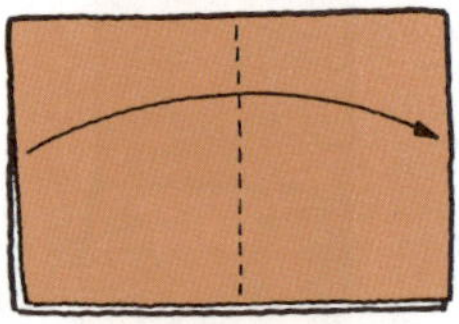

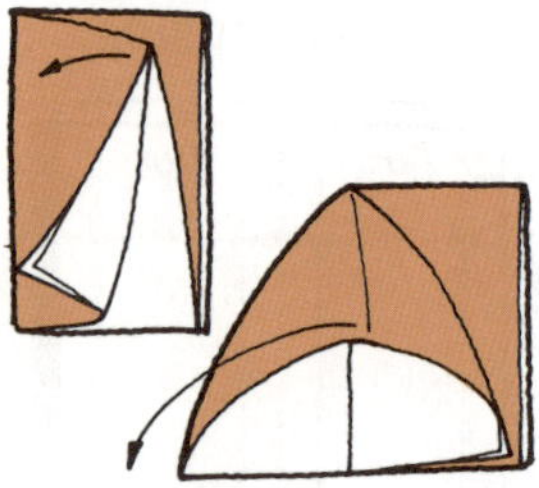

4 きちんと折り目をつける。
Make a sharp crease.

5 右の上の１枚を左のカドに合わせる。
Fold the right top flap to the left.

6 **3**と同様に、矢印の方向に開く。
Repeat steps **3**～**4**.

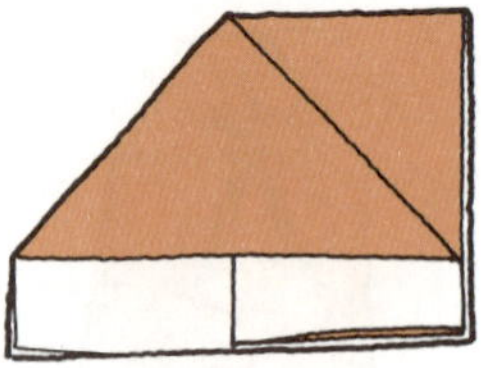

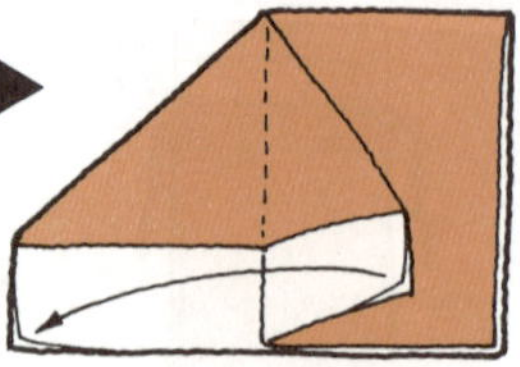

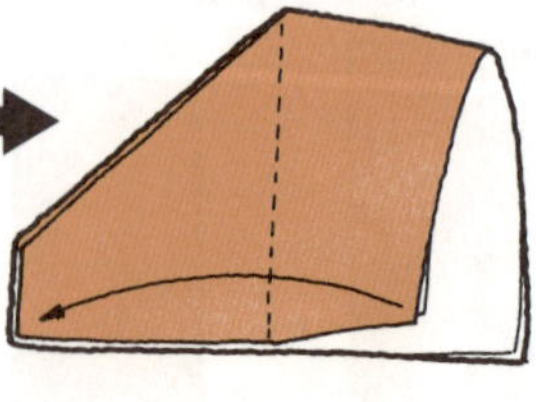

7 しっかり折り目をつける。
Make a sharp crease.

8 1枚右に戻す。
Fold the left top flap to the right.

9 向きを変える。1枚ずつ内側に向けて折り合わせる。
Turn upside down. Fold the upper flaps inside.

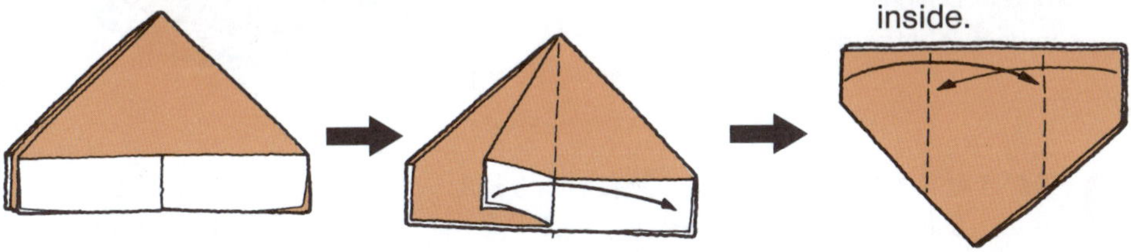

10 裏側も同様に折り合わせる。
Do the same with the reverse side.

11 折りすじをつけておく。
Make a crease on the bottom. Unfold.

12 上の部分を折り下げる。
Fold the upper flaps down.

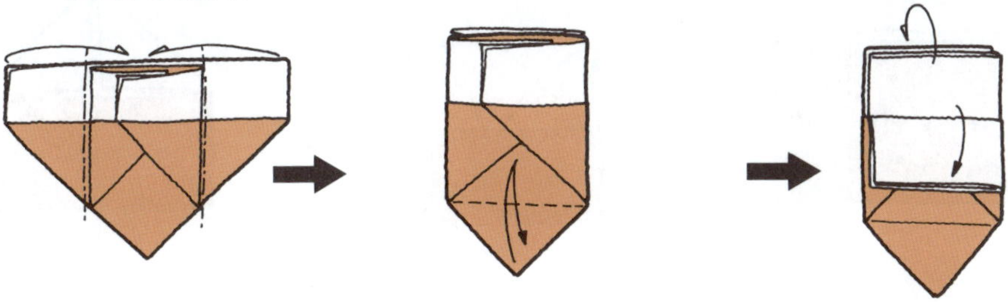

13 形を整えて、広げる。
Shape into a box.

Finished

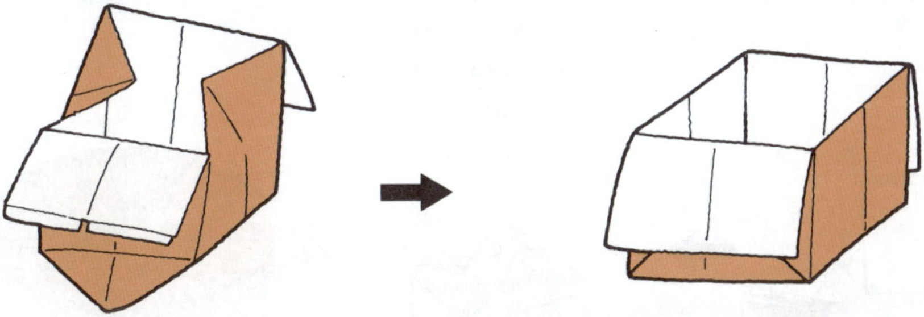

なべしき

Pot Mat

●材料　materials
はがき30枚前後
30pieces postcards

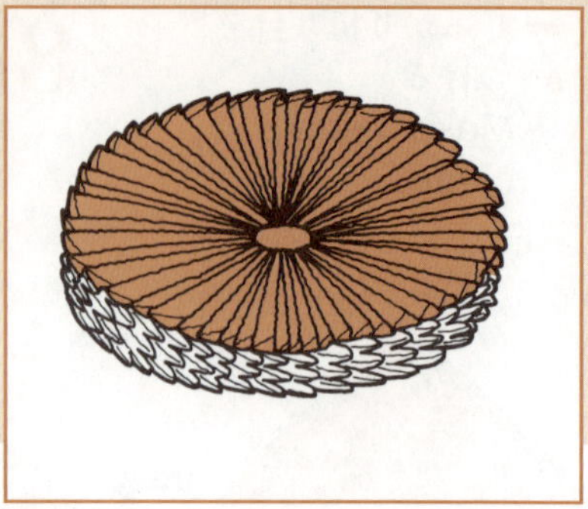

1 はがきを３等分に折り、もとにもどす。
Fold in trisection. Unfold.

2 ⅓だけ折り返し、上下のカドを中心に向けて折る。
Fold 1/3 down and fold corners to meet at the center.

3 半分に折る。
Fold in half.

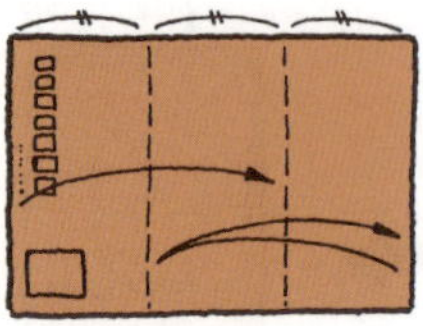

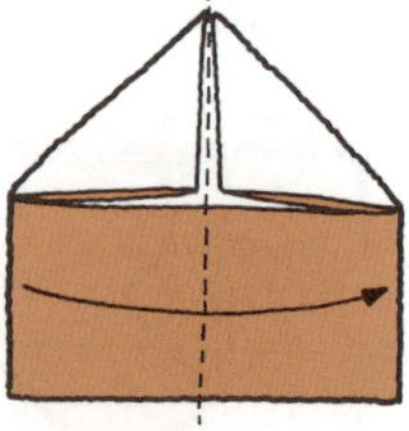

4 ●と●を合わせるように内側を開いて折る。
Fold ● inside to meet ● as shown.

5 別のひとつ（B）をAの間にはさむ。Aの上の三角をBの袋にはさみ込む。
Make another one (B). Put the upper triangle of A into B's pocket.

6 同様につなぐ。
Continue till you have a pot mat.

Finished

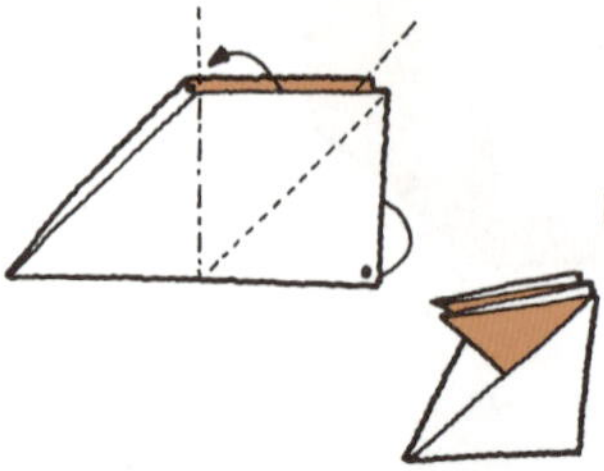

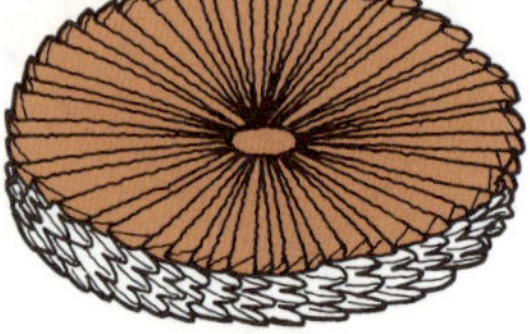

とりの小物入れ

Case

32×32㎝

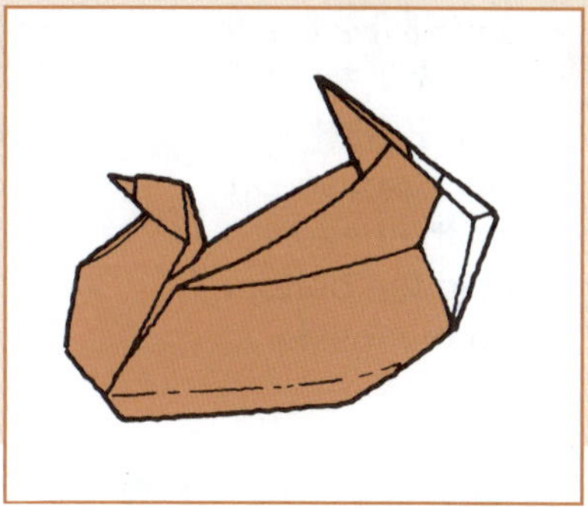

1 半分に折りすじをつけ、中心線に合わせて折る。
Make a crease in the center and fold both corners to meet at the center.

2 半分に折る。
Fold in half.

3 上から⅓のところで折る。裏側も同様に折る。
Fold the upper flap 1/3 of the way down. Do the same with the reverse side.

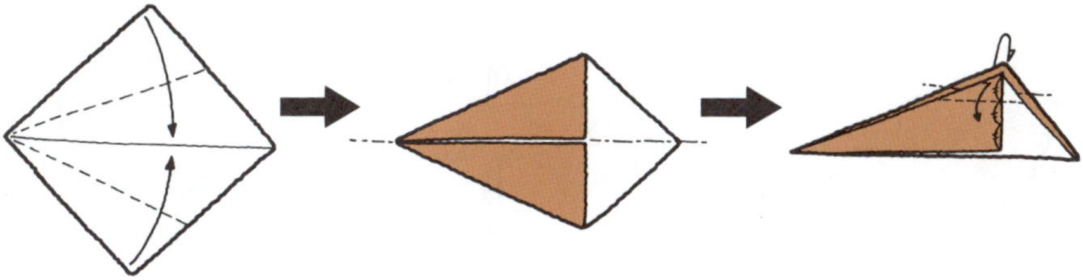

4 中わり折りをする。
Do "Nakawari-Ori" to form a neck.

5 かぶせ折りをする。
Do "Kabuse-Ori" to make a head.

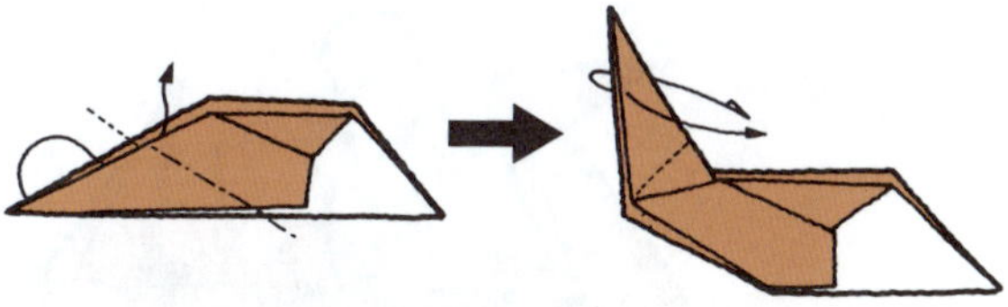

6 頭の部分をかぶせ折りをする。下のカドを内側に折る。
Do "Kabuse-Ori" on the head.
Fold the bottom corner inside.

7 だん折りで、口ばしをつくる。
Do "Dan-Ori" to make a bill.

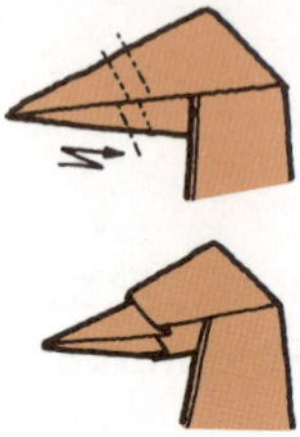

8 背の間を開くようにしながら、しっぽを持ち上げる。
Lift and open the tail.

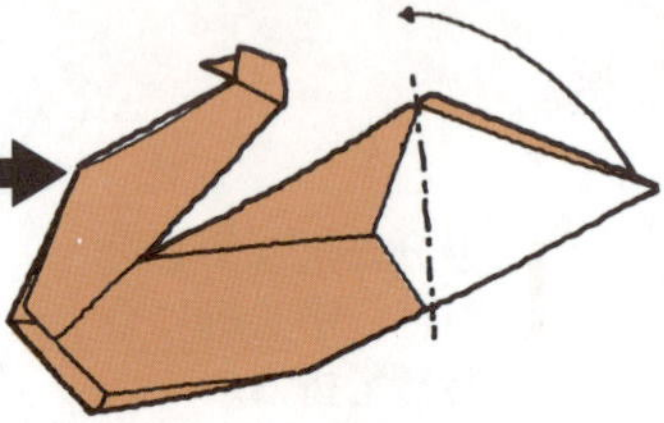

9 中心に合わせて折る。
Fold both corners in to the center line.

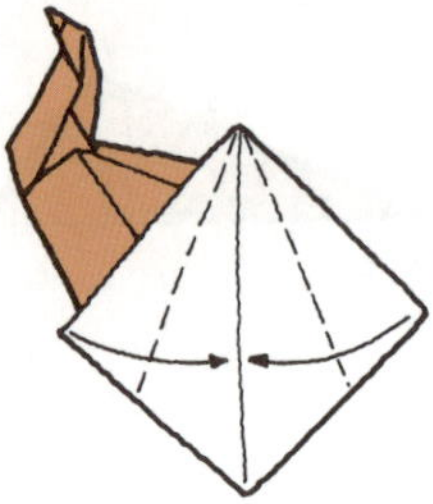

10 右カドを左カドに、重ねる。
Fold in half.

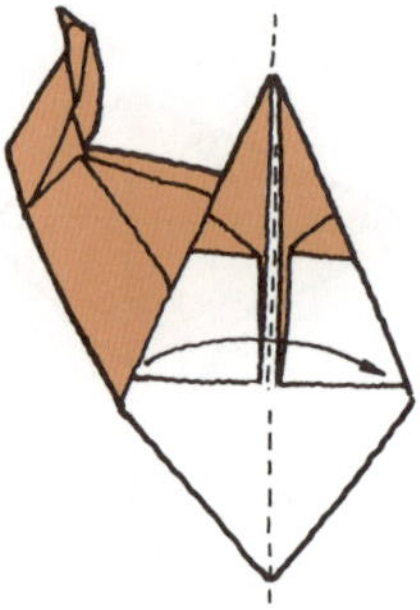

11 中の袋を整える。
Shape into a case.

Finished

花びらの入れ物

Case

●材料　materials

18×18cm

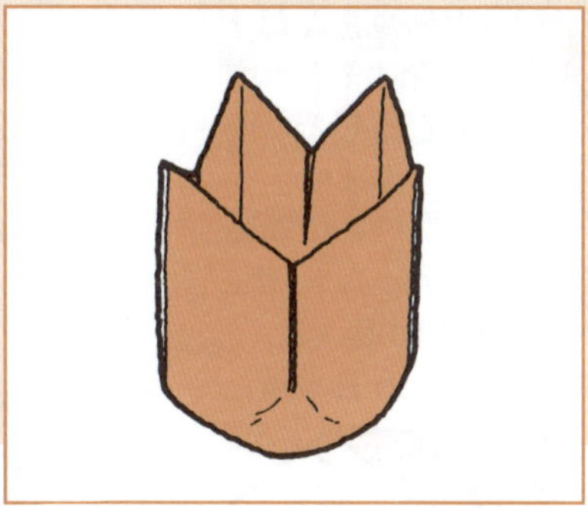

1 風船基本形（P 26参照）から始める。
Begin with "Basic Fūsen" (See P26).

2 左右のカドを折る。裏側も同様に折る。
Fold the left and right corners up to the top corner. Do the same with the reverse side.

3 左右のカドを折る。裏側も同様に折る。
Fold both corners in. Do the same with the reverse side.

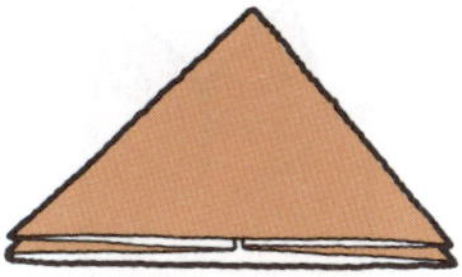

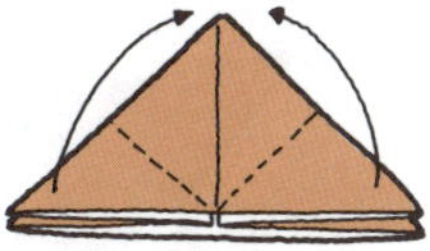

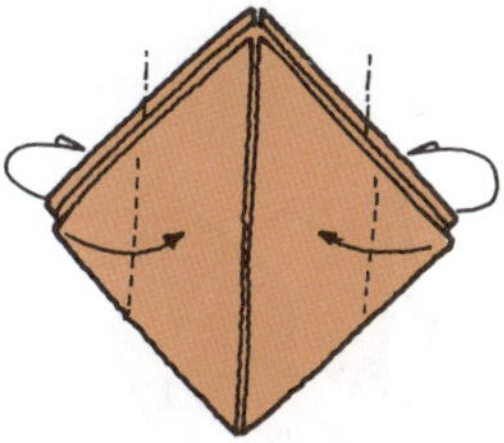

4 開いて、ざぶとん基本形（P 23参照）にする。
Open, then fold "Basic Zabuton" (See P23).

5 1枚開く。上から、Aの部分を山折りにつまむ。
Open one triangle. Pinch A by "Yama-Ori".

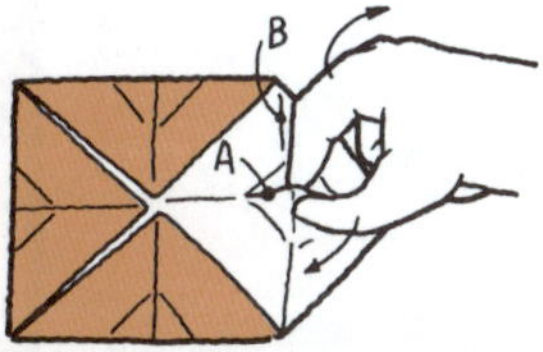

6 ①Aをつまんだまま、時計まわりでBまでねじる。
②Bもつまむ。
①、②の順で折る。
①Twist A to the right to B.
②Pinch B also.

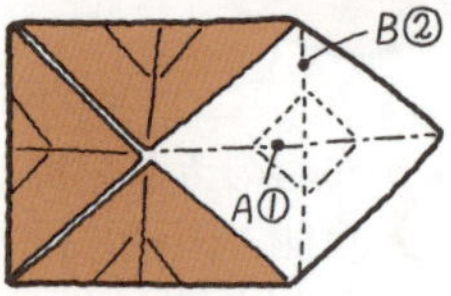

7 つまみながら、右の三角部分を色が出るように折る。
Fold the coloured face back while pinching.

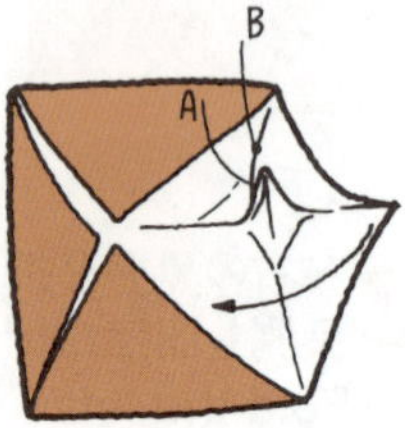

8 図のようになる。
It should look like this.

9 折った部分を横から見た図。
Side view.

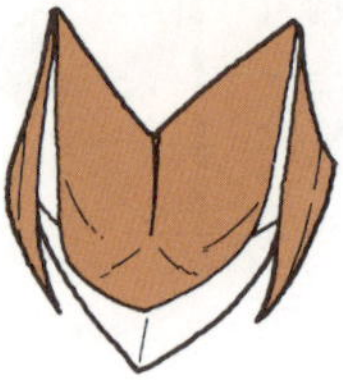

10 残りの3カ所も同様につまんで、折り返していく。
Repeat steps 5～7 on the other 3 sides.

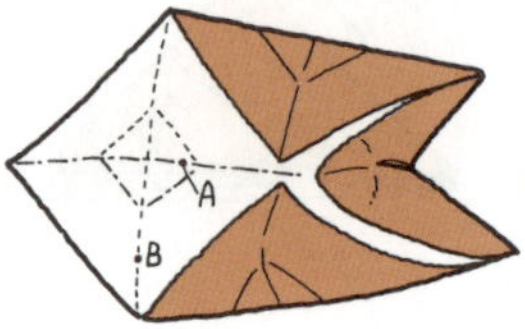

Finished

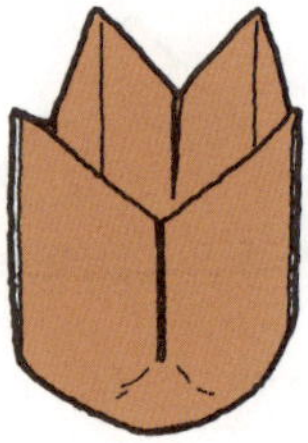

花のかご

Flower Basket

●材料　materials

厚手の紙　thick paper／27×27cm

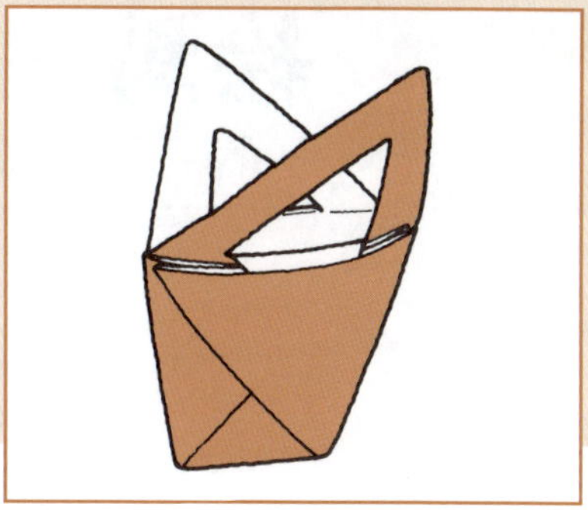

1 三角形に折る。
Fold in half to make a triangle.

2 A、Bの順でだき合わせるように、重ねる。
Fold the corner A to B′, and fold the corner B to A′.

3 半分に折るようにする。背をつまむようにしながら、切り込みを入れる。
Fold in half and cut as shown. Unfold.

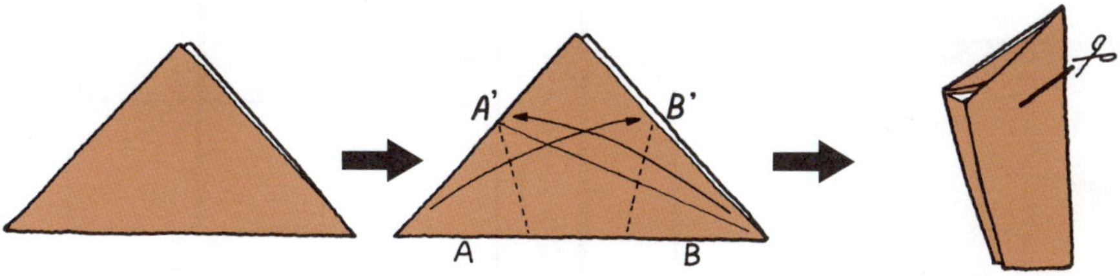

4 切り込んだ部分の２枚を手前側とうしろ側に開くように分ける。
Fold the 2 small triangles forward and backward.

5 手前部分は、前の袋の中に入れのりづけし、開く。
Put the small triangle into the front pocket, then glue it.

Finished

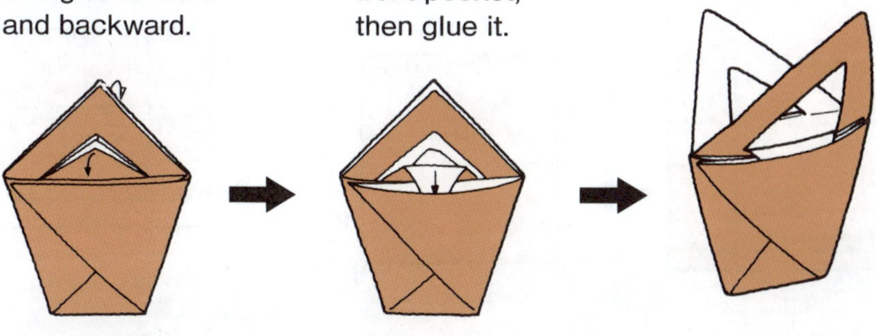

絵馬

Ema

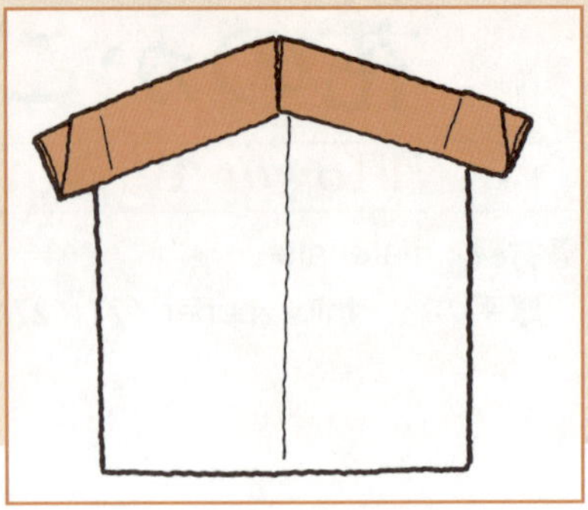

1 中心に折りすじをつけ、左右を折る。
Make a vertical crease. Unfold. Fold the left and right edges to the center.

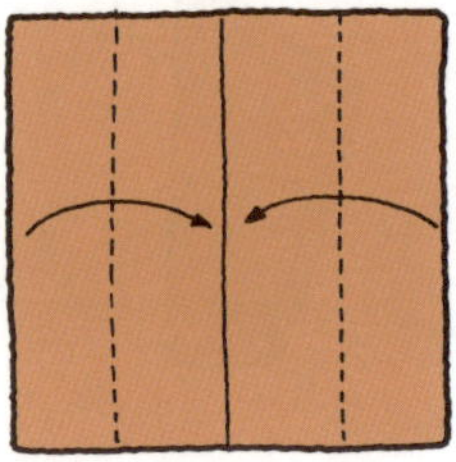

2 上の部分を折り、さらに折り上げる。
Fold the top edge down, fold the front bottom edge up to the top.

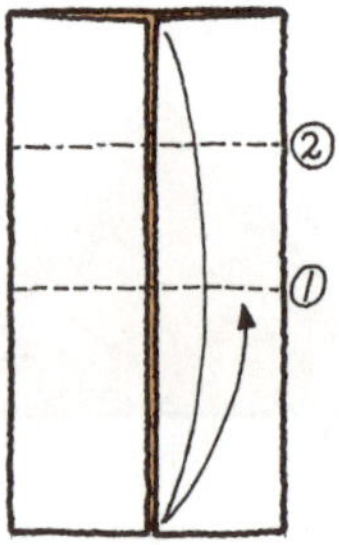

3 折り上げる。
Fold the bottom edge up to the center. Unfold.

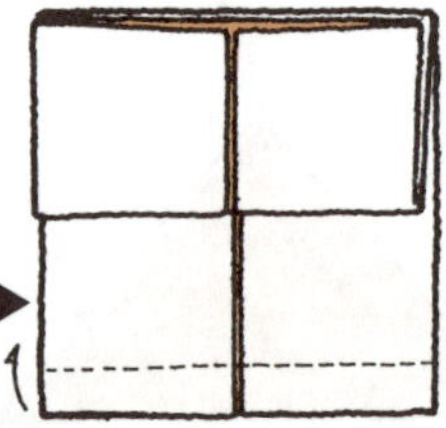

4 全部広げる。
It should look like this.

5 表を出して、図のように折りすじに合わせて折る。
Fold the top crease backward and fold the bottom crease up.

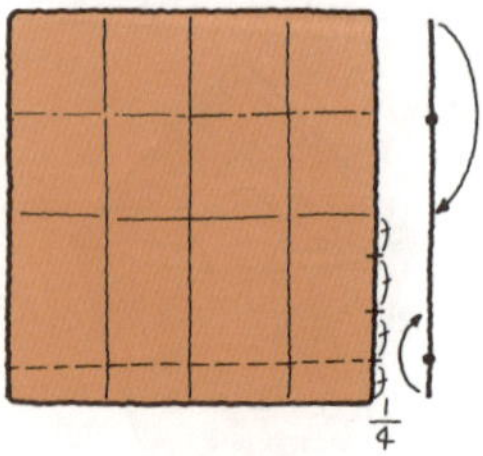

6 左右を中心に合わせて折る。
Fold the left and right edges to the center.

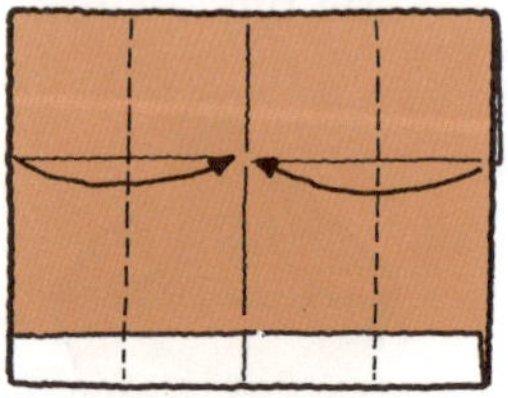

7

中を開き、外側に引っぱりながら折りつぶす。

Open the pockets and flatten to make triangles.

8

裏返して、折り下げる。

Turn over. Fold the upper part down in half.

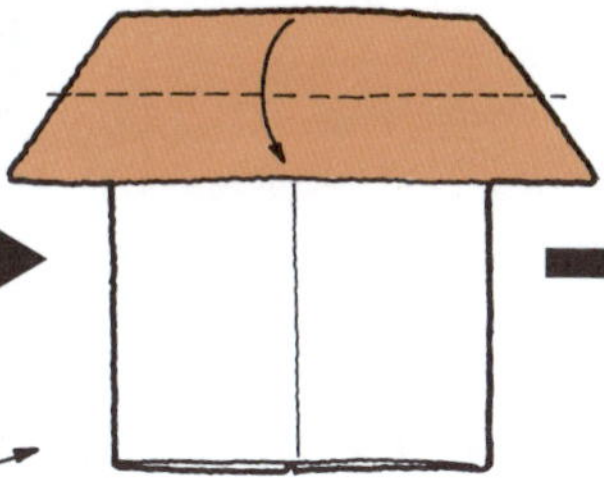

9

左右のカドを折り、上を折り下げる。

Fold both upper corners in to make a rectangle, then fold the top down in half.

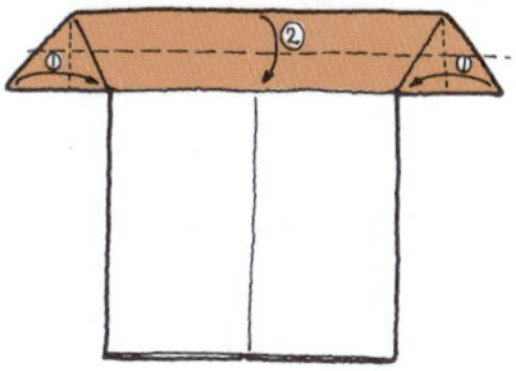

10

両カドを残して、あとは開いて戻す。

Unfold the top but not the corners made in step 9.

11

○を結ぶ対角線で折り、中心で重なる部分はつぶして右側にたおす。

Fold the diagonal lines through ○ as shown, then flatten the center part to the right.

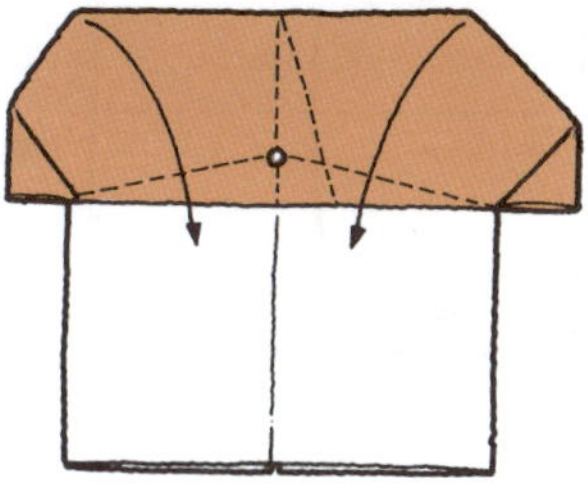

12

上の辺と下の辺を折りすじどおりに折る。

Fold the upper edge down and bottom edge up along the crease.

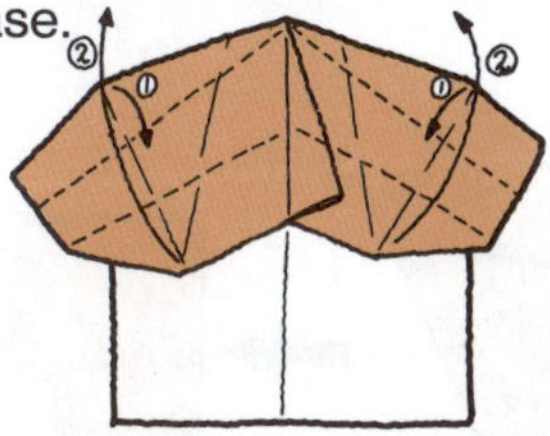

13

中心を整えながら、裏側へ折る。

Shape the center, then fold the flap backward.

Finished

- 絵馬は神社などに祈りやお礼のしるしとして、馬などをえがいて奉納する額のことです。
- People who come to pray at shrines, sometime write there wish on a votive picture and leave it as a kind of offering.

六角形のオーナメント

Hexagonal Ornament

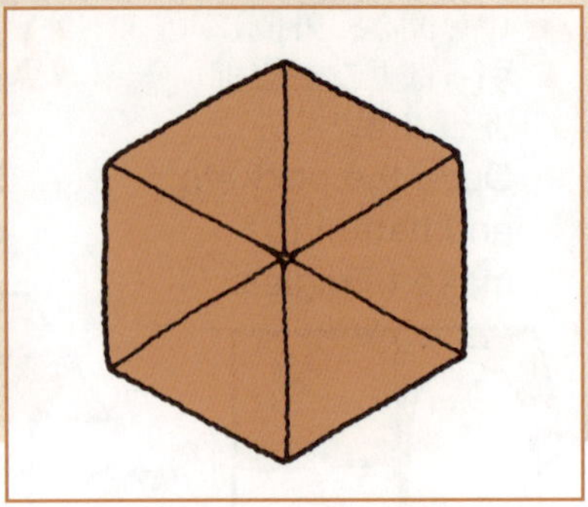

正六角形
Hexagon

1 半分に折る。
Fold in half.

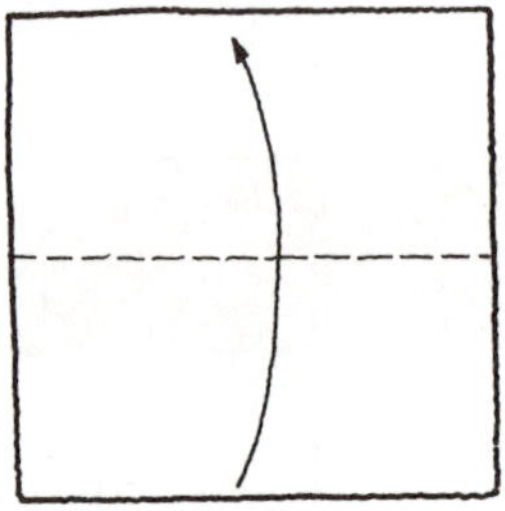

2 折りすじをつける。
Fold in half to the right. Unfold.

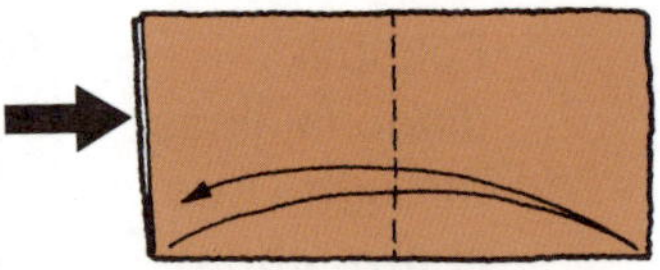

3 左側だけ折りすじをつける。
Fold in the left edge to the center. Unfold.

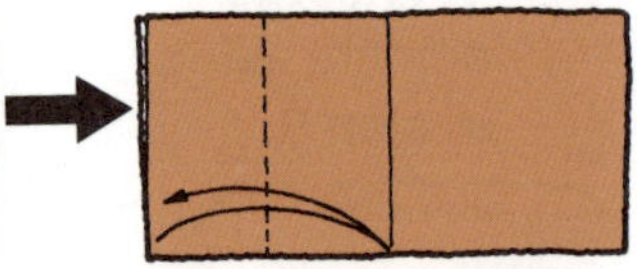

4 中心の折りすじを軸にして、右下のカドを3の折りすじに合わせて折る。
Fold the right bottom corner up diagorally to the quarter crease.

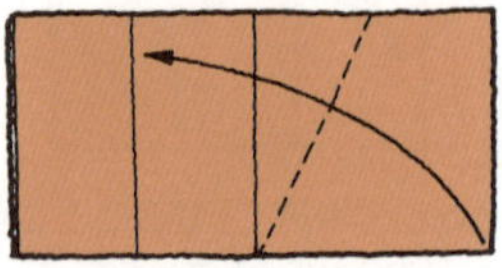

5 手前に折って、戻す。
Fold the left edge of the front flap to the right. Unfold.

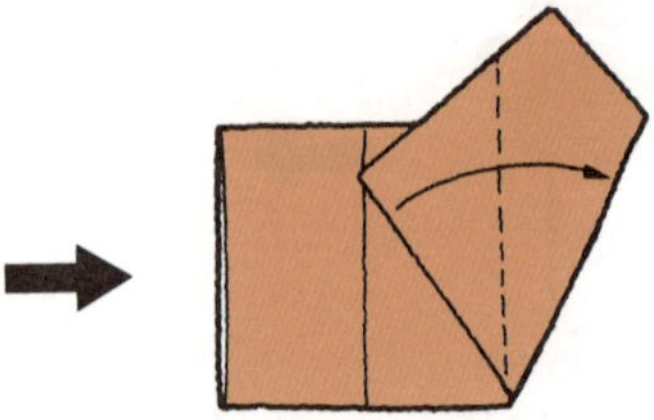

6 右に向かって折る。
Fold the left bottom corner up diagonally and lay it along the right edge.

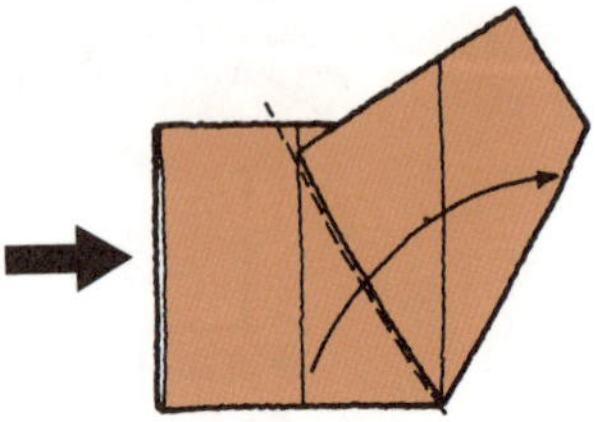

7 手前に折る。
Fold the front right flap to the left.

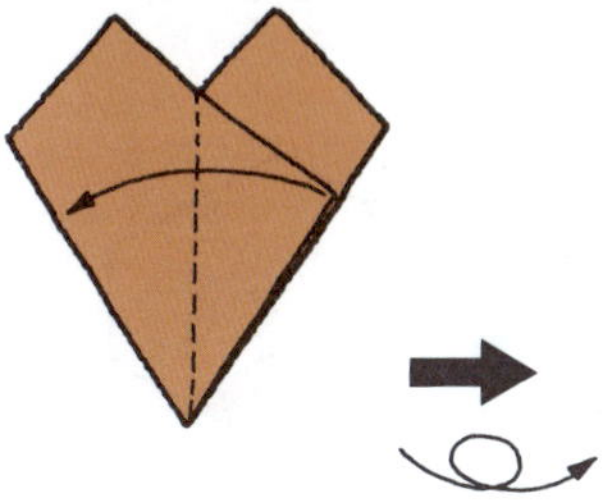

8 裏返して、中心で折る。
Turn over. Fold in half to the left.

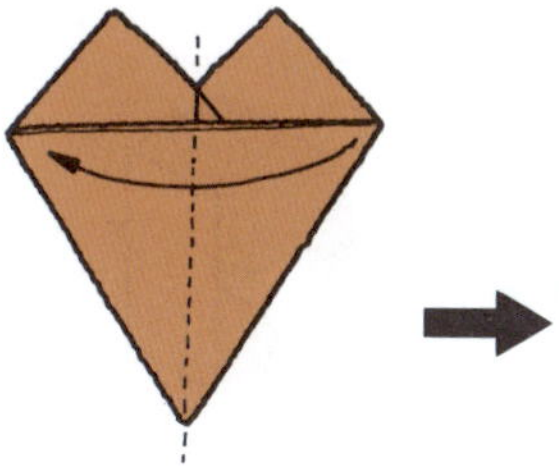

9 下の部分が直角三角形になるように折りすじをつける。
Fold the upper part down to make a right-angle triangle.

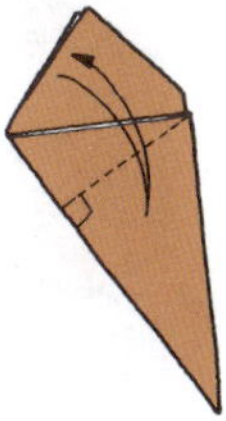

10 はさみで切る。
Cut along the crease.

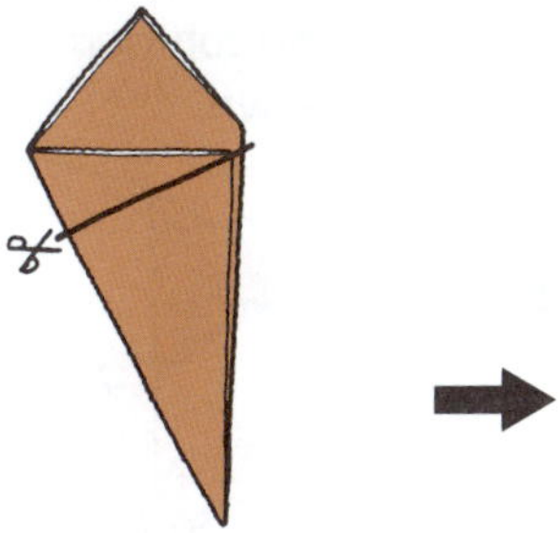

広げる。
Open the paper.

Finished

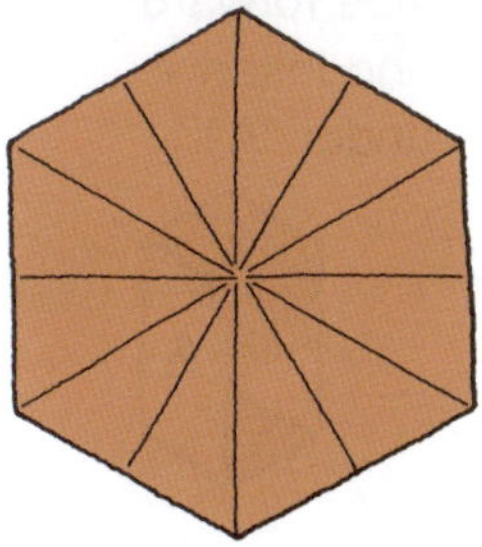

六角オーナメント
Hexagonal Ornament

1 正六角形の左側を中心に合わせ、折る。
Make a hexagonal paper. Fold the left side to the center.

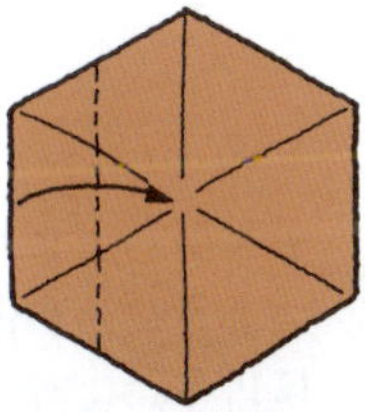

2 図のようになる。
It should look like this.

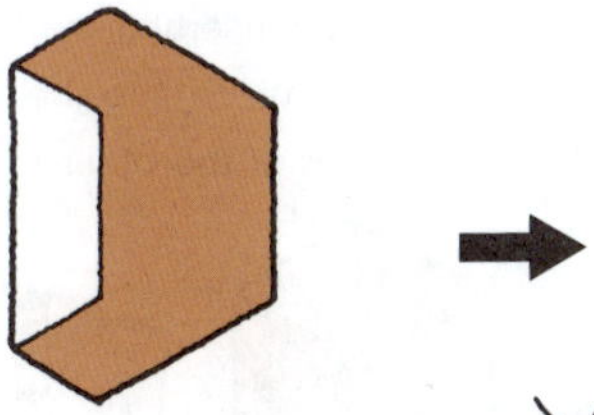

3 裏返し、カドを中心に合わせて折る。
Turn over. Fold the upper right side to the center.

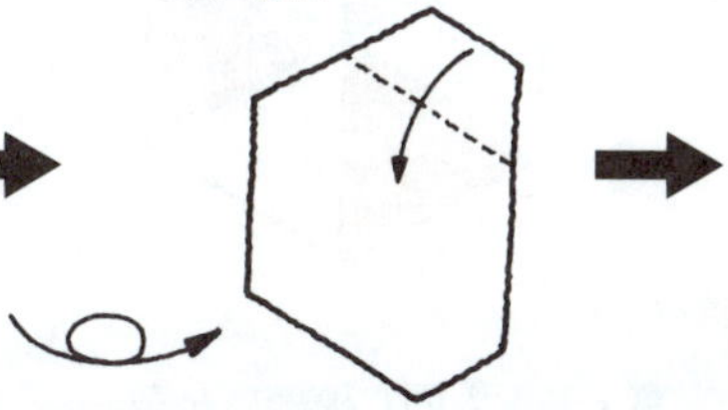

4 図のようになる。
It should look like this.

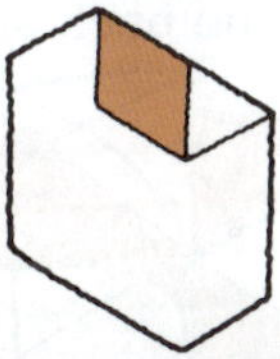

5 裏返して、下のカドを中心に合わせて折る。
Turn over. Fold the bottom left side to the center.

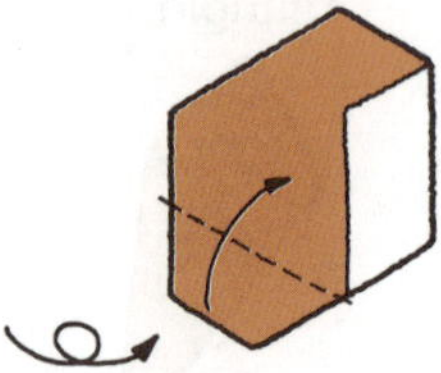

6 図のようになる。
It should look like this.

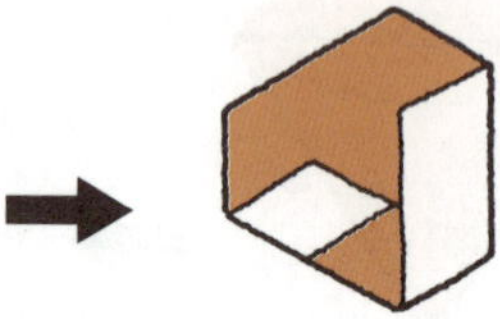

7 裏返して、中心に合わせて折る。
Turn over. Fold the right side to the center.

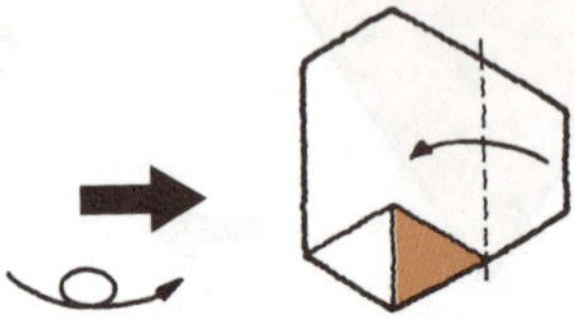

8 図のようになる。
It should look like this.

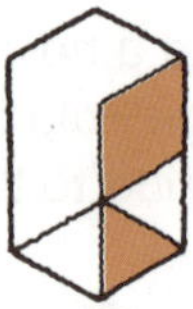

9 裏返し、手前に折りAの下に入れる。
Turn over. Fold the upper left side forward and insert it under "A".

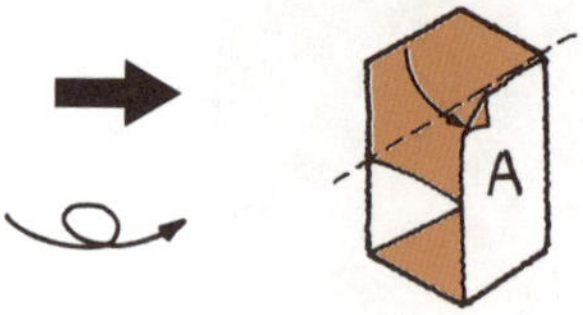

10 上の１枚を引きよせながら折る。
Raise the front top sheet, bring the top corner down.

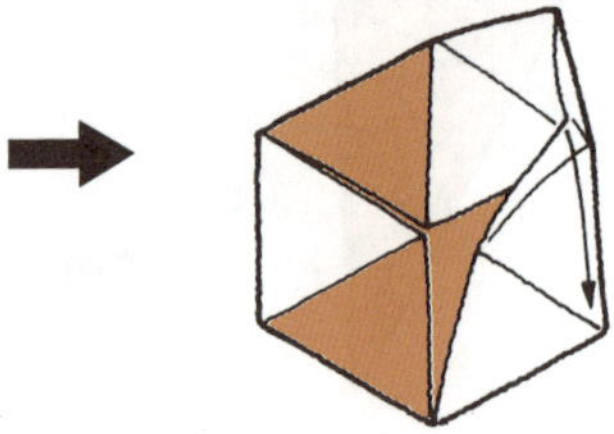

11 カドをつぶさないように、裏側に折る。
Fold the lozenge made in step 10 to the back side.

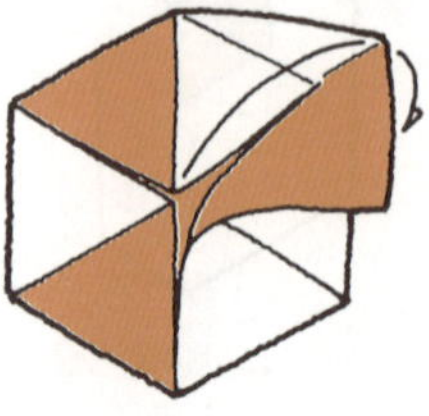

Finished

裏・表とも同じ模様になる。

※六角形のオーナメントをいくつか作り、図のようにつなぐとユニットになる。
※Make some more pieces. Join by inserting the flap of one piece into the pocket of the other.

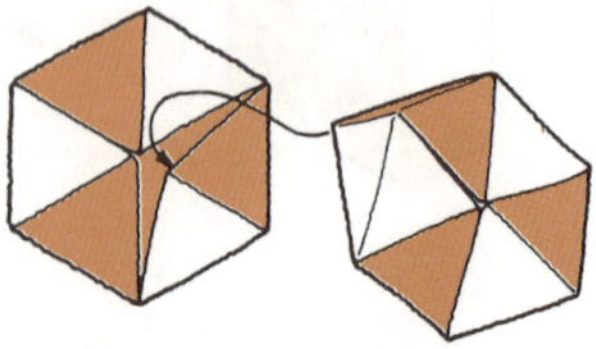

クリスマスのかざり

Christmas Decoration

●材料　materials

リース　wreath／3×3cm（金、緑　gold and green sheets）、ろうそく　Candle／3.5×3.5cm（銀、赤　silver and red sheets）、リボン　Ribbon／3.2×3.2 cm（金　gold sheet）

クリスマスリース
Christmas wreath

1 金と緑の折り紙を裏ではり合わせ、金を上にし、①②の順に折る。
Glue gold and green sheets together. Turn the gold side up and fold as shown.

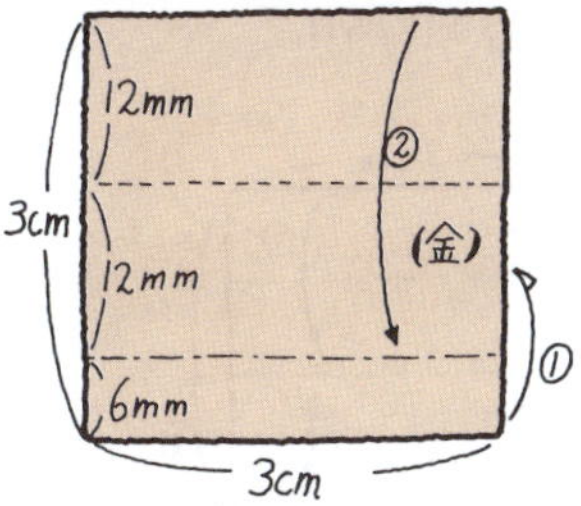

2 両カドを折る。同じものを8枚作って、さしこんでいく。
Fold both corners. Make 8 pieces, then join as shown. Make a ring.

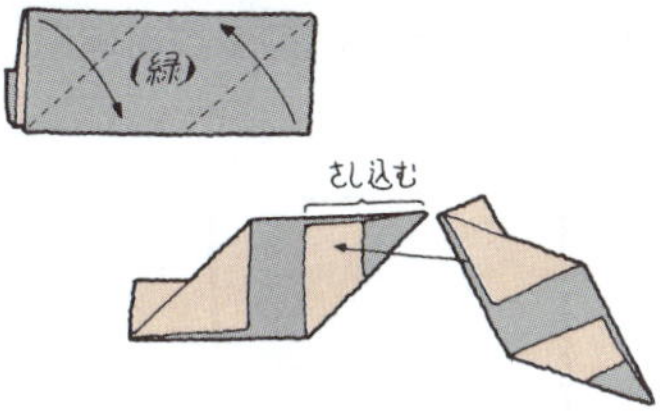

Finished

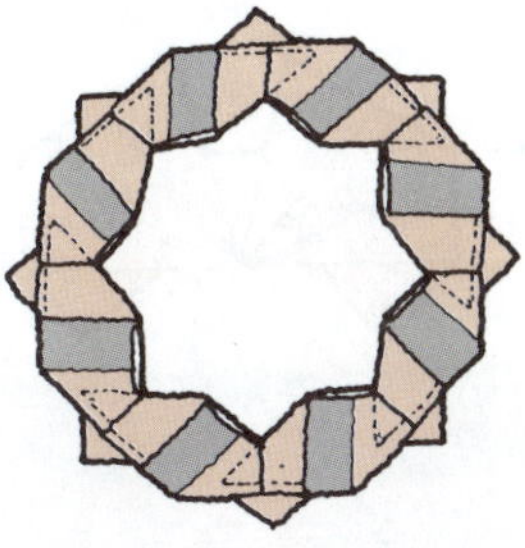

ろうそく
Candle

1 銀と赤の折り紙を裏ではり合わせ、赤を上にし、①②の順に折る。
Glue red and silver sheets together. With the red side facing up, fold as shown.

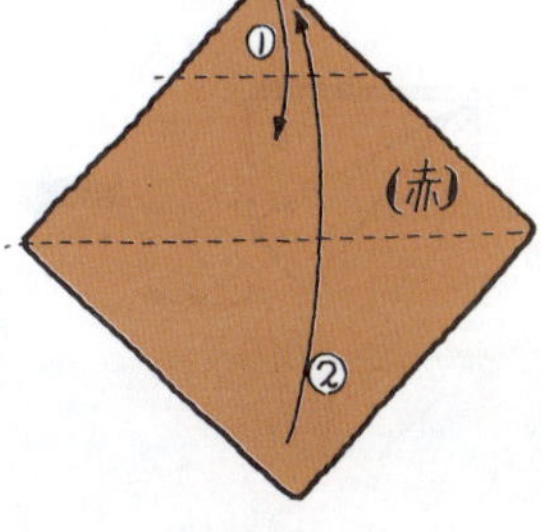

2 手前の１枚だけを中心線に合わせて折り合わせる。
Fold the front flaps in to meet at the center line.

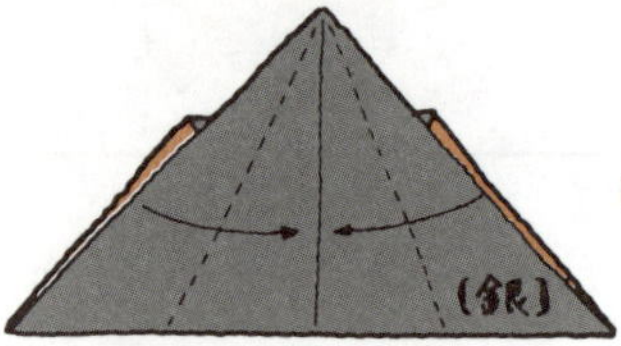

3 左右を折り合わせる。
Overlap the front flaps as show. Glue them together.

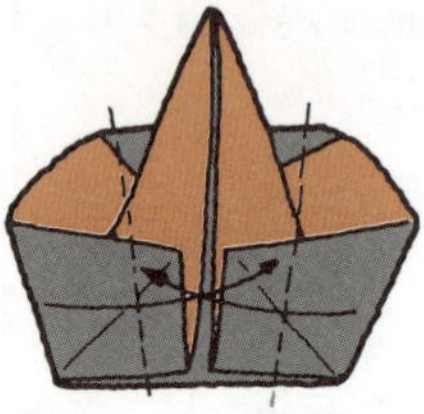

ひっくり返す。
Turn over.

Finished

リボン
Ribbon

1 折りすじをつけて、もどす。
Make a cross shaped crease on a piece of gold paper. Unfold.

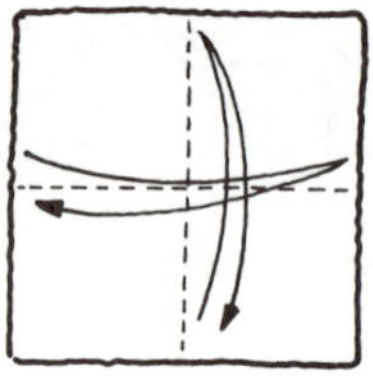

2 ①②③の順で折る。
With gold side facing down, fold as shown.

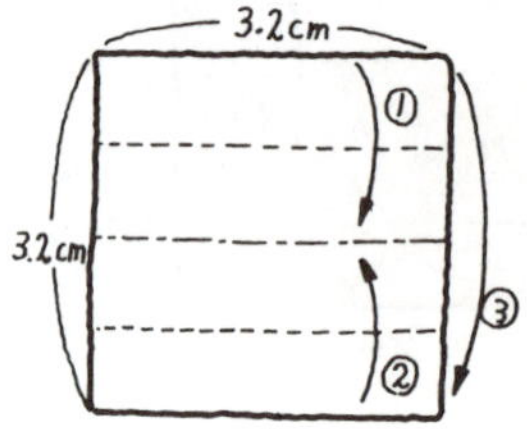

3 折り下げる。
Fold both corners down as shown.

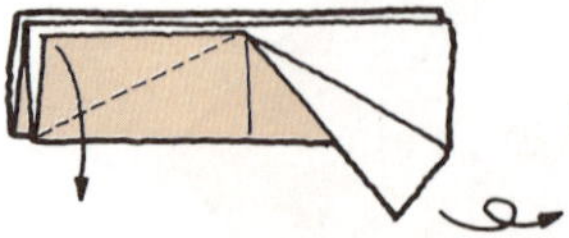

4 ひっくり返し、中心に折り上げる。
Turn over.
Fold both corners up as shown.

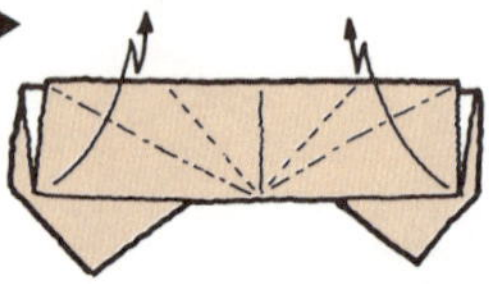

Finished

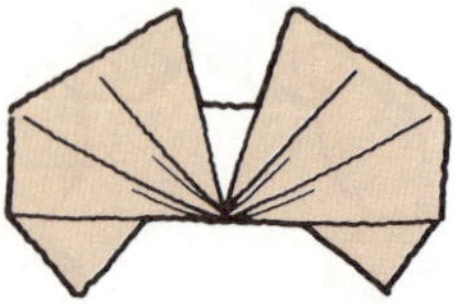

Chapter 3

花を折る
Flowers

つりがねそう

Bellflower

●材料　materials

つりがねそう　Bellflower／7.5×7.5㎝

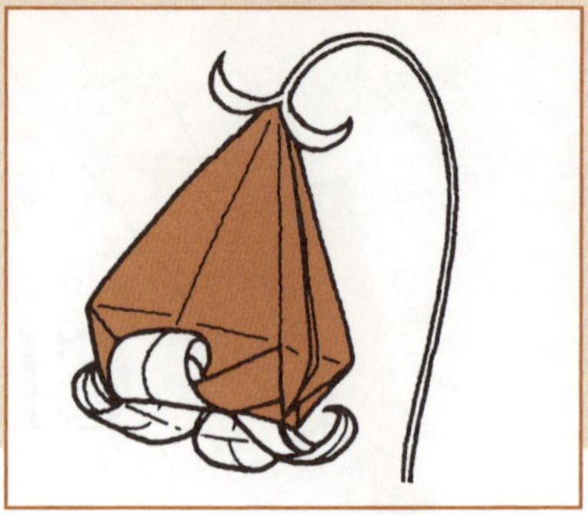

1 正方基本形（P25参照）から始め、左右を折る。裏側も同様に折る。
Begin with "Basic Square" (See P25). Fold the flaps. Do the same with the reverse side.

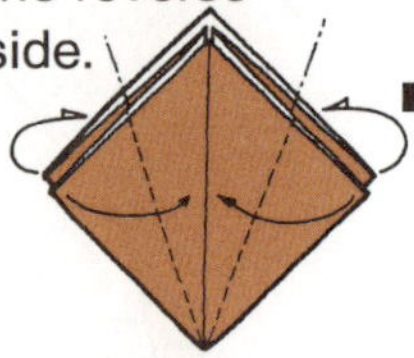

2 中心に合わせて、左右を折る。裏側も同様に折る。
Fold both corners in to meet at the center. Do the same with the reverse side.

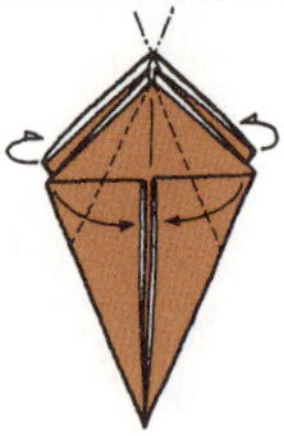

3 内側の袋を広げてつぶすように折る。裏側も同様に折る。
Open the inside pockets and flatten. Do the same with the reverse side.

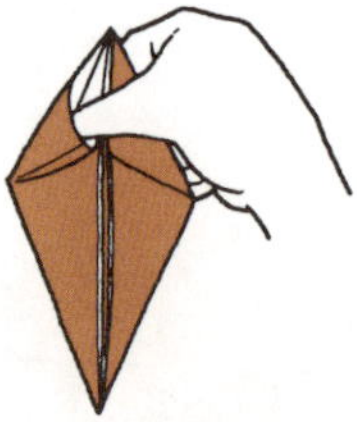

4 4カ所を内側に向けて折り込む。
Fold each pocket backward.

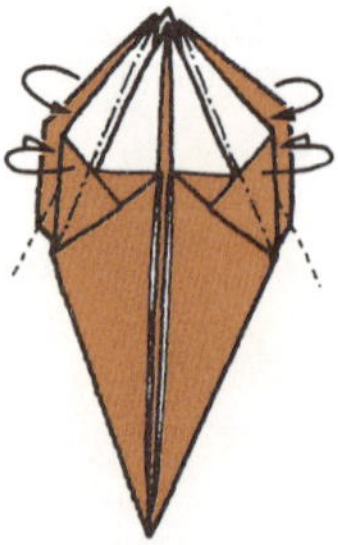

5 先をカールさせるように広げる。
Curl each tip, then spread.

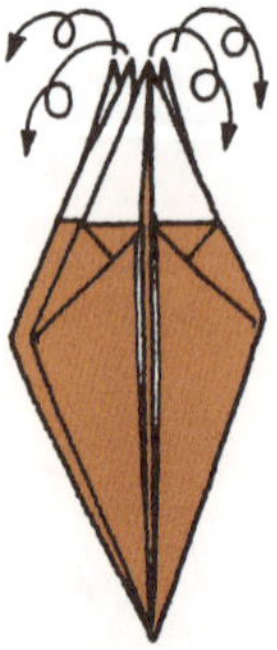

Finished

あやめ

Ayame

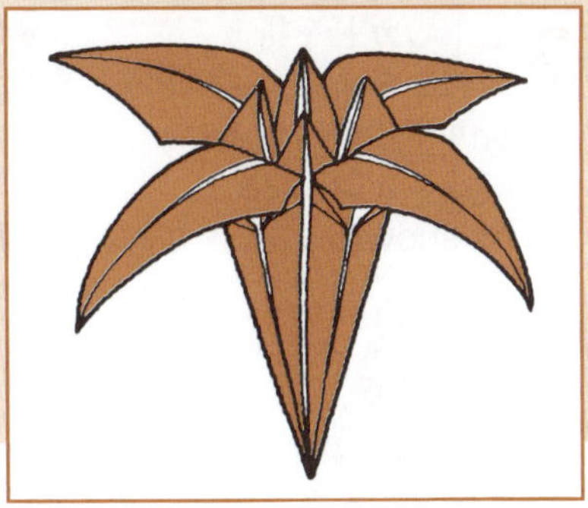

1 正方基本形（P 25参照）から始め、折りすじをつける。裏側も同様に。
Begin with "Basic Square" (See P25). Make creases. Do the same with the reverse side.

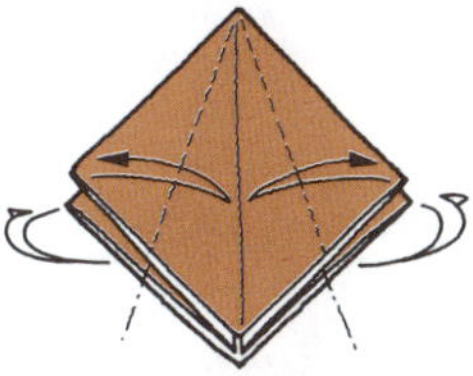

2 ●と●を合わせるように、右の袋を広げる。次につぶして折る。
Open the right pocket of the top flap, then flatten.

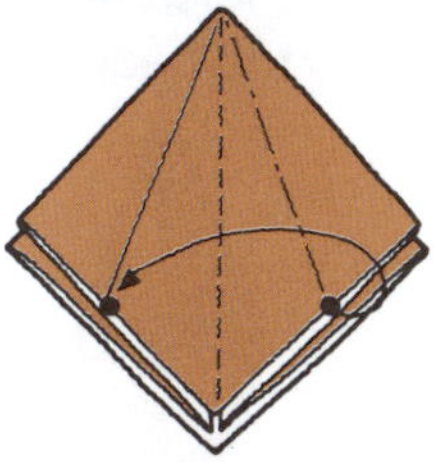

3 裏側も同様に折る。
Do the same with the reverse side.

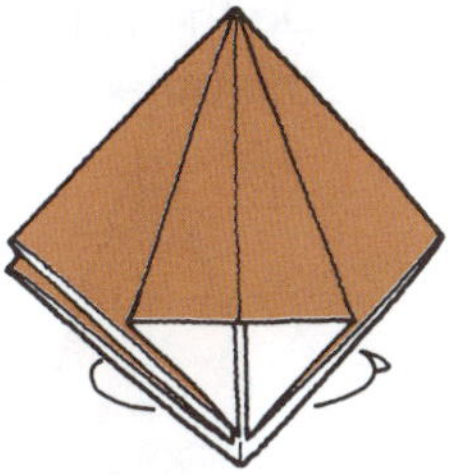

4 左に重ね合わせる。裏側も同様に折る。
Fold the right flap to the left. Do the same with the reverse side.

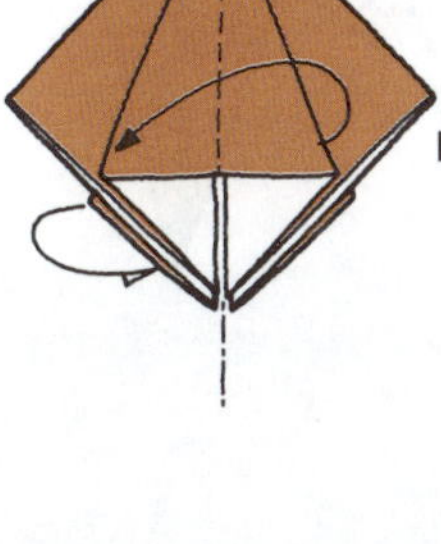

5 2と同様に広げてつぶして折る。
Repeat steps 2 ～3.

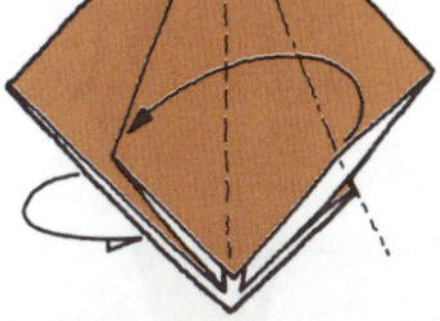

6 左右を中心に折り合わせ、戻す。
Fold both corners of the top flap in to the center. Unfold.

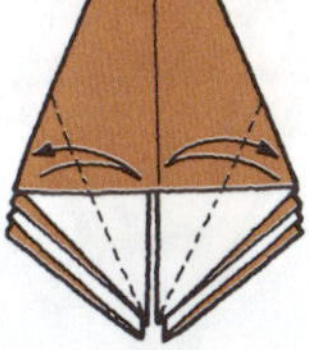

7 上下のカドを折り合わせるように、折りすじをつける。
Make a crease as shown.

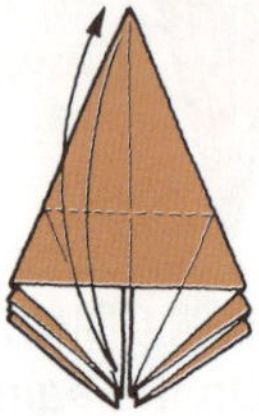

8 6、7でつけた折りすじを使って、開くように折る。
Open and flatten the bottom pocket.

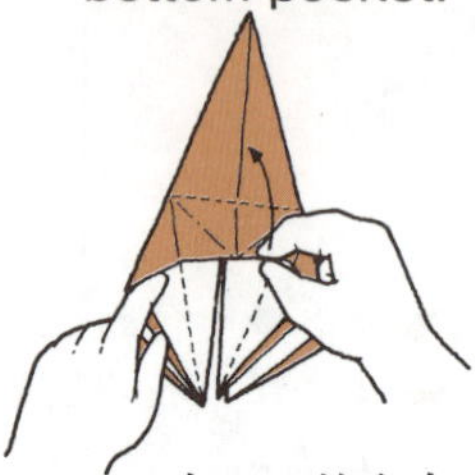

9 4面とも同様に折る。
Do the same with the other sides.

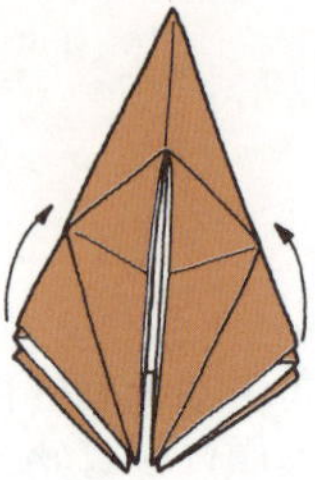

10 向きを変えてカドを折り上げる。4面とも同様に。
Turn upside down. Fold the flap up. Do the same with the other sides.

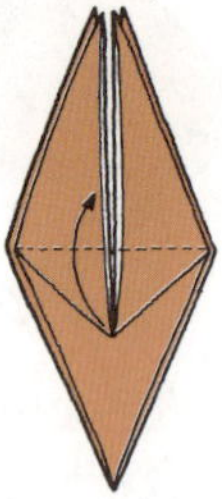

11 右の1枚を左に重ね合わせる。裏側も同様に。
Fold the flap to the left. Do the same with the back one.

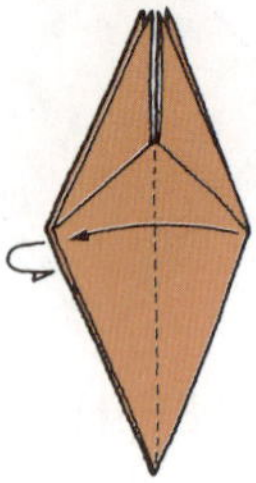

12 中心に合わせて、左右を折る。裏側も同様に折る。
Fold the corners in. Do the same with the back one.

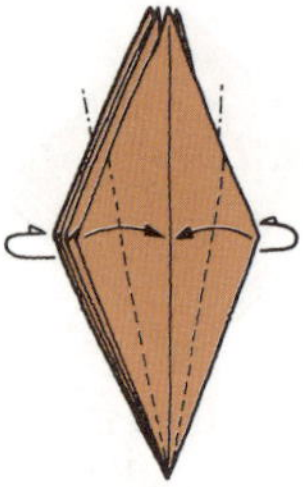

13 左右を内側に折り込む。
Fold the other flaps inside.

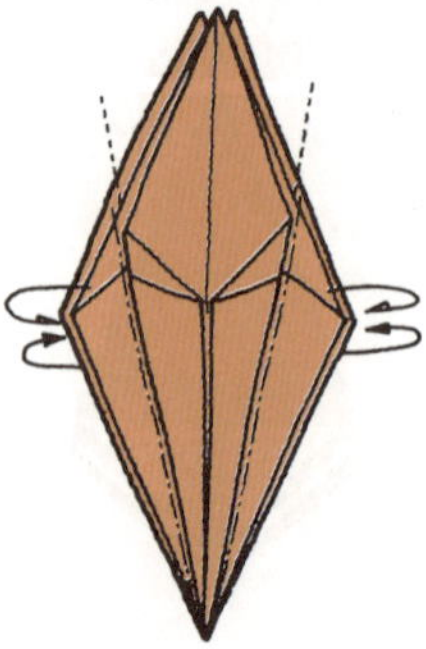

14 4カ所を、開くように折る。
Open the 4 tips and fold down.

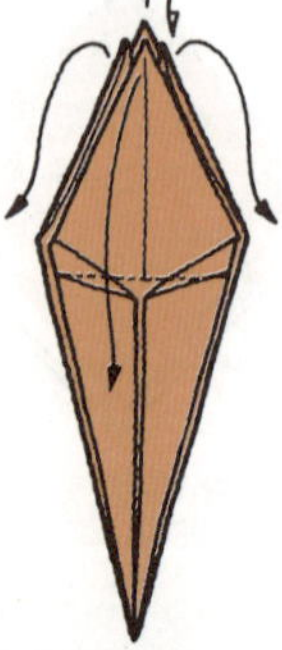

Finished

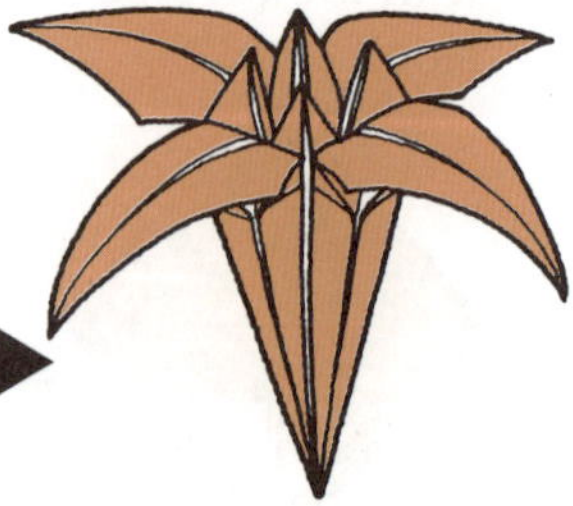

ゆり

Lily

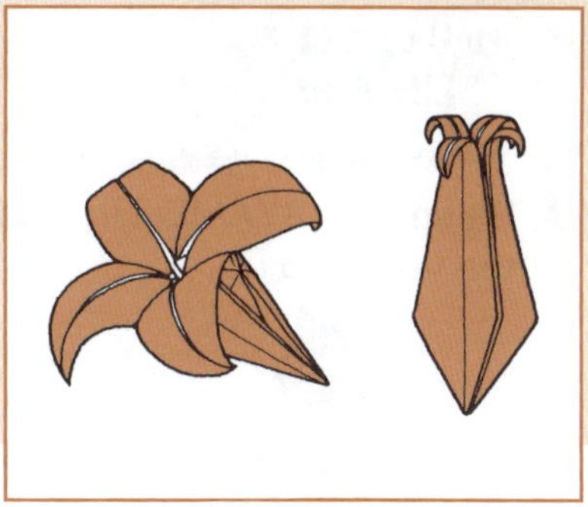

ゆり
Lily

1 あやめの10から始める。向きを変え、右の１枚を左に重ね合わせる。裏側も同様に折る。
Begin with AYAME-10. Turn upside down, and fold the front right flap to the left. Do the same with the reverse side.

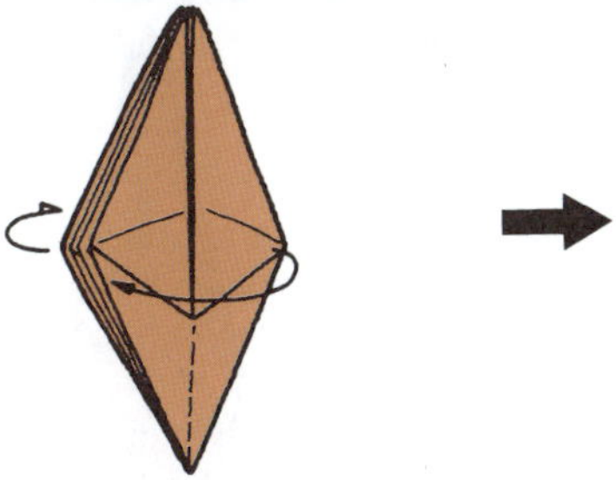

2 中心に合わせて、左右を折り合わせる。裏側も同様に折る。
Fold the top left and right flaps to the center. Do the same with the reverse side.

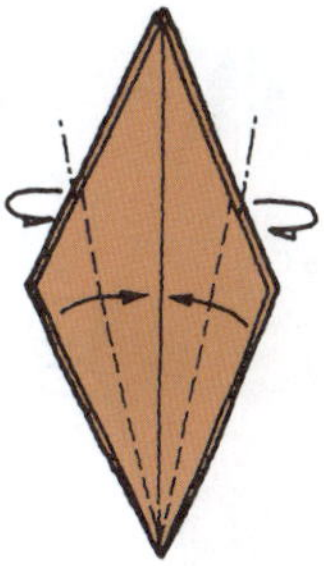

3 左右を内側に折り込む。
Fold the other flaps inside.

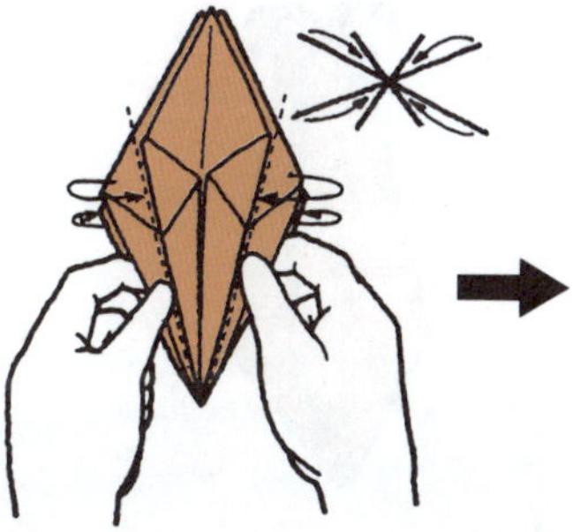

4 ４カ所とも下にカールしながら折り下げる。
Curl 4 tips with a pencil, and fold down.

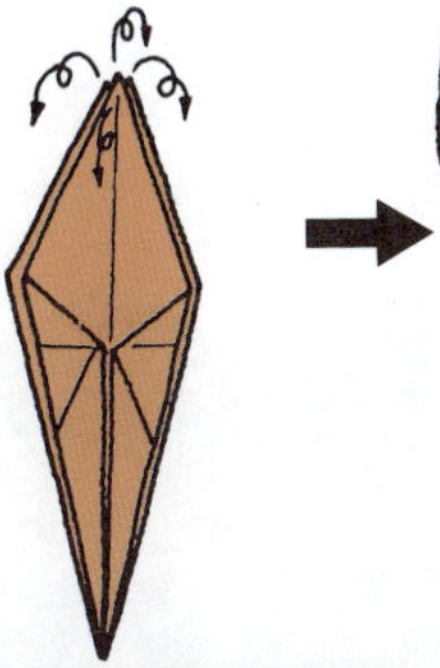

Finished

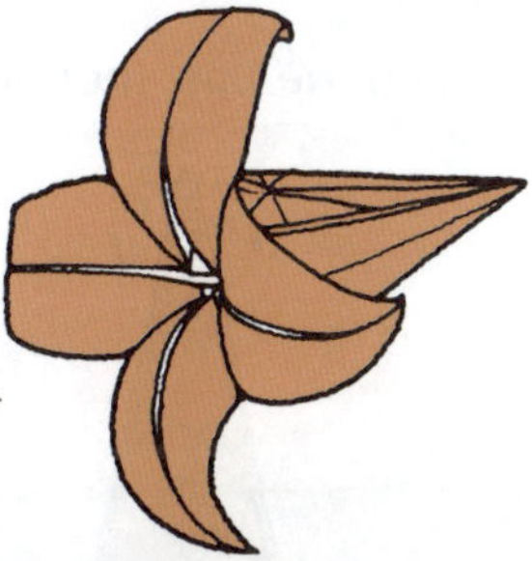

ゆりのつぼみ
Lily Bud

1 あやめの10から始める。
Begin with AYAME-10. Fold the front flap up.

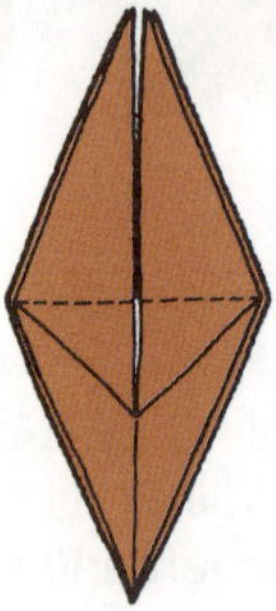

2 中心に合わせて、左右を折り合わせる。裏側も同様に折る。
Fold the left and right flaps to the center. Do the same with the reverse side.

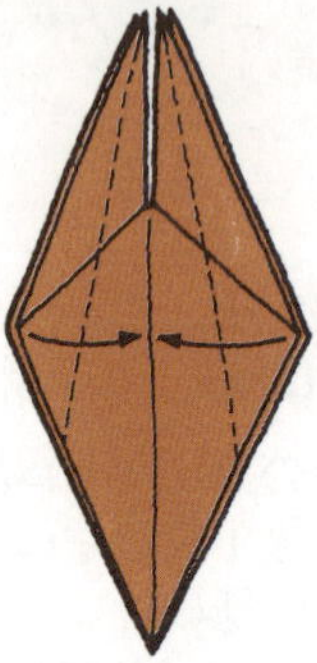

3 左右を内側に折り込む。
Fold the other flaps inside.

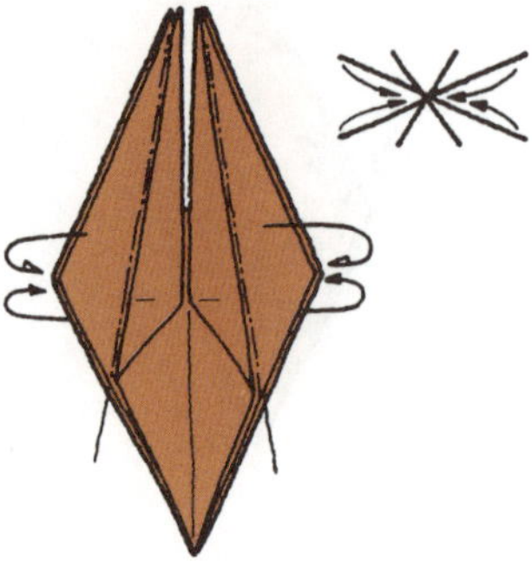

4 右の１枚を左に重ね合わせる。裏側も同様に折る。
Fold the right flap to the left. Do the same with the reverse side.

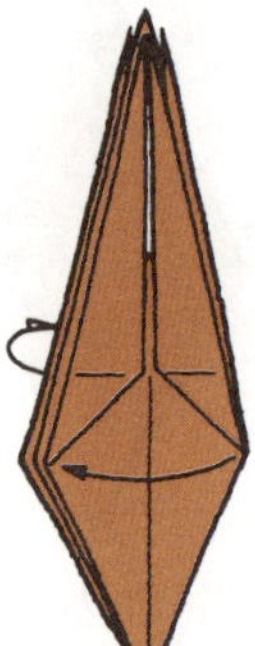

5 花びらの先をカールしながら折り下げる。
Curl the tips, then fold down.

Finished

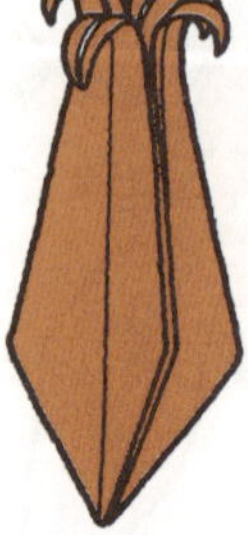

花・チューリップ・葉と茎

Flower・Tulip・Leaf & Stem

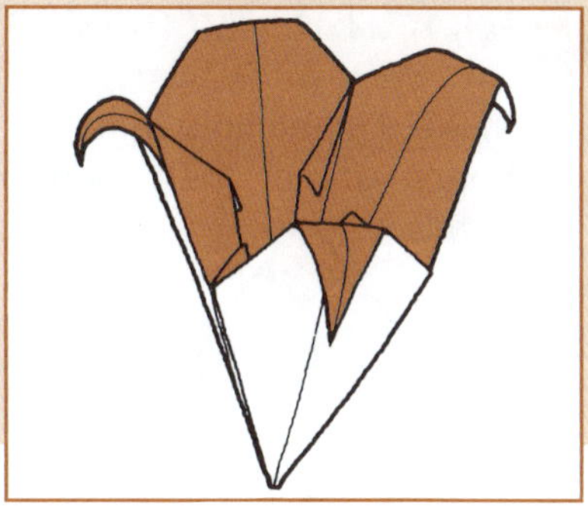

おはな
Flower

1 表を中にして、正方基本形（P25参照）を折り、左側を開いてつぶす。
Begin with “Basic Square” (See P25). Bring the front left flap to the center, and open and flatten.

2 4カ所とも同様に折る。
Do the same with the other flaps.

3 左側を右に重ね合わせる。裏側も同様に折る。
Fold the front left flap to the right. Do the same with the reverse side.

4 内側の4カ所を図のように折る。
Fold the edge of the short inside flap as shown. Do the same with the other inside flaps.

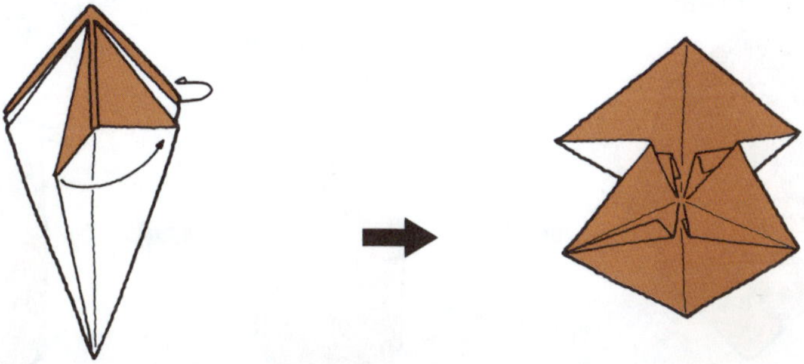

5 底に穴をあけ、花びらの部分を手前にそらせる。
Make a small hole in the bottom corner, then open the petals.

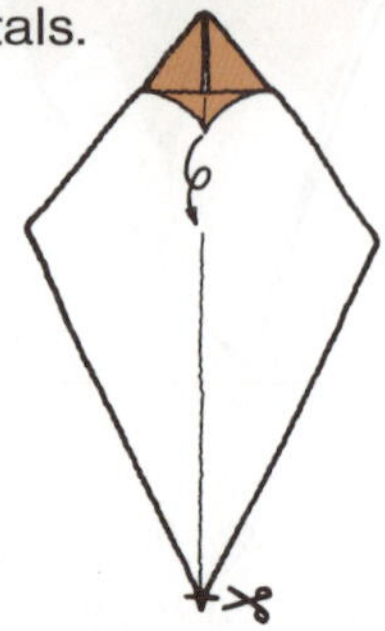

6 中を広げる。
Shape into a flower.

Finished

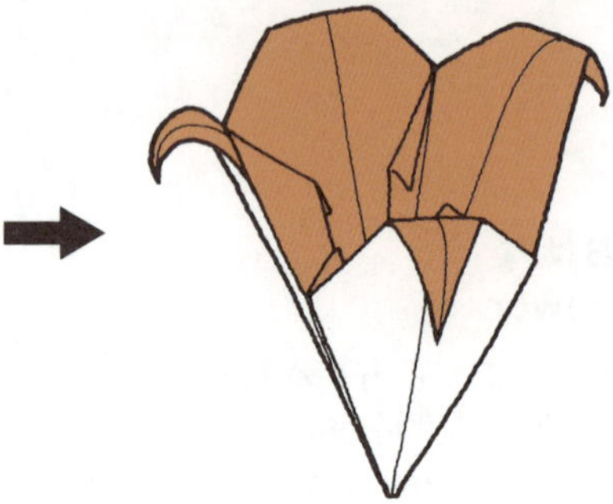

チューリップ
Tulip

1 色を表に出して、正方基本形を折る。中心に向かって左側は手前に、右側は裏側に 4 カ所折りすじをつける。
Begin with “Basic Square”. Fold the two left corners to the center. Unfold. Fold the two right corners backward. Unfold.

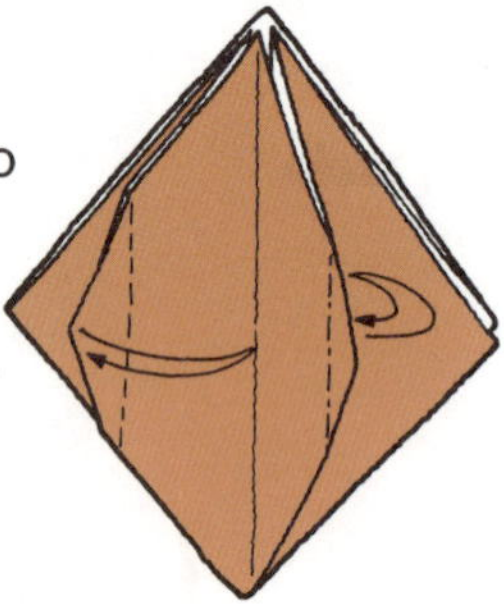

2 折りすじに合わせて折る。
Fold each corner to the crease.

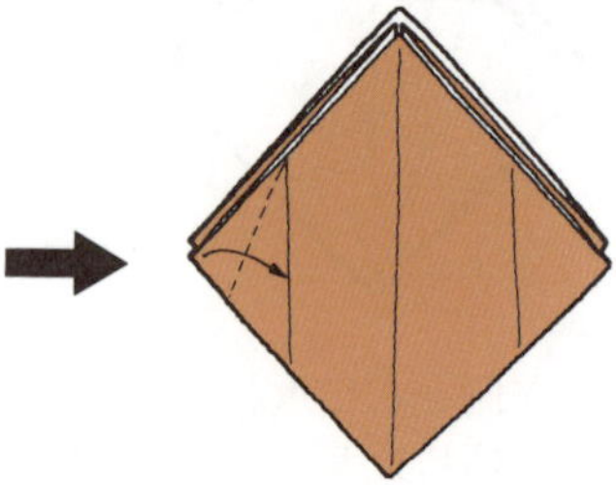

3 折りすじどおりに折る。
Fold each corner in again along the crease.

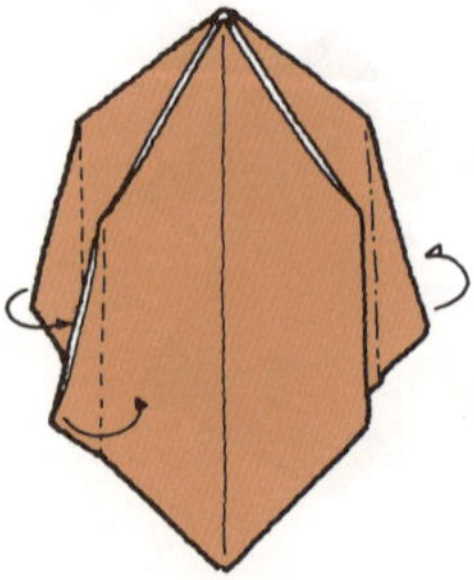

4 底に穴をあけ、花びらの部分を手前にそらせる。
Make a small hole, and open the petals.

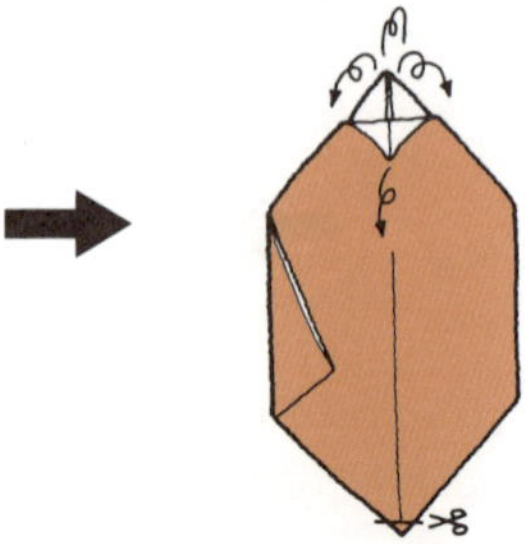

中を広げる。
Shape into a tulip.

Finished

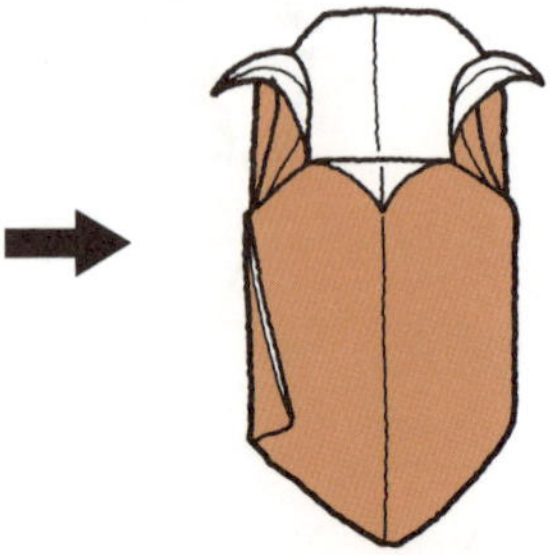

葉と茎
Leaf and stem

1 魚の基本形（P 130参照）から始める。左右をつまみ折りし、開いてつぶす。
Begin with “Basic Fish” (See P130).
Open the center flaps and flatten as shown.

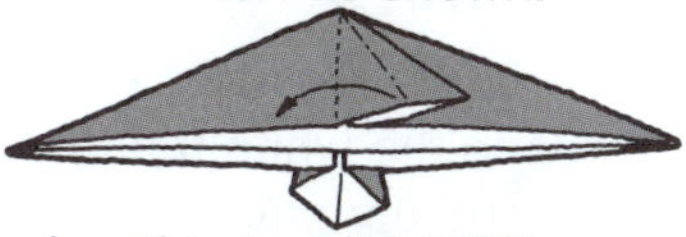

2 中わり折りする。
Do “Nakawari-Ori” on both ends.

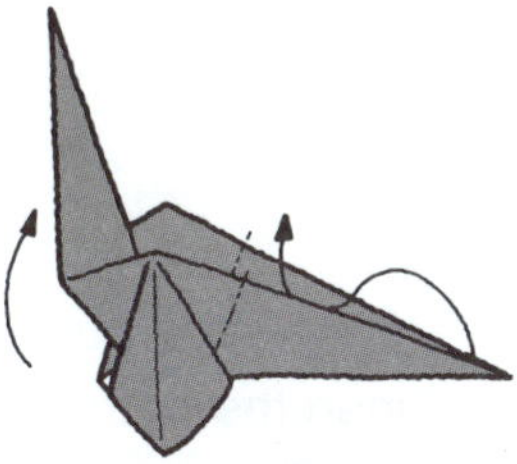

3 右へ重ねる。裏も同様に。
Fold the left flap to the right.
Do the same with the reverse side.

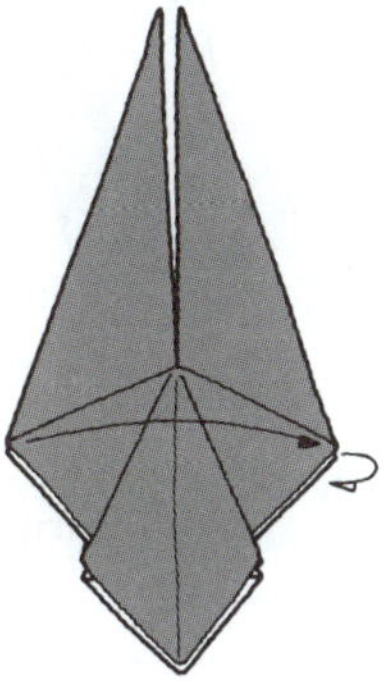

4 表は下、裏は上の部分を中心に向かって折る。
Fold the lower edges of the front flaps to the center, and fold the upper edges of the back flaps to the center.

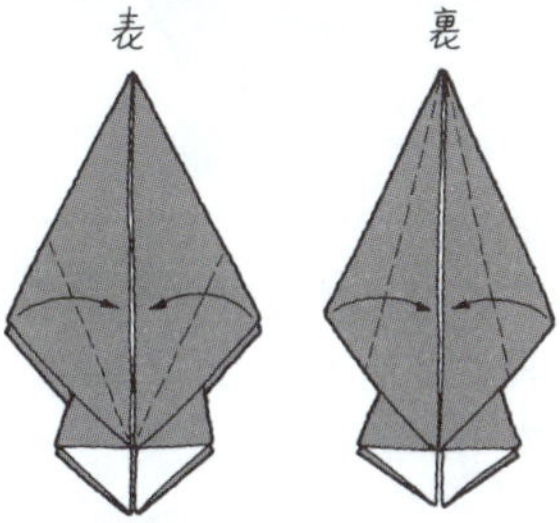

5 右へ重ねる。裏側も同様に(A)。もうひとつ同じものを作る(B)。
Fold the left flap(A).
Do the same with the reverse side.
Make another one(B).

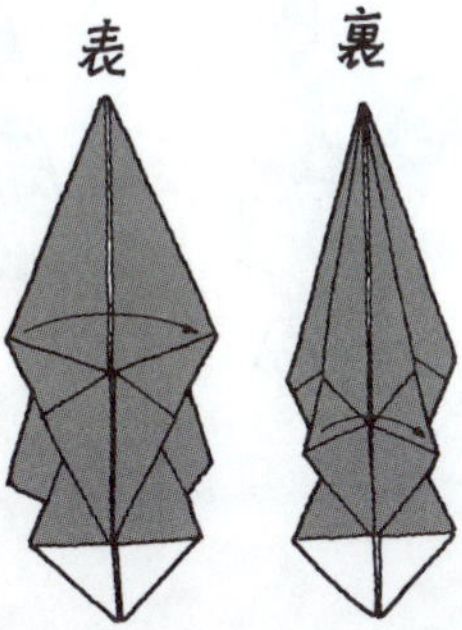

6 A：下の部分を内側へ折り込む。裏側も同様に。
A：Tuck the bottom inside. Do the same with the reverse side.

B：下の部分を手前に折る。裏側も同様に。
B：Fold the bottom triangle outside. Do the same with the reverse side.

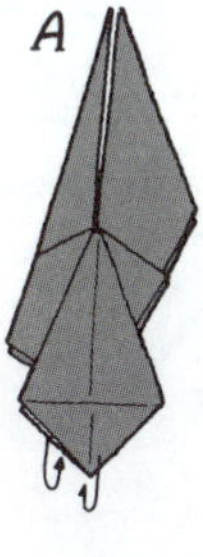

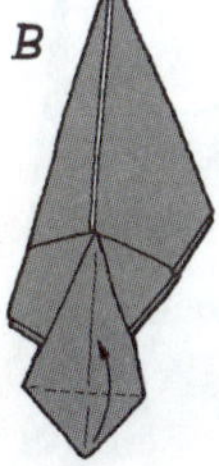

7 A・B：葉の部分を中わり折りにする。
A・B：Do "Nakawari-Ori" on the leaf as shown.

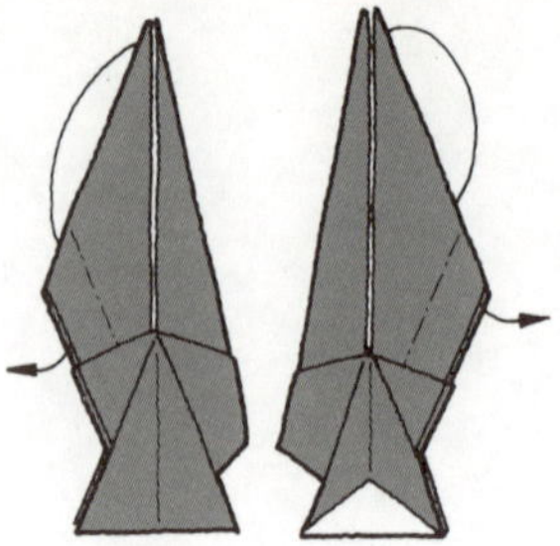

8 A　台の部分をふくらませて立てる。
A　Open the bottom and stand upright.

B　手前の部分を広げて立てる。
B　Open the white triangle and stand upright.

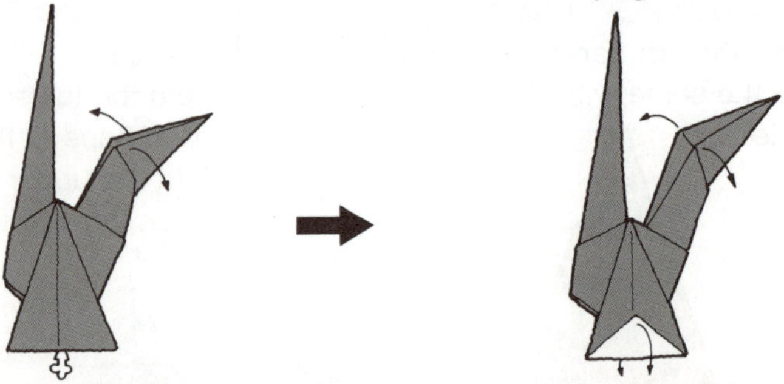

9 お花とチューリップを茎にさしこむ。
Stuck the flower and tulip in the stem.

Finished

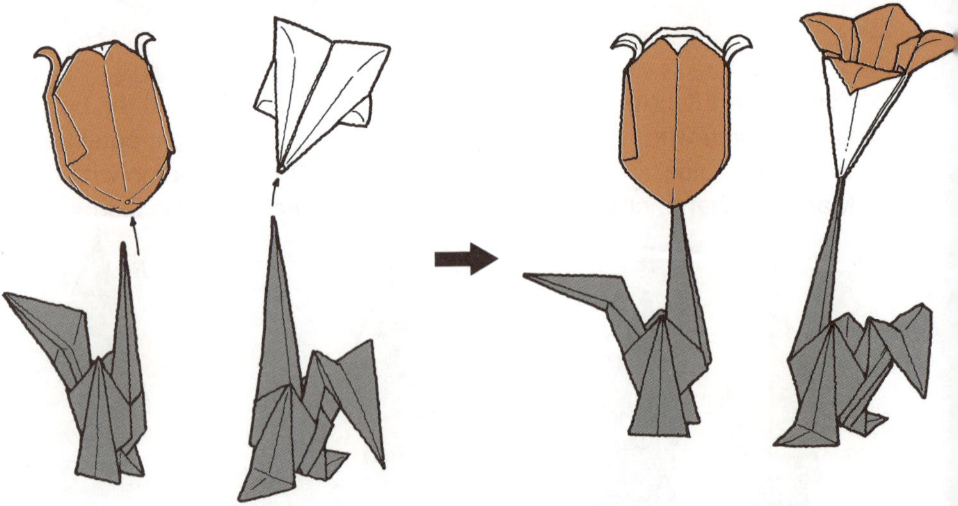

かきつばた

Iris

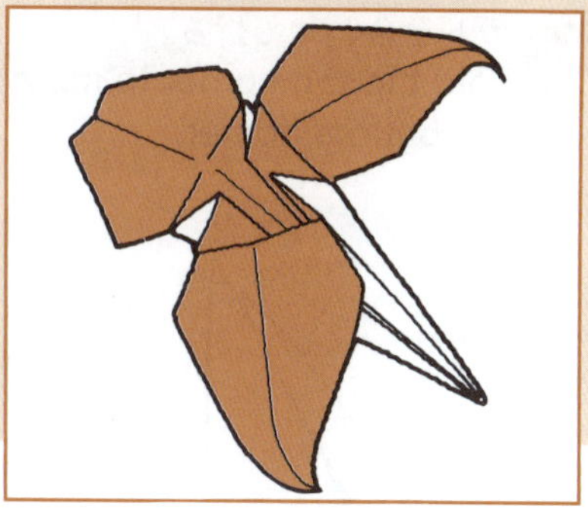

1 折りすじをつける。
Fold in half to make a crease. Unfold.

2 ○のところを合わせるように、折りすじをつける。
Fold the right bottom corner up to the center line. Unfold.

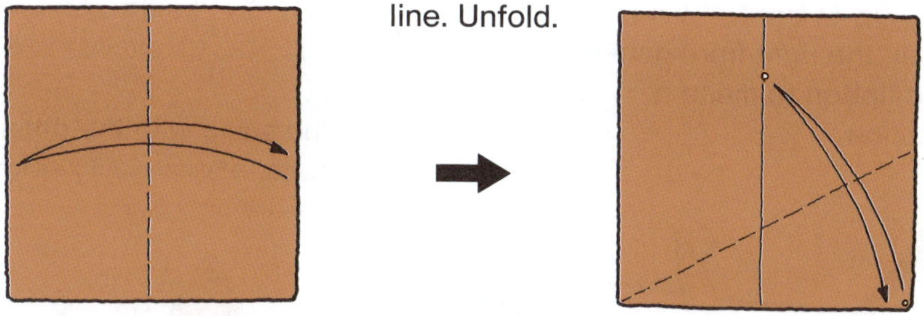

3 ●のところを合わせるように、折りすじをつける。
Fold the right top corner down to the center line. Unfold.

4 正三角形になっているところを切る。
Cut the creases as shown to make an equilateral triangle.

5 半分に折る。
Fold in half.

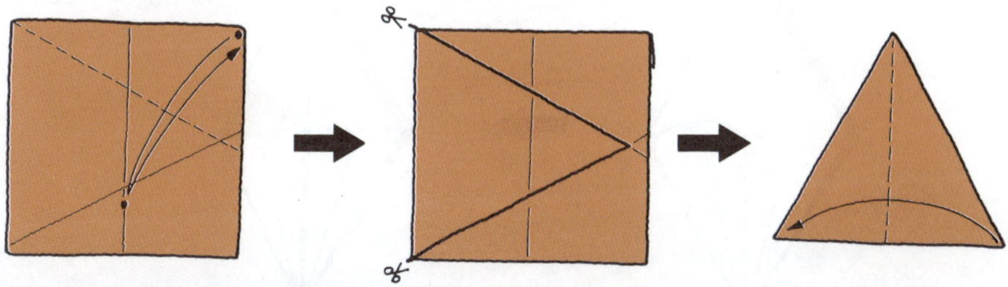

6 カドを合わせて折る。
Fold the top corner to meet the bottom corner.

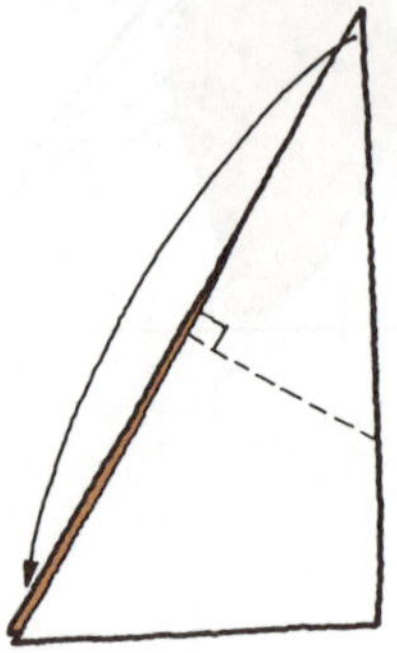

7 ひっくり返し、手前の１枚を開くように折る。
Turn over. Insert your forefinger in the top pocket and open, then flatten to make a triangle.

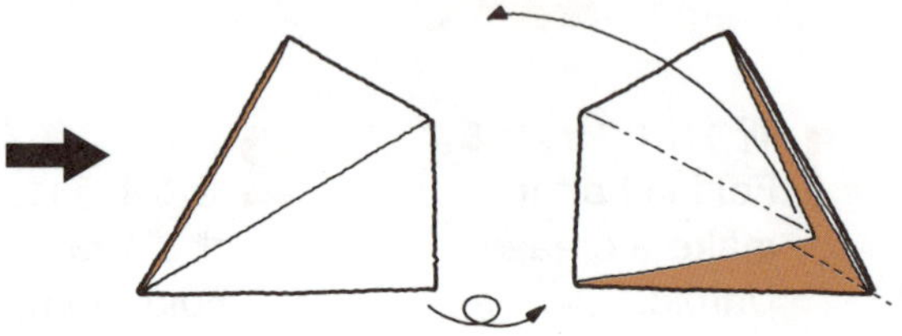

8 手前の１枚をつぶすように折る。
Open the right front pocket and flatten to make a lozenge.

9 ほかのところも同様に折る。
※三番目のひし形は他のふたつの間に入れる。
Do the same with the other pockets. ※Fold the 3rd lozenge between the other two.

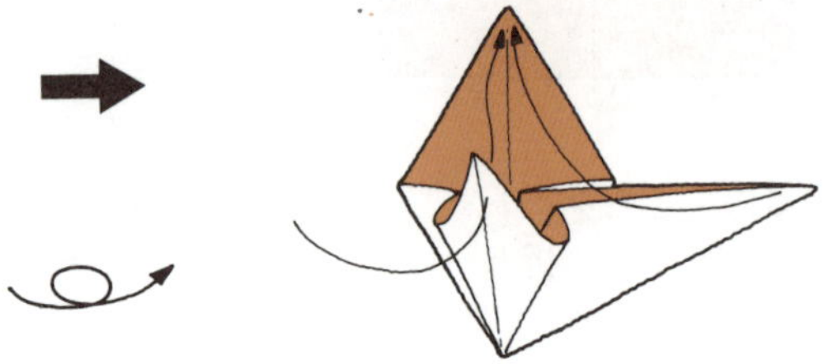

10 中心に合わせて折る。
Fold the flaps to the center.

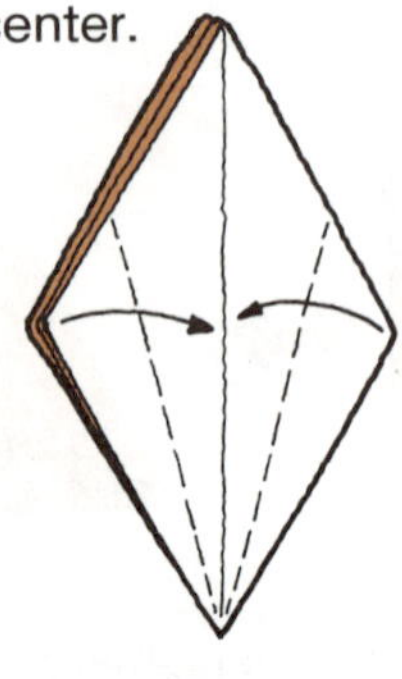

11 ほかのところも同様に折る。
Do the same with the other flaps.

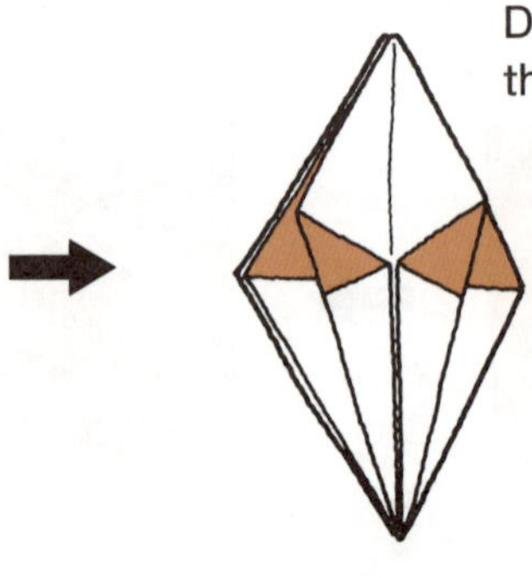

12 手前の1枚を折る。裏側も同様にする。
Fold the front flap down.
Do the same with the reverse side.

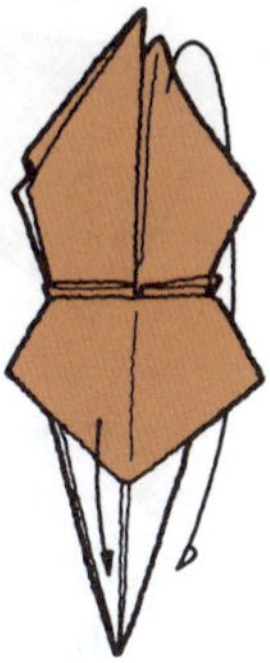

13 右へ開くように折る。
Fold the flap to the right.

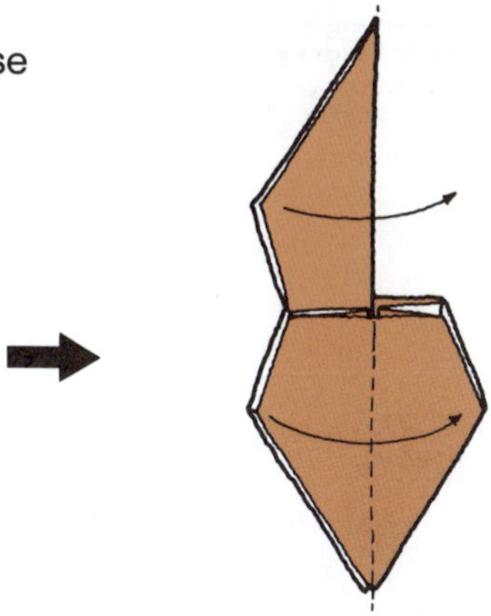

14 手前に折る。
Fold the top corner down to the bottom.

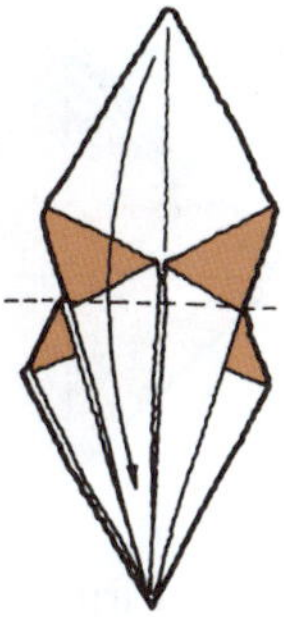

15 開く。
Bring the 3 flaps up to open the petals.

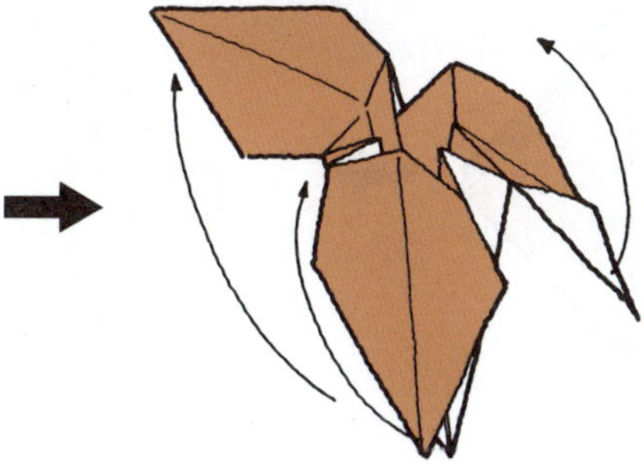

16 花びらの先端をカールさせる。
Curl each petal.

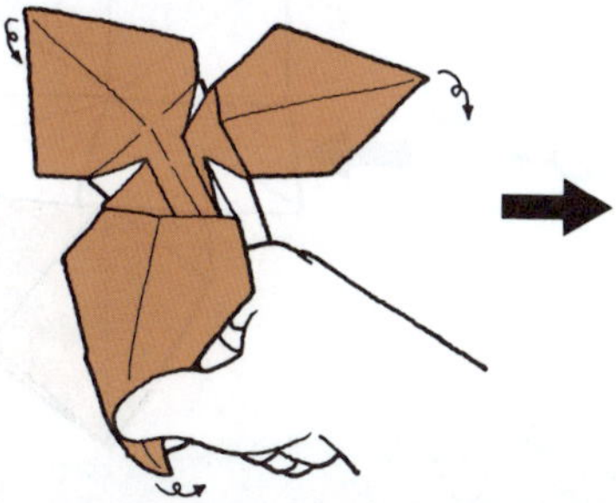

Finished

つきみそう

Evening primrose

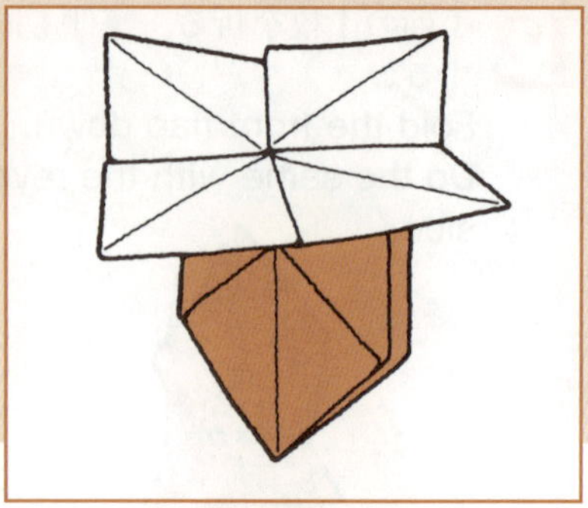

1 裏を出して、正方基本形（P 25参照）から始める。
Begin with "Basic Square" (See P25).

2 折りすじをつける。裏側も同様にする。
Fold the front flap down. Unfold. Do the same with the reverse side.

3 両側とも中心に合わせて折る。
Fold both corners in to the center. Do the same with the reverse side.

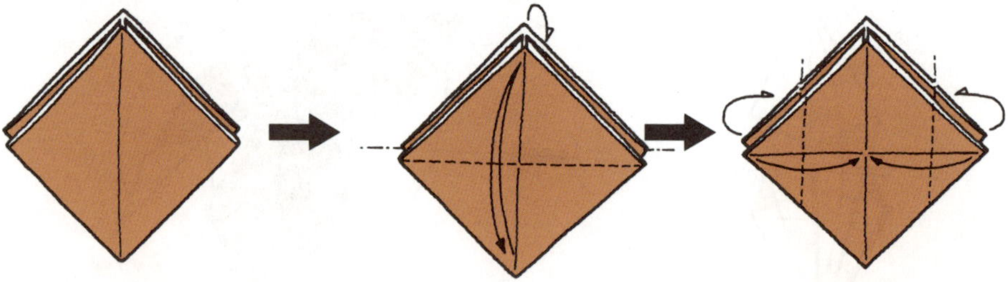

4 半分に折る。
Fold in half to the top corner.

5 広げる。
Spread the petals.

Finished

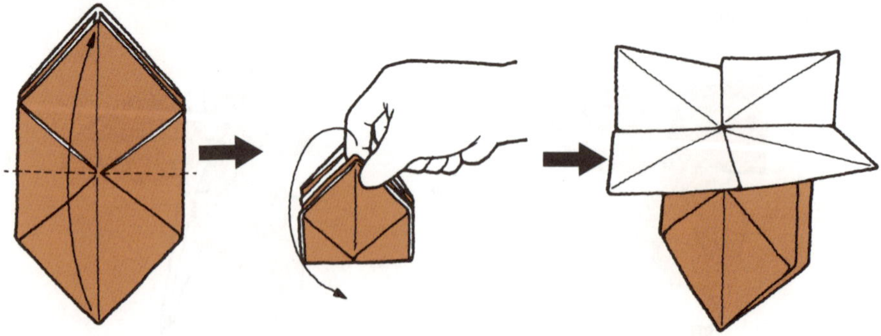

Chapter 4

かわいい動物たち
Animals

ライオン
Lion

1 中心に折りすじをつけ、カドを折る。上下も折る。
Make creases. Fold both corners, and fold the edges to the center.

2 ひっくり返し、折りすじに合わせて折る。
Turn over. Fold the left edge to the center.

3 半分に折る。
Fold in half.

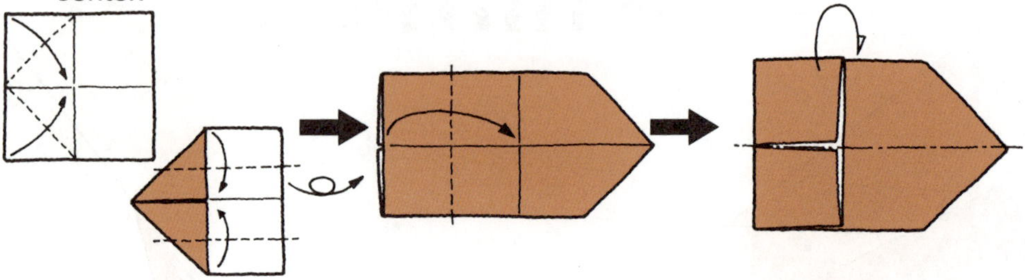

4 カドをつまんで引き上げる。
Pull the corner up to make a head.

5 頭のカドを内側に折り込む。2カ所にはさみを入れる。
Fold the corner of the head inside, then cut the paper as shown.

6 顔をかく。
Draw a Lion's face.

Finished

ぶた

Pig

1 折りすじに合わせて折る。カドも折りすじをつける。
Make a crease and fold the edges to the center. Then fold the corners to the center line. Unfold.

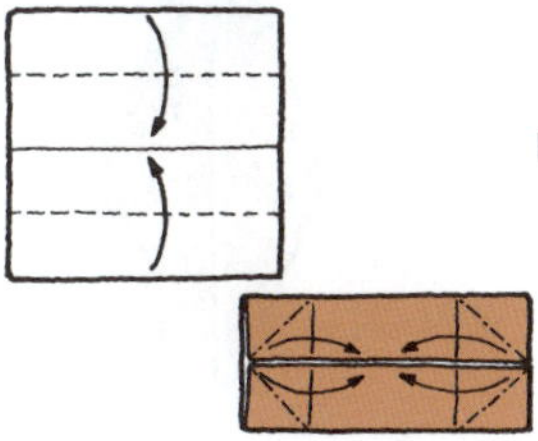

2 折りすじを使って、上の1枚を中心に移動させるように折る。
Open the end pockets and flatten.

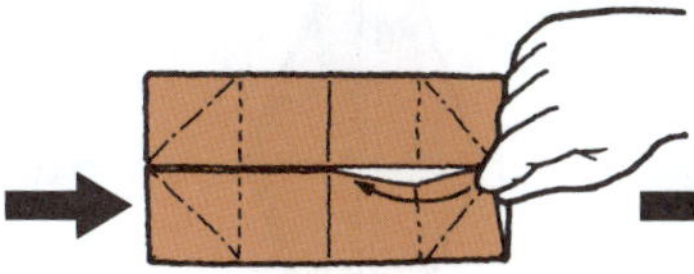

3 山折りをし、半分に折る。
Fold in half.

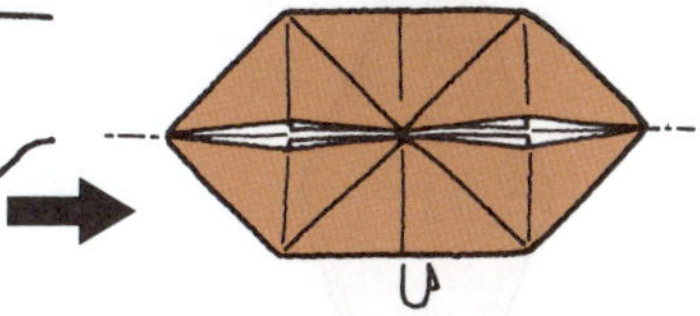

4 折りすじに合わせて、左右とも折る。裏側も同様に折る。
Fold the triangles along the creases to make legs.
Do the same with the reverse side.

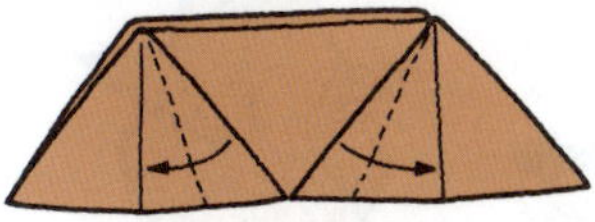

5 顔としっぽを中わり折りで作る。
Do "Nakawari-Ori" to make a head and a tail.

Finished

きつね・たぬき

Fox • Raccoon Dog

きつね①
Fox①

1 鶴の基本形（P27参照）から始める。
Begin with "Basic Turu" (See P27).

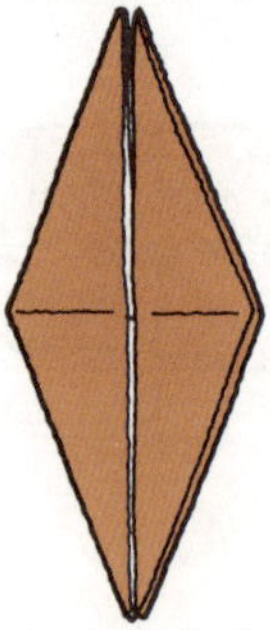

2 図のように２カ所に、２枚とも切り込みを入れる。
Cut the paper as shown.

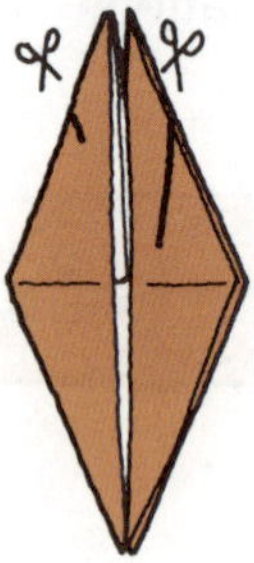

3 開くように折る。裏側も同様に折る。
Fold the upper right flap. Do the same with the reverse side.

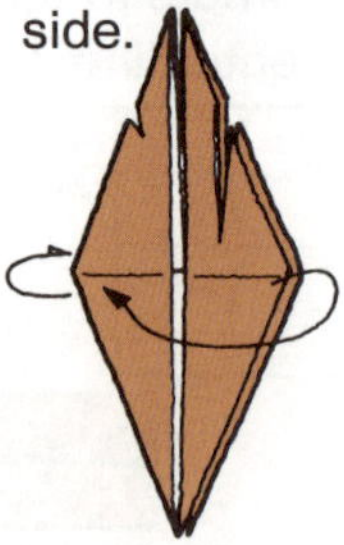

4 切り込みを入れた、上の１枚を斜め横に折り、手を作る。
Fold the front cuts diagonally to make hands.

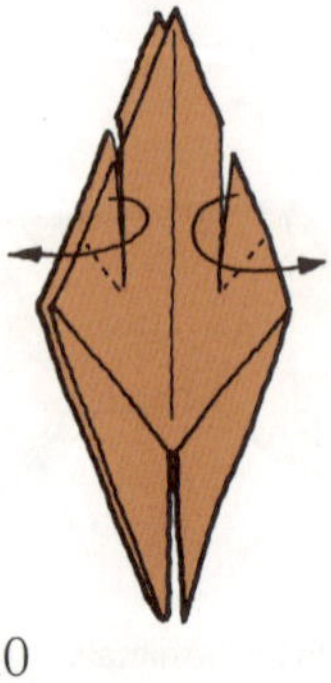

5 上の１枚を斜め下に折り下げ、しっぽを作る。
Fold the top flap down diagonally to make a tail.

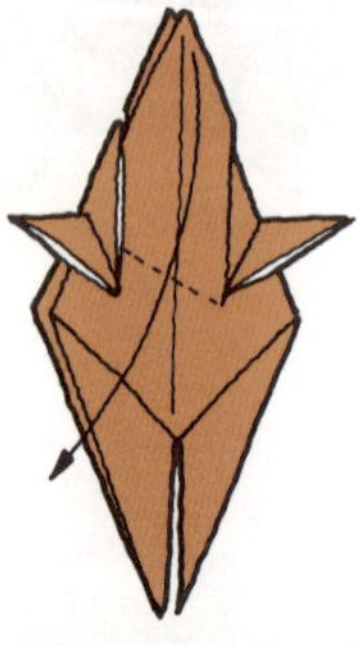

6 中わり折りをして、足を作る。
Do "Nakawari-Ori" on the lower flaps to make legs.

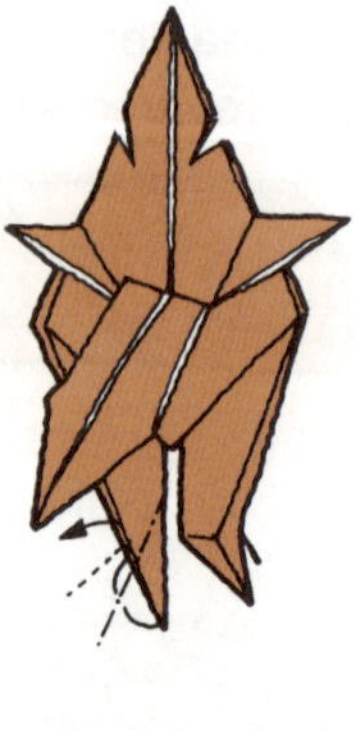

7 図のようになる。
It should look like this.

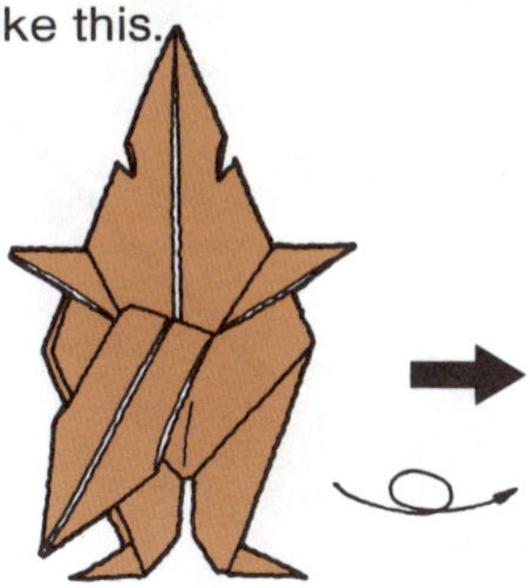

8 ひっくり返し、カドを折り下げる。
Turn over. Fold the top corner down.

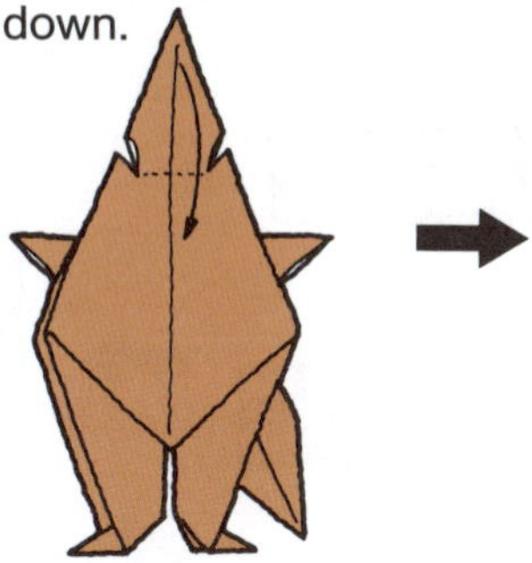

Finished

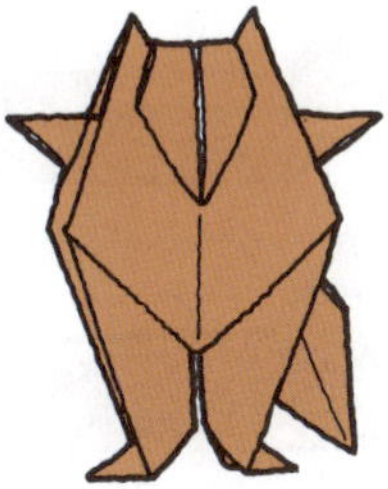

きつね②
Fox②

正方形を半分にした長方形の用紙を使う。
Use a rectangular piece of paper.

1 裏を出し、上下を折る。
Fold the top and bottom edges to the center.

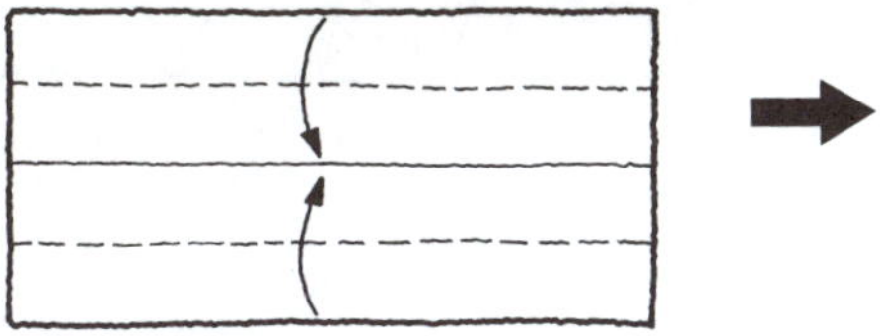

2 左側だけ中わり折りする。
Do "Nakawari-Ori" on both corners of the left side.

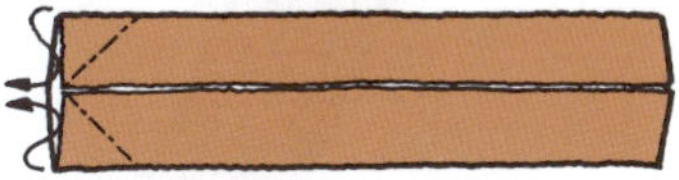

3 半分に折る。
Fold in half backward.

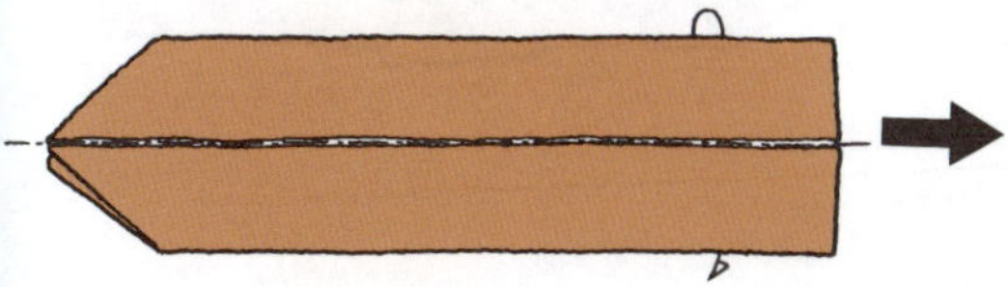

4 折り上げる。
Make a crease diagonally, Fold the left side along the crease to make the head.

5 顔の部分を広げてつぶし、かぶせ折りする。
Open the head, then do "Kabuse-Ori" as shown.

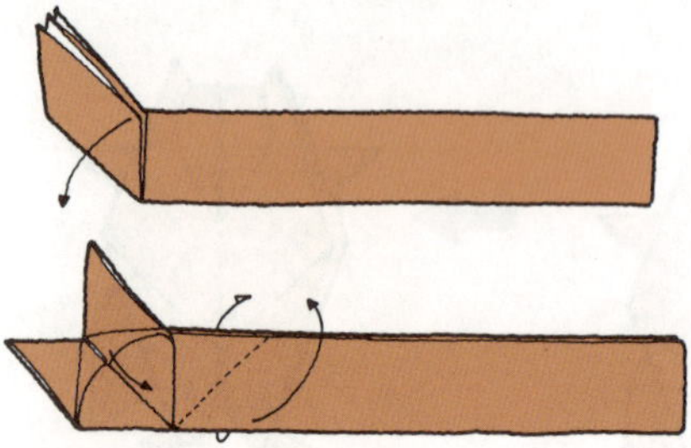

6 胴の部分をかぶせ折りする。
Do "Kabuse-Ori" again.

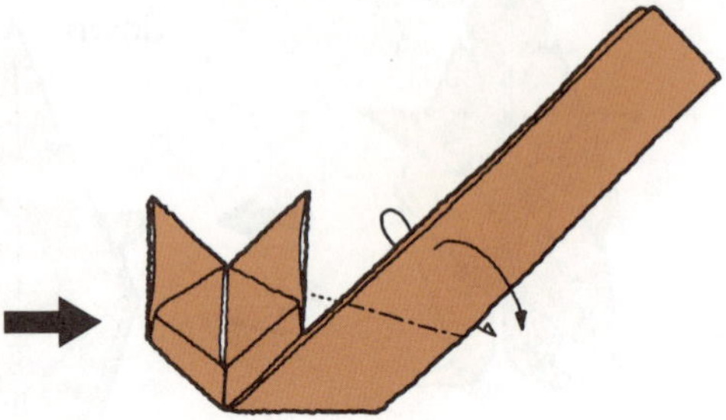

7 裏側に折る。
Fold the bottom backward diagonally.

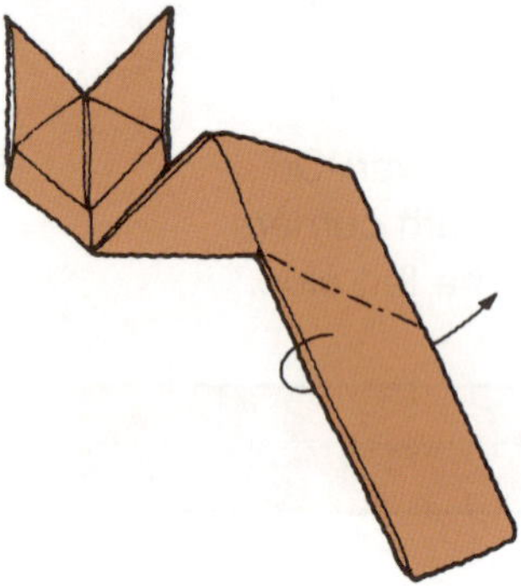

8 しっぽの先を中わり折りし、裏側に折り上げる。
Do "Nakawari-Ori" on the tip of the tail, and fold it backward again.

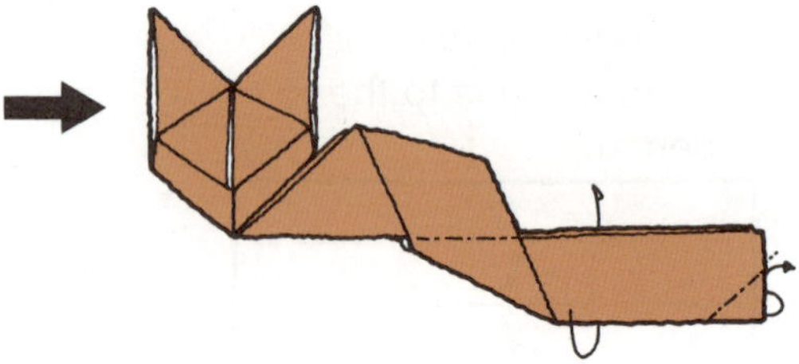

9 裏側に折る。
Fold a tail backward a little.

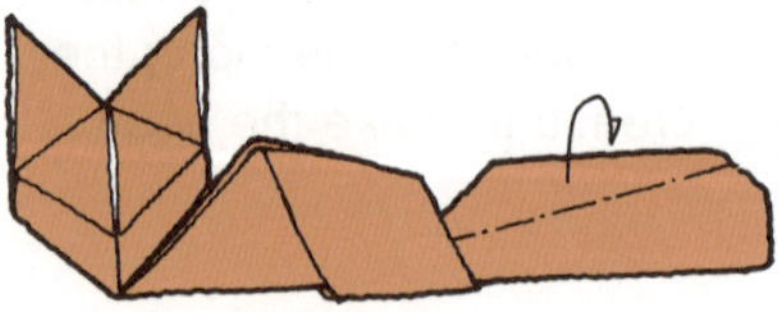

Finished

たぬき
Raccoon Dog

1 鶴の基本形（P 27参照）から始める。
Begin with "Basic Turu"(See P27).

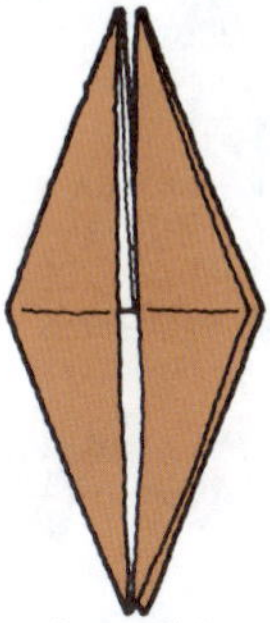

2 ２カ所、２枚とも切る。※右側は、きつね①より深めに切る。
Cut the paper as shown. Cut the right side deeper than fox①'s.

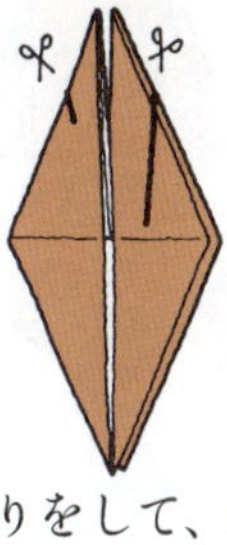

3 右の１枚を左に重ねる。裏側も同様に折る。
Fold the upper right flap to the left. Do the same with the reverse side.

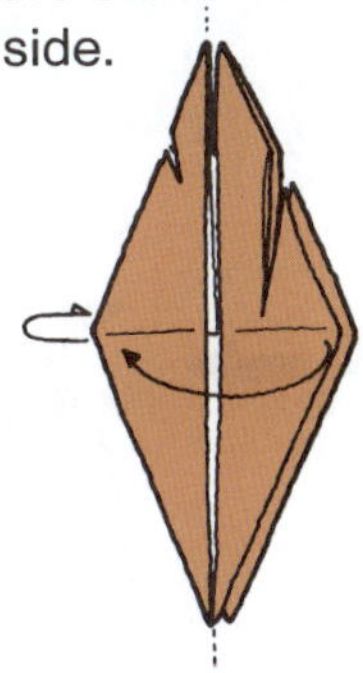

4 中わり折りをして、足を作る。
Do "Nakawari-Ori" to make legs.

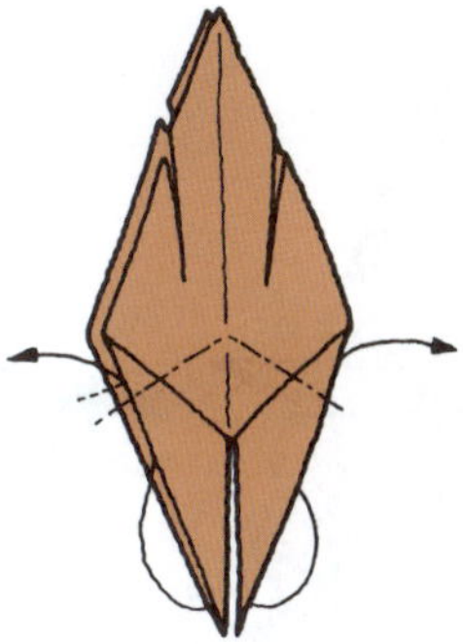

5 もう一度、中わり折りをする。
Do "Nakawari-Ori" again.

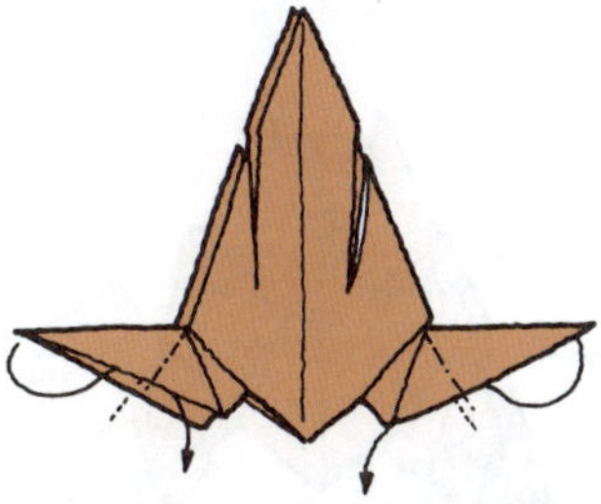

6 もう一度、中わり折りをして、足首を作る。
Do "Nakawari-Ori" once more to make ankles.

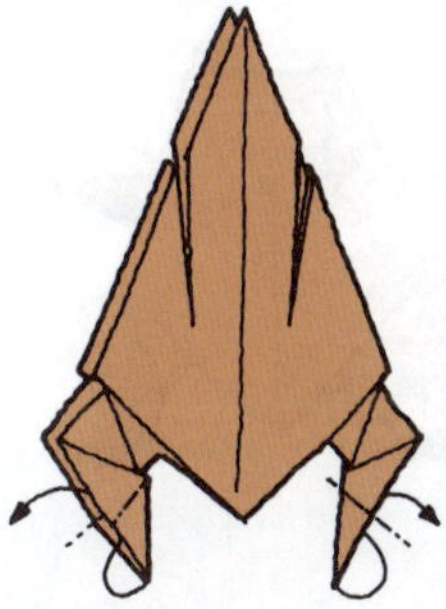

7 上の１枚を斜め横に折り、手を作る。
Fold the front cuts diagonally to make hands.

8 上の１枚を斜め下に折り下げ、しっぽを作る。
Fold the front top flap down diagonally to make a tail.

9 ひっくり返す。
Turn over.

10 カドを折り下げる。
Fold the top corner down.

11 内側にだん折りをする。
Do "Dan-Ori" to make a head.

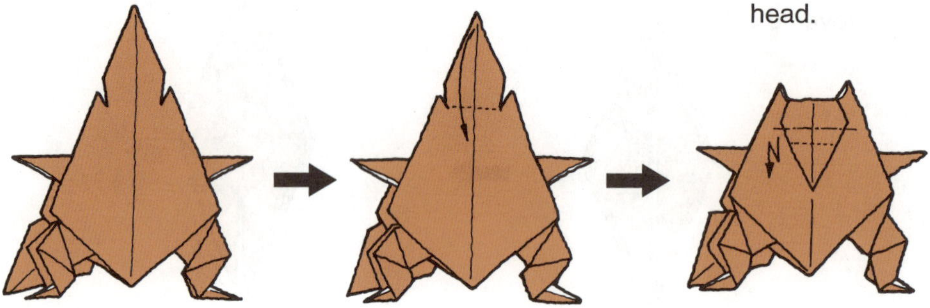

12 手のカドを前に折る。
Fold both hands forward.

Finished

ねずみ

Mouse

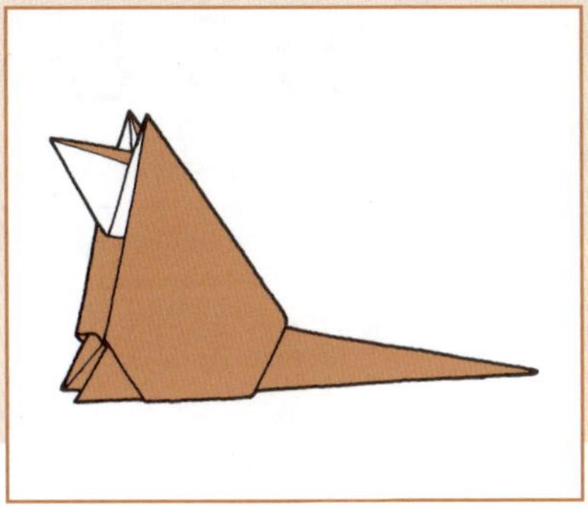

1 凧の基本形（P 22ページ参照）から始め、裏返して半分に折る。
Begin with "Basic Kite"(See P22). Turn over. Fold in half.

2 ひっくり返し、図のように折りすじをつけて、開く。
Turn over. Make creases as shown.

3 折りすじどおりつぶす。
Fold the triangle in half along the creases.

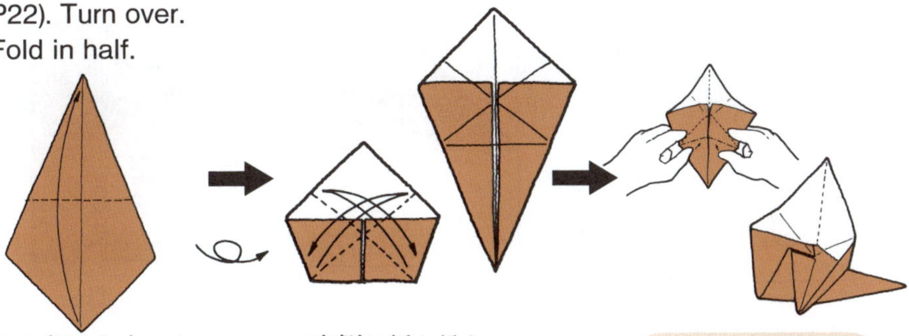

4 上の部分を中わり折りにする。下の部分を内側に折る。
Do "Nakawari-Ori" on the top corner. Fold the bottom inside.

5 内側に折り込む。頭、足の部分を、だん折りにする。
Fold the chest inside. Do "Dan-Ori" on the head and legs.

Finished

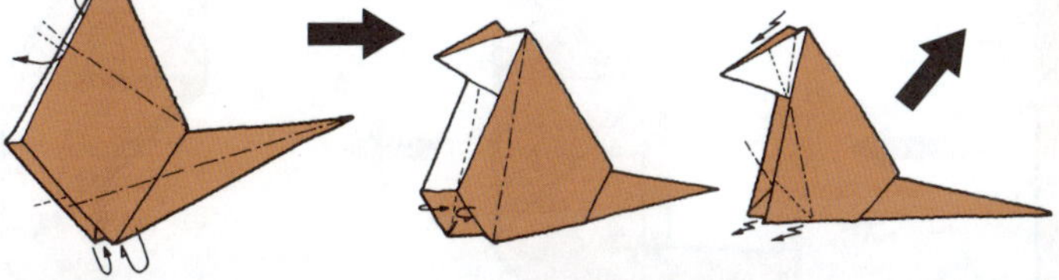

おうむ

Parrot

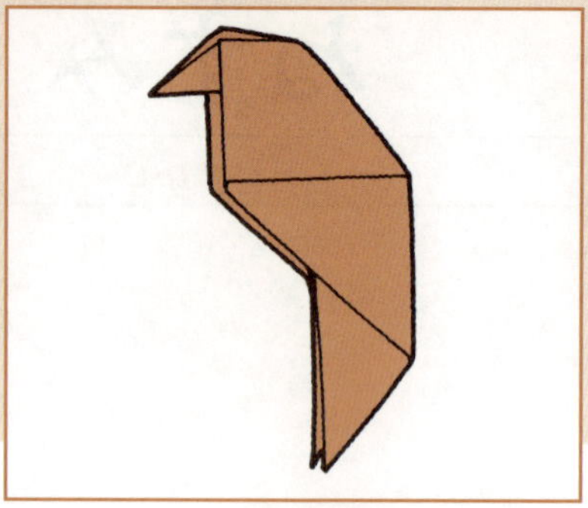

1 半分に折りすじをつけ、カドを折る。
Fold in half. Unfold. Fold the top corners down.

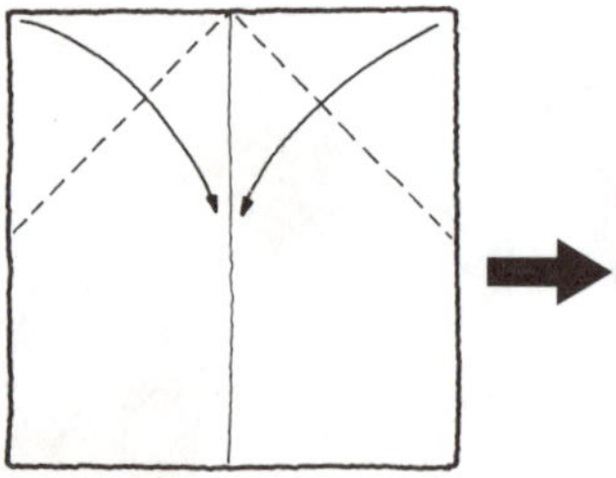

2 中心に合わせて折る。
Fold both sides to the center.

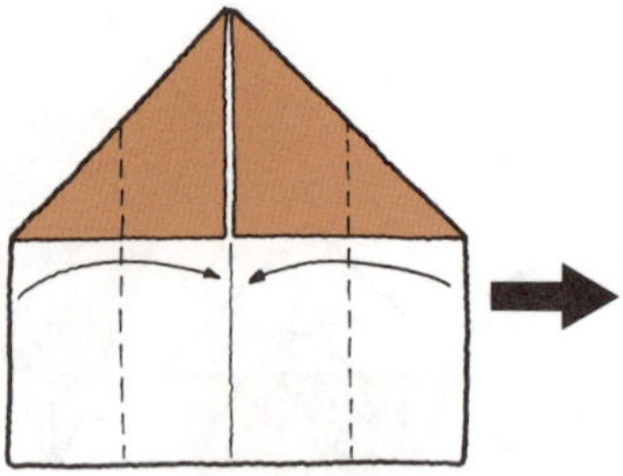

3 半分に折る。
Fold in half backward.

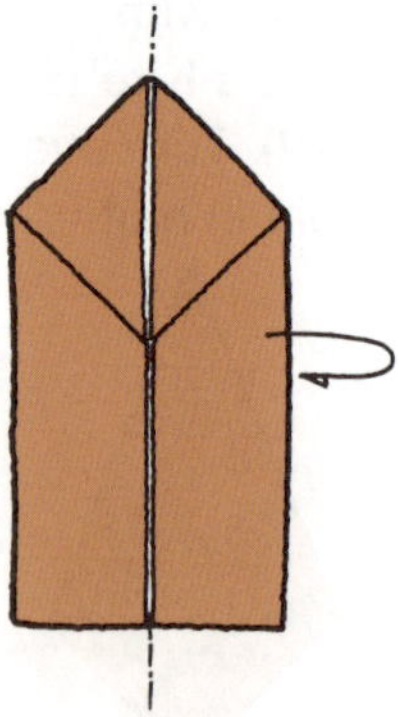

4 中わり折りをする。
Make a crease as shown. Do “Nakawari-Ori” using the crease.

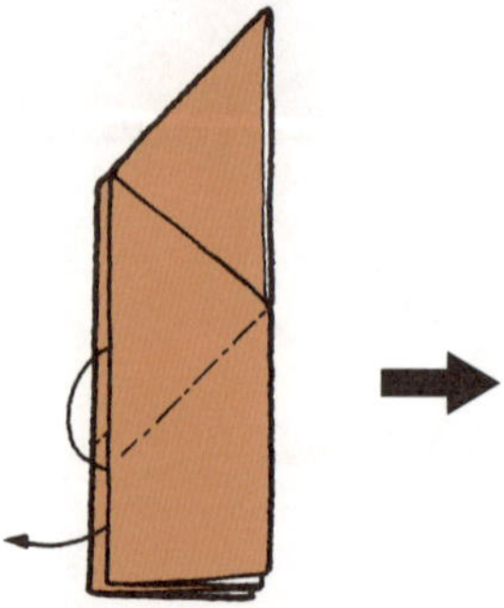

5 カドを内側に折る。先のところを中わり折りにする。
Fold the corner inside to make a triangle. Do “Nakawari-Ori”.

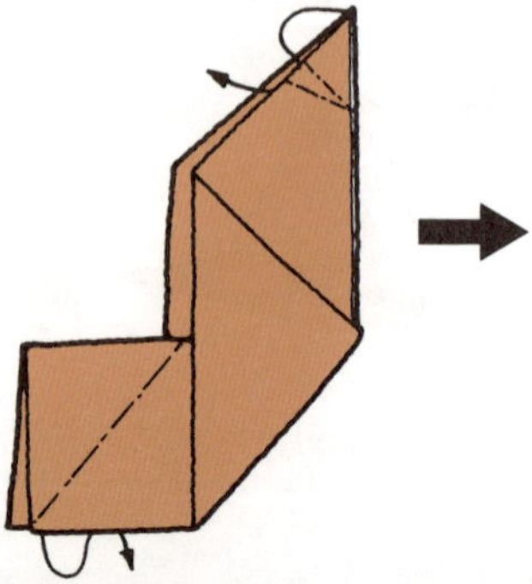

Finished

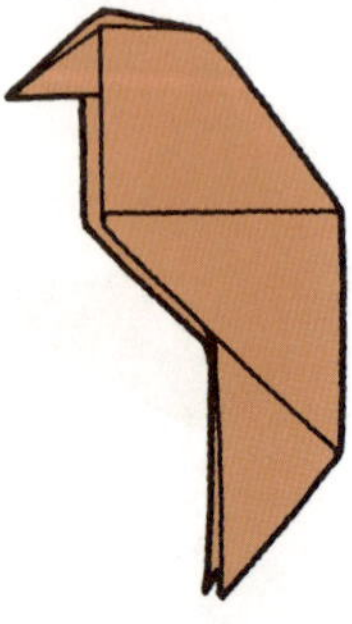

おんどり・ひよこ

Cock • Chick

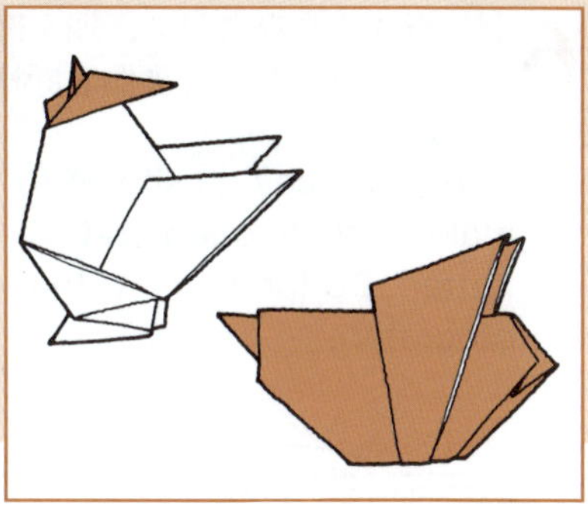

●材料　materials

おんどり　Cock／16×16cm（白　White）2×2cm（赤 Red）、ひよこ　Chick／7×7cm

おんどり
Cock

1 裏を出して赤い紙をはる。三角に折る。

Glue small red triangles on the corners. Fold in half to make a triangle.

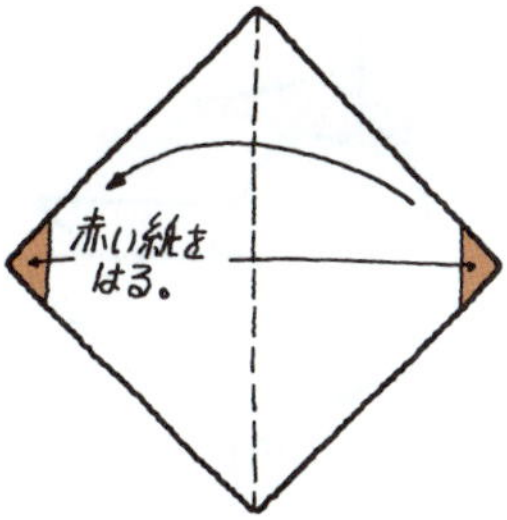

2 上の１枚を折って、裏の赤い紙を表に見せる。

Fold the top sheet back to expose the red triangle.

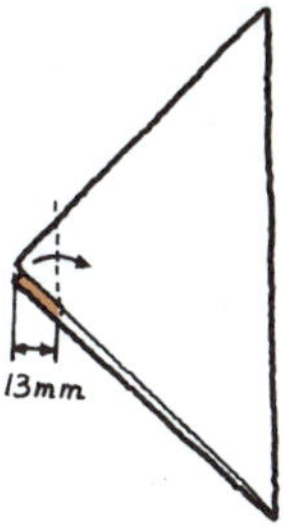

3 下の紙はだん折りにする。

Do "Dan-Ori" on the bottom paper.

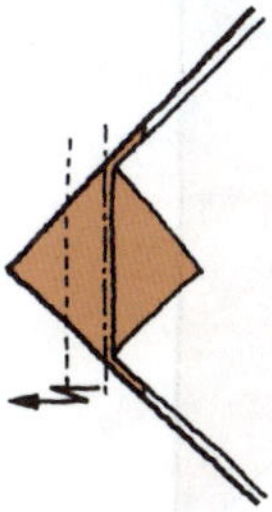

4 半分に折る。

Fold in half.

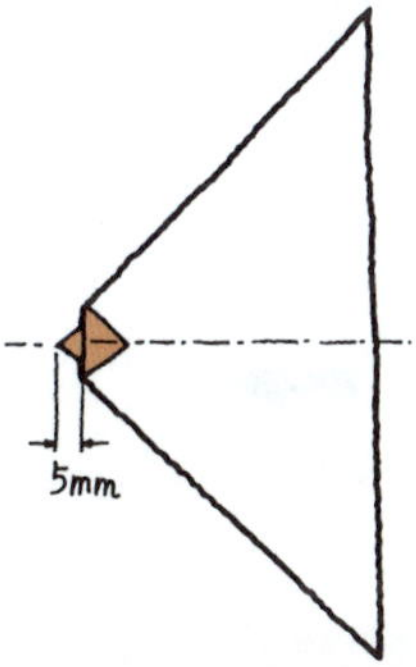

5 上の１枚だけ半分に折る。裏側も同様に折る。

Fold the top flap in half. Do the same with reverse side.

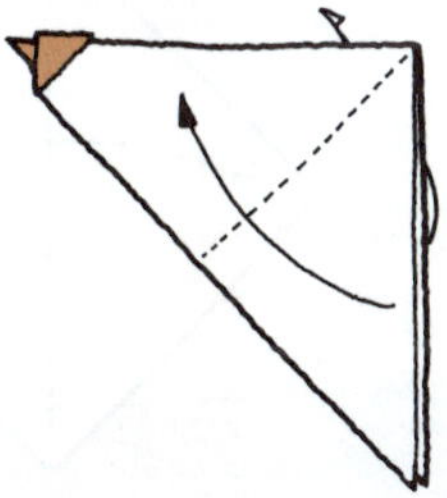

6 羽に折りすじをつけて、羽を開くようにしてたたむ。裏側も同様に折る。
Make creases as shown to make a wing, open and flatten. Do the same with the other flap.

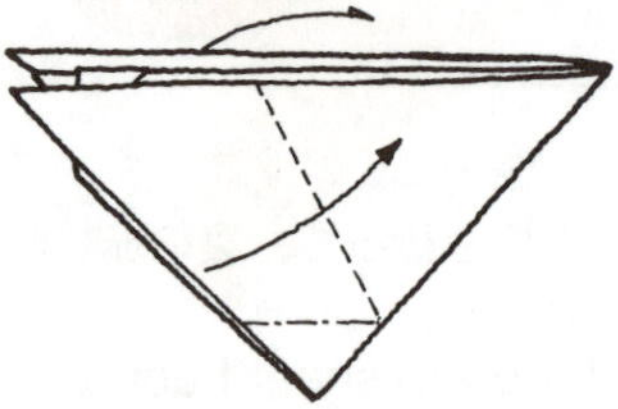

7 中わり折りにする。
Do “Nakawari-Ori”.

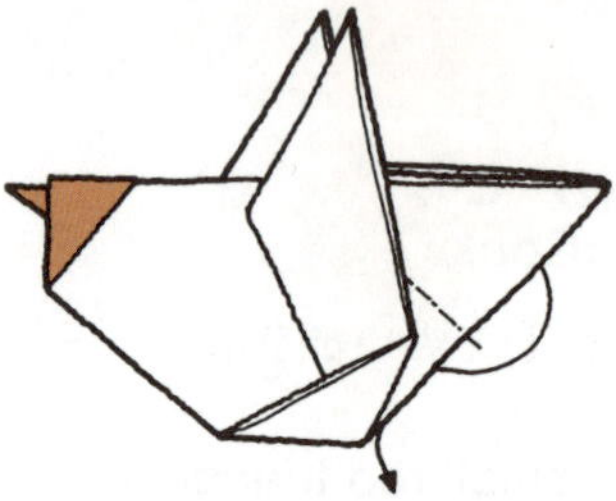

8 とさかをひっぱって立てる。
Pull the crest up.

Finished

ひよこ
Chick

1 裏を出し、三角に折る。
Fold in half to make a triangle.

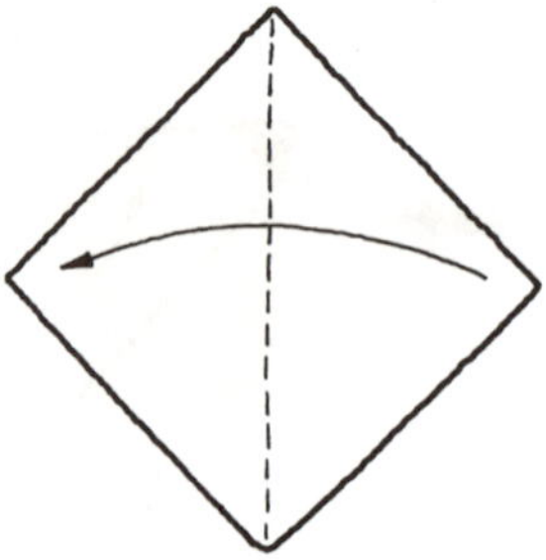

2 2枚いっしょにだん折りにする。
Fold the corner of both sheets together by “Dan-Ori”.

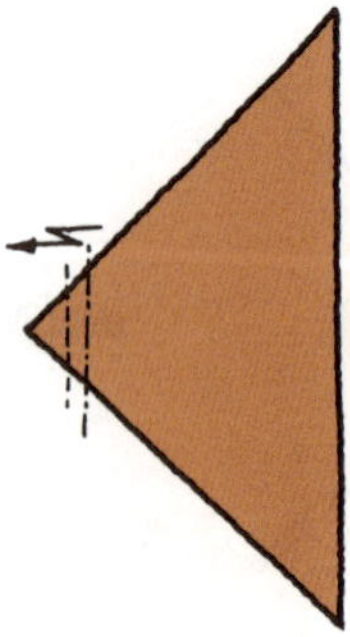

3 半分に折る。
Fold in half.

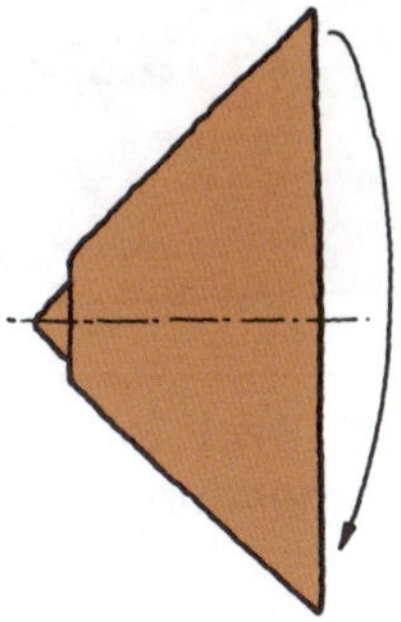

4 上の１枚だけ半分に折る。裏側も同様に折る。
Fold the top sheet in half. Do the same with the reverse side.

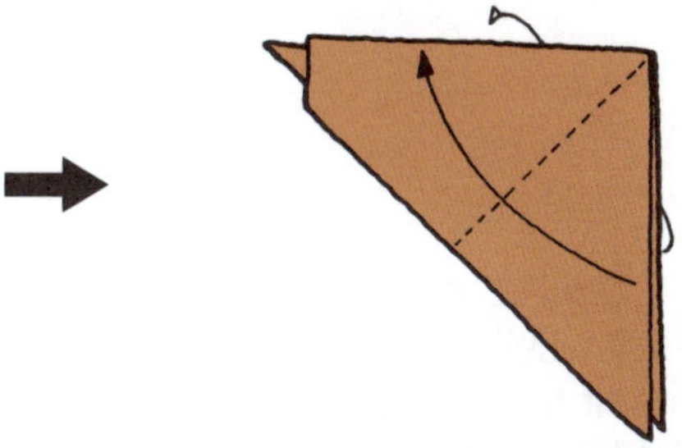

5 羽をななめに折り上げる。
Fold the wings up diagonally.

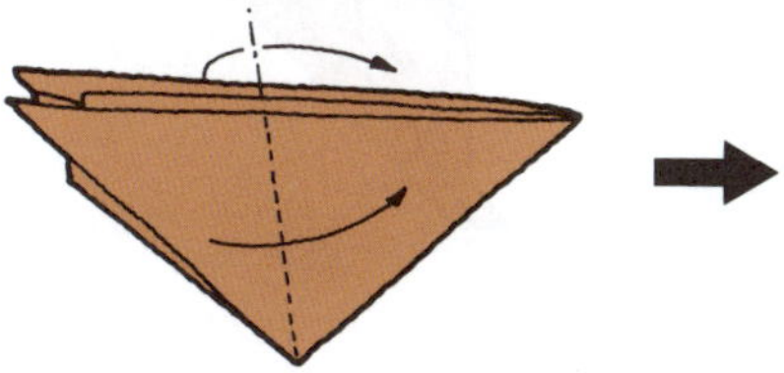

6 下のカドを内側に折る。裏側も同様に折る。
Fold the front bottom corner inside. Do the same with the reverse side.

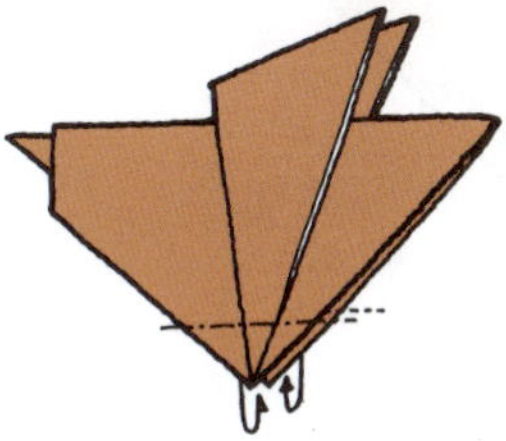

7 中わり折りをする。
Do "Nakawari-Ori".

Finished

うし
Cow

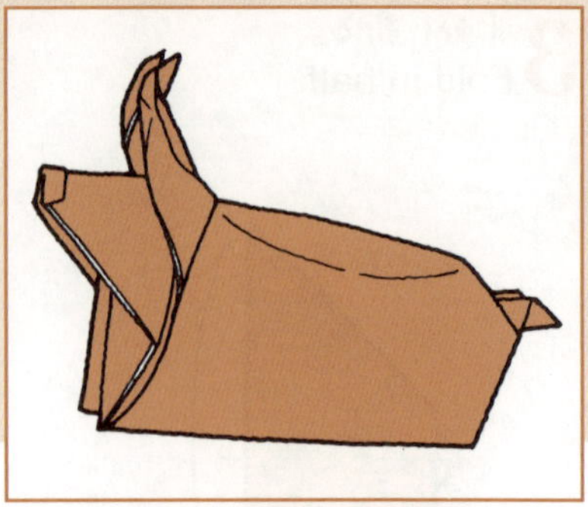

1 裏を出してカドとカドを合わせて折る。もう一度細い幅で折る。
Fold in half to make a triangle. Then fold in a narrow strip along the bottom edge.

2 三角に折って、カドを合わせる。
Fold the corners up to meet at the corner.

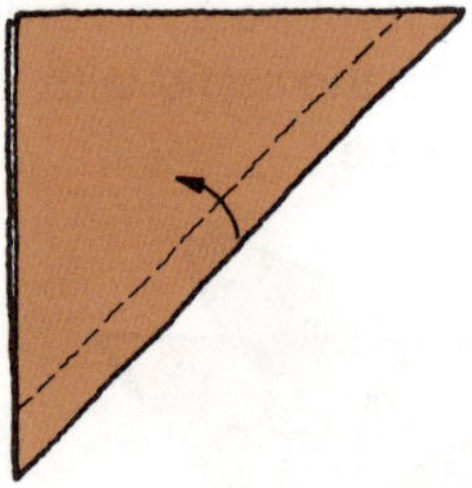

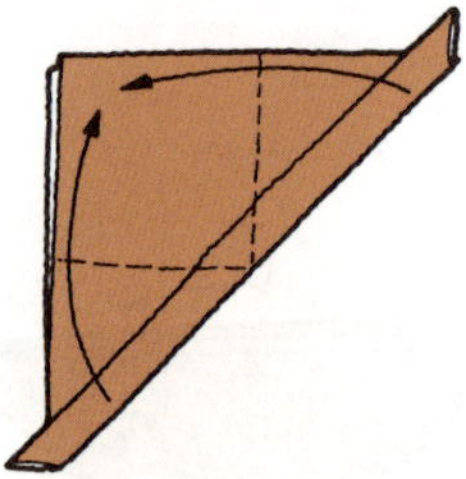

3 半分に山折りにする。
Fold in half by Yama-Ori.

4 内側に広げて、4枚いっしょにかぶせ折りをする。※体とのバランスを見ながら、かぶせ折りする。
Open and do "Kabuse-Ori" on the 4 sheets together. ※It is important for the head and the body to be in proportion.

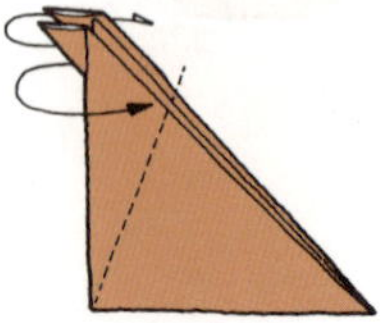

5 上の２枚だけ、かぶせ折りにする。
Do "Kabuse-Ori" on the upper 2 sheets.

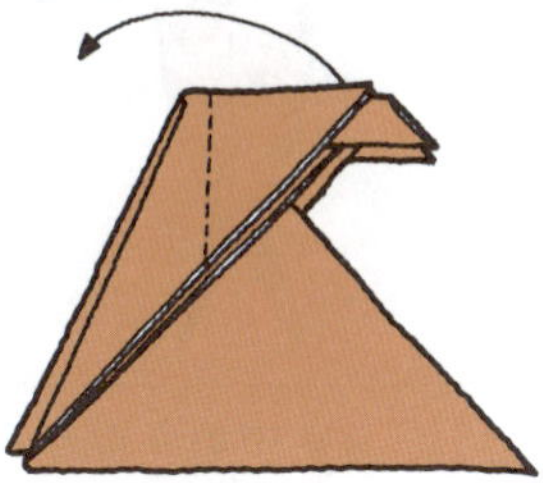

6 ひきよせ折りしてツノを立てる。しっぽは中わり折りのあと折り上げる。
Do "Hikiyose-Ori" to make the horns. Do "Nakawari-Ori" on the bottom corner and fold it up to make the tail.

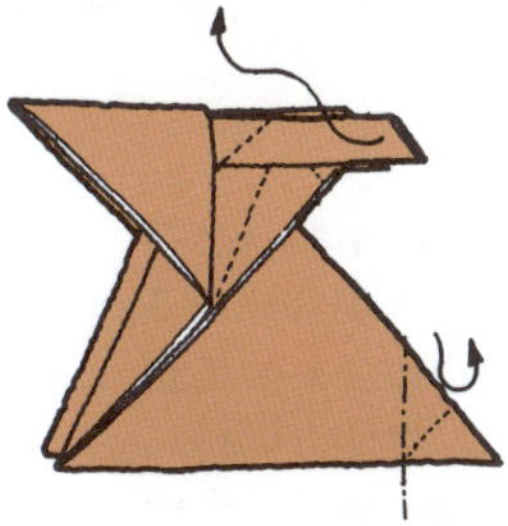

7 下の縁を内側に折り、鼻先を丸めるように折る。
Fold the bottom edges inside, and blunt the tip of the nose.

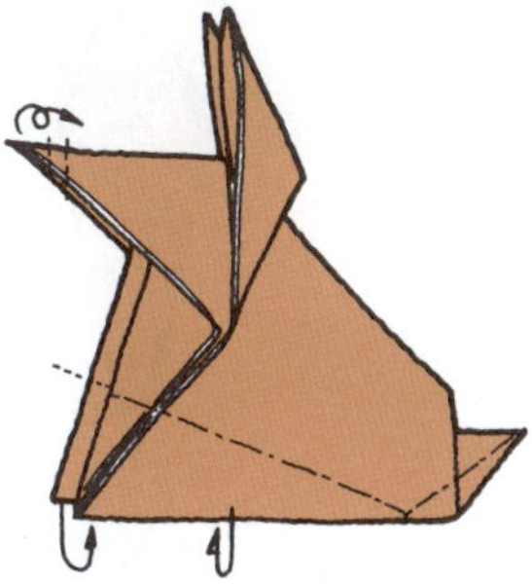

8 しっぽを中わり折りにする。背中をくぼませ、ツノは内側に巻く。
Do "Nakawari-Ori" on the tail, dent the back and twist the horns.

Finished

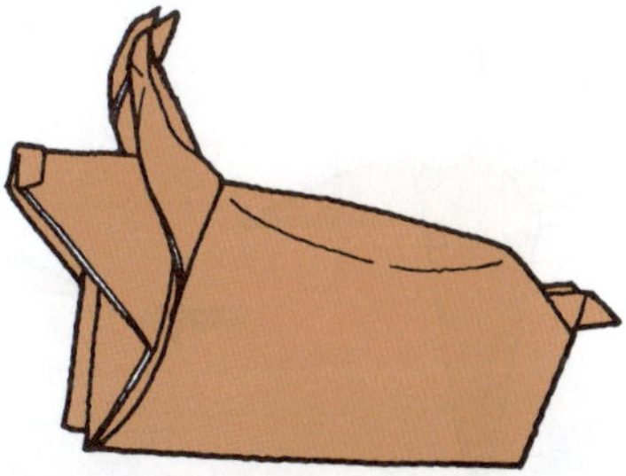

つばめ

Swallow

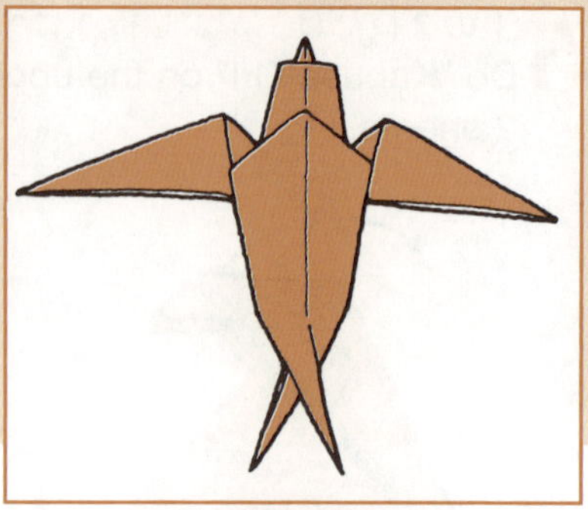

1 鶴の基本形（P27参照）から始める。中心に合わせて折る。裏側も同様に。
Begin with “Basic Turu”(See P27). Fold both sides in. Do the same with the reverse side.

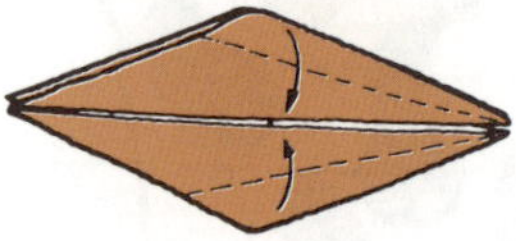

2 右の１枚を左に重ねる。裏側も同様に折る。
Fold the right flap to the left. Do the same with the reverse side.

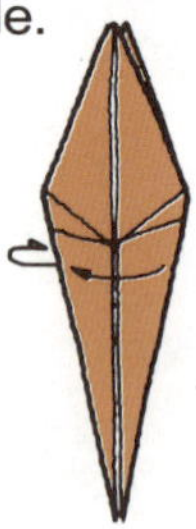

3 中わり折りで、羽を作る。
Do “Nakawari-Ori” on the upper flaps to make the wings.

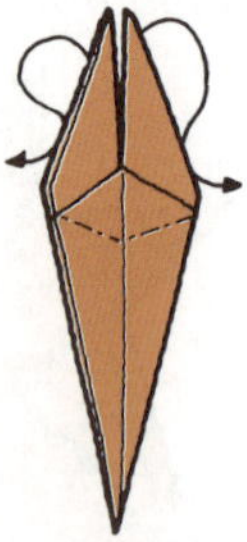

4 １枚を折り上げる。
Fold the front bottom flap up.

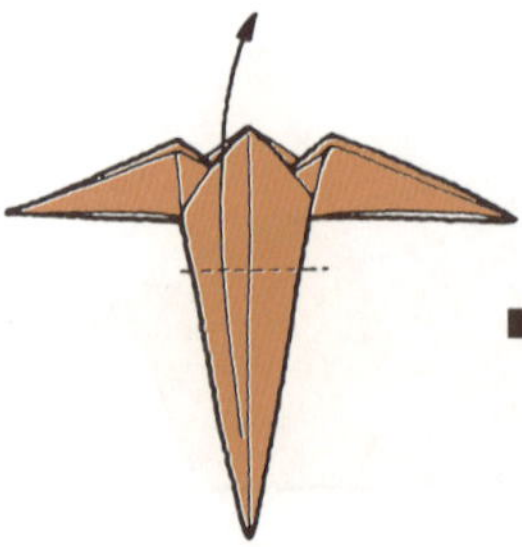

5 だん折りで頭をつくり、尾に３cm切り込みを入れる。
Do “Dan-Ori” to make the head. Cut 3cm from the bottom corner.

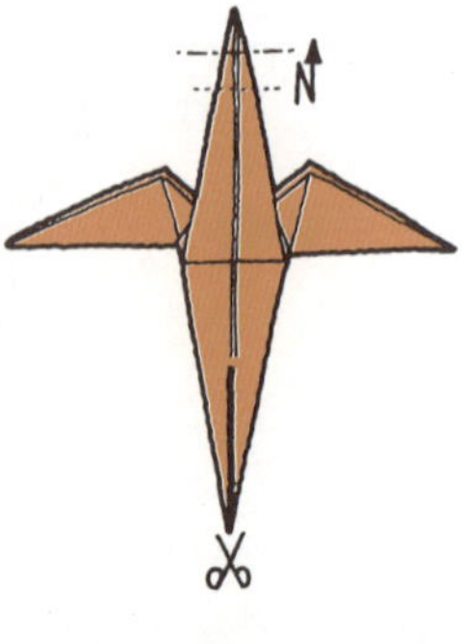

6 尾を交差させ、ひっくり返す。
Cross the tails and turn over.

Finished

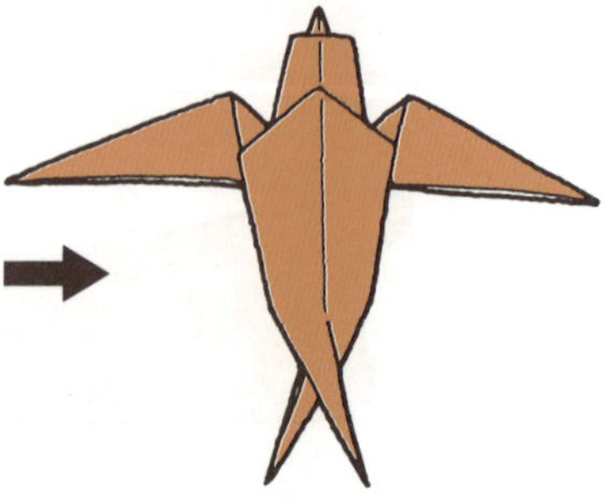

さる

Monkey

1 三角に折って上の１枚に、折りすじをつける。
Fold in half to make a triangle, then make creases on the front sheet as shown.

2 折りすじどおりに折って、ひっくり返す。
Fold it along the creases. Turn over.

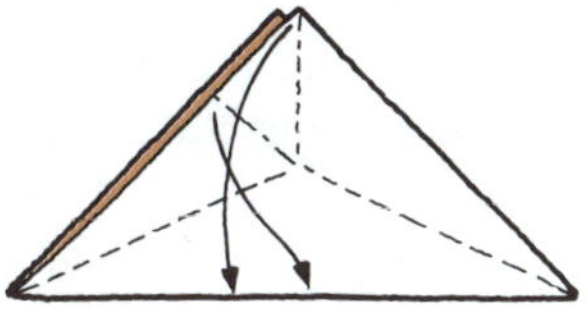

3 折りすじをつけ、折りすじどおりに、折り上げる。
Make creases as shown. Fold it along the creases.

4 ひっくり返す。
Turn over.

5 折りすじをつけ、内側を広げてつぶす。
Make creases as shown, then open the corner and flatten.

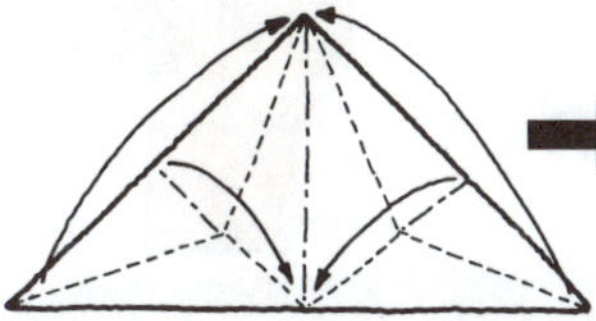

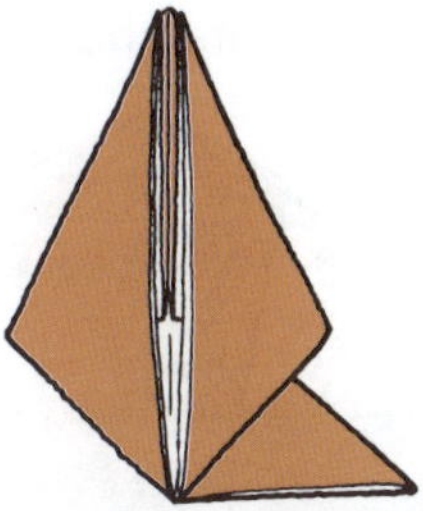

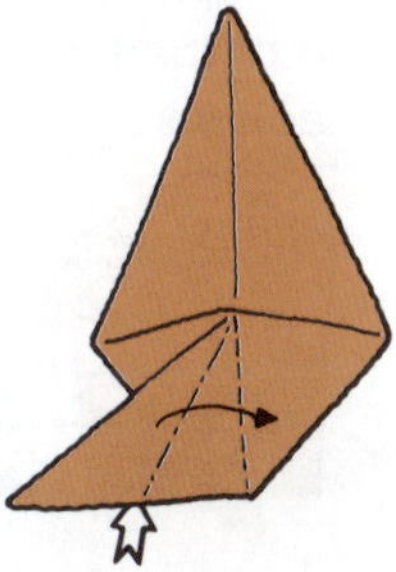

6 カドを内側に折り込む。
Fold the bottom corner backward.

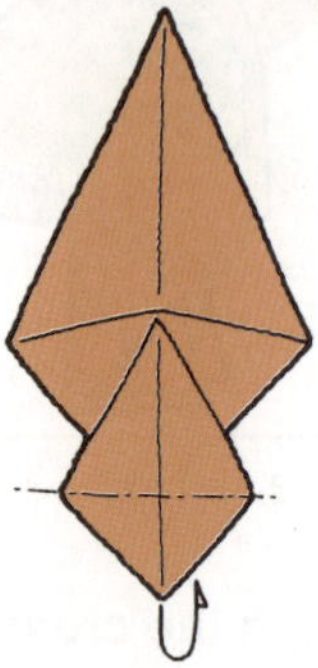

7 半分に折る。
Fold in half to the left.

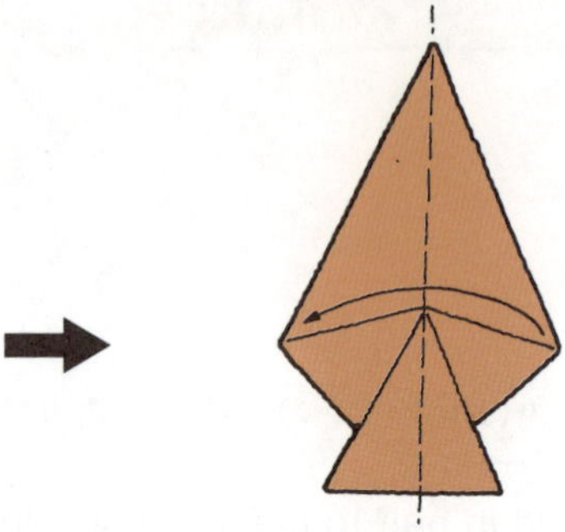

8 ななめに折り下げて腕をつくり、カドを内側に折り込む。
Fold the front flap diagonally and the back flap down diagonally. Fold both tips of the corners inside.

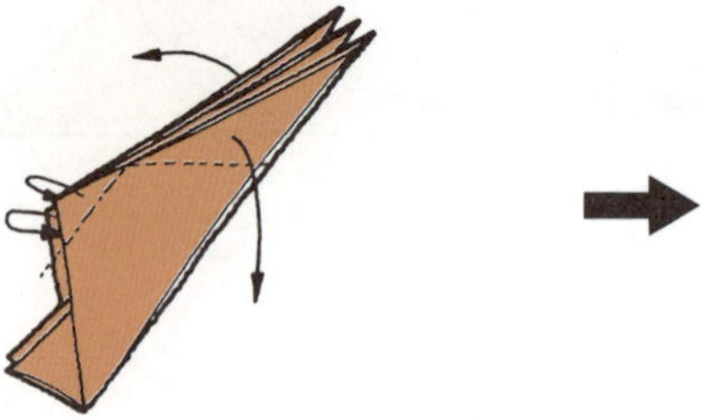

9 まん中の三角形を折りすじに合わせて折り、顔を作る。左右の腕は図のように折って動きを出す。
Make creases on the middle triangle, fold it along the creases. Fold the arms as shown.

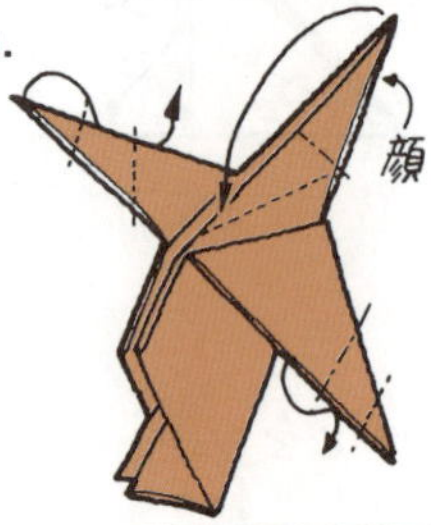

10 だん折りにして、カドを折る。
Do “Dan-Ori” on the face, then fold the tip of the face backward.

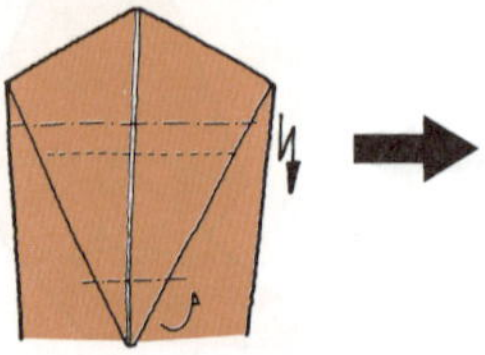

11 耳と鼻を、開くように折る。
Open the corners and flatten to from ears and nose.

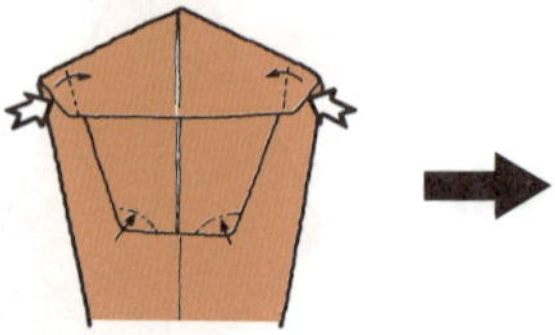

Finished

ダックスフンド

Dachshund

●材料　materials
長方形の紙　rectangular paper

1 裏を出して、中心に折りすじをつけ、上下を折る。
Make a horizontal crease in the center, then fold the top and bottom edges to the center.

2 4つのカドを折る。
Fold the 4　corners to the center.

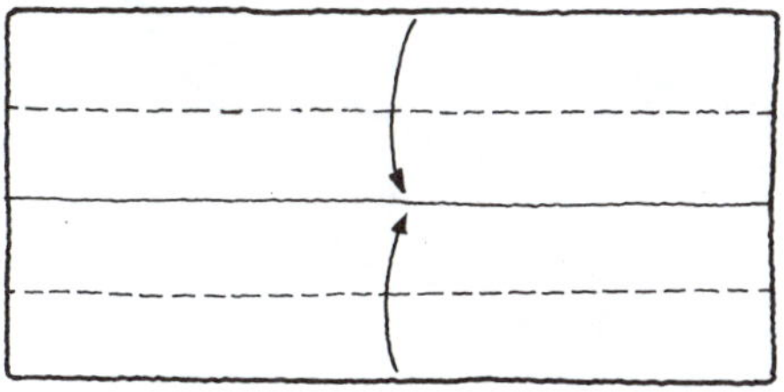

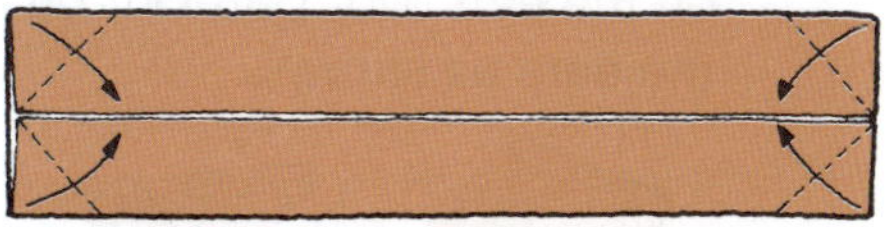

3 左側のカドを少しだけ裏側に折り、右側は中心に合わせて折る。
Fold the tip of the left side backward and fold both edges of the right corner to the center.

4 中心で手前に折る。
Fold in half to the front.

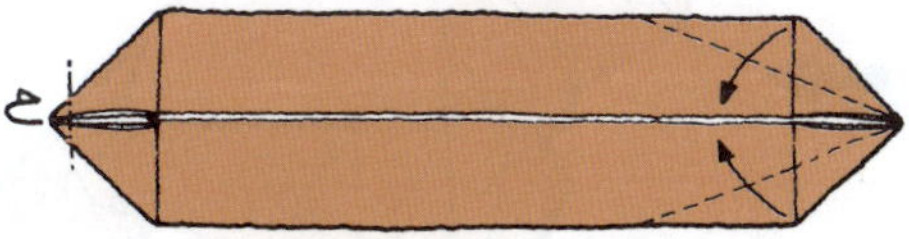

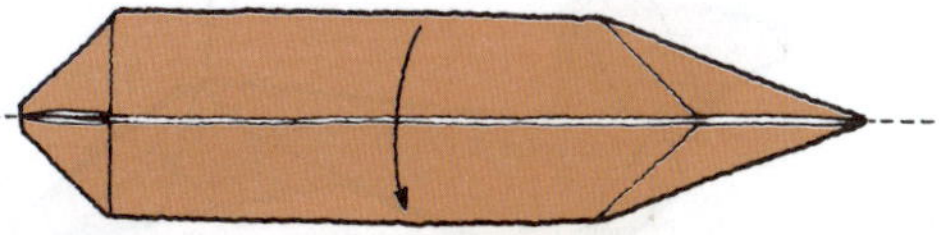

5 図の位置で中わり折りをする。
Do “Nakawari-Ori” as shown.

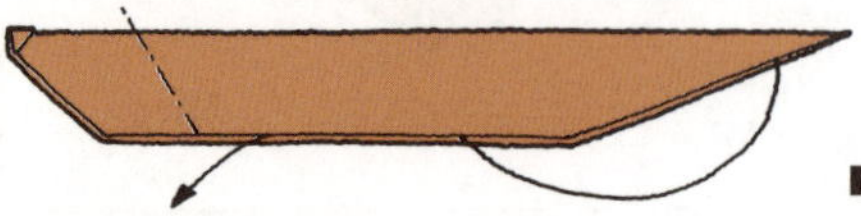

6 図の位置で中わり折りをする。
Do “Nakawari-Ori” again as shown.

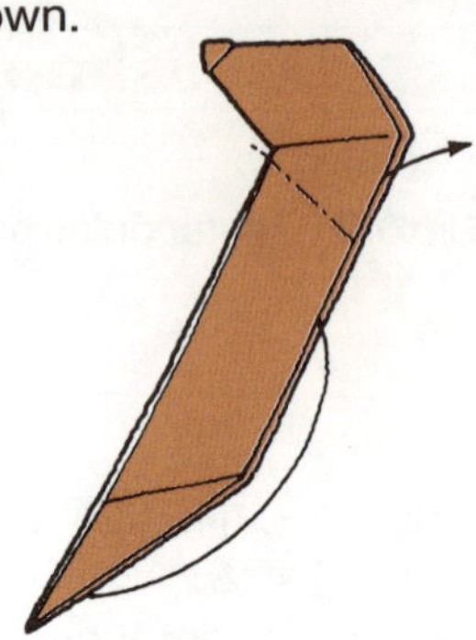

7 すき間を指で持ち上げながら引きよせ折りをし、さらにだん折りにする。
Raise the flap and fold it inside, and do “Hikiyose-Ori” on the ears. Do “Dan-Ori” on the ears as shown.

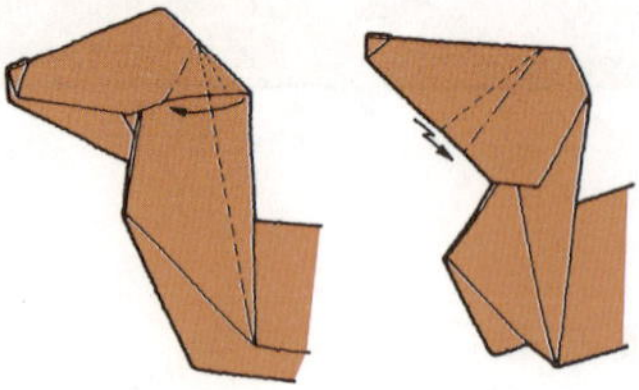

8 中わり折りをする。
Do “Nakawari-Ori” as shown.

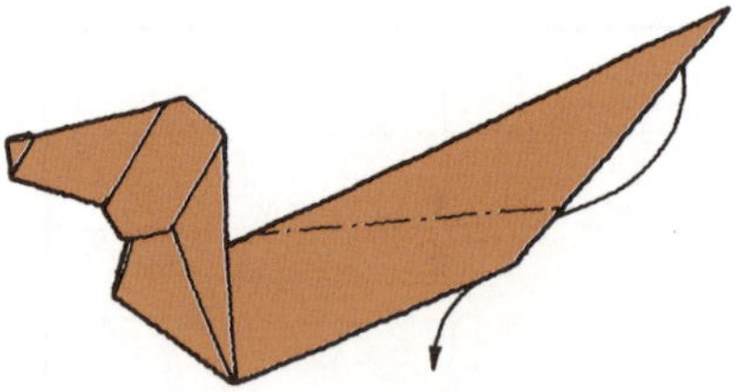

9 中わり折りをする。
Do “Nakawari-Ori” as shown.

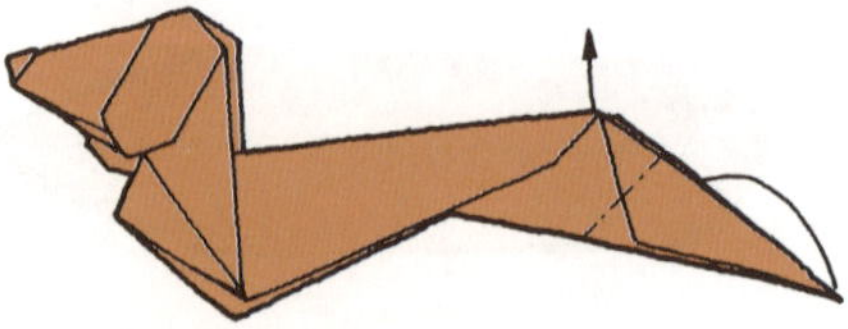

Finished

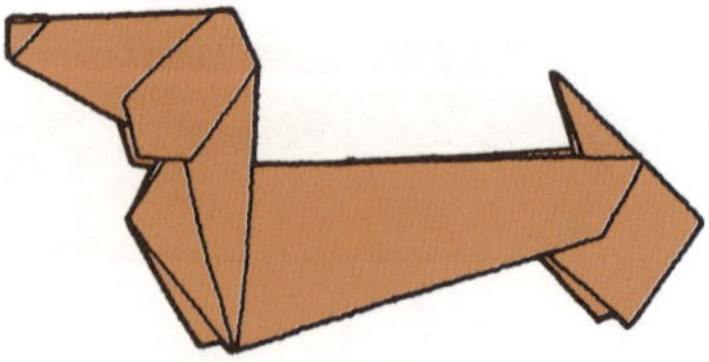

Chapter 5

水辺の生き物たち
Aquatic Animals

とび魚

Flying fish

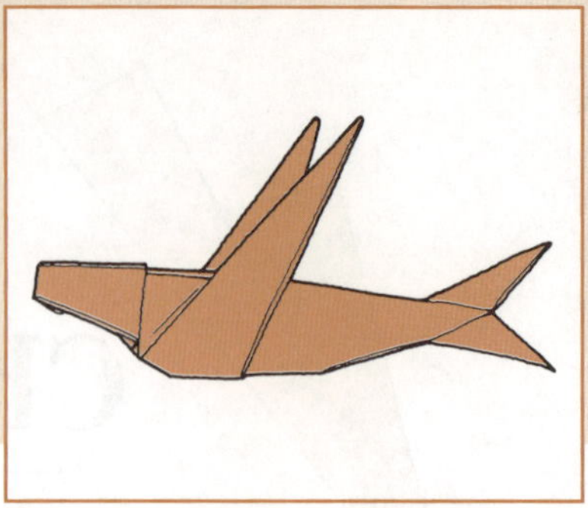

1 鶴の基本形（P27参照）を折り、下の部分を中わり折りにする。
Begin with “Basic Turu” (See P27). Do “Nakawari-Ori” on the bottom flaps.

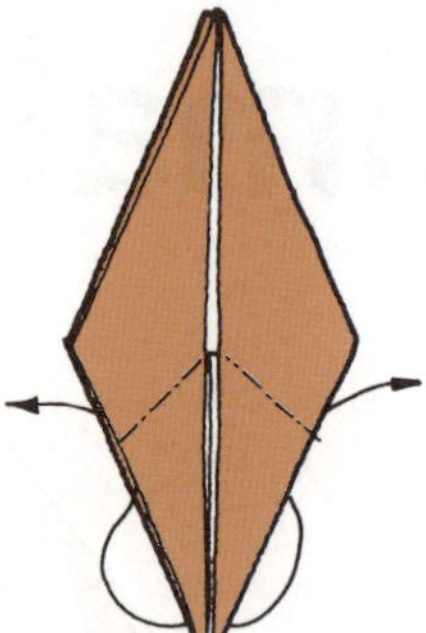

2 上の部分を折り下げる。裏側も同様に。
Fold the top corner down. Do the same with the reverse side.

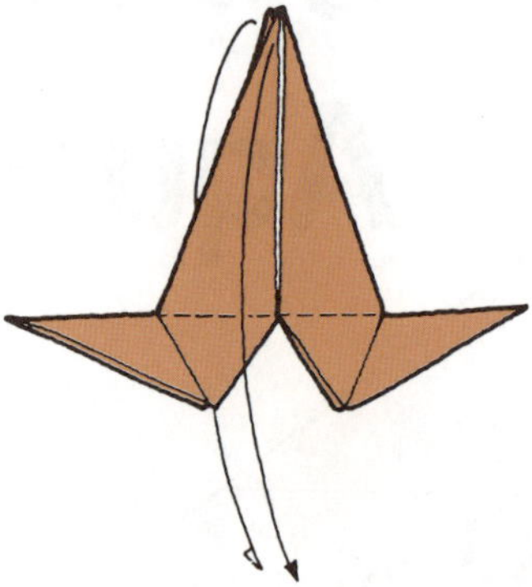

3 中心に合わせて折る。裏側も同様に。
Fold the upper edges of the front flap to the center. Do the same with the reverse side.

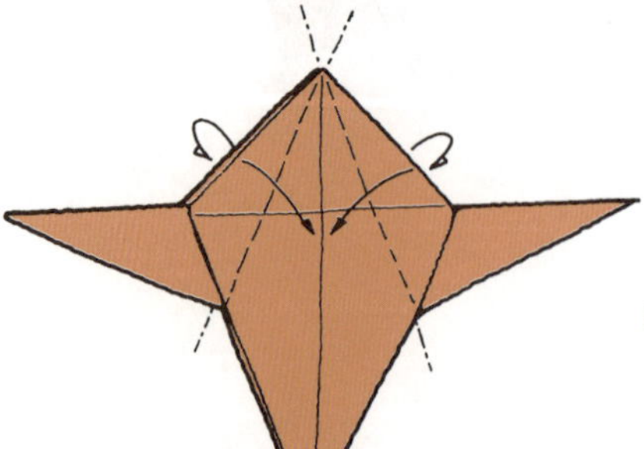

4 カドを少しだけ手前に折り、だん折りする。
Fold the tip of the top corner forward, then do “Dan-Ori” on the upper triangle.

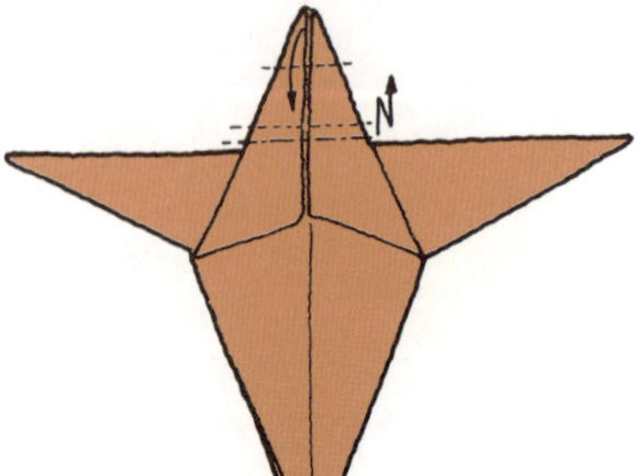

5 半分に折る。
Fold in half to the right.

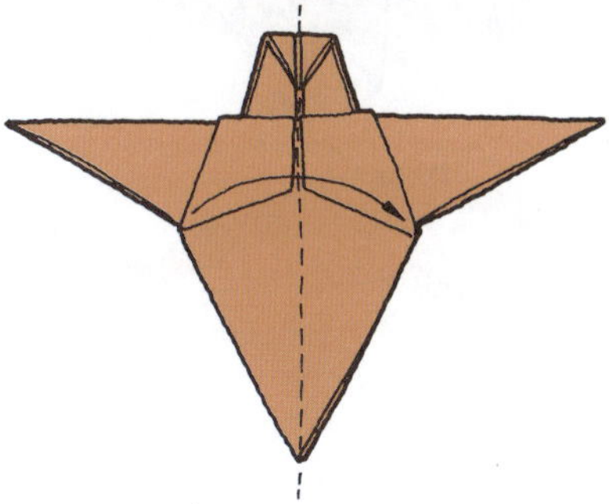

6 中わり折りにする。
Do "Nakawari-Ori" on the center of the body.

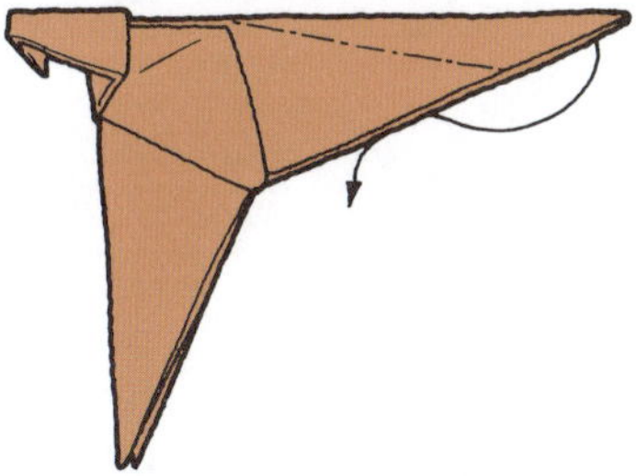

7 胸ひれの部分を折り、尾ひれの部分は上の１枚を中わり折りする。
Fold the fins up and do "Nakawari-Ori" on the upper tail fin.

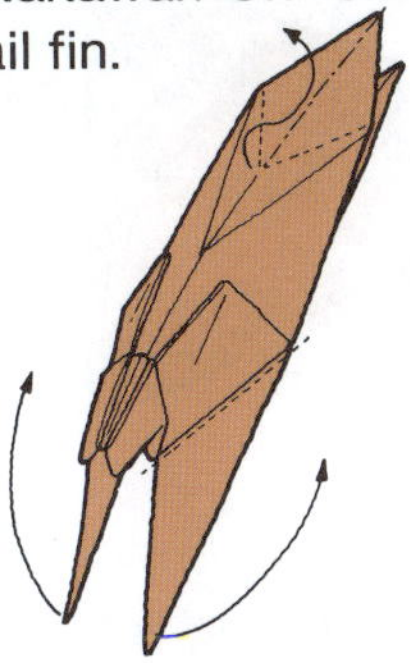

8 内側に折り込む。
Fold both sides inside.

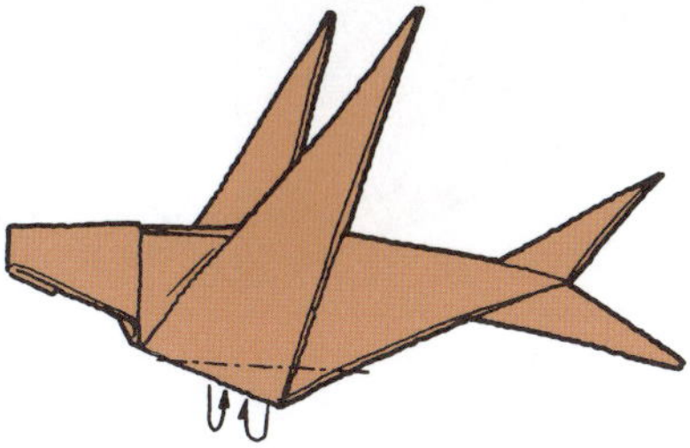

Finished

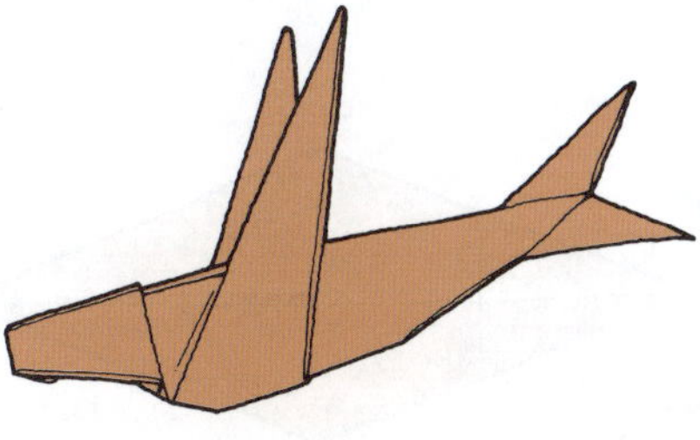

魚・シャチ

Fish • Orc

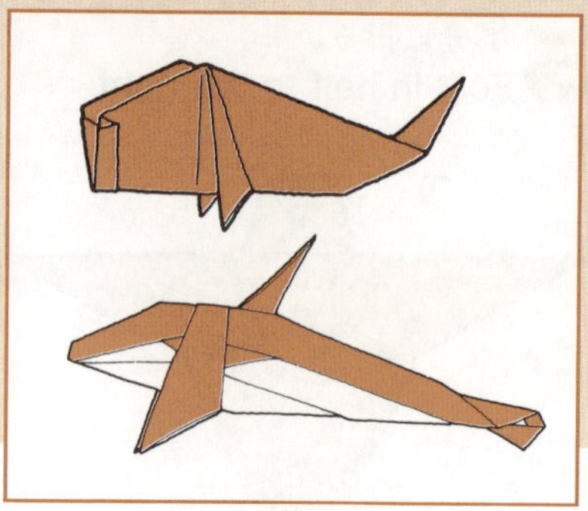

魚
Fish

1 凧の基本形（P22参照）から始める。
Begin with "Basic Kite"(See P22).

2 折りすじをつける。
Make creases as shown.

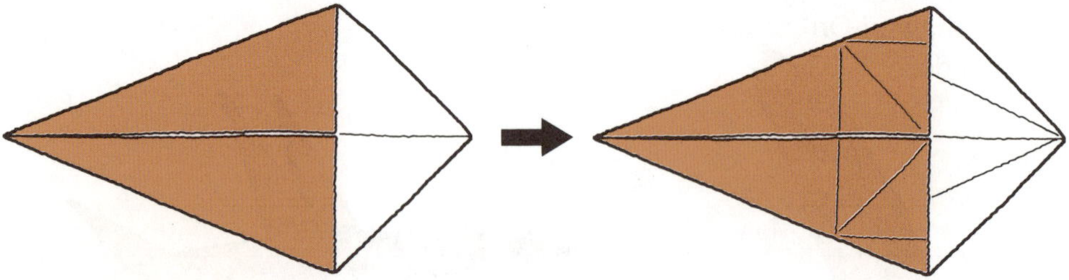

3 折りすじに合わせて折る。
Fold it along the creases.

4 カドを折る（魚の基本形）。
Fold the left corner backward.
(This is the "Basic Fish" form)

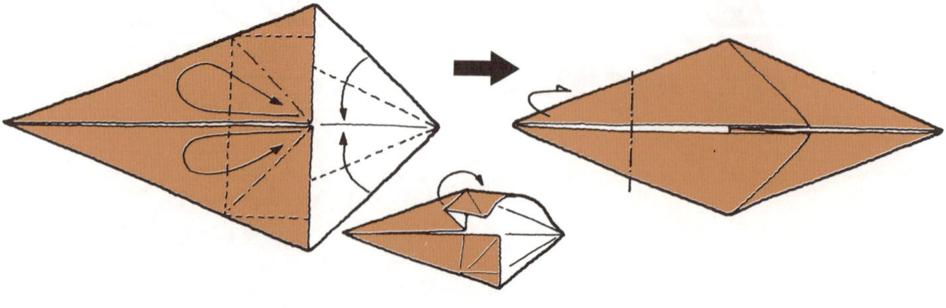

5 はしを少し折る。
Fold the left edge in a little.

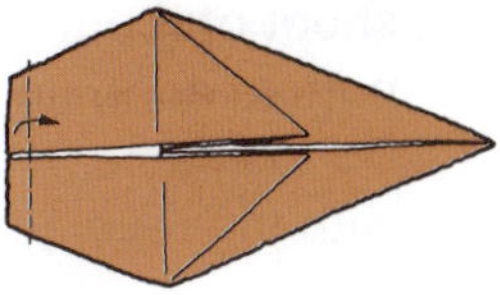

6 半分に折る。
Fold in half backward.

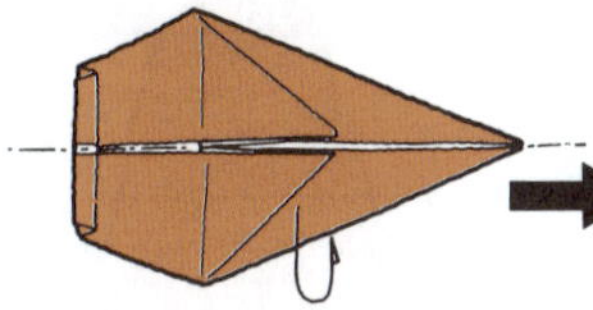

7 中わり折りをし、手前に折る。
Do "Nakawari-Ori" on the right corner, then fold the triangles in a little.

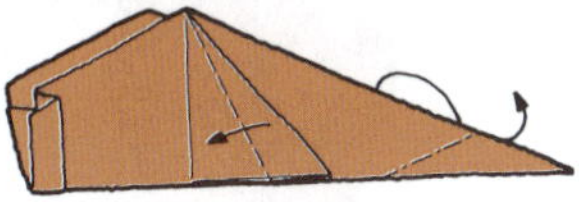

Finished

シャチ
Orc

1 裏を出して、魚の基本形（P130参照）から始める。
Begin with "Basic Fish" (See P130).

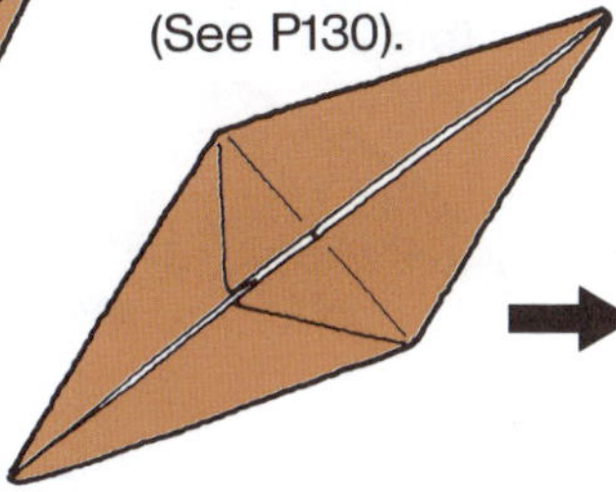

2 裏返して、折りすじをつける。
Turn over. Fold the top corner to the center. Unfold.

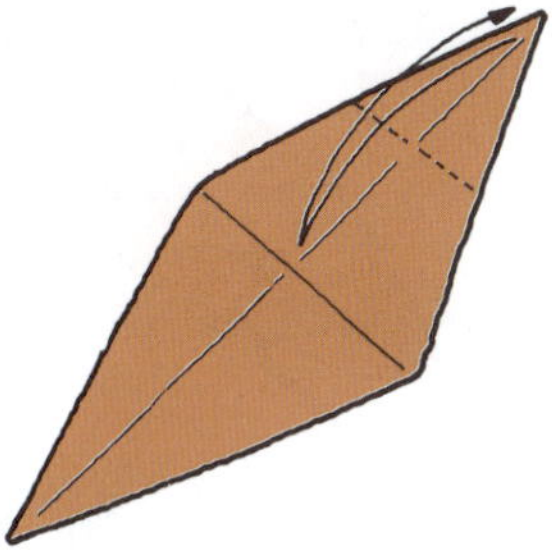

3 上のカドを折りすじに合わせて折り下げる。裏返して、三角の部分を中心に合わせて折り上げる。
Fold the top corner along the crease. Turn over. Fold the center flap up as shown.

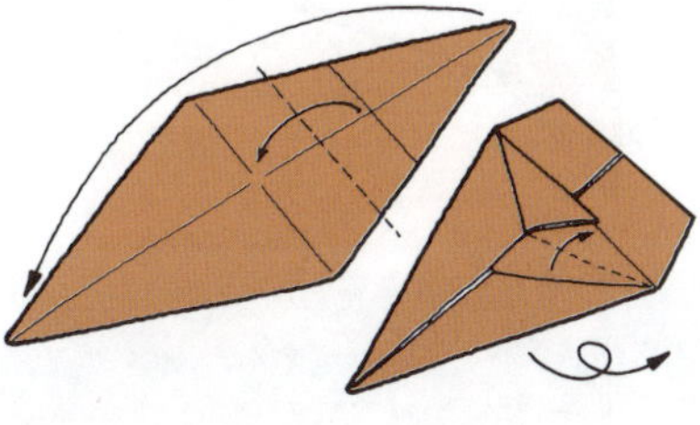

4 裏返して、中心に合わせて左右を折る。
Turn over. Fold the upper left and right edges to the center.

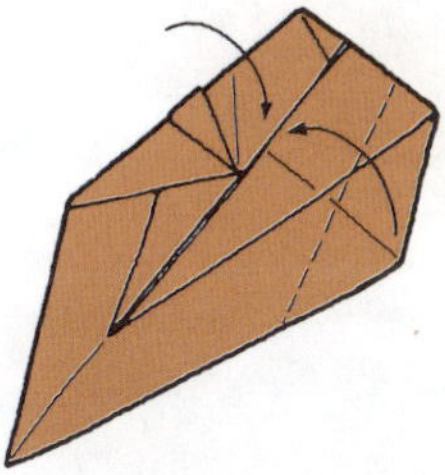

5 上のカドを折る。
Fold the top corners a little.

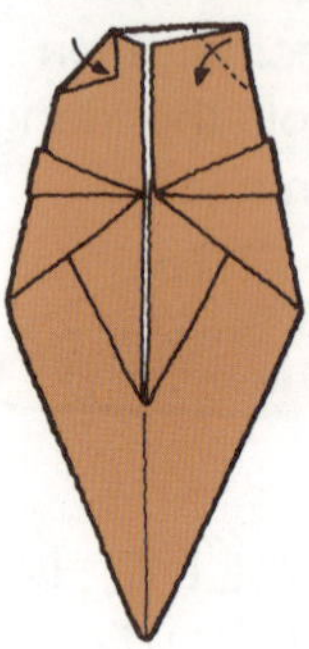

6 半分に折る。
Fold the left side to the right.

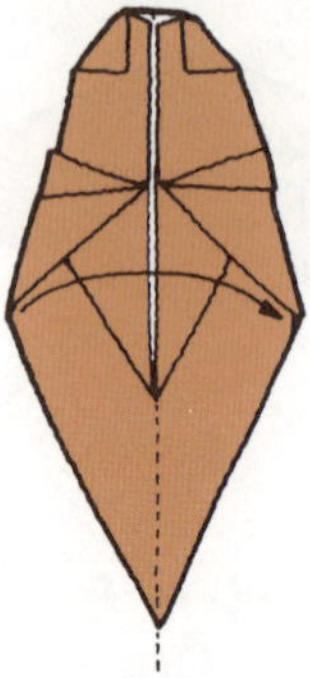

7 手前の１枚を折り上げる。裏側も同様に。
Fold the front sheet of the bottom edge up. Do the same with the reverse side.

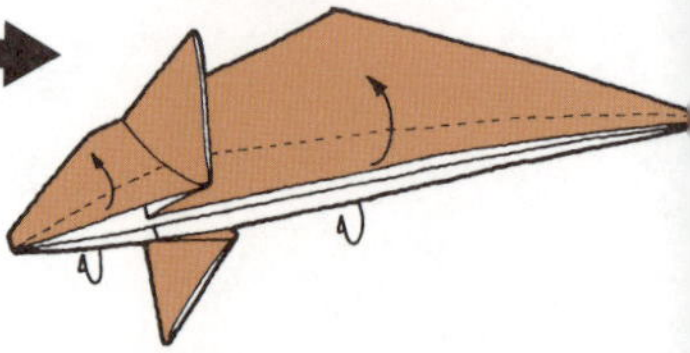

8 中わり折りする。
Do “Nakawari-Ori” on the top corner.

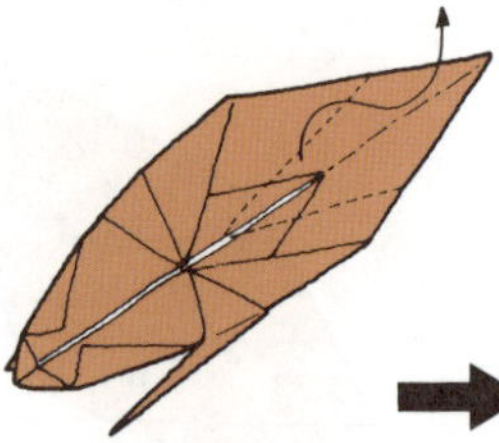

9 内側のとがった部分を立たせる。
Open the top, bring the inside triangle up and fold in half.

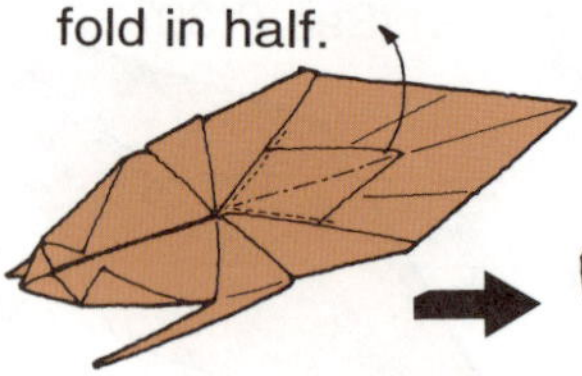

10 内側に折り込む。
Fold the top edges inside as shown.

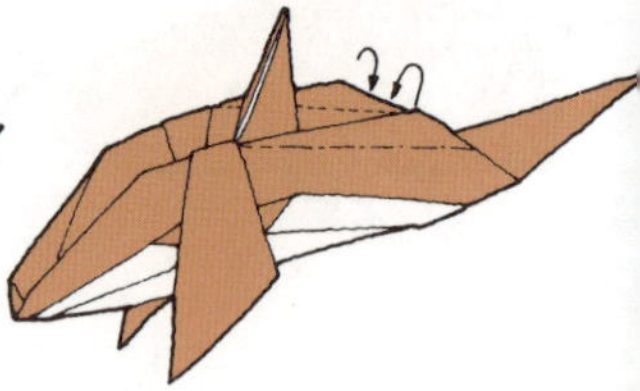

11 尾の先を内側に折り、さらに中わり折りにする。
Fold the tip of the tail inside.
Do “Nakawari-Ori” on the tail.

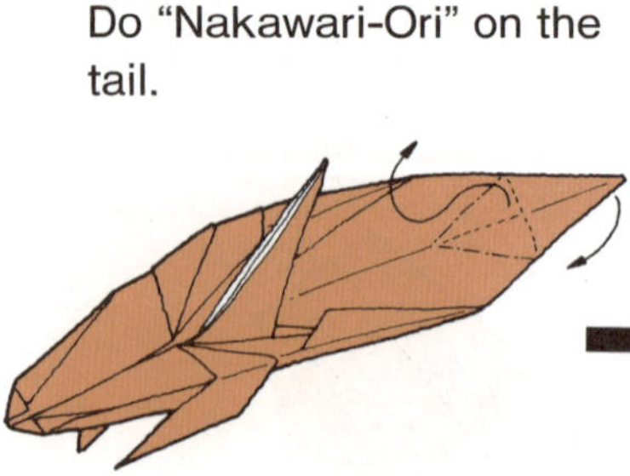

Finished

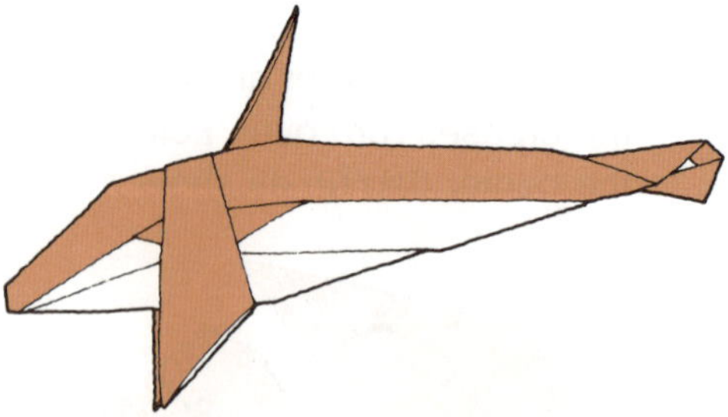

かめ

Turtle

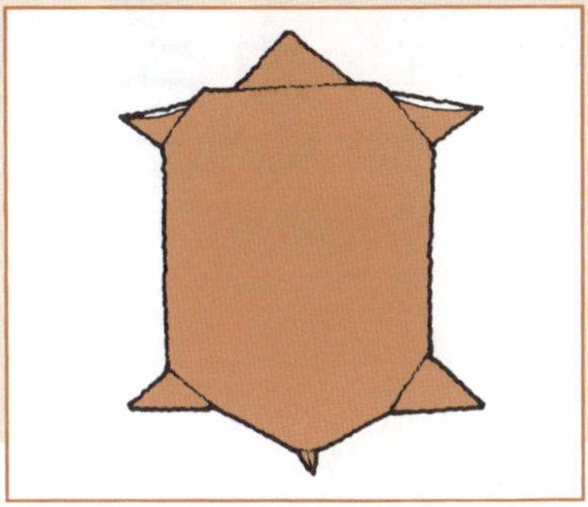

1 三角形に折り、左右を折り下げる。
Fold in half to make a triangle, then fold the corners down to make a square.

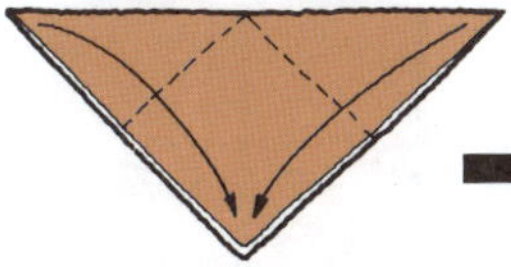

2 真上に折り上げる。
Fold the flaps up to meet at the top corner.

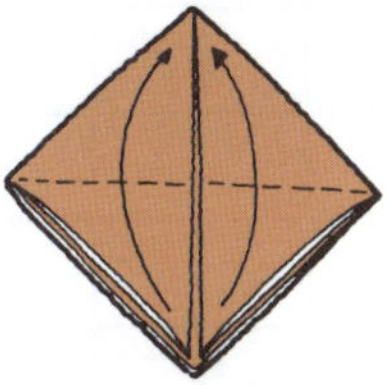

3 上の１枚に切り込みを入れ、４カ所を同様に折る。
Cut the top sheet to the center. Then fold the 4 flaps.

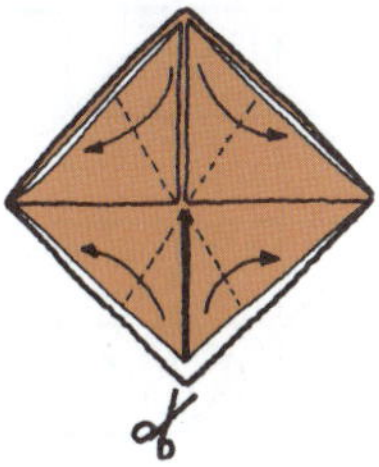

4 左右を中心に向けて折る。頭の部分をだん折りする。
Fold the left and right flaps to the center. Do “Dan-Ori” to make a head.

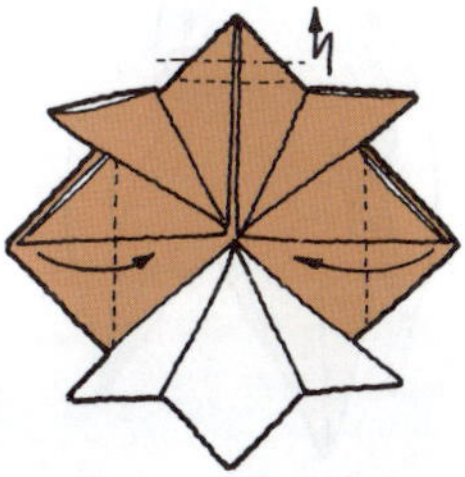

5 しっぽをつまむように折る。
Twist the tip a little to make a tail.

6 ひっくり返す。
Turn over.

Finished

カニ

Crab

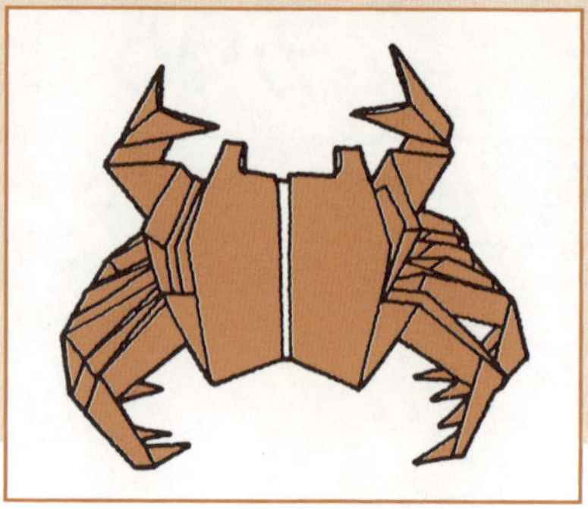

1 折り紙の裏を出して図のように折りすじをつける。
Make creases as shown.

2 切り込みを入れる。
Cut as shown.

3 折りすじどおりにたたむ。
Fold the paper in along the creases to make a square.

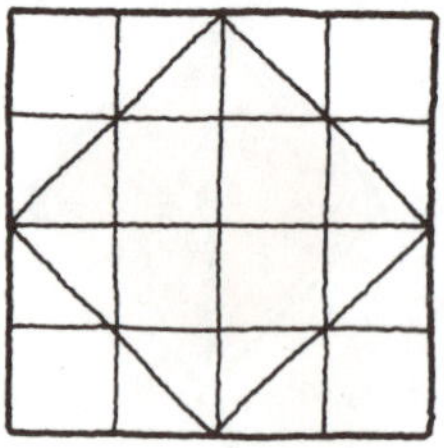

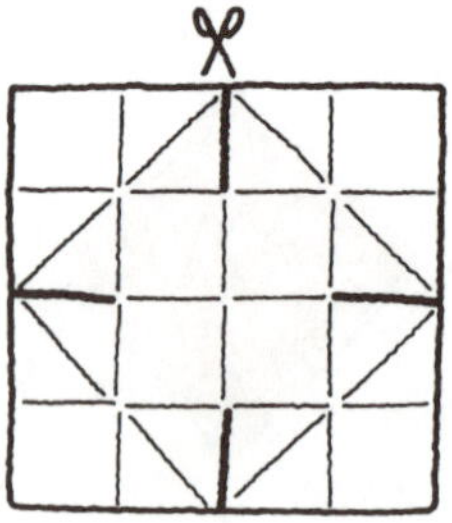

4 4カ所で、鶴の基本形（P 27参照）を折る。
Using “Basic Turu”(See P27) make a lozenge in each corner.

5 裏返して、図のように4カ所に折りすじをつける。
Turn over. Make creases as shown.

6 立てるようにして、折りすじを使って鶴の基本形を作る。
Fold each corner by using creases to make “Basic Turu”.

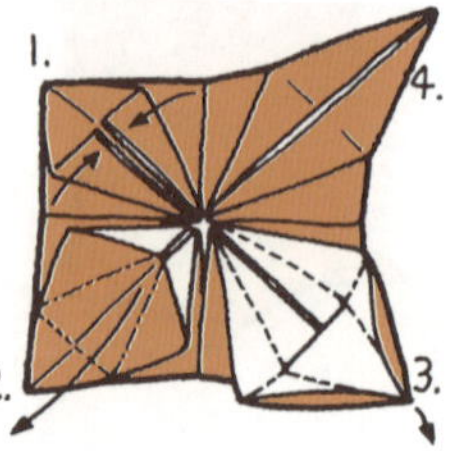

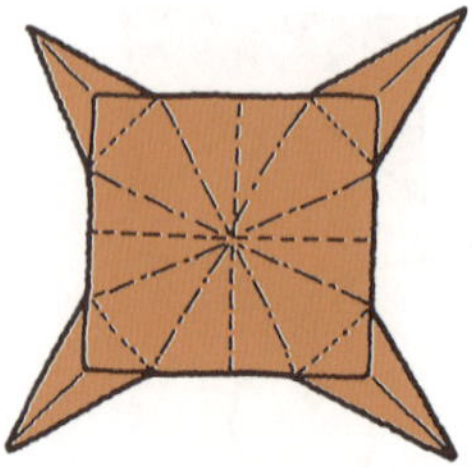

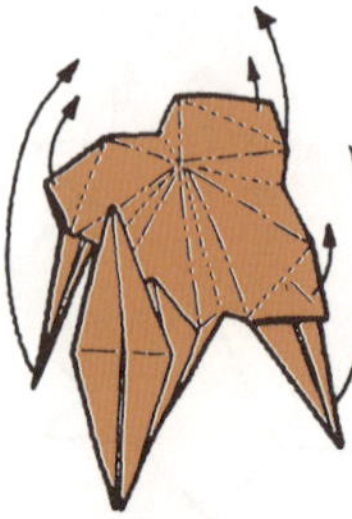

7 4カ所で鶴の基本形を作る。
Make "Basic Turu" as shown.

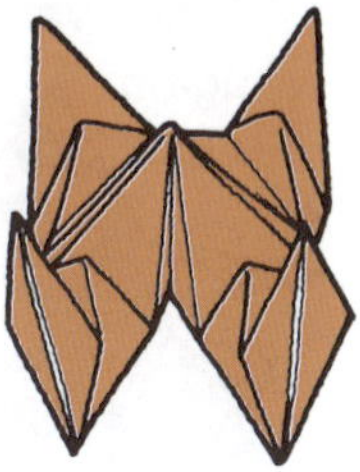

8 左右8枚ずつに折りたたむ。右の1枚を左にめくる。
Fold over to make 8 lozenges, then fold the front right flap to the left.

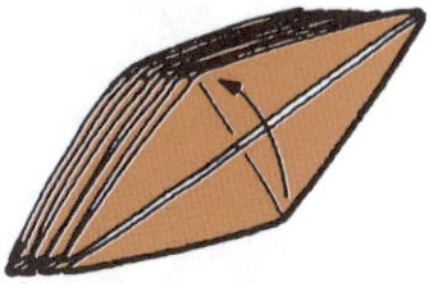

9 左右を中心で折り合わせる。
Fold the front flaps to the center.

10 外側の右の1枚を左にめくる。
Fold the outer right flap over to the left.

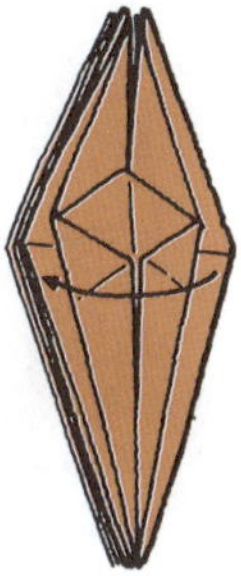

11 9から同様に8カ所とも折る。
Repeat steps 9-10 on the other flaps.

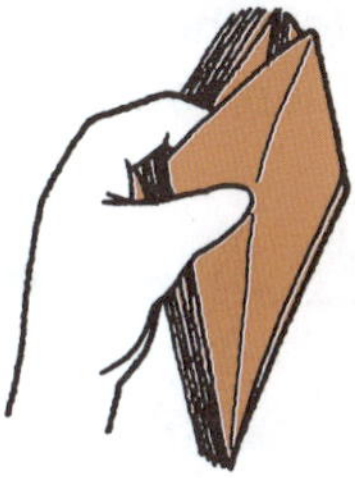

12 左右の足を4本ずつ中わり折りで折り上げる。
Fold the 8 flaps up by "Nakawari-Ori" to make legs.

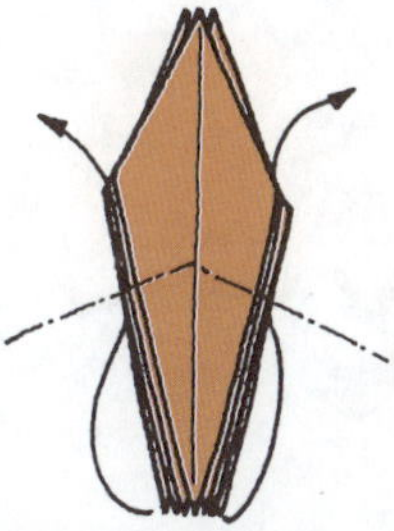

13 左右の足を中わり折りで折り下げる。
Fold each leg down by "Nakawari-Ori".

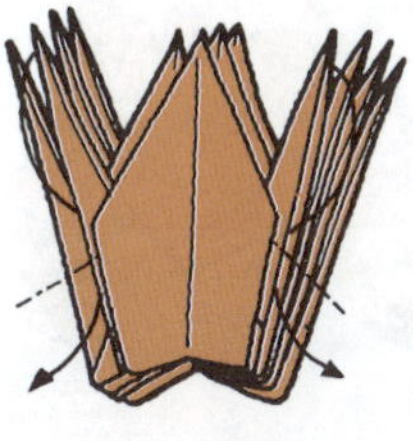

14 8本とも、かぶせ折りをする。
Do "Kabuse-Ori" on the 8 legs.

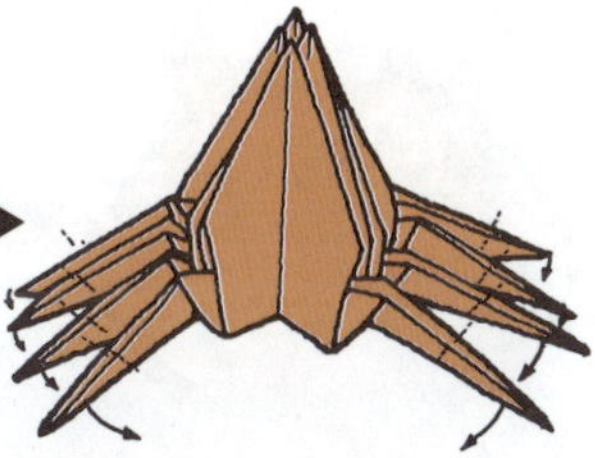

15 ８本とも、中わり折りをする。
Do “Nakawari-Ori” on the 8 tips of the legs.

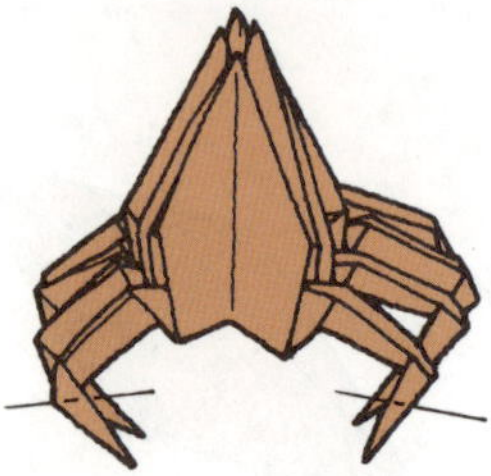

16 まん中の紙を中わり折りで左右に出す。
Pull the middle flaps out by “Nakawari-Ori” to make claws.

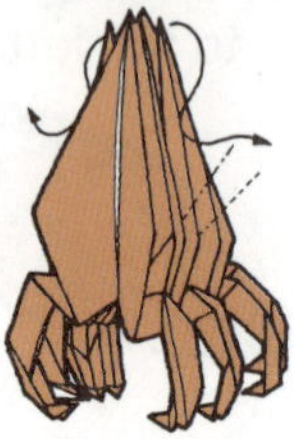

17 中わり折りで上に向ける。
Fold the claws upward by “Nakawari-Ori” again.

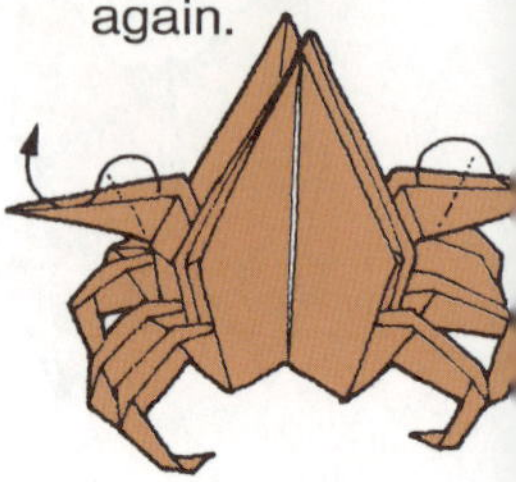

18 手前の１枚を折り下げ、後ろ１枚も折り下げる。
Fold the front flap down, then fold the back flap down.

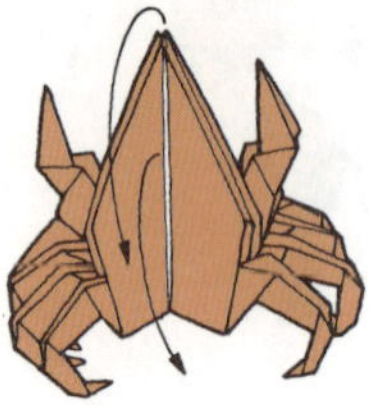

19 図のようになる。
It should look like this.

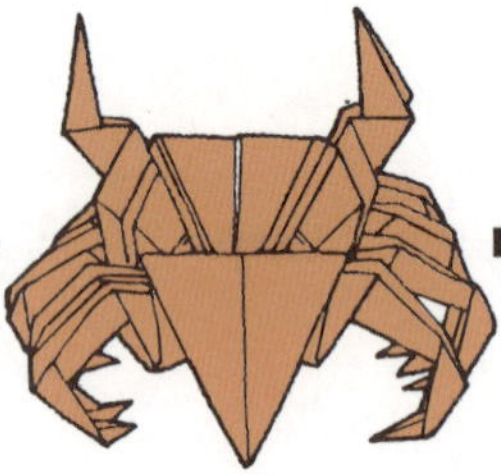

20 図のように、切り込みを入れる。
Cut the paper as shown.

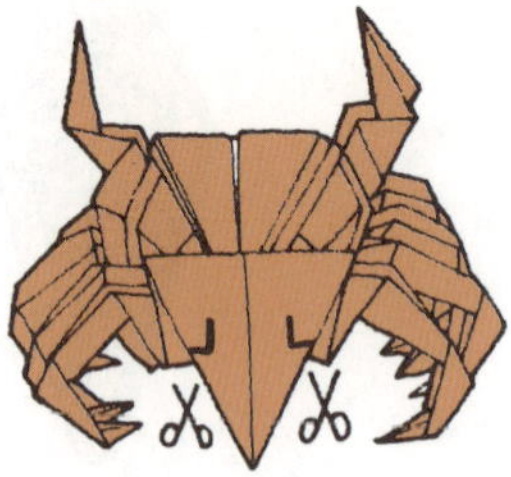

21 後ろ側にかぶせ、のりづけする。
Fold the flap to the back and glue it.

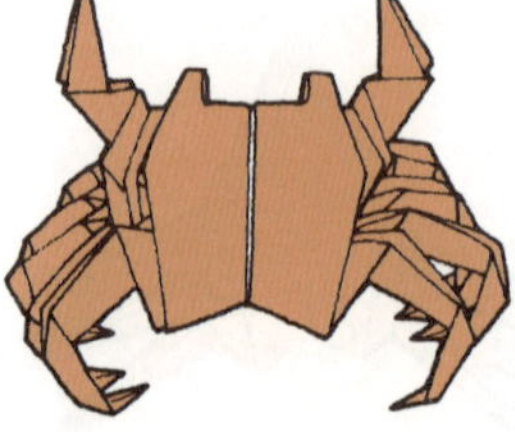

22 はさみで切り込みを入れる。
Cut the tips of the claws.

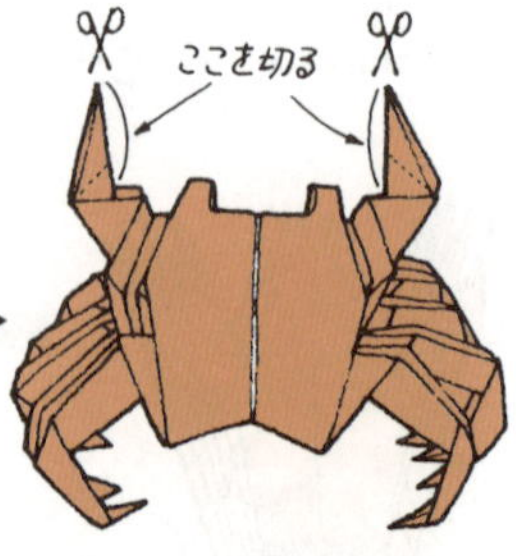

23 切り込みを開く。
Open the tips of the claws.

Finished

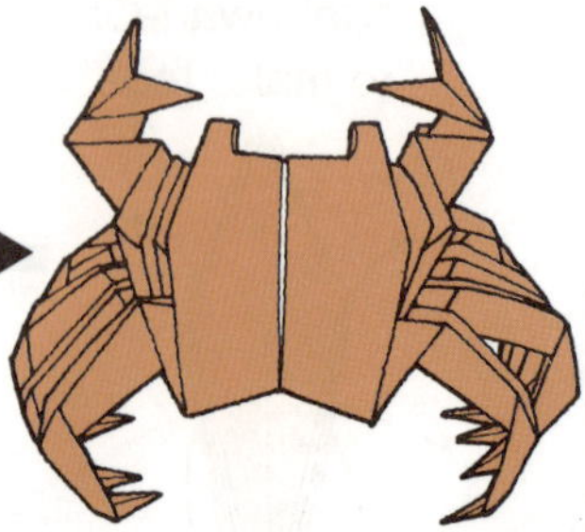

白鳥

Swan

1 凧の基本形（P 22参照）から始める。
Begin with "Basic Kite"(See P22).

2 ひっくり返し、中心に合わせて折る。
Turn over, and fold both sides to the center.

3 たてに半分に折る。
Fold in half.

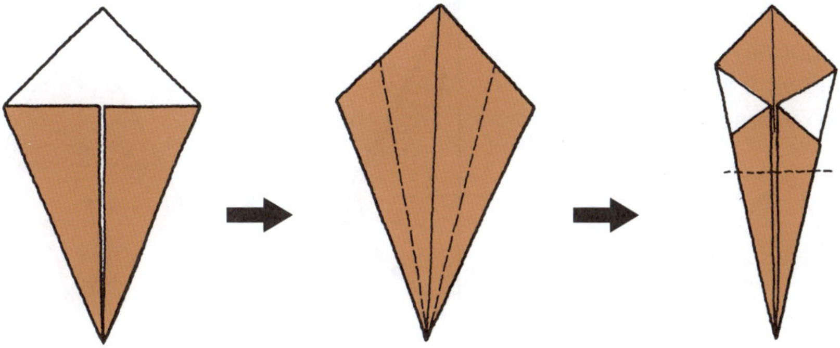

4 よこに半分に折る。
Fold in half.

5 首を引き上げ、かぶせ折りをする。
Pull the neck up, then do "Kabuse-Ori" to make the head.

6 だん折りで、くちばしを作る。
Do "Dan-Ori" to form a bill.

Finished

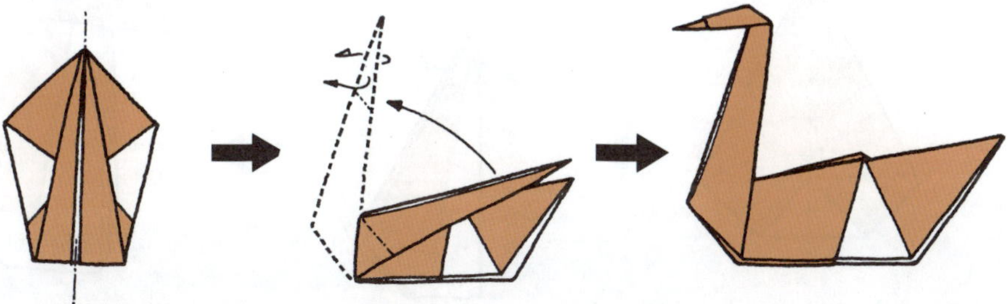

ペンギン

Penguin

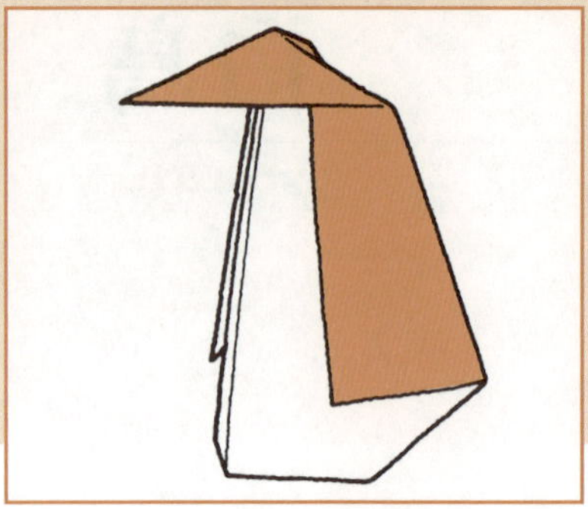

1 中表にして折る。
1枚を折り下げる。
裏側も同様に。
Fold in half.
Fold the upper sheet down diagonally. Do the same with the reverse side.

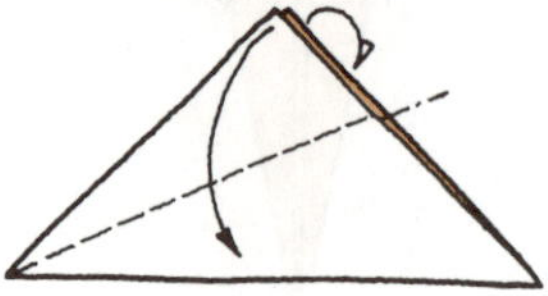

2 広げる。
Open it to the left.

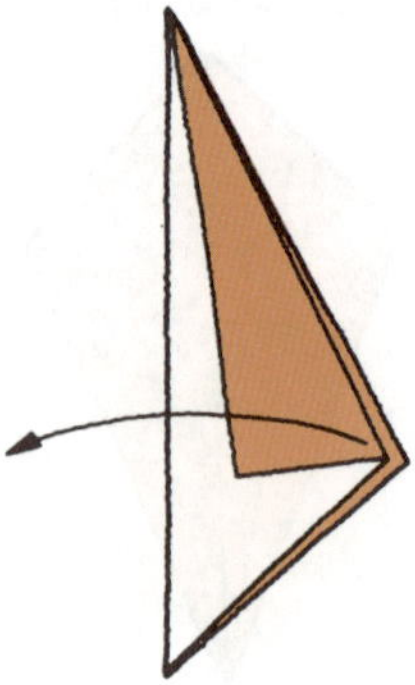

3 下のとんがった部分を折り上げる。
Fold the bottom corner up.

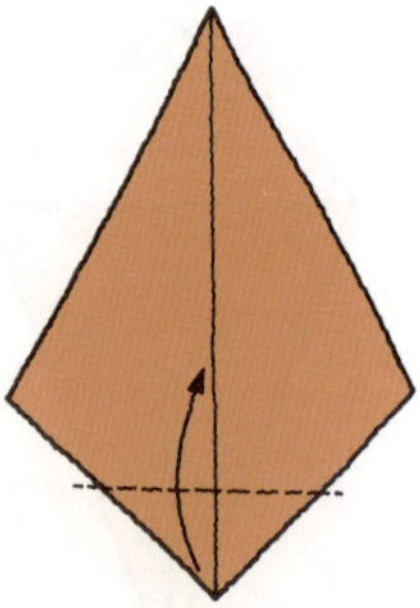

4 もう一度、半分に折る。
Fold in half to the right.

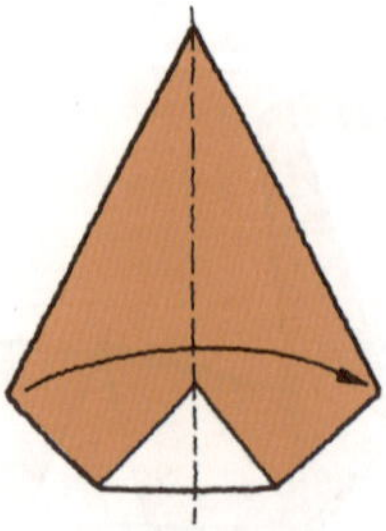

5 図のようにすじをつけ、かぶせ折りする。
Make a crease on the top corner. Do "Kabuse-Ori".

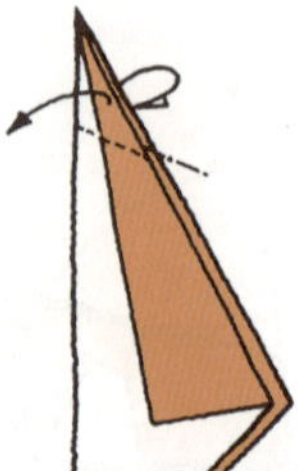

Finished

たこ
Octopus

1 鶴の基本形（P 27参照）から始める。切り込みが入っているほうを下に置く。
Begin with "Basic Turu" (See P27). Place Origami as shown.

2 1枚を、折り下げる。裏側も同様に折る。
Fold the upper flap down. Do the same with the reverse side.

3 上と下の2枚だけに切り込みを入れる。
Cut the top and bottom flaps (2 sheets each) as shown.

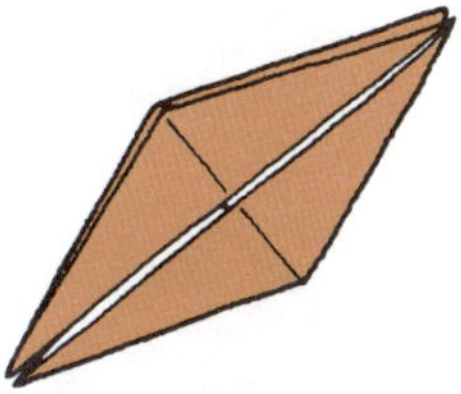

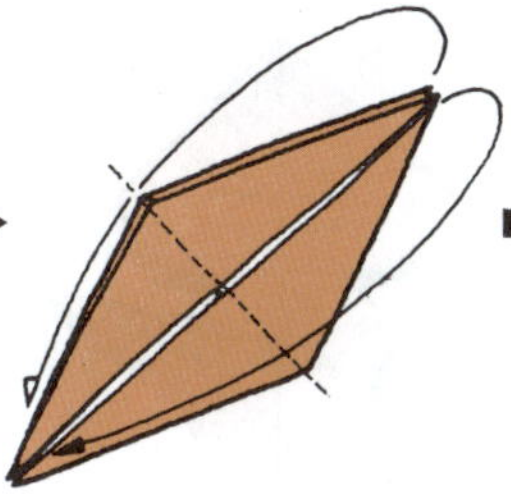

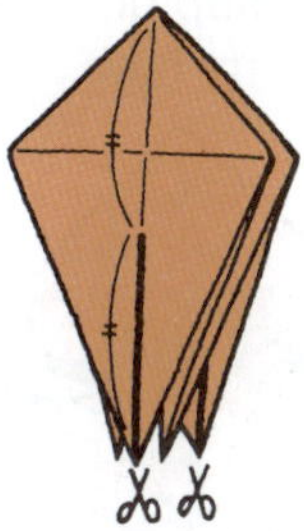

4 右の1枚を左に移動させる。裏側も同様に折る。
Fold the right flap to the left. Do the same with the reverse side.

5 3と同様に切り込みを入れる。
Cut as in step 3.

6 図の部分を切る。
Cut out the sides as shown.

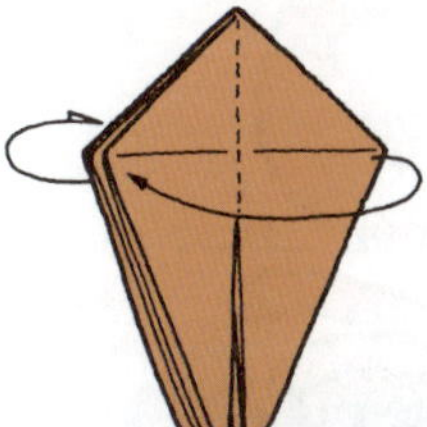

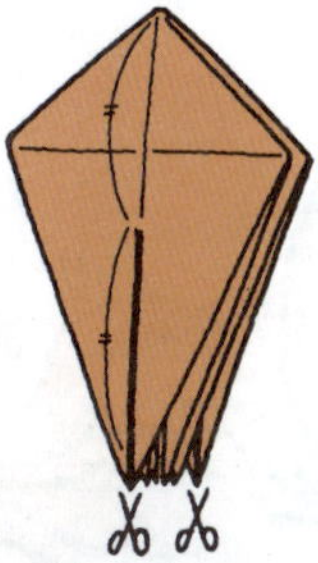

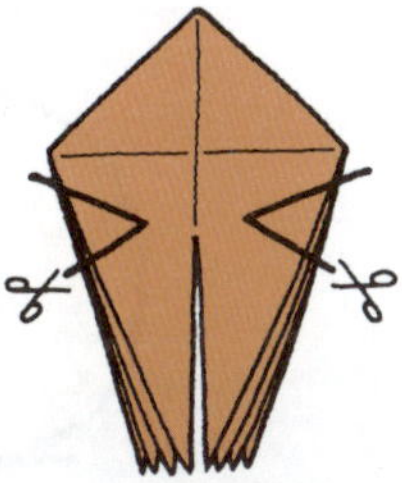

7 カドを４枚とも斜めに折り上げる。
Fold the 4 right flaps up diagonally.

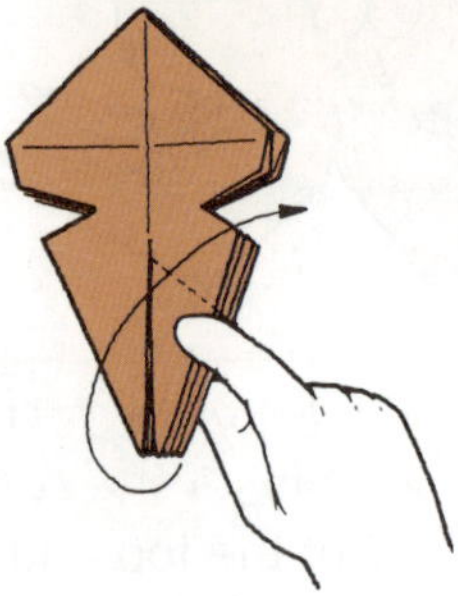

8 戻す。
Unfold.

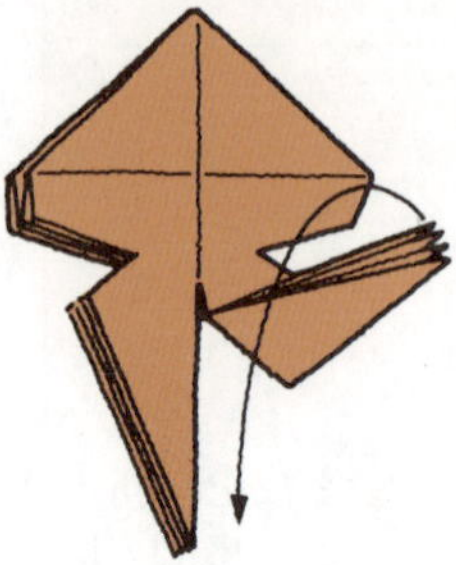

9 上の１枚だけを、折りすじに合わせて折る。
Fold the top flap along the crease.

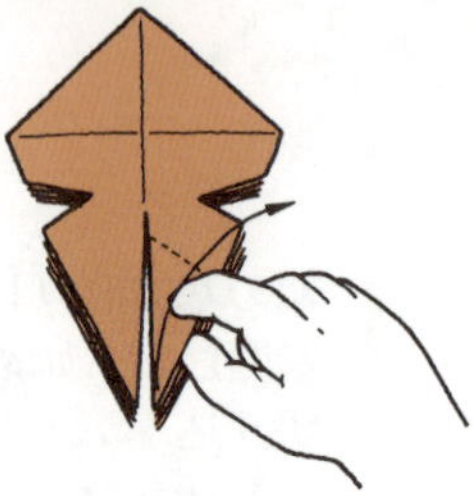

10 ２枚目は、１枚目の下に折る。
Fold the 2nd flap under the 1st flap.

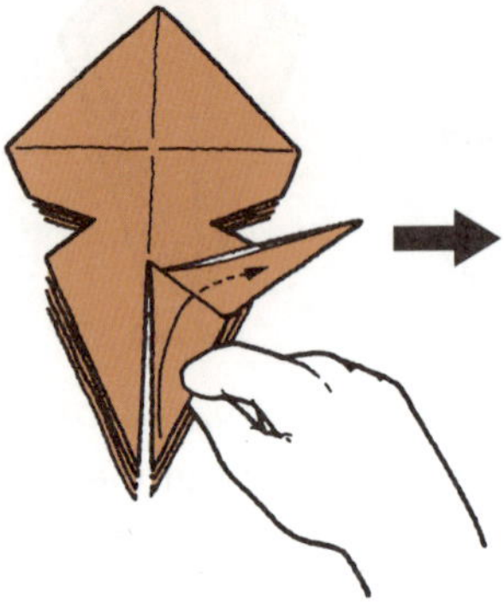

11 残りも同様に折る。
Do the same with the others.

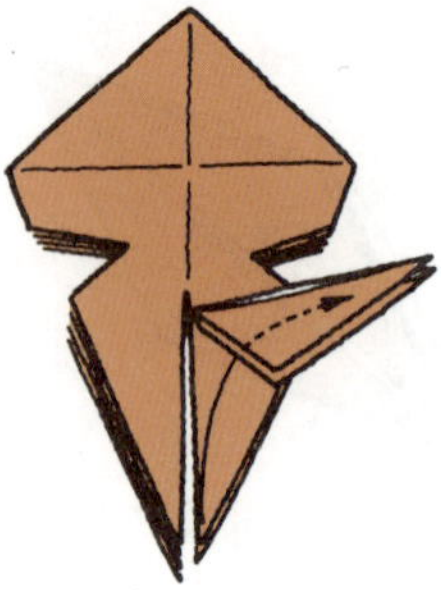

12 左側も同様に折り、顔をかく。
Repeat steps **7-11** on the left flaps.
Draw the face.

Finished

金魚

Goldfish

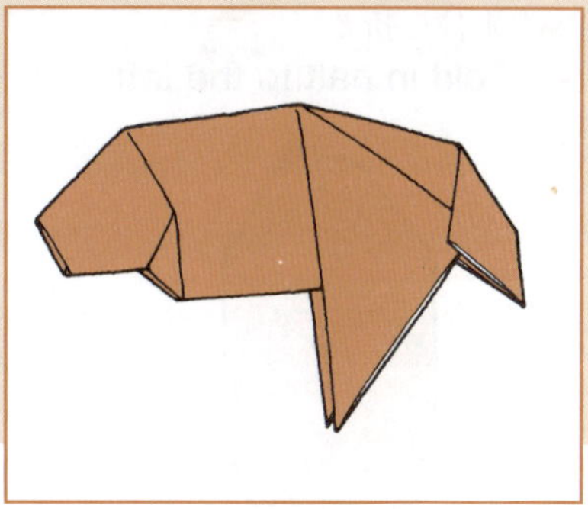

1 半分に折る。
Fold in half to make a triangle.

2 中心に合わせて折る。
Fold both corners down to the bottom corner.

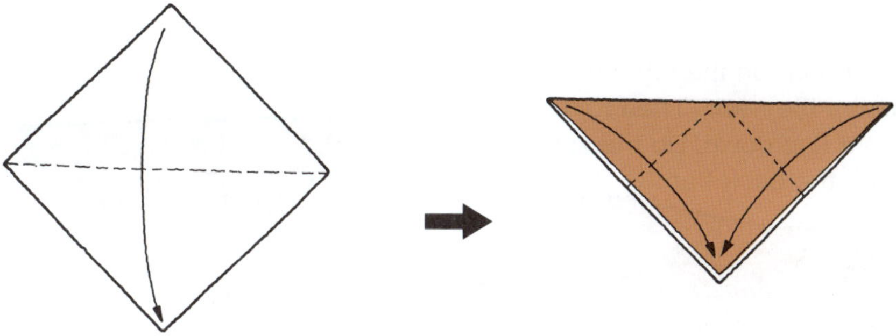

3 図のようになる。
It should look like this.

4 カドをそれぞれ折る。
Fold the corners in to the center, then fold the top corner a little.

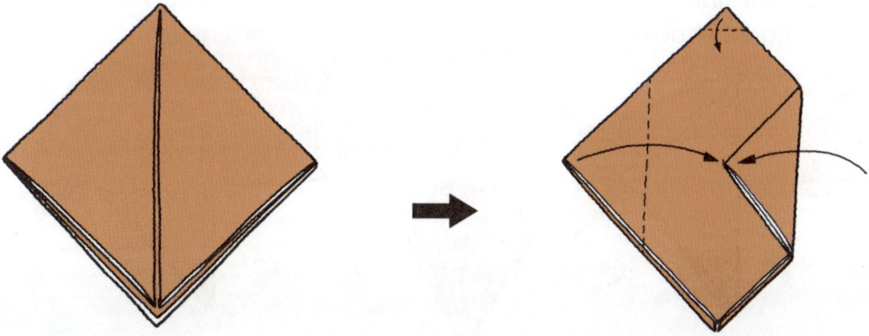

5 半分に折る。
Fold in half to the left.

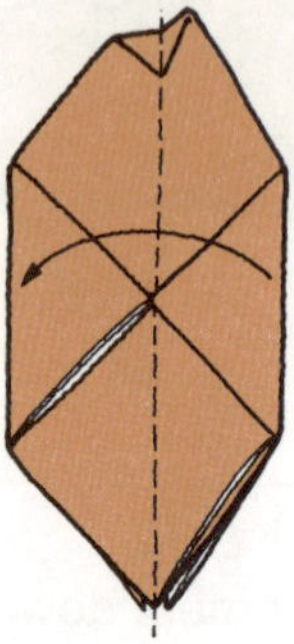

6 図のようになる。
It should look like this.

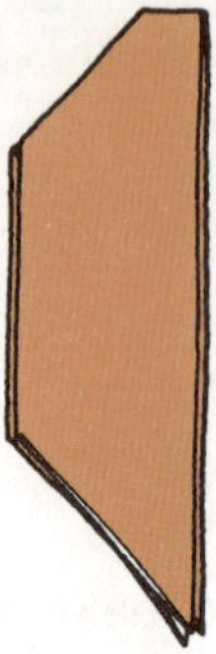

7 頭になるほうを段折りし、手前の１枚だけ折る。裏側も同様に。
Rotate 90°to the left. Do "Dan-Ori" on the left side to make the head. Then fold the front flap down. Do the same with the back flap.

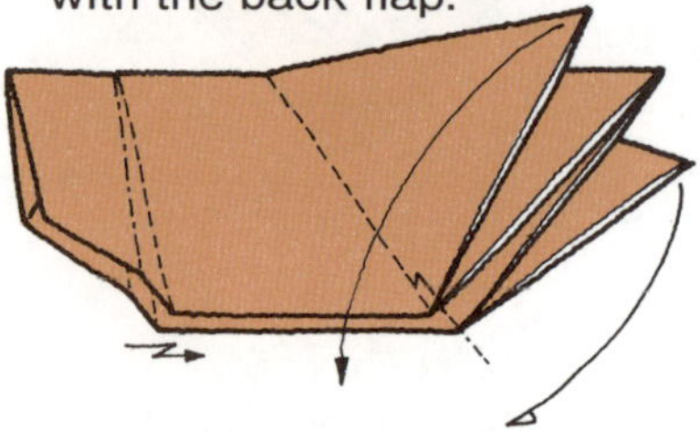

8 中わり折りをする。
Do "Nakawari-Ori" on the center flap.

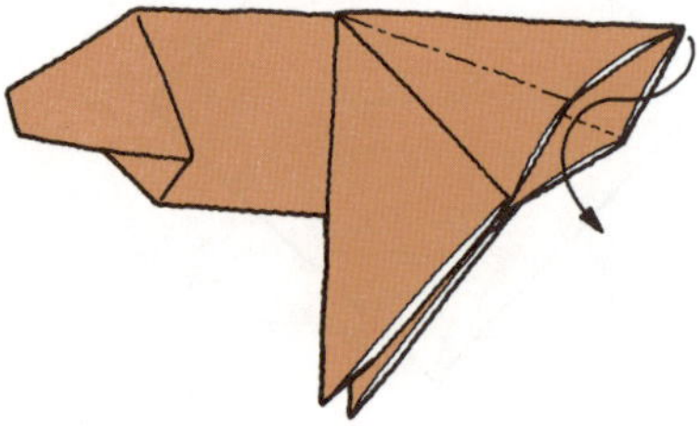

9 かぶせ折りをする。頭のところを少し折る。
Do "Kabuse-Ori" on the tip of the center flap. Fold the head in a little as shown.

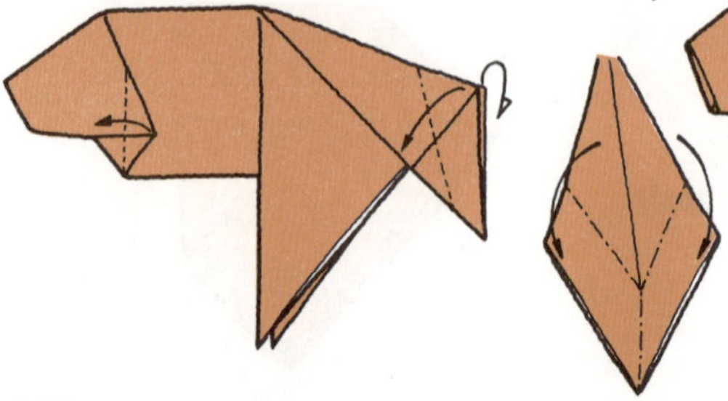

Finished

海ガメ

Sea Turtle

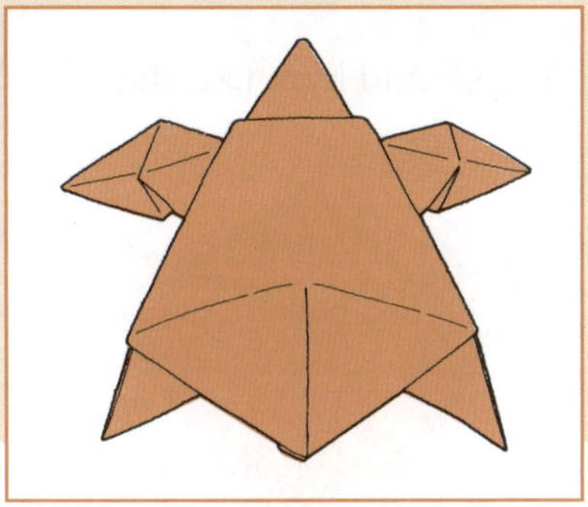

1 風船基本形（P26参照）から始める。
Begin with "Basic Fūsen".

2 半分に折りすじをつける。
Make a crease at halfway up the left edge.

3 さらに半分に折りすじをつける。
Make another crease halfway between the first crease and the bottom corner.

4 Cのところを通るように折る。
Fold the right front flap up and across to C.

5 反対側も折る。
Fold the left front flap up and across.

6 半分のところでだん折りをする。
Do "Dan-Ori" on the remaining flaps as shown.

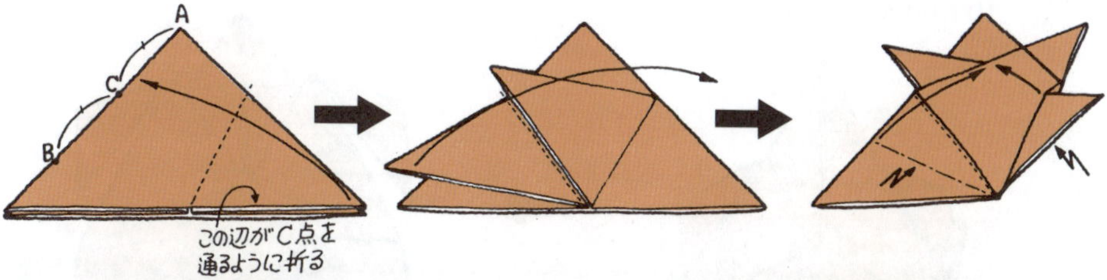

7 図のようになる。
It should look like this.

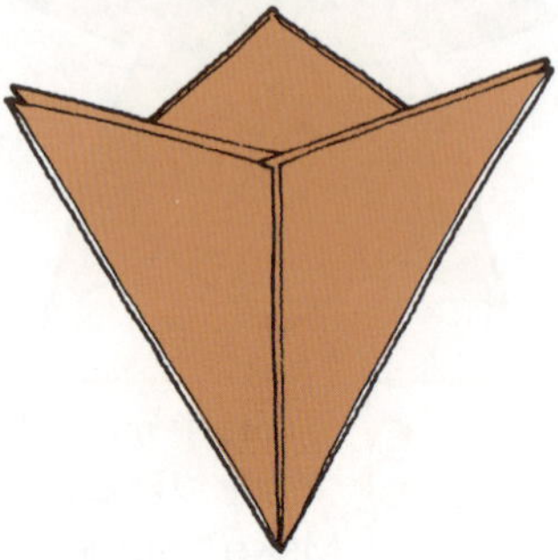

8 さかさにし、折り線どおりに折り上げる。
Turn upside down. Crease each flap as shown, then fold both corners up along the crease.

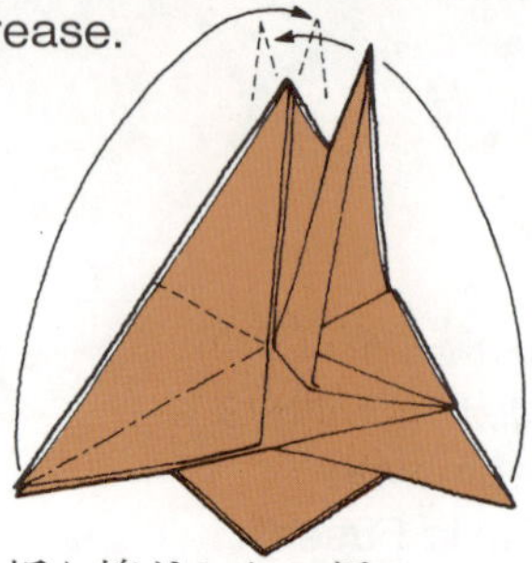

9 カドを外に出すように折る。
Do “Yama-Ori” on the top flaps to make forelegs.

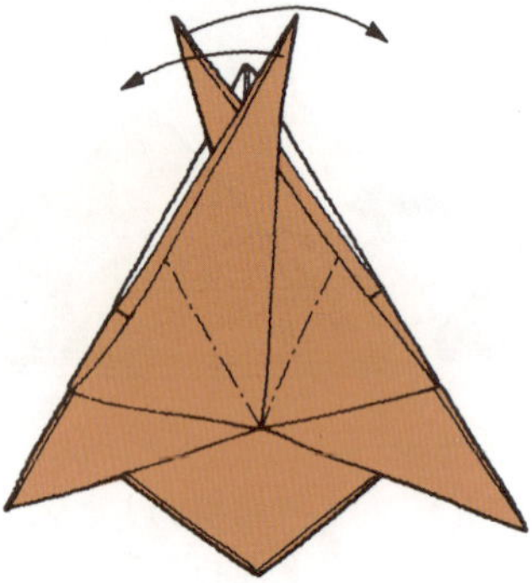

10 折り線どおりに折る。
Do “Tani-Ori” as shown to form forelegs and hind legs.

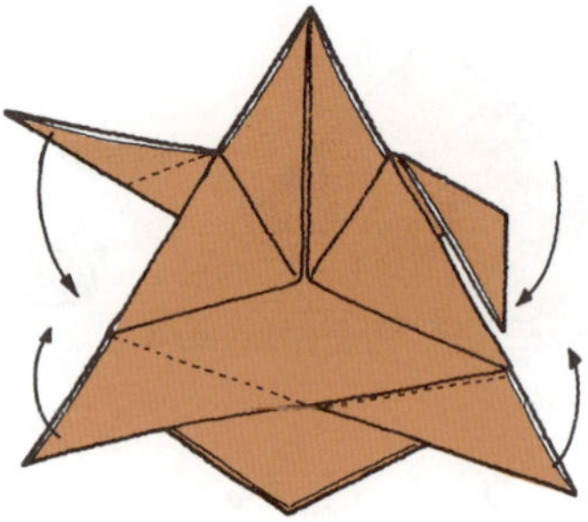

11 先のとがった部分はだん折りに、左右は折り下げる。
Fold the hind legs down. Do “Dan-Ori” on the top triangle to make the head.

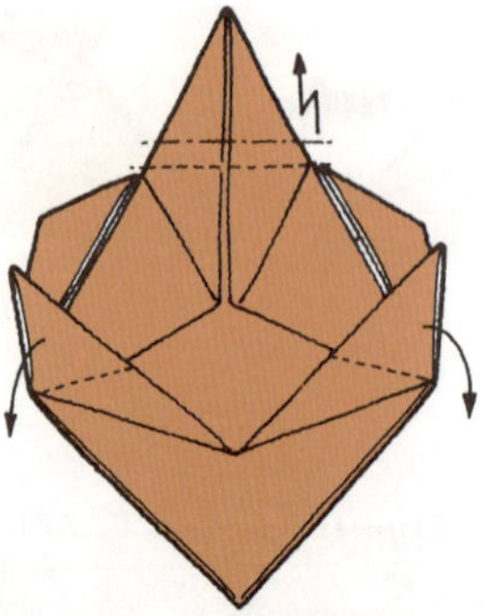

12 図のようになる。
It should look like this.

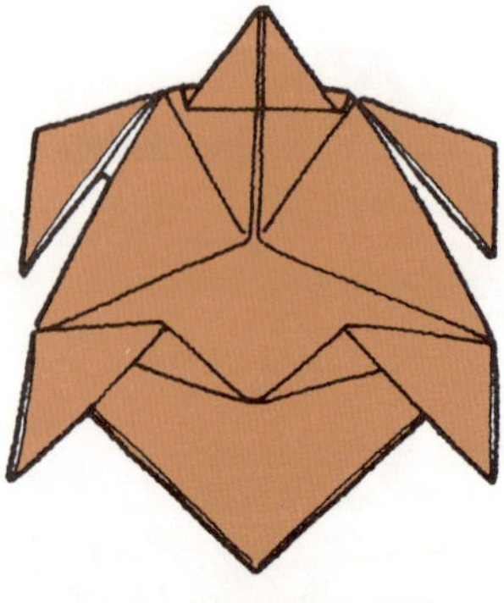

13 先の部分を折り上げ、開いてつぶす。
Open the tip of the foreleg and flatten.

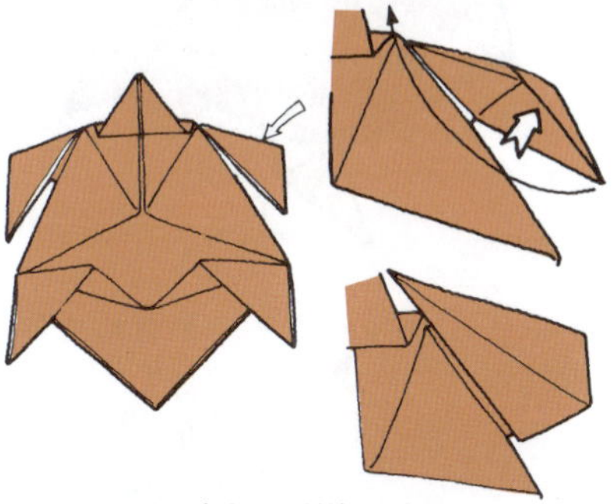

14 折り下げる。
Fold it downward as shown.

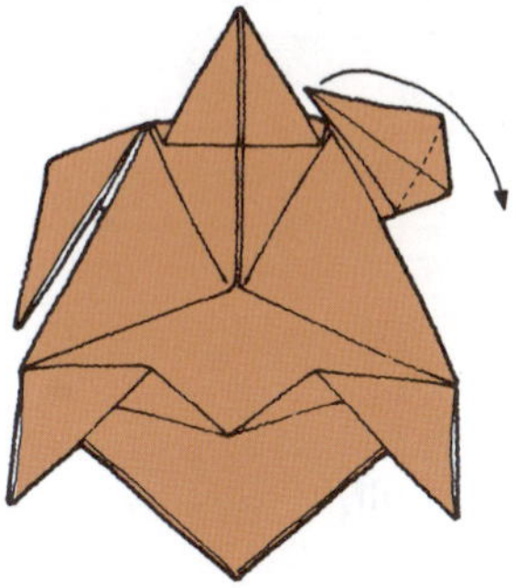

15 反対側も同様にする。
Do the same with the other one.

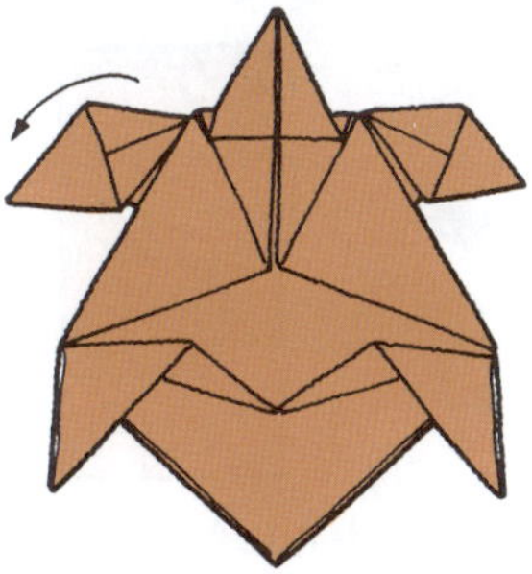

16 だん折りをする。
Do "Dan-Ori" on the bottom corner.

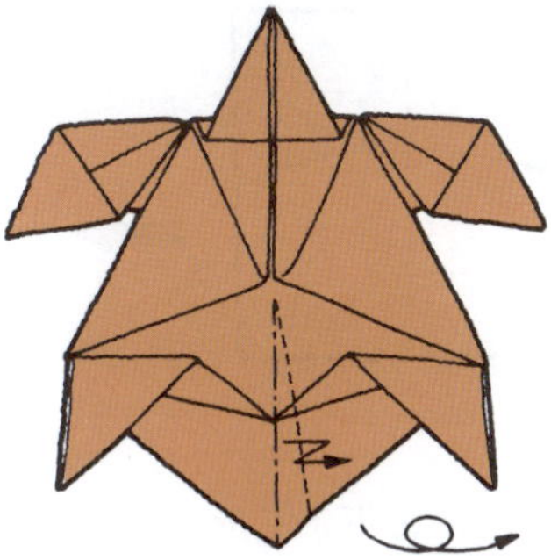

17 ひっくり返し、間に差し込むようにする。
Turn over. Tuck the tip in.

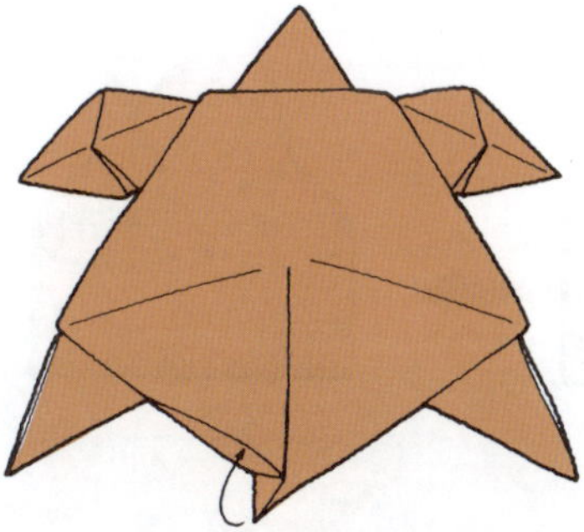

Finished

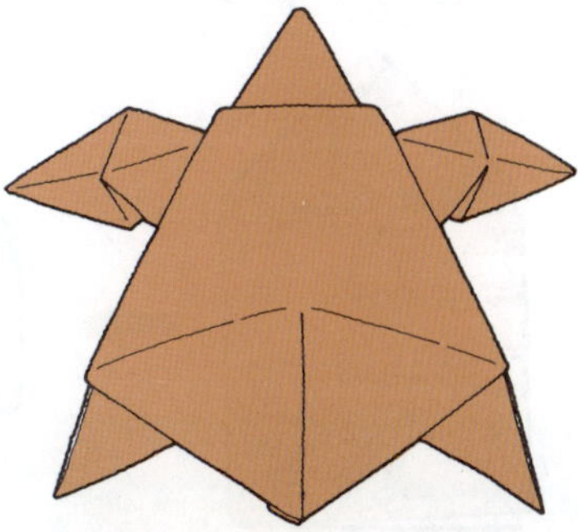

ピョンピョンがえる

Jumping Frog

1 半分に折る。
Fold in half.

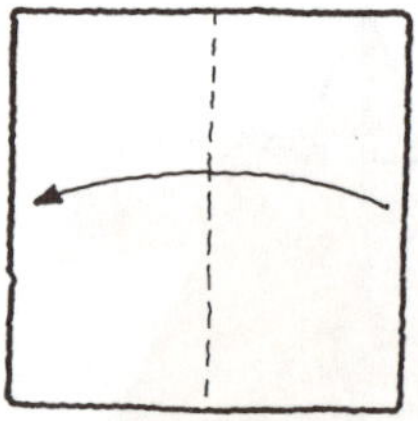

2 両カドを三角形に折り、もとに戻す。
Make creases as shown. unfold.

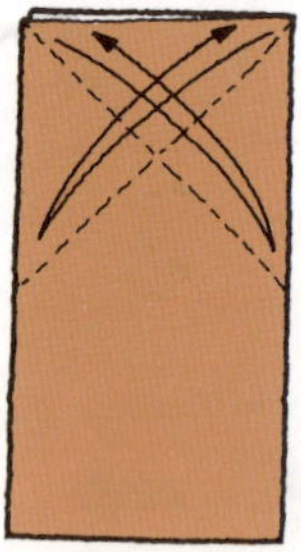

3 ○と○を合わせるようにして、三角形に折りたたむ。
Fold ○ and ○ in to meet at the center and fold the top down.

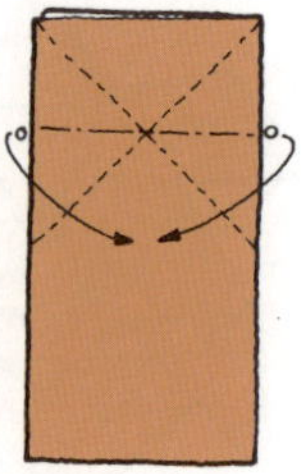

4 三角形の下まで折り上げる。
Fold the bottom edge up to the bottom of the triangle.

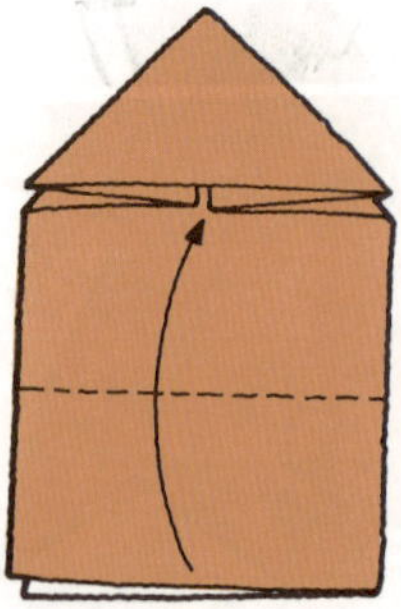

5 斜めに折り上げる。
Fold both corners of the top triangle up diagonally.

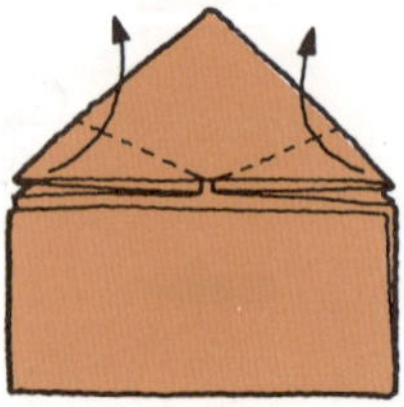

6 中心に合わせて、左右を折り合わせる。
Fold both sides to the center.

7 半分に折り上げ、またもとに戻す。
Fold the bottom up to the center. Unfold.

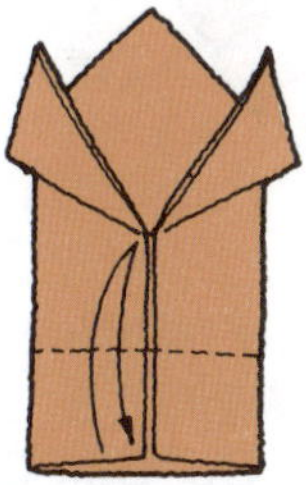

8 左右に押し広げる。
Open the pockets outside as shown.

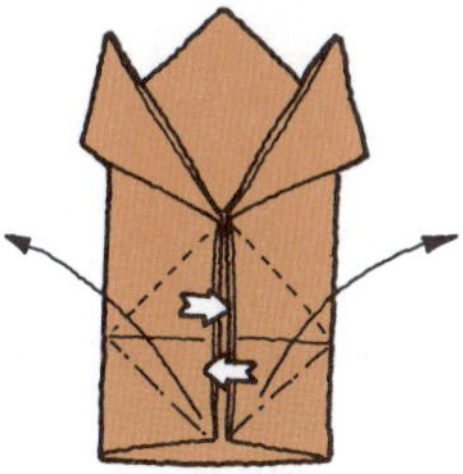

9 指を間にはさむと、広げやすい。
Inserting your forefinger in the bottom corners makes it easier.

10 左右を折り下げる。
Fold both corners down along the creases.

11 斜めに折る。
Fold the bottom flaps outside diagonally.

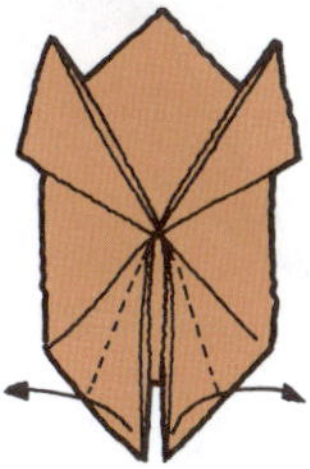

12 半分に折る。
Fold in half.

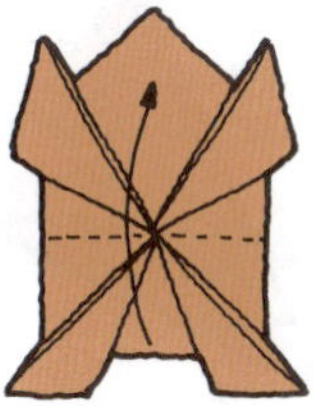

13 半分に折る。
Fold the top rectangle down.

14 図のようになる。
It should look like this.

15 裏返して、目をかく。
Turn over. Draw the eyes.

Finished

えび

Shrimp

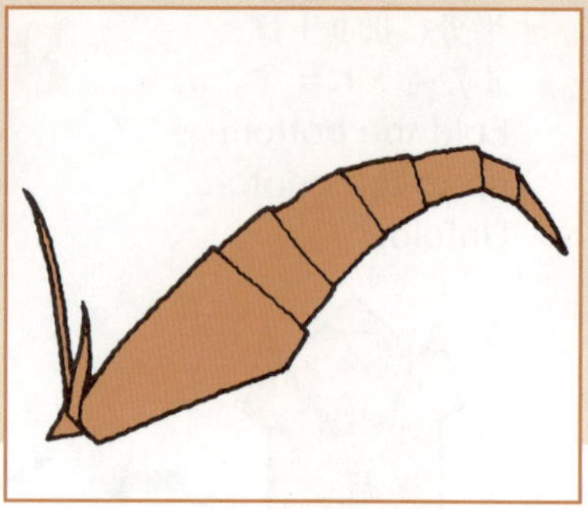

1 凧の基本形（P22参照）から始める。中心線に合わせて折る。
Begin with "Basic Kite"(See P22). Fold both sides to the center.

2 上の三角形も中心線に合わせて折る。
Fold the top corners to the center line.

3 だん折りで、頭部をつくる。
Do "Dan-Ori" to make the head.

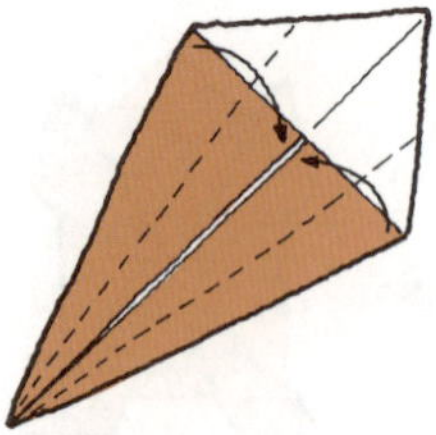

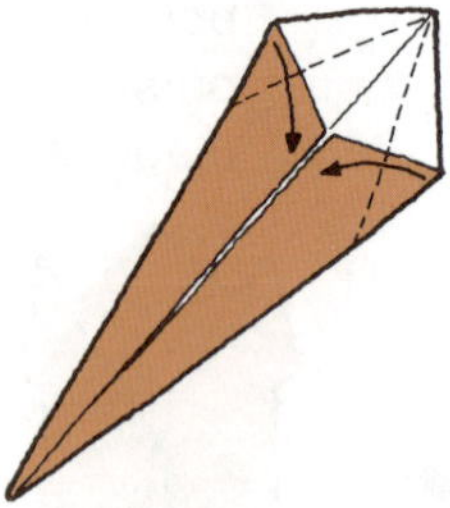

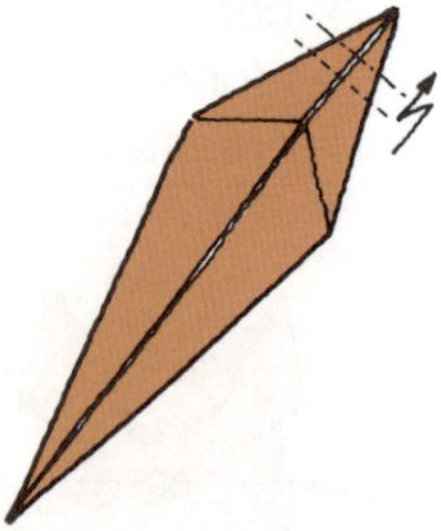

4 上の２枚を図のように切る。
Cut the 2 flaps as shown.

5 ひげを上に折り返す。背になる部分を図のように折る。
Fold the flaps upward. Do "Dan-Ori" and "Tani-Ori" as shown.

6 形を整える。
Arrange as shown.

Finished

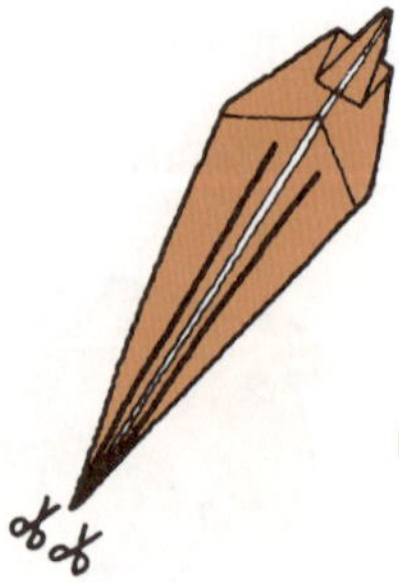

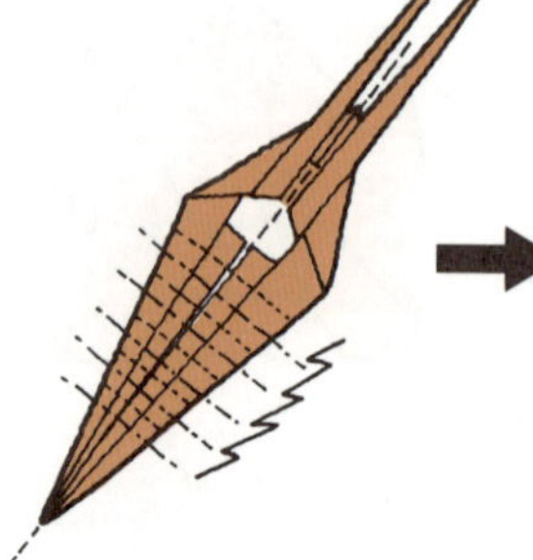

カジキマグロ

Tuna

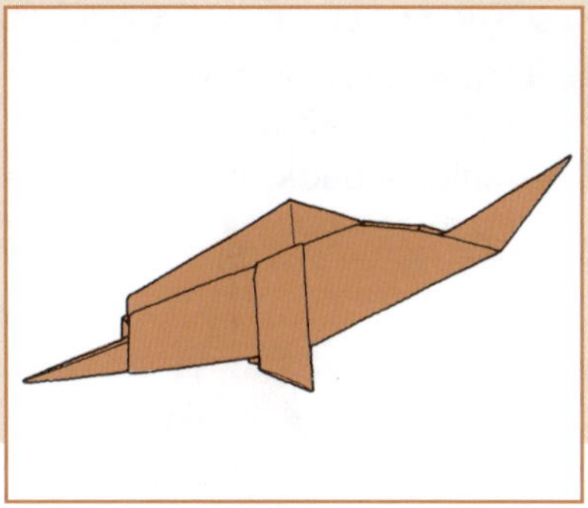

1 裏を出し、魚の基本形（P 130参照）から始める。図のように折りすじをつける。
Begin with “Basic Fish”. Make a crease as shown.

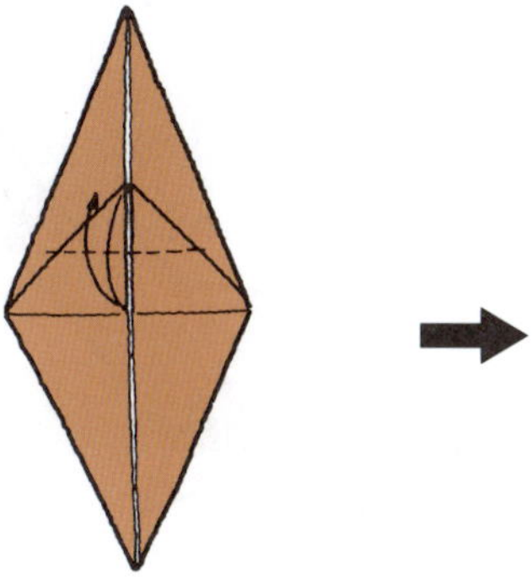

2 1の折りすじ、中心に合わせて２本の折りすじをつけ、だん折りにする。
Make 2 creases as shown, do "Dan-Ori”.

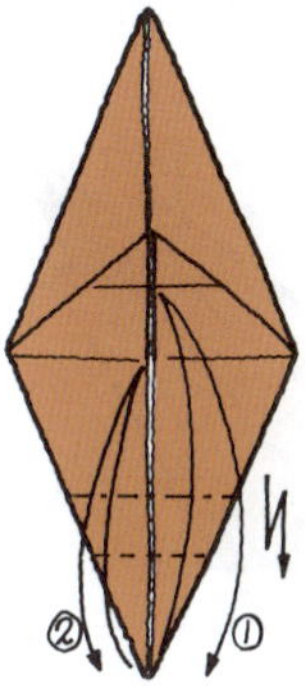

3 A：中央の三角形を中心に向かって折り下げる。
B：裏返し、ひきよせ折りにする。
A：Fold the center flaps to the center line as shown.
B：Turn over. Do “Hikiyose-Ori”.

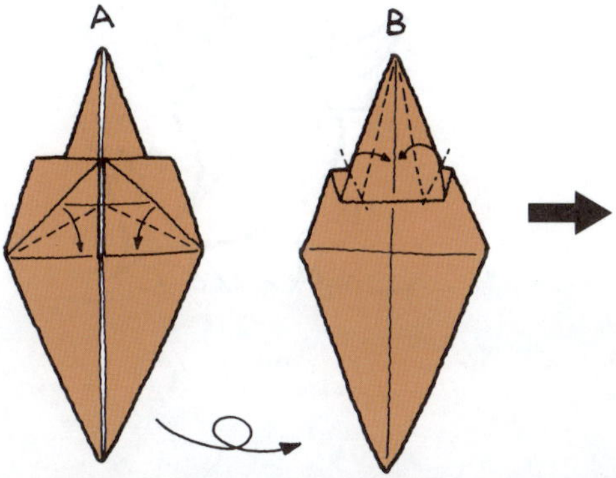

4 中心に向かって折る。
Fold the upper edges to the center.

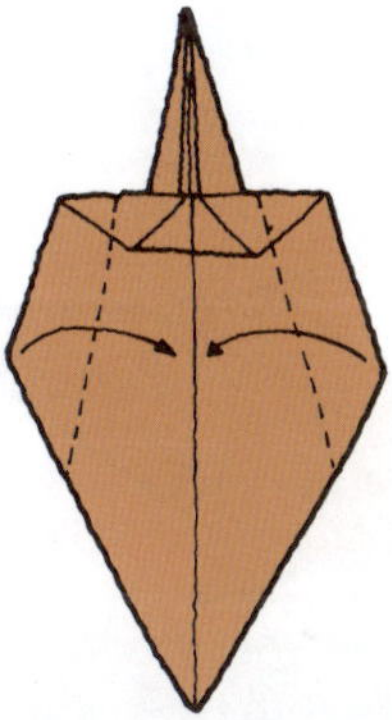

5 左側だけ外に出るように折る。※背ビレをできるだけ大きくとる。
Fold the left side outside to make a back fin. ※Make it as big as possible.

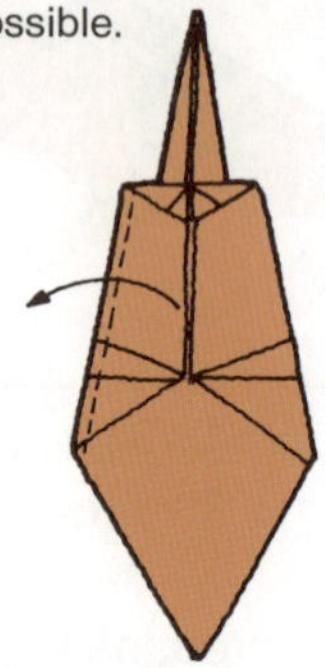

6 半分に折る。
Fold in half to the left.

7 中わり折りにする。
Do “Nakawari-Ori” on the bottom.

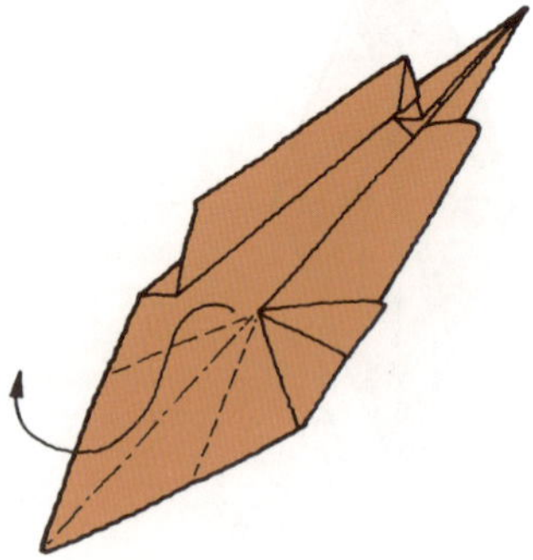

8 それぞれ内側へ折り込む。
Fold both sides inside.

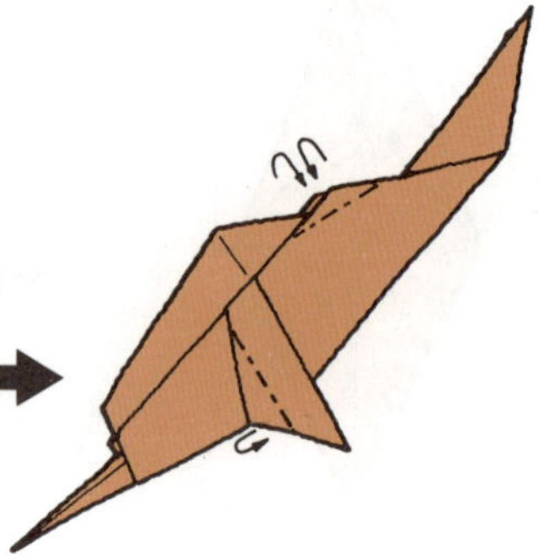

Finished

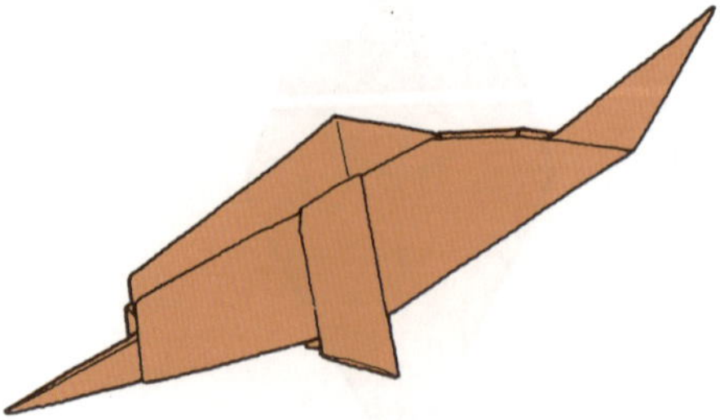

エイ

Ray

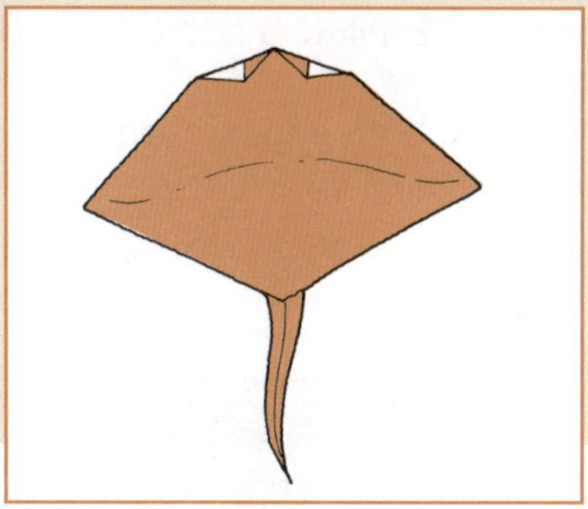

1 凧の基本形（P 22参照）から始める。
Begin with “Basic Kite”(See P22).

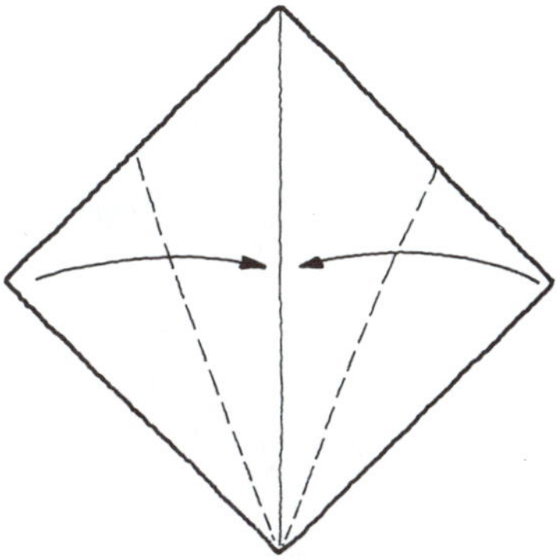

2 折り線どおりに折り上げる。
Bring the right edge up and lay it along the bottom edge of the white triangle, then fold the left corner up.

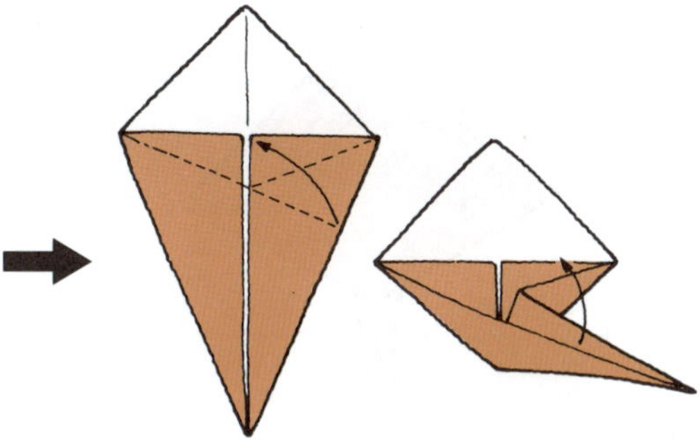

3 中心に戻して開いてつぶす。
Bring the right corner to the center, then open and flatten.

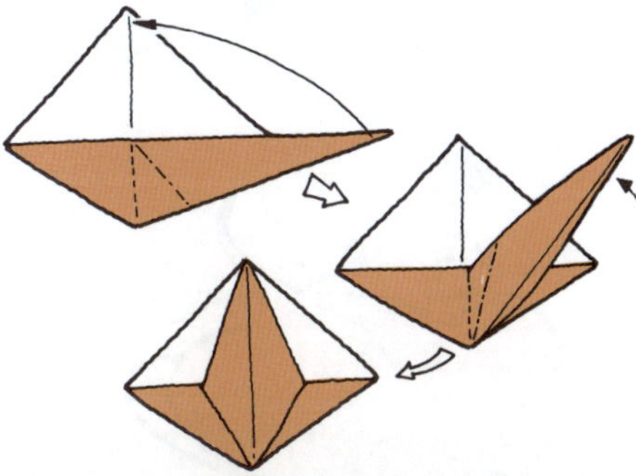

4 折り鶴の羽を折るように折り下げる。
Fold it downward, then fold both edges in to the center.

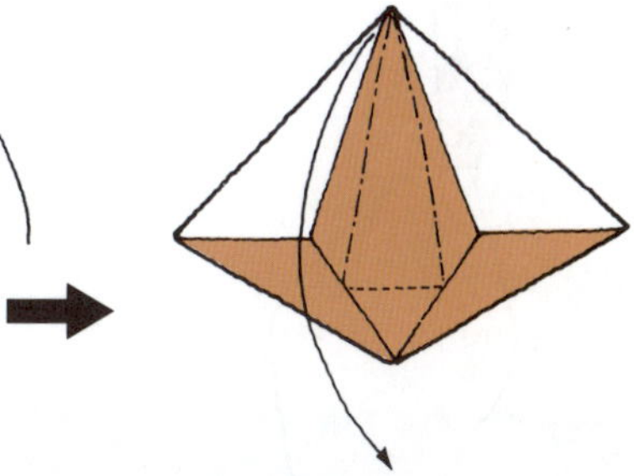

5 左右を中心に合わせて折って細くする。
Fold both edges in again.

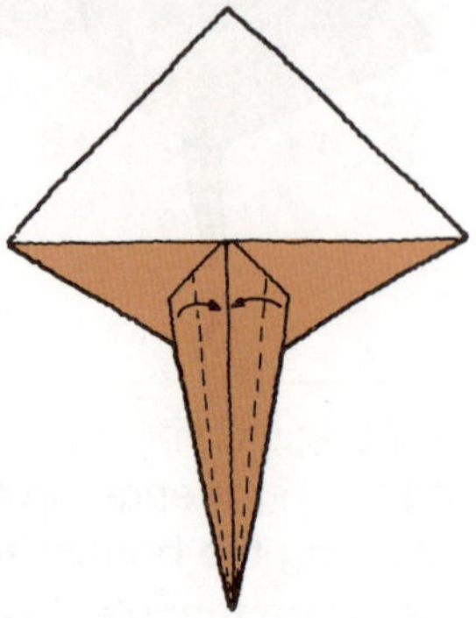

6 カドを折り下げる。
Fold the top corner frontward.

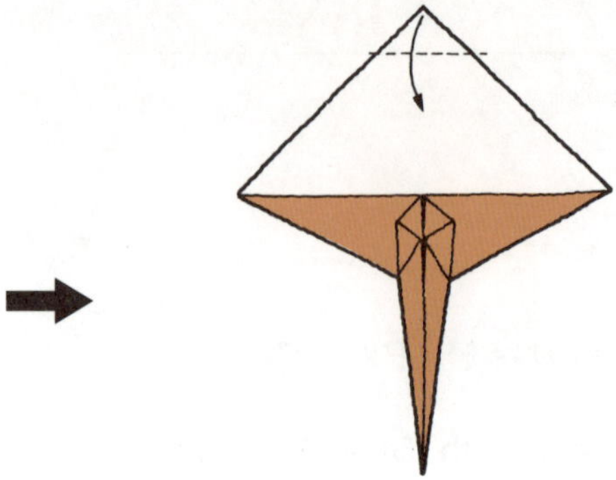

7 ひっくり返して、カドを折る。
Turn over. Fold both tips of the top corners to make eyes.

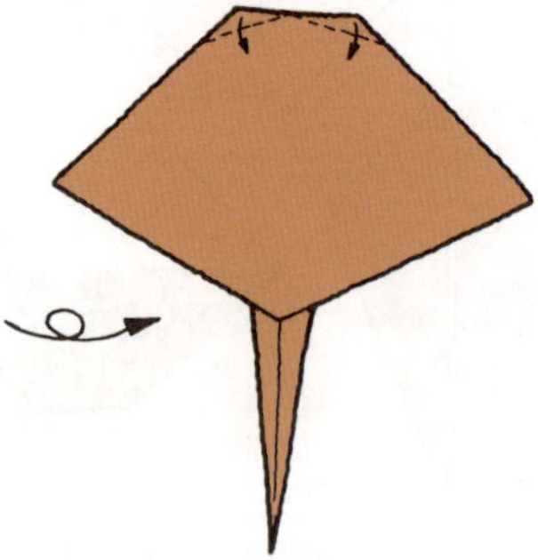

8 しっぽをしぼるようにして形を作る。
Fold the tail in half along the center, then undulate slightly.

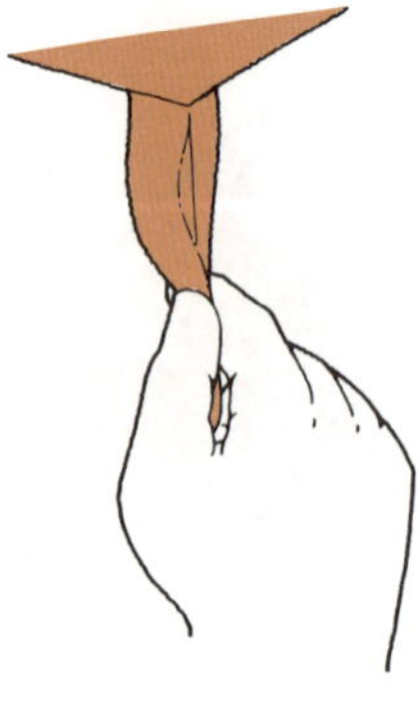

Finished

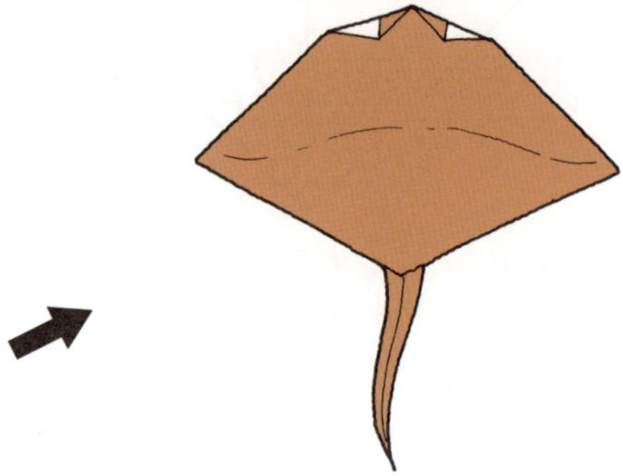

Chapter 6

昆虫
Insects

かたつむり

Snail

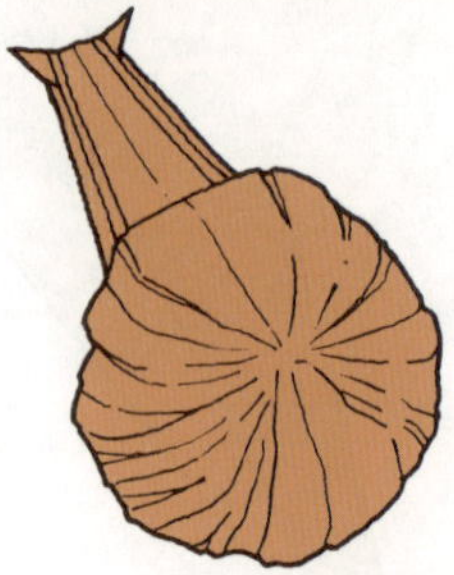

1 正方基本形（P 25参照）から始める。
Begin with "Basic Square" (See P25).

2 左右を中心線に合わせるように折る。裏側も同様に折る。
Fold both corners to the center. Do the same with the reverse side.

3 もとにもどす。
Unfold.

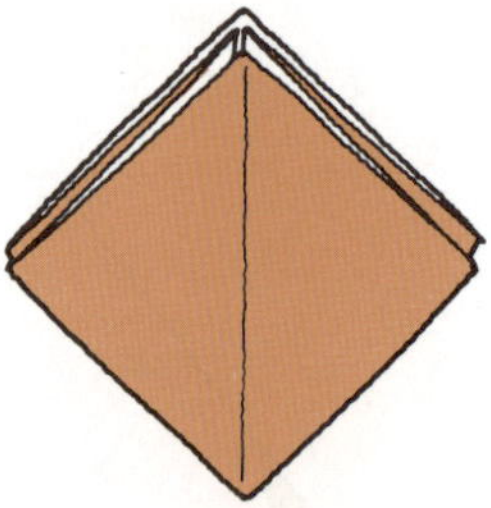

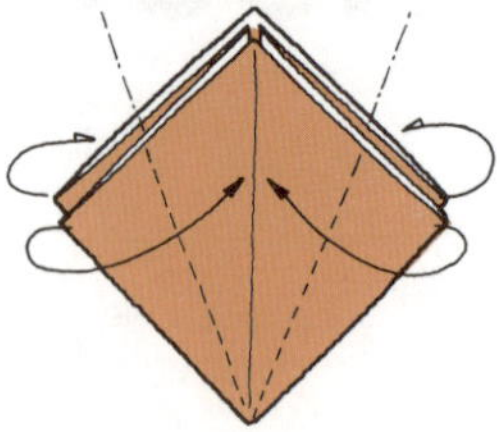

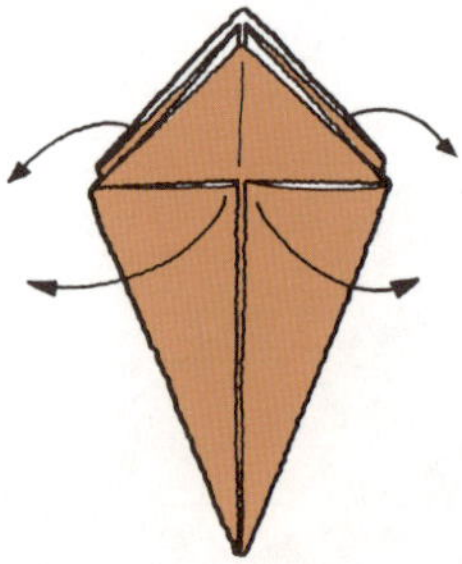

4 内側を広げて、つぶすように折る。
Open the top sheet and flatten to make a triangle.

5 右の内側の１枚を左に重ねる。
Fold the right flap to the left.

6 右の袋になっている部分を、**4**と同様に折る。裏側も同様に折る。
Repeat steps **4-6** on the other sheets.

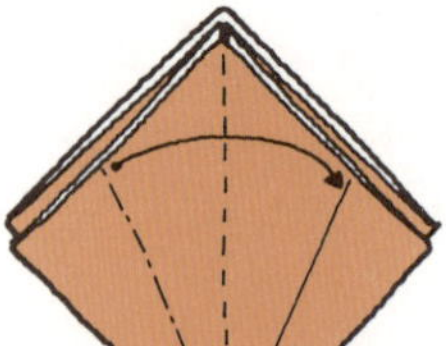

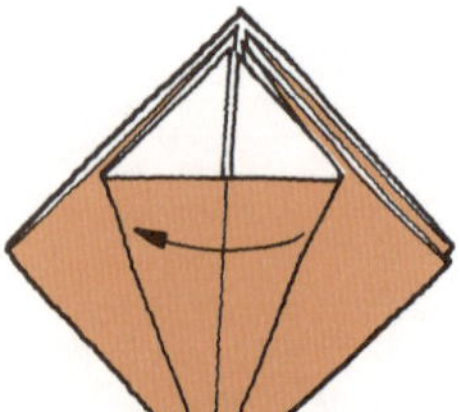

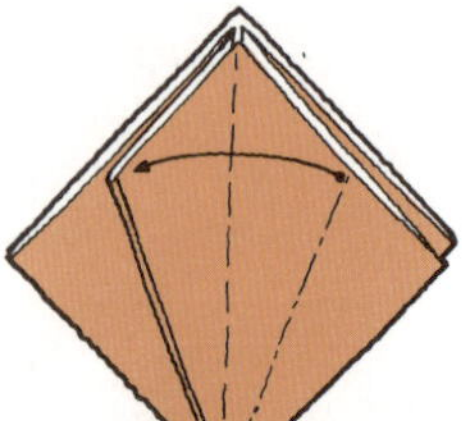

7 右側だけ３等分した角度で折る。
Trisect the top right flap.

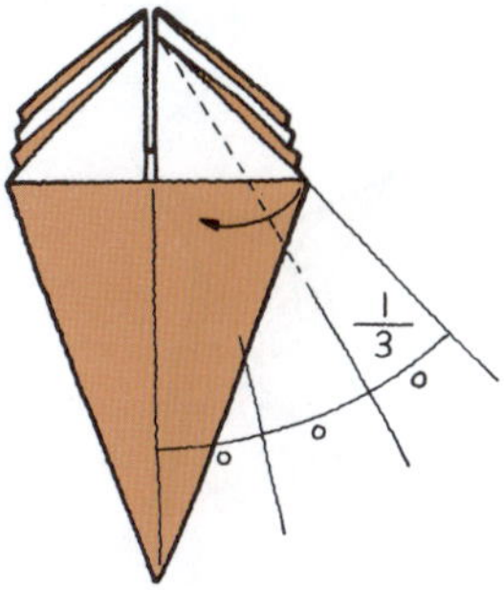

8 中心に合わせるようにして、折る。
Fold it to the center.

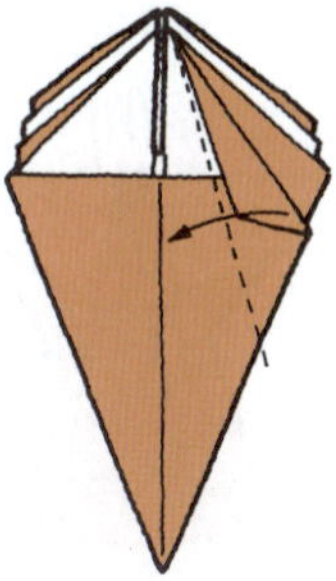

9 左側は、中心の線に合わせて折る。
Fold the top left flap to the center.

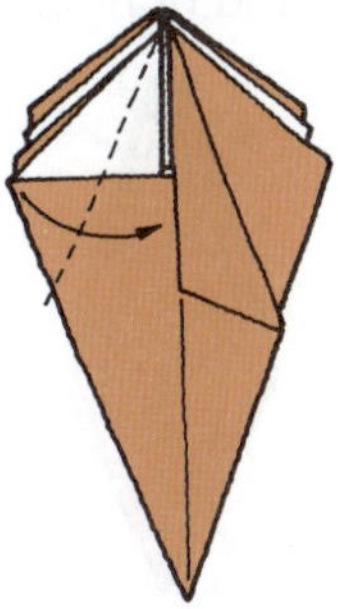

10 半分に折る。
Fold in half again.

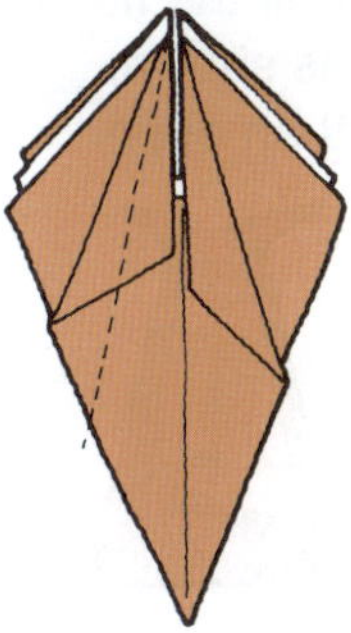

11 裏側も7から10の順に折る。
Repeat steps 7～10 on the reverse side.

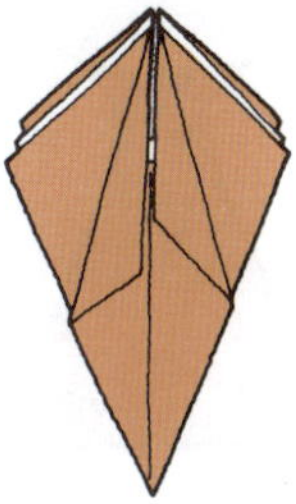

12 右の１枚を折る。裏側も同様に。
Fold the right flap over to the left. Do the same with the reverse side.

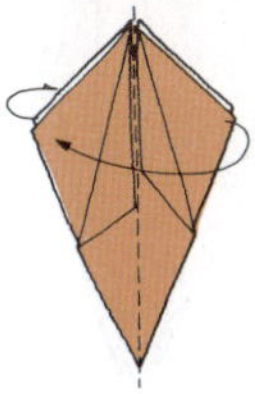

13 右側を半分、左側を３等分に、7～10の順で折る。裏側も同様に。
Fold the right side in half and trisect the left side. Repeat steps 7～10. Do the same with the reverse side.

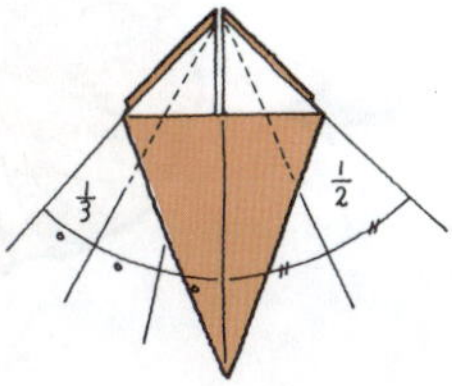

14 上の１枚を左に重ねる。裏側も同様に折る。
Fold the top right flap over to the left. Do the same with the reverse side.

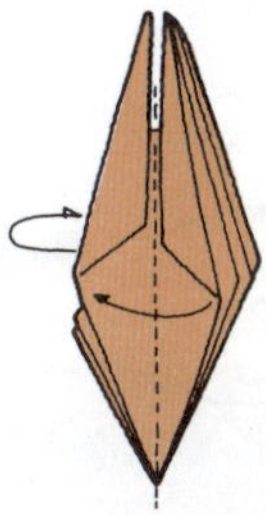

15 左右を中わり折りにする。
Do "Nakawari-Ori" on the left and right sides.

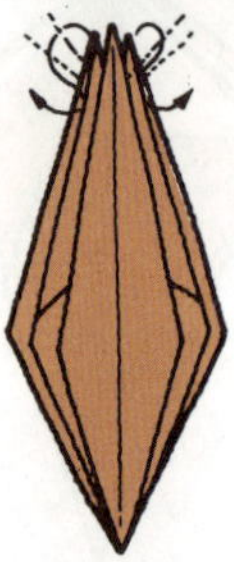

16 それぞれカドを内側に折り込む。
Fold the tips inside.

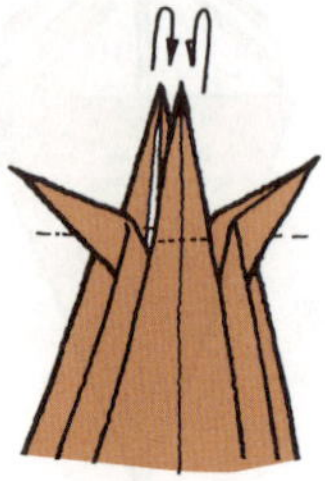

17 図のようになる。
It should look like this.

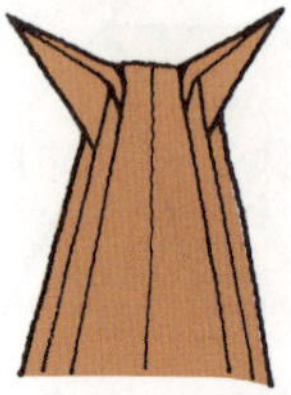

18 半分に折り目をつける。
Fold in half.

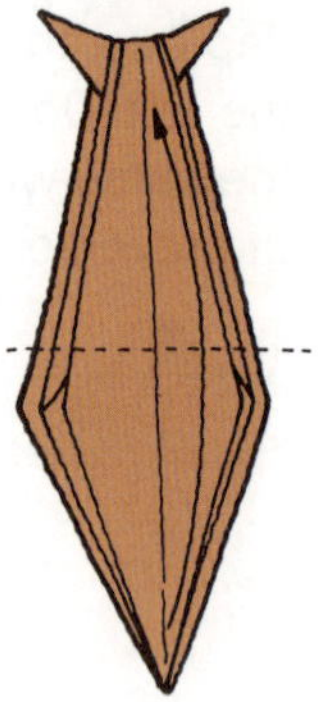

19 戻す。
Unfold.

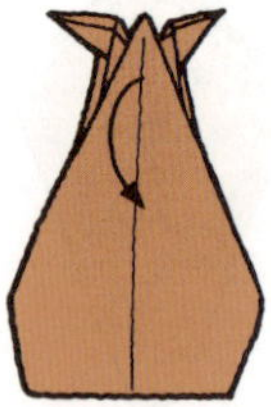

20 矢印の方向に引っぱりながら開く。
Pull the flaps as shown, then open.

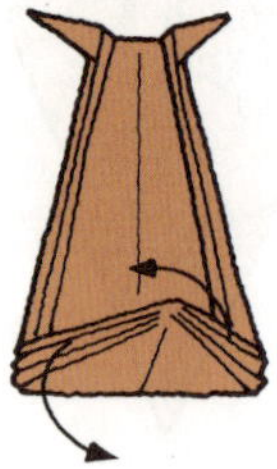

21 からの部分を丸くする。
Round out the bottom.

22 形をきれいに整える。
Shape into a snail

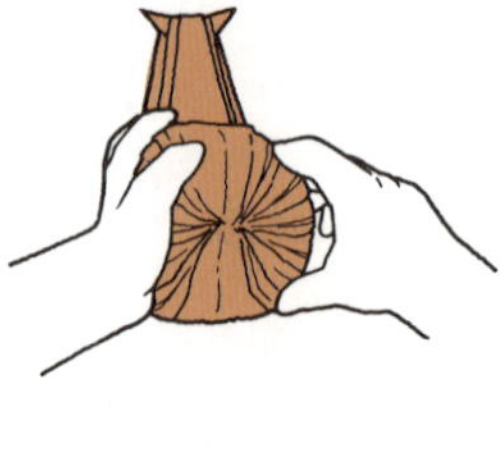

Finished

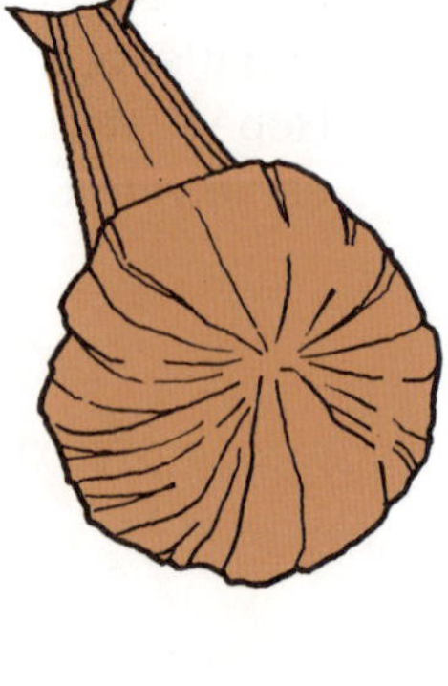

とんぼ

Dragonfly

1 鶴の基本形（P 27参照）から始める。
Begin with "Basic Turu" (See P27).

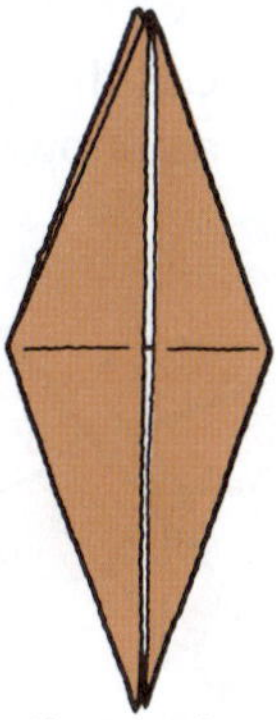

2 中心に合わせて折る。裏側も同様に。
Fold the front flaps to the center. Do the same with the reverse side.

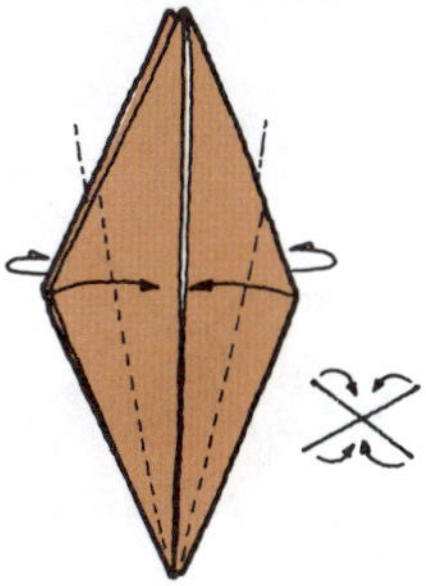

3 開くように折る。
Fold the left flap to the right.

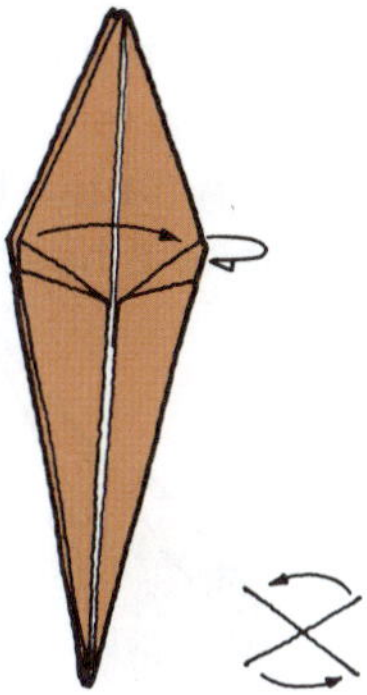

4 手前のカドを折る。
Fold the front bottom flap upward.

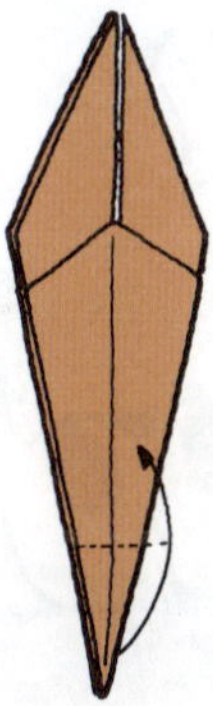

5 開くように折る。
Fold the right flap to the left.

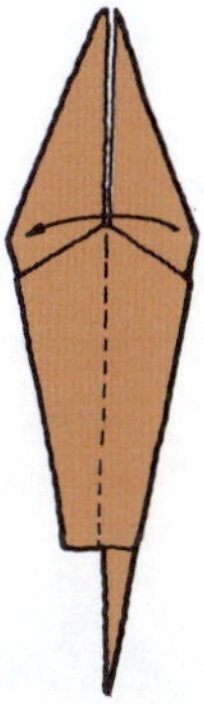

6 中わり折りをする。
Do "Nakawari-Ori" on the bottom flap.

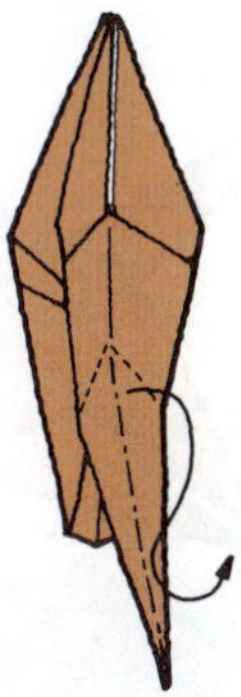

7 反対側も中わり折りをする。
Do “Nakawari-Ori” on the left side.

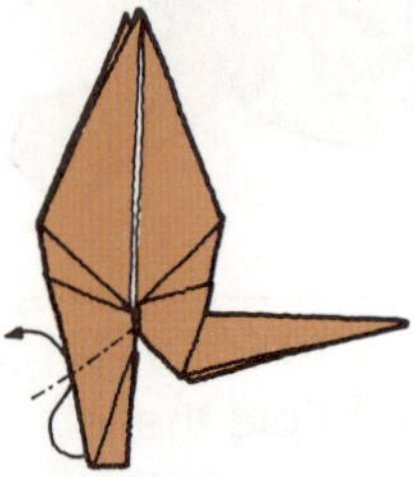

8 折り下げる。裏側も同様に折る。
Fold the top flap downward. Do the same with the reverse side.

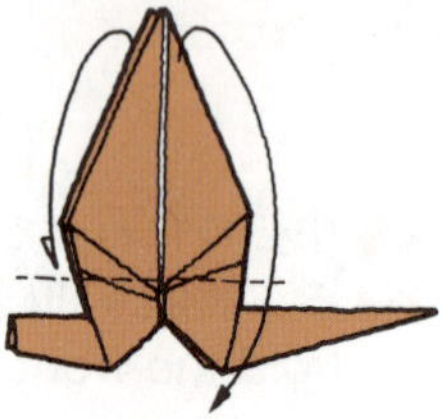

9 カドをすきまに折り込むようにする。
Put the top triangle into the front pocket.

10 つまむように折る。
Open the tip on the left, then flatten to make a head.

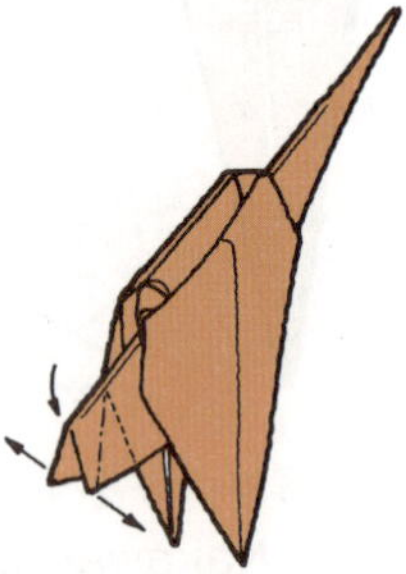

11 羽の部分を広げる。
Bring the center flaps up.

12 図のようにはさみで切る。
Cut the wings as shown.

Finished

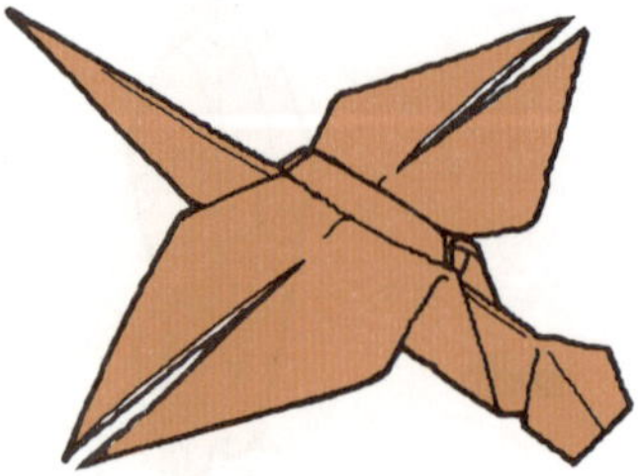

バッタ

Grasshopper

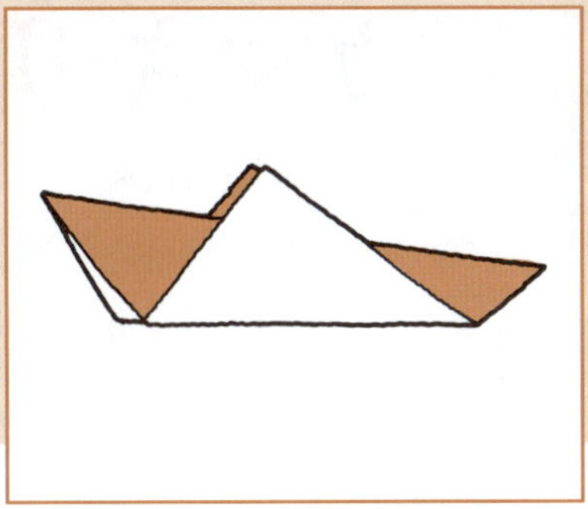

1 半分に折る。
Fold in half to make a triangle.

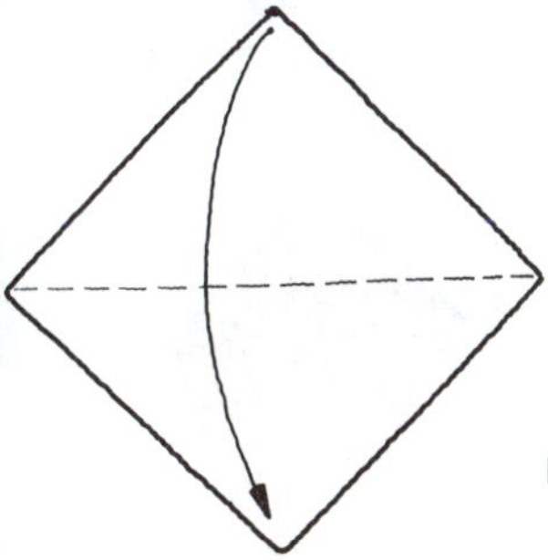

2 斜めに折り上げる。
Fold the front sheet up diagonally as shown.

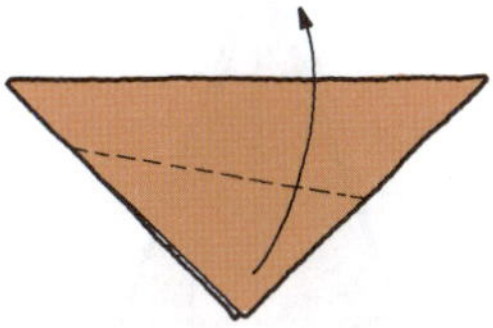

3 図のようになる。
It should look like this.

4 ひっくり返し、裏側に合わせて折る。
Turn over. Fold the bottom corner up to meet the top corner.

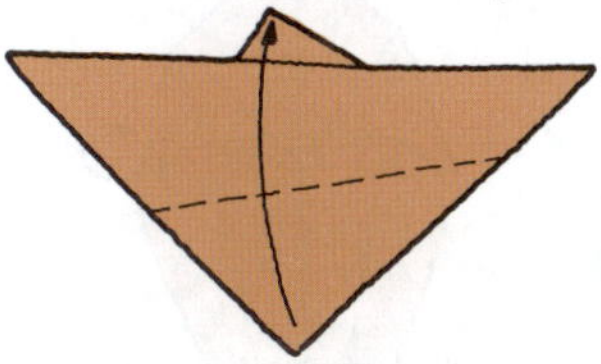

Finished

※カドをはじくようにすると、はねる。小さい紙で折ると、よく飛ぶ。

※Flick the head and it jumps. It works best if you use small size paper.

カマキリ

Mantis

1 鶴の基本形（P 27参照）から始める。
Begin with "Basic Turu" (See P27).

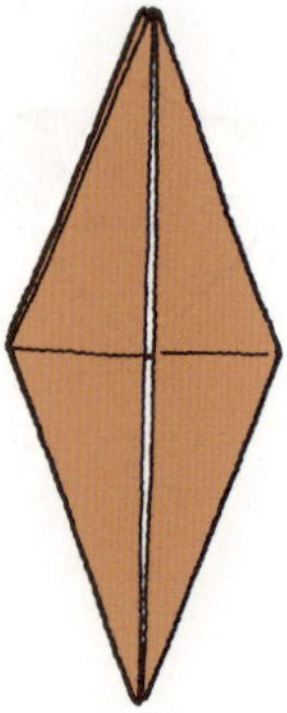

2 半分に折る。
Fold in half.

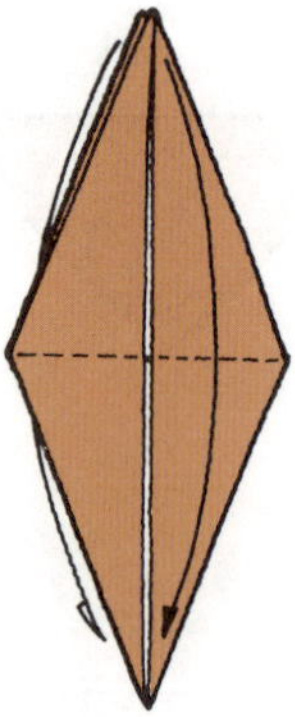

3 中心に合わせて折る。裏側も同様に。
Fold the front flaps. Do the same with the reverse side.

4 折りすじをつける。
Fold both corners of the front flaps outside. Unfold.

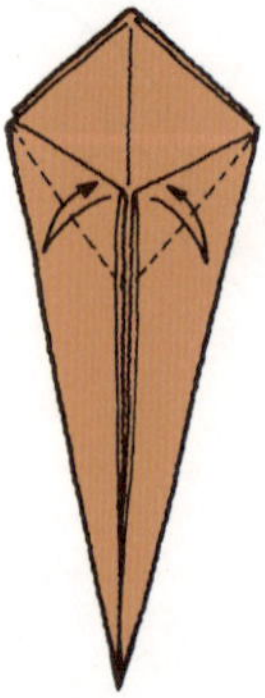

5 カドを開く。裏側も同様にする。
Open the front flaps and flatten. Do the same with the reverse side.

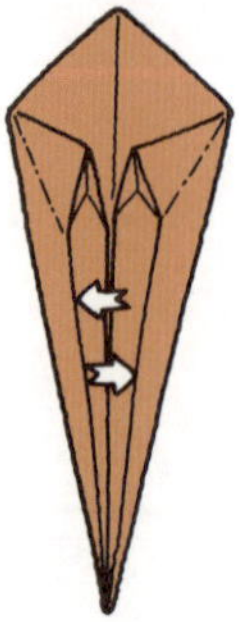

6 半分に折る。裏側も同様に折る。
Fold the left flap to the right. Do the same with the reverse side.

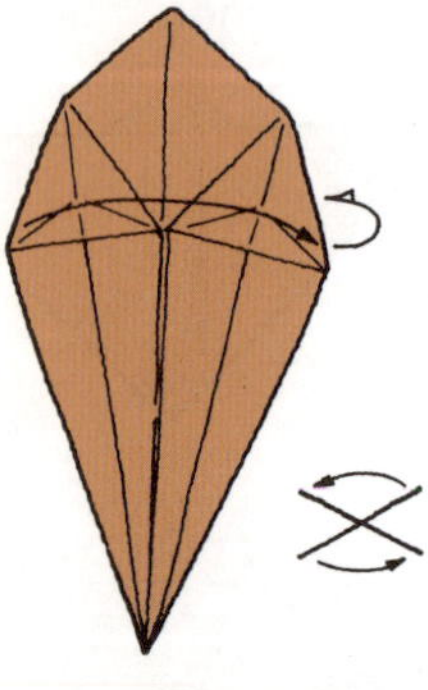

7 中心に合わせて折る。
Fold both flaps to the center.

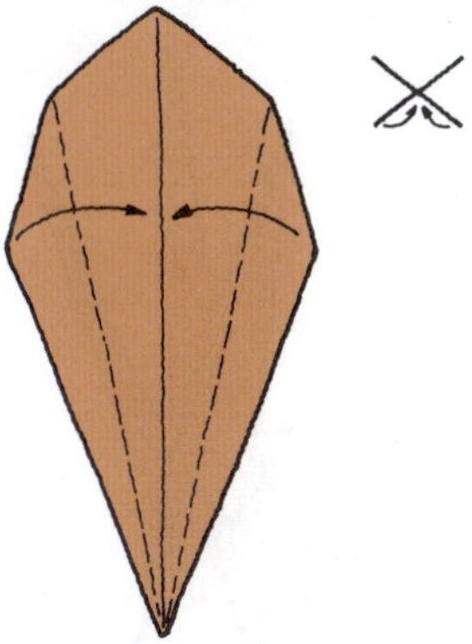

8 図のようになる。
It should look like this.

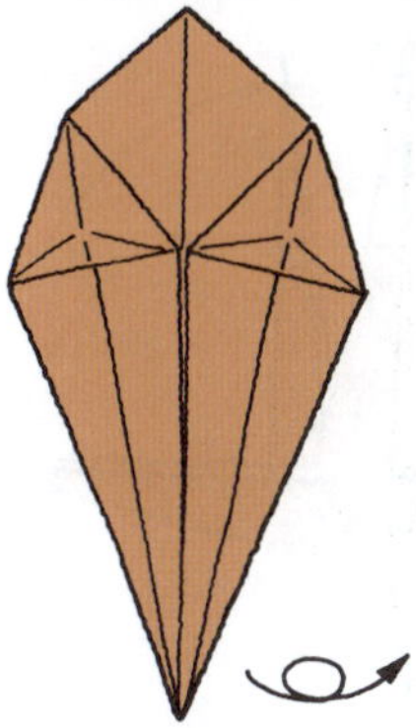

9 ひっくり返し、折り上げる。
Turn over. Fold the front flap up.

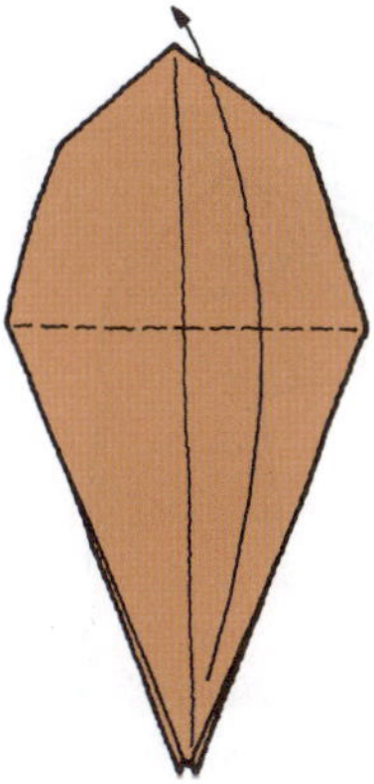

10 カドを折り下げる。
Fold the top corner down.

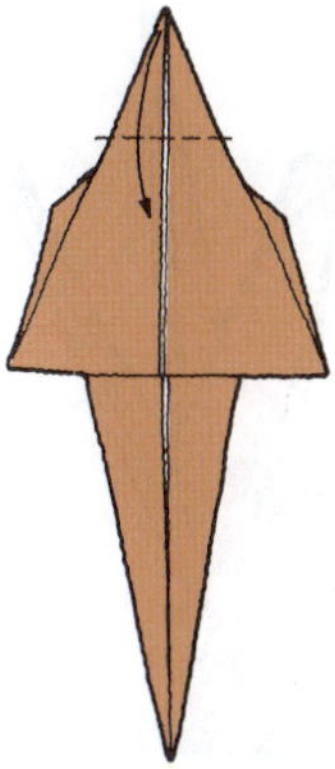

11 半分に折る。
Fold in half to the right.

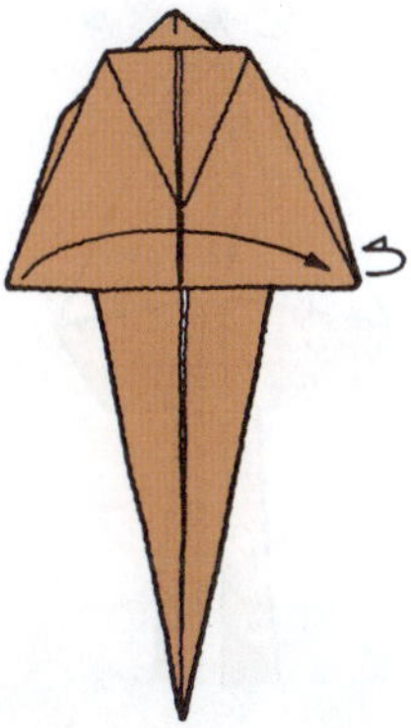

12 かぶせ折りをする。
Do “Kabuse-Ori” as shown.

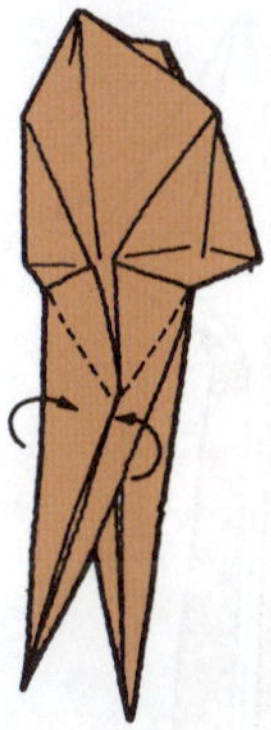

13 図のようになる。
It should look like this.

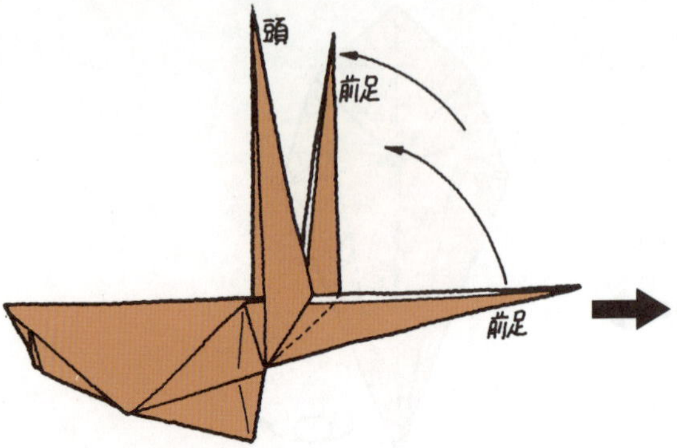

14 頭のところを中わり折りする。
Do "Nakawari-Ori" on the head.

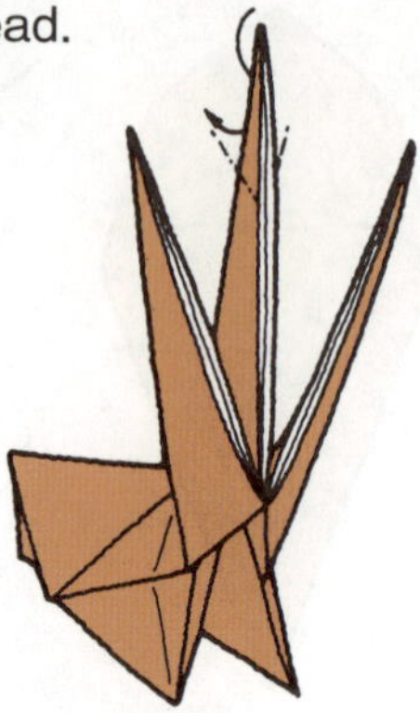

15 開くように折る。
Open the corner and flatten.

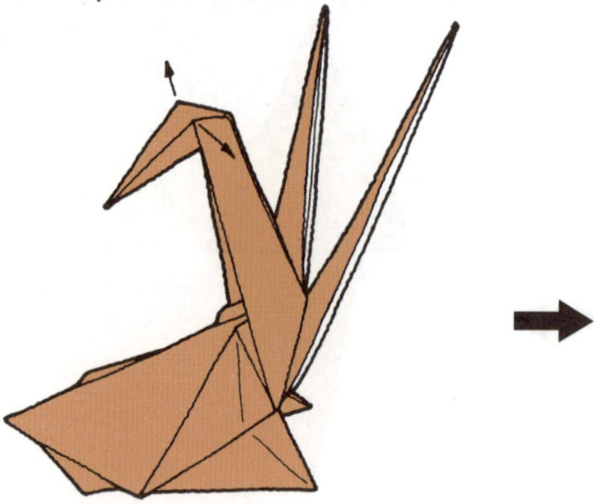

16 反対側に折る。
Fold the left corner to the right.

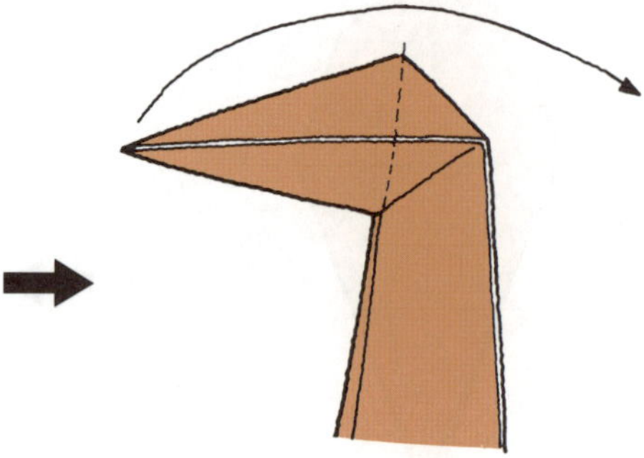

17 裏側を引き出すようにする。
Pull out the backside.

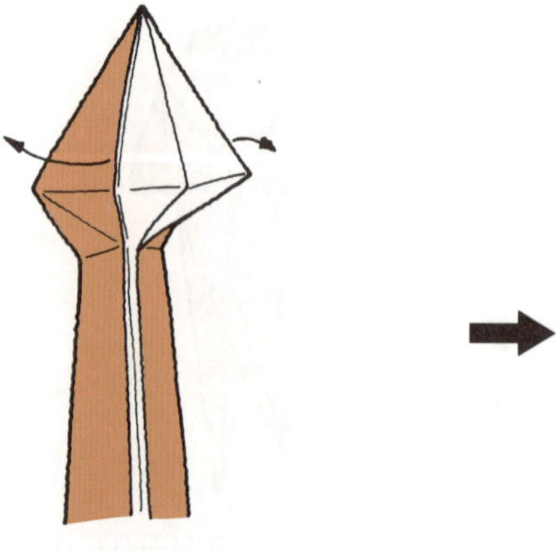

18 半分に折る。
Fold in half to the bottom.

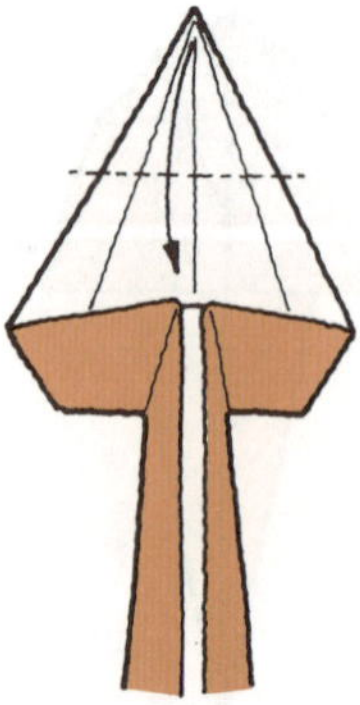

19
内側に折る。
Fold both corners in to the center.

20
裏側に折る。
Fold both sides backward a little.

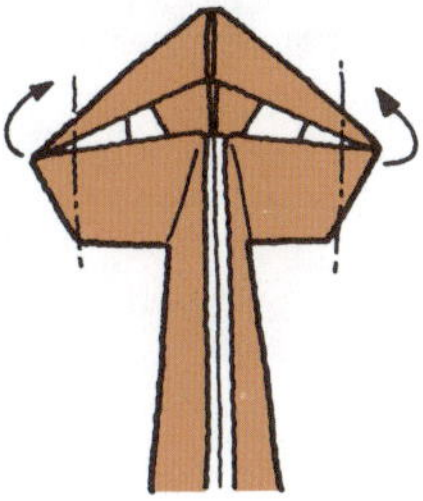

21
前足のところを折り下げる。
Fold the forelegs downward.

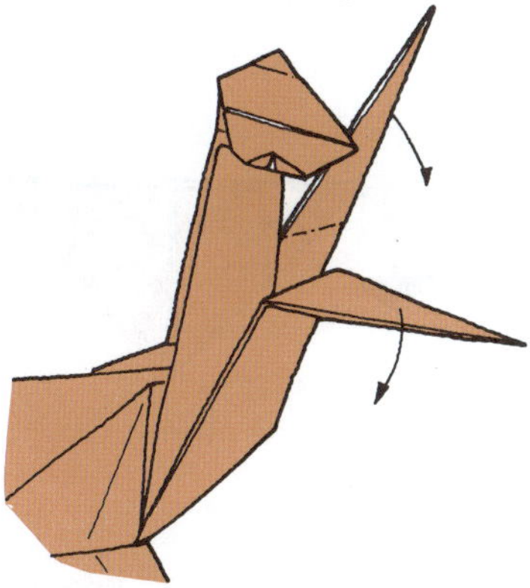

22
中わり折りをする。
Do “Nakawari-Ori” on the tips of the forelegs.

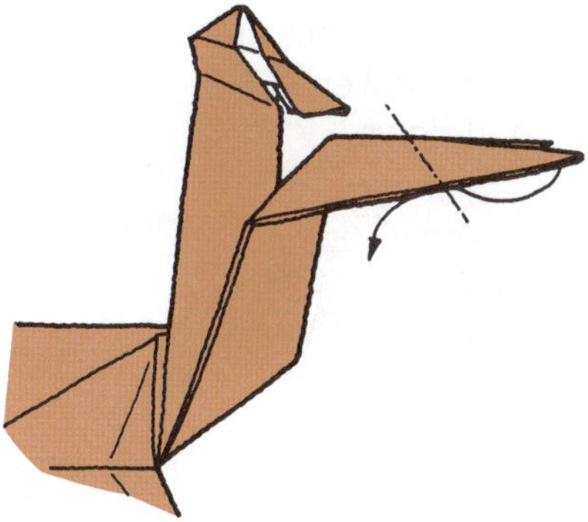

23
だん折りをする。
Do “Dan-Ori” on the bottom.

Finished

ちょうちょう

Butterfly

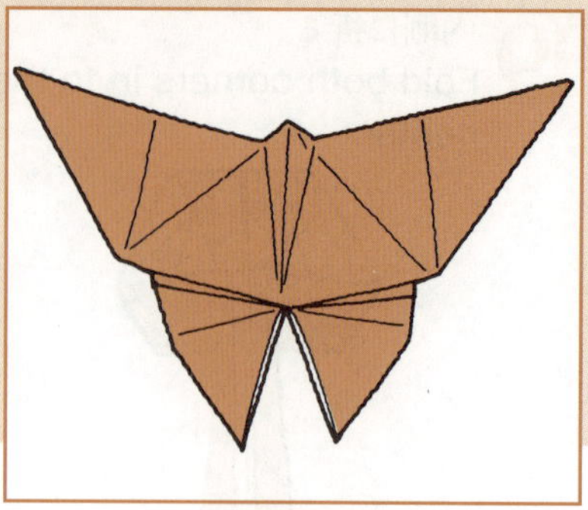

1 二そう舟基本形（P 23参照）から始め、端を折る。
Begin with "Basic Nisoubune" (See P23).
Fold the left and right corners of the lower part down.

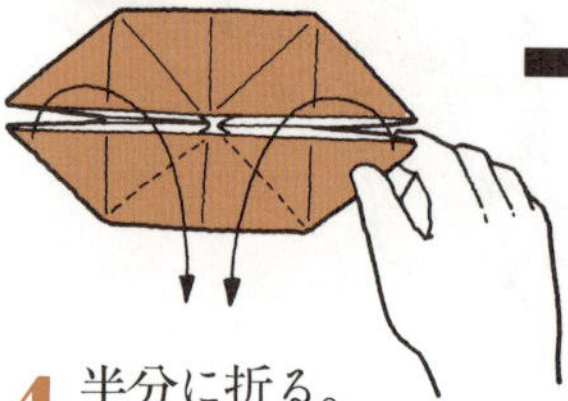

2 裏側へ折る。
Fold the upper part backward.

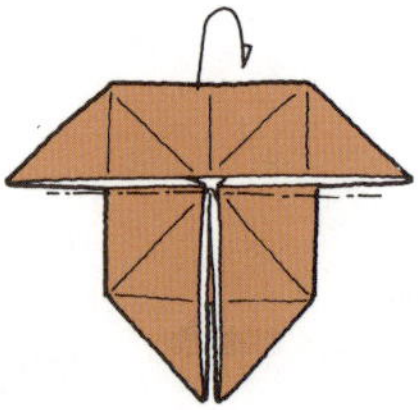

3 左右の上の１枚を折る。
Fold the corners of the front flaps in as shown.

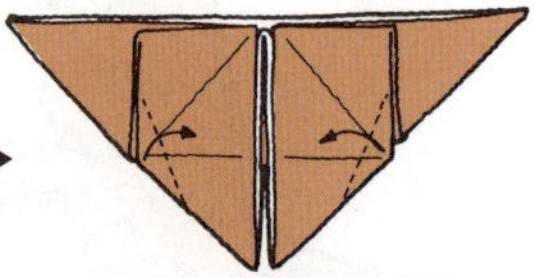

4 半分に折る。
Fold in half to the left.

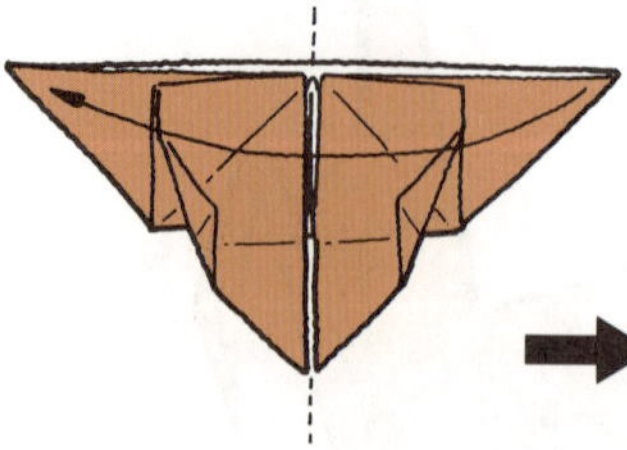

5 谷折りをしたあと、山折りもし、折りすじをつけ開く。
Make creases by "Tani-Ori" and "Yama-Ori", then open.

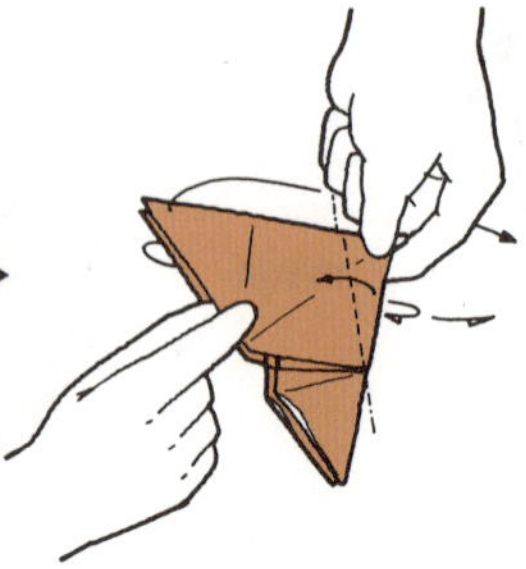

Finished

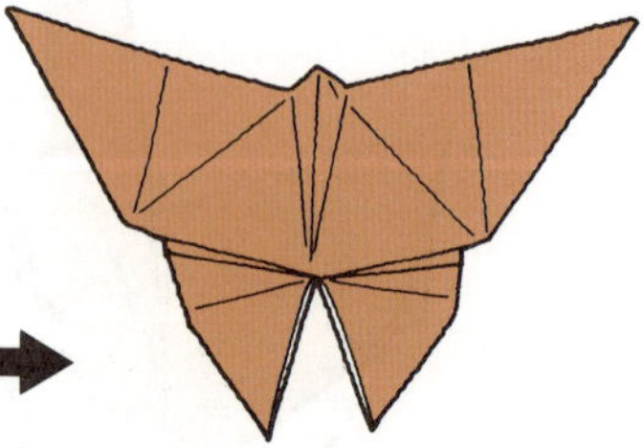

飛ぶちょうちょう
Flying Butterfly

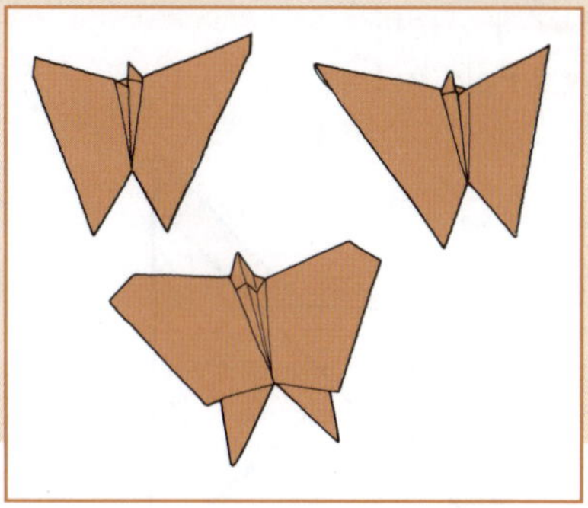

飛ぶちょうちょう①
Flying Butterfly①

1 裏を出して折りすじをつける。
Make diagonal creases.

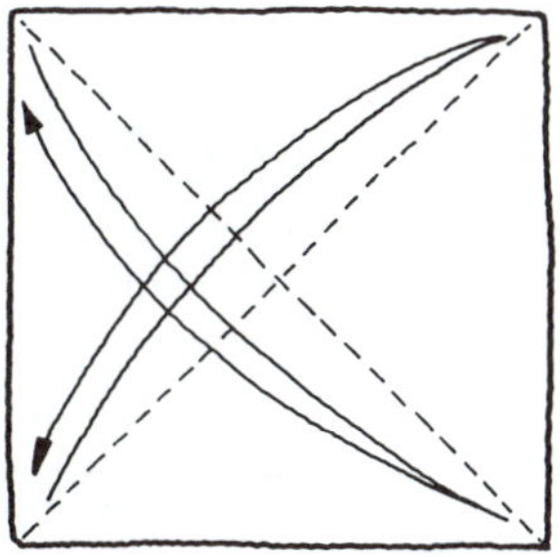

2 図のように折りすじをつけ、中央の折りすじに合わせるように折る。
Fold in half to the center to make a crease. Unfold. Fold the left corner in along the crease.

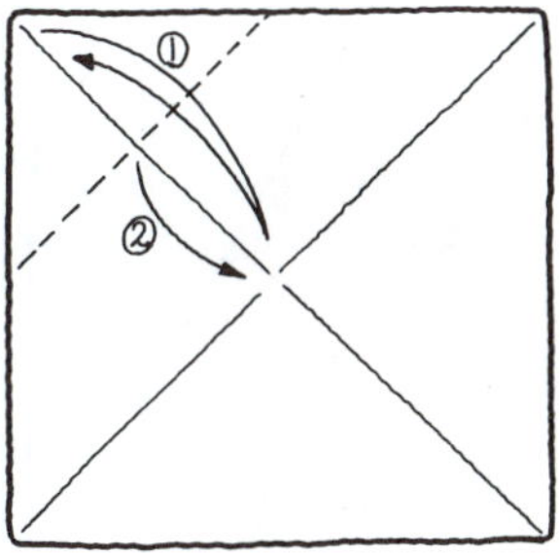

3 巻くように２度折る。
Fold in half to the center. Fold it in once more.

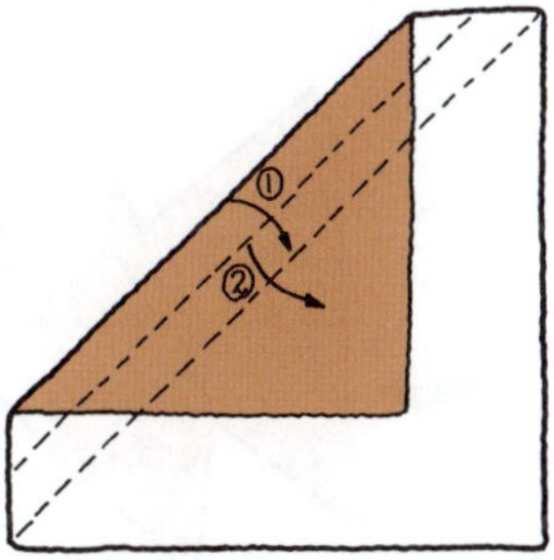

4 ○まではさみで切る。中央の三角形を折り上げる。
Cut the paper to the tip of the small triangle, then fold the small triangle to the left.

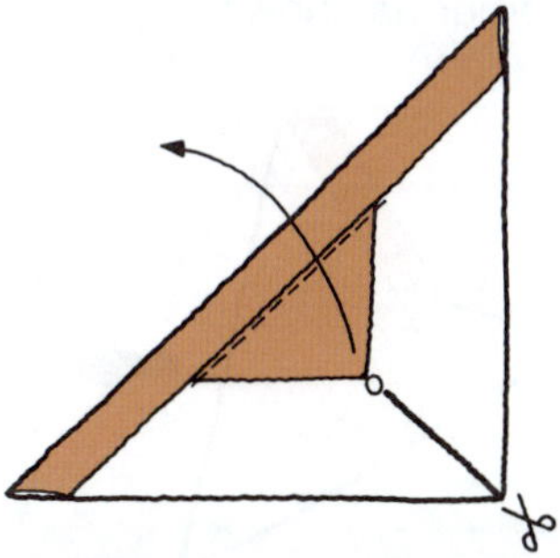

5 半分に折る。
Fold in half.

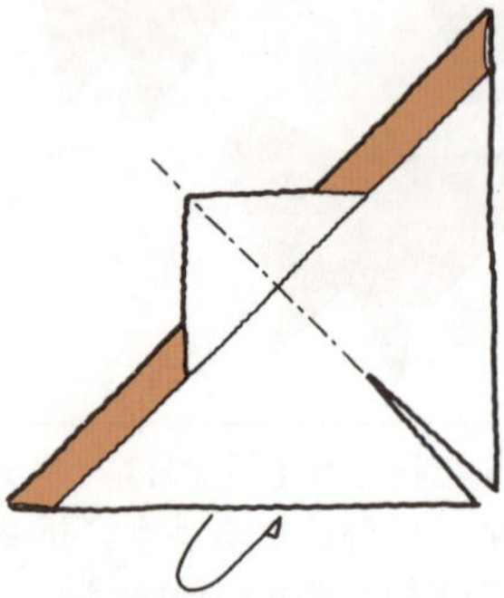

6 はねの部分を折る。※はねを広げる角度は120°。
Fold the front flap down diagonally. Do the same with the reverse side. ※Spread the wings at a 120° angle.

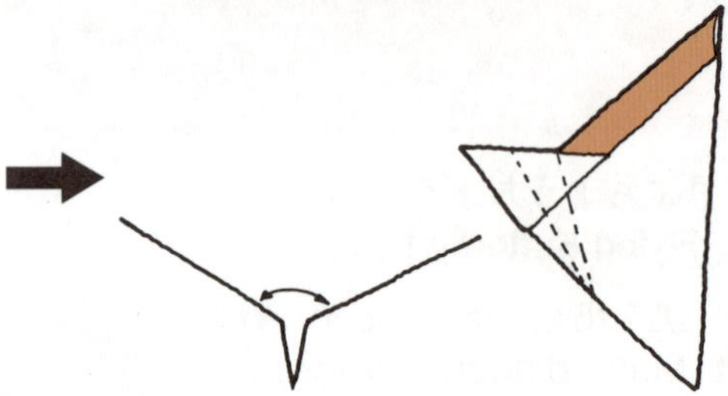

Finished

飛ぶちょうちょう② Flying Butterfly②

1 飛ぶちょうちょう①の**2**まで折る。
Repeat ①-steps **1-2**.

2 カドを折ってから、飛ぶちょうちょう①の**3～5**をくりかえす。
Fold both corners in, then repeat ①-steps **3-5**.

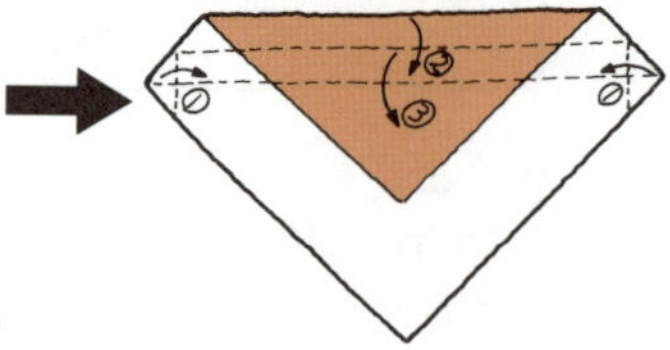

3 中わり折りする。
Do "Nakawari-Ori" on the left corner as shown.

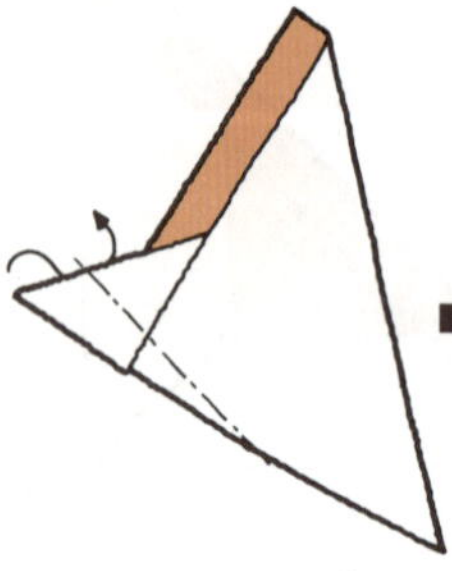

4 はねの部分を折る。
Fold the wings down.

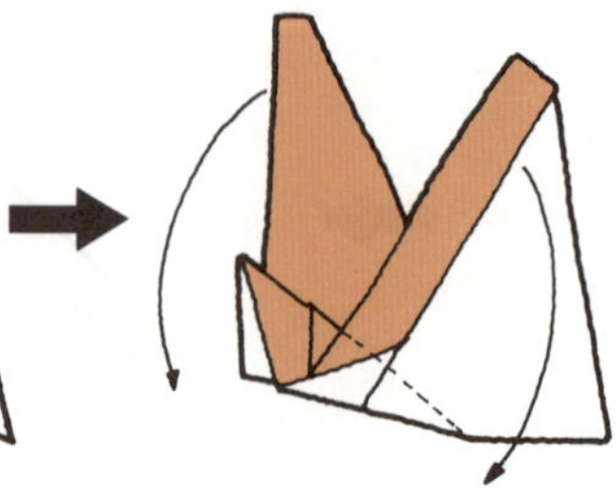

Finished

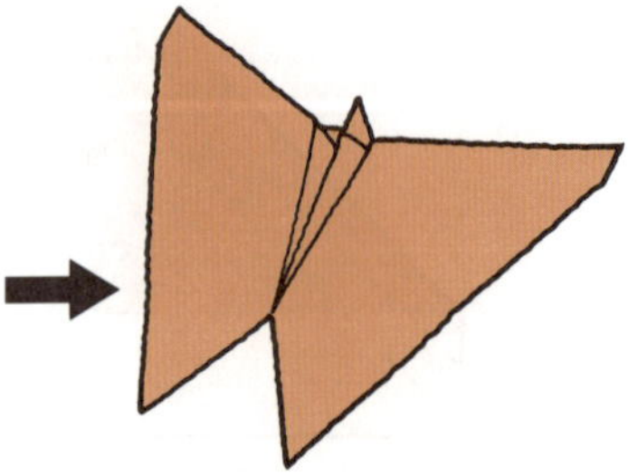

飛ぶちょうちょう③
Flying Butterfly③

1 飛ぶちょうちょう①の**3**まで折る。
Repeat. ①-steps **1**-**3**.

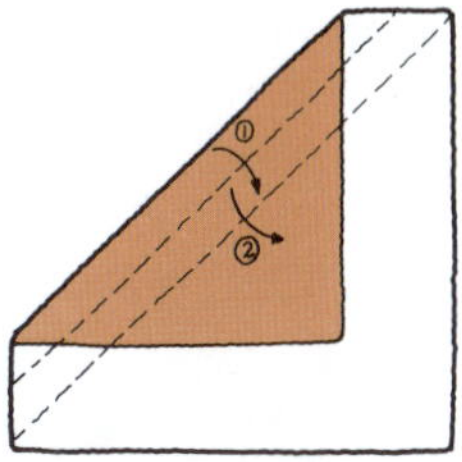

2 三角を折り上げる。
Fold the small triangle to the left.

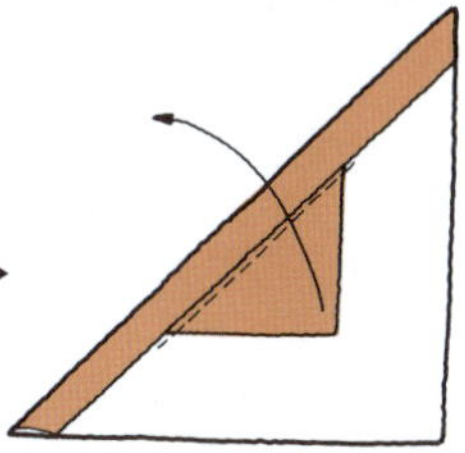

3 カドを中わり折りし、○まで切る。
Do “Nakawari-Ori” on both sides, then cut the paper as shown.

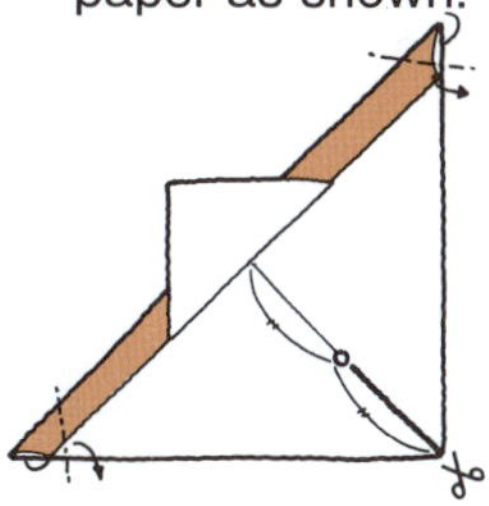

4 飛び出た部分を中に折り込み、切った部分をだん折りにする。
Fold the tips of both sides inside, then do “Dan-Ori” on the 2 flaps.

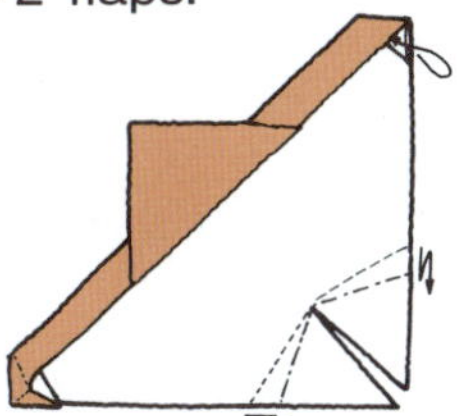

5 半分に折る。
Fold in half to the top.

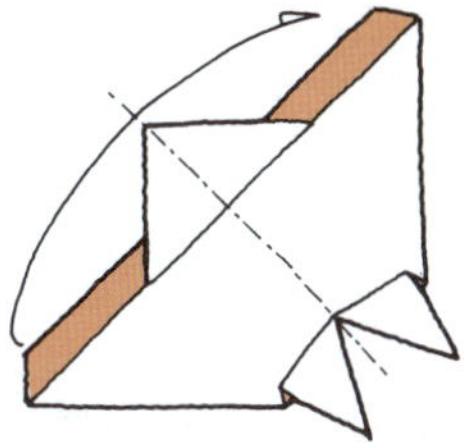

6 中わり折りにする。
Do “Nakawari-Ori” on the left corner.

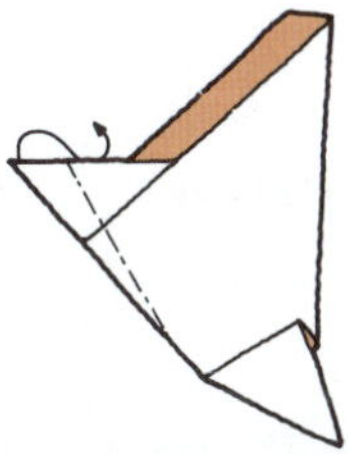

7 先を折り上げ、はねの部分を折る。
Fold the tip of the head and fold the wings down.

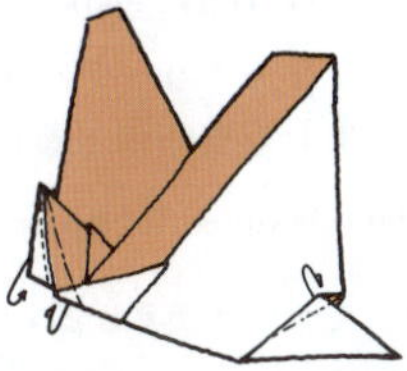

Finished

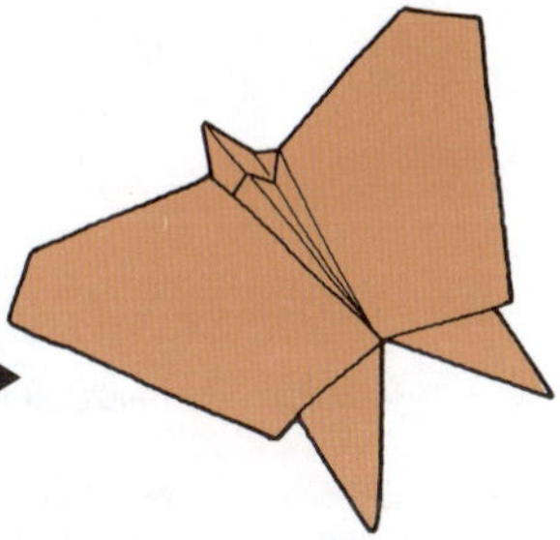

●監修

奥田光雄

創作折り紙歴30年。動物、花など、立体感ある作品は海外にも幅広く紹介されている。著書に『動物の折り紙』（ブティック社）などがある。

連絡先：〒356-0036　埼玉県上福岡市南台2-4-7

英語で楽しむ折り紙

1998年10月18日　発行

監修者　奥田光雄

発行者　佐藤龍夫

発行所　株式会社　大泉書店

住所　〒162-0805 東京都新宿区矢来町27

電話　東京（03）3260-4001（代）

振替　００１４０－７－１７４２

印刷　半七写真印刷工業(株)／製本・(株)明光社

落丁・乱丁本は本社にてお取り換えします。

ISBN 4-278-08319-X　C0071　R28